THE PACIFIC RIVALS

THE

PACIFIC RIVALS

A Japanese View of Japanese-American Relations

by the staff of the Asahi Shimbun

with a foreword by EDWIN O. REISCHAUER

WEATHERHILL/ASAHI

New York & Tokyo

This book is a translation from the Japanese
of *Nippon to Amerika* (Japan and America),
published in the fall of 1971 by the Asahi Shimbun-sha, Tokyo.
The English version, based upon Ken'ichi Otsuka's translation
for the *Asahi Evening News*, is the work of
Peter Grilli (Assistant Editor, John Weatherhill, Inc.)
and Yoshio Murakami (Staff Reporter, *Asahi Shimbun*).

First edition, 1972

*Published jointly by John Weatherhill, Inc., 149 Madison
Avenue, New York, N.Y. 10016, with editorial offices
at 7-6-13 Roppongi, Minato-ku, Tokyo; and the Asahi
Shimbun-sha, 2-3 Yuraku-cho, Chiyoda-ku, Tokyo.*
*Copyright © 1971, 1972, by the Asahi Shimbun-sha;
all rights reserved. Printed in Japan.*

LCC 75-185601   ISBN 0-8348-0070-5

Table of Contents

PHOTOGRAPHS

CREDITS: All photographs are from the files of the *Asahi Shimbun* except the following: 1, 3, and 5, from *The Black Ship Scroll* by Oliver Statler (Weatherhill, 1963); 9, 22–23, 27, 30–35, 42, 47, 55, and 61, from Kyodo Photo Service; 17, 53, 56, 61, 63, 66, and 69, from World Wide Photos; and 49, from the *New York Times.*

Foreword

THIS VOLUME presents in book form the series of articles on Japanese-American relations that everybody has been talking about—that is, everybody in Japan, but unfortunately no one in America or anywhere else in the world. These articles first appeared serially in the huge *Asahi* newspaper, which has a daily circulation of over six million throughout Japan and could reasonably claim to be not only the largest and most prestigious Japanese newspaper but possibly the greatest newspaper in the world in terms of a measurement of circulation times quality. Next the articles were published by the *Asahi* in book form, and sold over 50,000 copies in the first three weeks after publication. They are currently being serialized in English translation in Tokyo's *Asahi Evening News.*

Based on thousands of interviews and skillfully written in the factual, anecdotal style much appreciated by the Japanese, the series has proved a triumph of reporting in depth. It lays out through brief topical glimpses the whole vast panorama of relations between Japan and the United States over the past century and conveys an intimate feel of that relationship from the Japanese side. For its millions of Japanese readers it has probably served as an interesting reminder of things they already half know or feel. For Americans and others, it could be much more deeply revealing. But typically, these articles have remained all but unnoticed by the outside world.

This is a curious situation. A similar series of articles in a German paper on German-American relations, let us say, would have drawn wide comment in the United States, throughout Europe, and in Japan too, for that matter. Books and articles by opinion makers or significant stories in major magazines and newspapers anywhere in the West draw a world audience and bring worldwide repercussions. The *Asahi* is not only a mammoth newspaper but the leading member of a small group of nationwide or regional dailies in Japan that together constitute probably the most influential national press in the world. The subject of the series—Japanese-American relations—is one of the handful of international relationships that will help shape the future of the whole world. But the articles remained hidden behind Japan's high language barrier, completely overlooked by the rest of the world. Even the English translations in the *Asahi Evening News* have gone unnoticed outside Japan.

There is a great need for communication between Japan and the outside world and especially with the United States. Instead of a true dialogue, however, there is a flow of words in only one direction. The Japanese diligently study the world. Their magnificent mass media— television and magazines as well as newspapers—report extensively on all areas and most assiduously of all on the United States. Literally thousands of books, articles, and newspaper stories are translated annually from Western languages and published in Japanese. The insatiable, dogged Japanese readers struggle through reams of strange names and clumsy literal translations in their eagerness to perceive what is in the foreign mind.

Thus, there is a torrent of information and opinion pouring into Japan from the outside world, but the reverse flow is only a trickle. Newsmen find that to get even a little of their copy about Japan printed, they must stress the exotic or spectacular, not what may be really important. Some Japanese literature is beautifully translated, but it tells us more about the psychological and esthetic perceptions of a few unusual, talented individuals than about Japan as a whole. Some foreign observers attempt to interpret Japan, and, being one of them, I trust that they do it well, but their accounts at best are interpretations—more like a scientific analysis of love or hate, let us say, than the real emotions themselves. A relatively small group of Japanese write in Western languages for foreign consumption or participate in international conferences, but their accounts tend to be simplified, sanitized, and tactfully slanted for what is assumed to be a relatively ignorant, insensitive, and uninterested audience. Their product is a bit like editions of Shakespeare prepared for very young children. What the Japanese are saying to one another about their own country or the rest of the world remains unheard abroad.

Everyone is the loser from this situation. The harm to the outside world is obvious, for it learns little of what Japanese feel and think. But the Japanese too are hurt. Their views elicit from other countries no stimulating reactions of agreement or disapproval. Their misinterpretations are not corrected; their concepts are not challenged; their analysis is not honed by the friction of contrary views. There is none of the give and take that is necessary to define problems, isolate areas of disagreement, and produce the sort of understanding in depth that will be increasingly necessary if mankind is to survive in this crowded, complex world.

In the nineteenth century it may not have been necessary for others to know what Japanese really thought. Japan was far away and the world system to which it had been forced to accomodate was of Western manufacture. But this is no longer the case. Even in the 1920s and 1930s adequate communication between Japan and the United States might have avoided or at least mitigated the tragedy of the 1940s. Today Japan is the third largest economic unit in the world. It is also the fastest rising and in many ways the most smoothly functioning unit. Its economy has come to have a global impact in a world in which economic factors increasingly take precedence over military and the destiny of all mankind has become inextricably intertwined. What Japanese feel and think will become a steadily growing element in determining the fate of men everywhere. In particular, the huge, complex, and emotionally ambiguous relationship with the United States will be a major factor in determining the future of the world.

Japan and the United States stand at a turning point in their relations. Japanese no longer are satisfied with a position of subordination to American policies which they perceive to have been the product of the American defeat of Japan in World War II, seven years of American military occupation and direction, and the aftermath of the occupation in which, at least for a while, Japan remained extremely dependent on the United States both economically and for its defense. Such a situation, whether real or only a mistaken assumption surviving from conditions in the past, is no longer tolerable for a proud, successful people who find themselves rising rapidly to superpower status, at least in the economic sphere. In searching for a new place in the world and a relationship with the United States more befitting their present position as the world's third greatest economic power, they keep wondering how compatible are Japanese and American national interests, how basically friendly the United States is to Japan, how trustworthy American commitments to Japan may be, and above all whether Americans and other Occidentals are really prepared to accept a non-Western, non-white nation as a full equal. They remember a somewhat parallel moment in their recent history, when Japan,

xi

accepted as one of the four great victor powers at the Versailles Conference to settle World War I, asked that the peace treaty include a statement of racial equality—and was refused.

At a time like this, it is imperative that there be a full and frank interchange of views and feelings between Americans and Japanese. But it cannot take place unless we hear what the Japanese are saying. The appearance of this volume, therefore, is very welcome. For once, writings that have had a large impact in Japan are being presented in undoctored translation to a wide audience abroad. There may be more unfamiliar Japanese names than the Westerner finds palatable. The points of view may seem odd or distorted. The disjointed presentation may at first seem less enlightening than more sweeping or smoother generalizations. But such complaints are like a baby's early distaste for a diet beyond the mashed, strained, tasteless mush that emerges from baby-food bottles. This is the real thing—what Japanese write for one another and find significant and interesting. We owe it to ourselves to develop a more robust taste for Japanese perceptions, opinions, emotions, and even names. We will find it in the long run much more tasty than the baby food on Japan that has satisfied us in the past—and a great deal more intellectually nourishing.

Let us hope that this book represents the start of a new flow abroad of Japanese opinion and information to balance the heavy flow of opinion and information into Japan. We are in desperate need of a true dialogue. It is high time that it started.

Edwin O. Reischauer

Editors' Preface

ON JANUARY 3, 1971, a new series began appearing on page four of the *Asahi Shimbun*, Japan's largest and most influential newspaper. It continued for seven months, about four times a week, and many of the *Asahi*'s more than six million readers were to find themselves falling into the habit of turning immediately to that page as soon as they picked up their morning paper, so keen was the interest in the series.

What was this series that so many Japanese newspaper readers became addicted to? A new novel by a modern Japanese Dickens? A popular horoscope? It was called *Japan and America* and was an account of the relations of the two great Pacific nations, from their first meetings in the middle of the nineteenth century to the tensions of the present. Dull and academic, one might guess at first, and bristling with statistics and documentation and names. The names, dates, and numbers were there, but they were contained in a journalistic tour de force forming a saga of events and personalities that proved to be of constant fascination. Responsible reporting at its best, the articles managed to be both informative and eminently readable.

Disturbed by the almost visibly worsening relations between the United States and Japan, in the fall of 1970 the editorial directors of the *Asahi* had assembled a *"Japan and America* task force" from the huge manpower resources of the many departments of the newspaper. The seventeen men on the force—correspondents, news analysts, social, political, and scientific reporters—were charged with the formidable task of reinvestigating all aspects of the long and complex relationship of the two countries.

They did their job thoroughly and well. Beginning with a study of original documents and secondary sources, they then augmented the

xiii

information gathered from written materials with the less formal spoken words of more than two thousand individuals, whom they interviewed in Japan and abroad. Generalized statistics on what the people of the two countries thought about each other were compiled from numerous, specially commissioned opinion polls conducted among people of all ages and all social backgrounds in both Japan and the United States. The task force was constantly encouraged in its activities by the great interest and excitement inspired in everyone they spoke with. Each person had his own outlook on the Japanese-American relationship, colored by particular assumptions and opinions and enlivened by personal experience. And each welcomed the interview as an opportunity to rethink what the binational relationship meant to him. That the articles had an equally strong effect upon newspaper readers was demonstrated by the lively and sometimes heated correspondence and discussion they engendered.

One month after the newspaper serialization was complete, the articles were brought out in book form. The book's large first printing sold out almost immediately, and during the next few months, several more printings were sold out. The articles also began to appear in English translation in the *Asahi*'s English-language subsidiary newspaper, the *Asahi Evening News*.

*   *   *

Such, then, was the genesis of the present book. In preparing it for an English-speaking audience, we have made a few small adjustments. We have added the short introductory paragraphs that appear in italics at the beginning of each part, setting the stage for readers unfamiliar with the events to be described in the articles themselves. We have changed the order of some of the articles in the interest of a more logical progression, and have omitted several that were of current, but somewhat ephemeral, interest. In dealing with Japanese names, we have followed a practice that now seems fairly widespread even among Japanese when writing in English: taking the date 1868 as the beginning of the modern period of Japanese history, we give modern names in the Western order, surname last, while older names are given in the traditional Japanese order, surname first. The title of the book has been changed from the original *Japan and America* to avoid confusion with other, similarly titled books. Finally, we have occasionally departed slightly from the original text, adapting and rewriting where it seemed necessary to convey understanding to a Western audience of names, events, and terms that a Japanese editor could count on his readers recognizing immediately. Where it was possible to accomplish such elucidation smoothly, additional information has been incorporated directly into the text. Occasionally, explanations have been inserted parenthetically.

In short, we here present what we believe is an entirely honest translation: all the facts given and opinions expressed are those of the original writers. But the eager student who might want to compare the Japanese and English versions should be warned in advance that this is not a literal, word-for-word translation. Our aim has been simply to make the material as easily grasped in English as it originally was in Japanese.

The book is organized in seven parts, as it was in the original. First, by way of introduction, comes a series of articles on various private individuals who today are acting as points of contact between Japan and the United States. The second part is a rapid chronological survey of important aspects of the relationship during the ninety-odd years between 1853, when Perry arrived to "open Japan," and 1945, when Japan fell in military defeat to the United States and her allies. The articles in the third part penetrate the intricacies of the Occupation, the critical seven-year period when, under direct American rule, Japan's institutions and social values were fundamentally transformed. Part Four deals with the post-Occupation American and Japanese diplomats and officials who stage-managed the official relations of the two countries and arranged for Japan's re-entry into the international arena. Part Five describes the new image that Japan has evolved for herself in American eyes in recent years. The sixth part investigates in some depth the problems—political, military, economic, social, and cultural—that the two countries face today as they stand on the threshold of the future. The concluding group of articles looks briefly toward that future and speculates on the possible courses the two Pacific nations might follow as they move ahead.

Unavoidably fragmentary and sometimes seemingly incohesive, this series may disturb some readers by its lack of a unifying thread of analysis or a lofty overview from a single, fixed vantage point. Here, however, the reader will find many insights and perceptions— unconnected and fragmentary, to be sure, but perhaps, for that very reason, closer to reality—of the innumerable facets of an international relationship that defies quick summarization and facile analysis. It is to be hoped that these many glimpses of the interactions of Japan and the United States will lead to a deeper understanding and appreciation of this difficult, complicated, but vital—and enormously important—relationship.

*　　*　　*

A work of this size and scope requires the efforts of many persons, far too numerous to list here with the specific thanks that each of them is due. The tasks of some may have been larger or more onerous or time consuming than those of others, but—just as the two nations described here are the aggregates of numerous individuals—this book also could not be considered complete without the contribution of each person who worked on it.

The original *Japan and America* task force was headed by Tadashi Kitani, deputy managing editor of the Tokyo office of the *Asahi Shimbun*. Its members, in alphabetical order, were Tetsuya Chikashi, Takashi Hamada, Toshio Hatano, Tsugio Kato, Yoichi Kawakami, Ikuzo Kikuchi, Yasunari Magami, Tomonori Matsumoto, Yukio Matsuyama, Yoshio Murakami, Satoshi Otani, Tetsuji Shibata, Hiroshi Shinohara, Kensaku Shirai, Toyozo Tanaka, and Eiji Tominomori. In doing their work, these men relied upon the assistance of scores of other researchers, writers, photographers, and members of the *Asahi* editorial staff. They, and we, are also grateful for the enthusiastic response of the many Japanese and Americans who were approached with requests for interviews and information.

The translations of the articles that appeared in the *Asahi Evening News* were done by Ken'ichi Otsuka. Substantially adapted and revised along the lines already explained, his translation has formed the basis of the present English version. Nobuo Dodo and Tei Teruyama, of the photography section of the *Asahi Shimbun*, were particularly generous with their time in guiding us through the massive photo files of the *Asahi* and helping us select the illustrations for this book.

Finally, we would like to thank Ralph Friedrich, Meredith Weatherby, and John Wheeler for reading the entire English manuscript in its final stages of preparation and offering many useful suggestions for stylistic and organizational improvements. But none of their excellent help can relieve us of final responsibility for the errors that must, inevitably, remain in this translation. The amount of checking and rechecking required by a book of this size and detail has seemed endless at times, but we have been constantly encouraged by the knowledge that the material we were working on was of real value and lasting importance.

PETER M. GRILLI
YOSHIO MURAKAMI

THE PACIFIC RIVALS

PART ONE

Nations Are People

How does one great nation meet another? In an era of rapid global travel, telecommunication, and simultaneous translation, what are the settings for international contact and what are the languages by which nations communicate with one another? Diplomatic channels of official communication continue to exist as they always have, but between two nations of the wealth, power, and variety of Japan and the United States, the diplomatic route cannot be counted on to carry the full burden of international intercourse. And between these two nations in particular, formal diplomacy has shown itself, on numerous occasions in the past, singularly inadequate to the task of reponsible communication. Real communication still lies in the unheralded encounters of ordinary people.

Americans and Japanese other than the diplomats and governmental representatives are today crossing the Pacific in both directions in greater numbers, meeting for a greater variety of purposes, and talking more about more complex matters than ever before. Whether or not Americans and Japanese are understanding each other better is another question, one far too subtle to be answered by stastistics. Other questions must be asked and answered first.

It is enough, for the moment, to ask who is meeting whom, where they are meeting and why, and how they talk to each other. This section offers brief glimpses of some of the myriad activities of Americans in Japan and Japanese in the United States at the present time. These are ordinary citizens, going about their business or pursuing their interests, unwilling to be labeled "unofficial envoys" or "ambassadors of good will" or any other such specious titles that are the creations of official public relations men. Still, to the extent that each of these private individuals is living in an alien land, speaking or hearing a language that is not his mother tongue, he is a representative of his country with an unavoidable, if often only subconscious, tendency to compare his present surroundings to "home." Whether he is an American businessman or lawyer trying to open an office in Tokyo, a high-powered Japanese international-affairs expert flying to a conference in New York or Geneva, an American scholar struggling to master the elusive complexities of the Japanese language, or a hippie communicating without language with his similarly attired fellows in the global youth culture, his thoughts on who he is and why he is where he is are vital to any understanding of the whole vast panorama of Japanese-American relations today.

An Alliance of Heretics

"JAPAN AND AMERICA seem very much alike at a glance, but culturally they are totally different societies," observes Robert Guillain, Far Eastern correspondent of *Le Monde* and long a resident of Japan. "For more than a quarter of a century the two nations have been close allies, but how amazingly little they know about each other! In Europe, such a thing would be inconceivable." Cultural anthropologist Yoshiro Masuda puts a similar thought a bit differently: "When compared to the rest of the world, the Japanese and the American cultures are each extremely peculiar, if not unique. I think of the close Japanese-American ties as a relationship linking two eccentrics or two heretics."

Until quite recently, the similarity of Japanese and American societies was a popular theme, harped on by many Japanese. Both were new societies. Both were mobile societies, allowing the individual to seek his proper place. Both were fluid societies, enthusiastic in their receptivity to novelty and innovation. Today, however, everyone emphasizes the cultural and social differences between the two countries. Both in Japan and elsewhere a flood of books and articles discussing Japan, the Japanese, and Japanese culture "from new angles" is deluging the reading public. One explanation lies in the mounting foreign curiosity about the secret of Japan's "economic miracle," which in turn has prompted the Japanese to take a new interest in themselves and their country. Another is that their new nicknames, inspired by Japan's high rate of economic growth—"economic animals" or "Yellow Yankees"—are prodding Japanese to re-examine themselves critically. It has been said that the Japanese are now sufficiently well fed and well clothed to tolerate self-analysis and self-criticism.

It is clear that the "honeymoon years" in Japanese-American relations are over, and that increased friction between the two countries has brought about American reappraisals of Japan. Just as Ruth Benedict's book *The Chrysanthemum and the Sword* was a product of a military war, Herman Kahn's *Emerging Japanese Superstate* and James Abegglen's *Japan, Inc.* are products of the new economic war.

[5]

Samuel Jameson, Tokyo correspondent of the *Los Angeles Times*, points to conflicting views of competition as the greatest difference between the Japanese mentality and the American. "American society is built on competition. The Japanese, however, are bound by a sense of community so strong that they don't know what competition means. To a Japanese, 'competition' means 'cooperation.' Only 'excessive competition' would compare to what Americans call 'competition.' " To Americans, only naked competition seems to be considered fair, but to the Japanese even competition should be controlled by rules. The difference in attitude may be due, in part, to historical and geographical factors. An American, dissatisfied with conditions wherever he might be, thinks nothing of picking up and going off to seek his fortune somewhere else. But a dissatisfied Japanese can only remain in his tiny, cramped country where there is hardly room for him to stand up straight. Asked "What is fair competition?" the Japanese and the American can hardly be expected to come up with the same answer. Many people would agree with Jameson that a fundamental cause of the souring in Japanese-American economic relations lies in just this crucial difference in attitude toward competition and fairness.

"The path to wealth and social position is open to all in both countries," says Makoto Saito, professor of American political and diplomatic history at Tokyo University. "But an American feels compelled to go on competing even after he has attained those goals. A Japanese, once he buys his 'ticket' to wealth and fame, feels confident and secure that he will be able to enjoy his 'reserved seat.' I wonder whether the Japanese people, confident that they have bought their 'ticket' for American friendship, are not taking for granted that the Americans will remain obliging and willing to understand every problem the way the Japanese wish them to."

History has shown that true friendship between nations cannot survive one nation's forcing her culture on another or one nation's forsaking her own culture in favor of another's. A generous recognition of different cultural patterns and mutual respect for them are essential to harmonious international relations. This certainly does not apply exclusively to Japan and the United States. In order to develop good relations with China, in particular, Japan must rid herself of the myth that the two nations share the same culture, simply because they use the same writing system. John Hall, professor of Japanese history at Yale University, has called this mutual recognition and respect for cultural differences "the imperative of cultural democracy." He also points out that American competitive values are currently being challenged and that many Americans find something to be learned from the Japanese emphasis on community.

Viewed in light of the history of world civilizations, China and Japan now seem to be conducting enormous experiments in diametrically opposed approaches to life and social organization. "American social scientists, increasingly skeptical of the control systems in their own country, are now looking toward the Orient," says Jun Shimokabe, a member of the Economic Planning Agency. "They are seeking new systems in China and Japan which may prove applicable to the United States as well." Futurologist Alvin Toffler adds to the interest in China by speculating that China's development has skipped the industrial stage and is heading directly into a post-industrial stage.

The future relations of Japan, the United States, and China will not be simply political and economic. Cultural intercourse will certainly become increasingly important. And it is clear that flower arrangement, tea ceremony, and traditional drama—Japan's standard stock in trade for cultural exchange—will no longer fill the bill. What else of interest and benefit can Japan offer the international community of nations? Kyozo Mori, an *Asahi* editorial staff writer, credits Japan with two things, and only two, that will prove of lasting benefit to the world. These are the Japanese spirit of tolerance and Article Nine of her constitution. "Japanese tolerance will make for peaceful coexistence, and the spirit behind the no-war covenant in the constitution denies forever the absolutism of state sovereignty."

A New Generation
of Japan Experts

"FOR A SUPPOSEDLY nature-loving country, Japan's pollution is terrible. . . ." "Japan is a rich country now. . . ." "But half of Japan's traditional culture still survives. . . ." These are scraps of conversation—carried on in sure, rapid-fire Japanese—that caught the ear of an *Asahi Shimbun* reporter when he visited students at the Inter-University Center for Japanese Language Studies in downtown Tokyo. In the decade since it was jointly founded by eleven U. S. universities and a Canadian one, the Center has been producing some of the most promising young Western scholars in all areas of Japanese studies. About two-thirds of all American students aspiring to doctorates in Japanese studies take the ten-month language course offered there.

Gerald Curtis, a graduate of the Inter-University Center, is perhaps representative of the new breed of young American Japan specialists. At thirty, he is an assistant professor of political science at Columbia University. His grasp of the intricacies of Japanese politics is so thorough as to amaze Japanese politicians and political scientists. The mechanism of public elections in Japan holds few mysteries for him, nor is he bewildered by the factionalism and divisions of Japanese parties.

After completing the Center course, Curtis lived for a year and a half in the home of Fumio Sato, a member of the ruling Liberal-Democratic party. Traveling the campaign route with Sato, talking with voters, and attending sakè parties with party regulars, Curtis observed at first hand the election of a Japanese politician to the Lower House of the National Diet. The experience was recorded in his doctoral thesis, which later formed the basis of his book, *Election Campaigning Japanese Style*; the book has been translated and published in Japanese.

The Pacific War spurred phenomenal advances in American research on Japan. While the Japanese government was prohibiting all use of English as an enemy language, the American government was recruiting men of talent for intensive training at Japanese-language schools run by the military. The graduates of these wartime language schools are often considered second-generation American Japanologists, distinguishing them from the first generation, which is comprised largely of the children of American missionaries born or raised in Japan, and also from the third generation, which has learned its Japanese since the war. The first generation includes such familiar names as Edwin O. Reischauer, who was to return to Japan as American ambassador in the early sixties, and professors Otis Carey, Hugh Borton, and John Hall. Among second-generation Japanologists well known in Japan are professors Donald Keene, Edward Seidensticker, and Herbert Passin, as well as David Osborne, former minister of the American Embassy and currently U. S. consul in Hong Kong. The second generation far outnumbers the first, and its members played major roles in the implementation of Occupation policies in the years immediately following the war.

After the Occupation, many of the men who had learned their Japa-

[8]

nese at military language schools turned to academic careers and led the development of Japanese studies at major American universities. Many who quit their study of Japan with the signing of the peace treaty in 1951 have returned as businessmen, drawn back by the great expansion of Japanese-American commercial relations. One such alumnus of the language school is A. E. Klauser, Asian-area general manager for Dow Corning International. In the autumn of 1970, he arranged a get-together in Tokyo for his former classmates. When more than 120 of them showed up for the reunion, he was surprised once again at the numerical strength of the second-generation Japanologists.

Members of the second and third generations are aware of sharp differences between themselves. Professor Passin points to the experience of the war as the primary source of their differences. Describing the second-generation scholars, he says: "We are unavoidably influenced, to a greater or lesser degree, by our memories of the war. Our sense of closeness to the Japanese as former adversaries and our sense of responsibility to them during the Occupation, combined with the feelings of caution remaining at the back of our minds, operate at times to make us appear officious or to be saying one thing to Americans and another to the Japanese. The attitudes of the third-generation Japanologists, in contrast, are more distant and more abstract." To the third generation, war means only the Vietnam war. They are aware of no lingering shadows of the Pacific War. "The second generation often talks of a 'revival' of Japanese militarism," says Professor Curtis characteristically. "We don't think that way. If Japan becomes militarized again, it will be a completely new type of militarism, not just a revival of the old."

Observers agree that the third generation approaches Japan directly, coolly, and objectively, as an object of study. It shares none of the patronizing "let us teach you and guide you" attitude of its predecessors. The second generation is apt to pass judgments or make sweeping generalizations about Japan as an entity, but the younger scholars try to analyze separate phenomena one by one. "Our teachers have written books directed at an audience that has an interest in Japan in general, but not in any particular subject," they say. "We write instead on specific subjects—politics, anthropology, or whatever—for people interested in the subject, making special reference to Japan in relation to the subject." Indicative of this are the topics they choose for their research: the rice-price policies of the Japanese government, the Maritime Self-Defense Force, a political study of the Ashikaga shogunate, an ethnological study of shoppers in a small Japanese village, a local chapter of a new religious group, and the like.

Ruth Benedict's book *The Chrysanthemum and the Sword* is highly rated by second-generation Japanologists, but the succeeding generation finds it almost worthless, complaining that the views expressed in it are far too simple to apply to all one hundred million Japanese people. Written toward the end of the war at the request of the U. S. Office of War Information, the book was completed in only slightly more than a year with very limited data based on Japanese residents in America. Despite these handicaps, it became one of the strongest influences on postwar evaluations of Japan.

Language remains the greatest single obstacle for American students of Japan. "We learned our Japanese from Nisei farmers in America who had no experience in teaching the language systematically," recalls Donald Keene. He adds enviously: "The third-generation students learn Japanese by a well-organized method and with the aid of well-prepared teaching materials in the home of the language. They can polish their conversational ability every evening at the public bath if they want to."

Despite the improved facilities for those American students who choose to go into Japanese studies, the popularity of the field is steadily declining at American universities. Many students find China more exciting these days. Another reason for the decline is that scholarship funds for Japanese studies are being slashed drastically. Kenneth Butler, director of the Inter-University Center, commenting on the suspension of support from the Ford Foundation, says: "The money has been cut off at a critical time. Japanese studies in America in the past has been tinged with exoticism and racial prejudice. But young scholars of the third generation have no particular interest in the exotic and are free of prejudice. Real Japanese-American understanding, uninfluenced by the past relations of the two countries, is only beginning to develop, and the third-generation scholars have a major role to play in building it."

Cocktail-Circuit Regulars

THERE IS a fixed group of young Japanese academics who seem to turn up at nearly every international conference involving the

[10]

United States and Japan. They all teach government or international relations, and nearly all of them studied in the United States during the late 1950s and 1960s, observing at first hand the new trends in American political science that were emerging during those years. They watched American intellectuals rally around the banner of the Kennedy administration and found the atmosphere of that period well suited to their own political philosophy, which is preoccupied with nuclear war and based on a hard-boiled, realistic vision of world politics.

The group includes professors Masataka Kosaka (Kyoto University), Yonosuke Nagai (Tokyo University of Technology), Fuji Kamiya (Keio University), Shinkichi Eto (Tokyo University), Michio Royama and Kinhide Mushakoji (both of Sophia University), and Kei Wakaizumi (Kyoto Industrial University). Most of them are in their forties.

"It sometimes occurs to us to recruit some new faces, but we don't dare," says Tadashi Yamamoto, secretary general of the Japanese Commission for International Friendship, which frequently sponsors Japanese-American conferences. "The fact is that it's so much safer to rely on these familiar men that we are afraid to experiment with new people." All the young professors are fluent in English and feel perfectly at ease dealing face to face with both foreign dignitaries and Japanese politicians. In addition to the conferences, they put in such frequent appearances at receptions and cocktail parties that they have been dubbed "the cocktail-circuit regulars." Another nickname for them in Japan is "American-type academics," for they travel widely, look realistically at things, and do not hesitate, in their informal capacity as contact points between Japan and the United States, to assist the government. Former ambassador to Washington Takezo Shimoda says of the group: "They can put across their messages to the Americans better than any other Japanese." The professors themselves are confident that they know America better than anyone else in Japan.

Wakaizumi currently holds the record for frequency of trips abroad; he has traveled to the United States and elsewhere as many as eight times in a single year to attend international conferences or to accept invitations to lecture. Kosaka shuttles between Tokyo and Kyoto weekly. They and most other members of the group employ secretaries to keep track of their appointments and schedules.

The Japanese-American Conference on Okinawa and Asia, held in Kyoto in January, 1969, was a clear example of the usefulness of these men to the government. The purpose of the conference was to influ-

[11]

ence in Japan's favor the critical negotiations on the reversion of Okinawa. This was to be done through prior discussion with certain Americans whose opinions were likely to be heeded in Washington. In name it was a private conference, but the tab of thirty million yen was shared by the Japanese government and private industry. The first important function of the professorial group was to draw up the list of American delegates to be invited to the conference. At their suggestion, the wives of the Americans were also invited. Each American couple was accompanied by a refined young Japanese lady who acted as guide, interpreter, and general assistant. And care was taken to provide each delegate's hotel room with his wife's favorite flowers.

The gracious manner in which the professors staged the conference no doubt contributed much to its success. The meetings are credited with paving the way for the eventual agreement to return Okinawa to Japan on a so-called *hondo nami* basis. (This is the popular term to indicate the return of Okinawa completely free of nuclear arms, with the U. S. bases there operating under the same restrictions as those in Japan proper. There are supposedly no nuclear weapons on the *hondo*, the four main islands of Japan.) At the Kyoto conference, an American hawk rejected "the two extremes" of the reversion issue, which he defined as maintenance of the status quo, on the one hand, and a *hondo nami* return of Okinawa, on the other. Kamiya was instantly on his feet. "The two extremes," he argued, "are maintenance of the status quo and total withdrawal of American troops from Okinawa. *Hondo nami* is not one of them." Royama argued that Okinawa had no need of nuclear arms, and Eto persistently denied the real existence of a China threat. Wakaizumi engaged tirelessly in private discussions with individual delegates in the hallways between formal sessions, continually requesting that they use all their influence in Washington to bring about a favorable settlement. Last-minute disputes over the wording of the final communiqué were smoothed over by Kosaka's polished phraseology.

Toshio Kimura, deputy chief cabinet secretary at the time of the Kyoto conference and now director of the Economic Planning Agency, praises the manner in which the professors operate: "They bypass the rigid framework that restricts foreign policy discussion to the Foreign Ministry and the State Department and manage to develop direct influence on the White House. They are valuable people indeed." But they are not without critics. Some call them "government agents," and Masatsugu Ishibashi, secretary general of the Socialist party, dismisses them as "fodder for the government's self-serving claim that it listens to intellectuals too."

[12]

"It's hard to say who exerts greater influence on the government," comments Hajime Shinohara of Tokyo University, "its friends on the inside or its critics outside. Friends always run the risk of being lured around to the government's position rather than influencing it. I rather doubt that the professors have as much influence on the government as they would like to think." "Although they consider themselves realists," remarks Professor Kanji Seki, "their political philosophy is actually a forced application of nineteenth-century theories to present-day events. They deal in concepts of superpowerism that neglect Asia."

That they are undisturbed by criticism like this is another distinguishing characteristic of the group. Rather, they find in their rebellion from the Japanese academic establishment a source of energy for their widening activities. The group has, however, been brought up short by a difficult obstacle. Theories of all-out nuclear war have been increasingly discredited by the progress of the Vietnam war, which defies definition according to their logic. And throughout the United States, numerous intellectuals, among whom the Japanese have close friends, have grown so frustrated by Vietnam that they are rapidly losing interest in international issues. In Japan too, the fierce campus crises and the pollution problem have generated intense skepticism of government policies.

In this altered situation, the professors are tending toward an interdisciplinary approach to international relations. Wakaizumi's interests have shifted from military affairs to the study of culture and civilization. He admits that the worldwide campus struggles were the largest factor behind this change. "I have come to realize that security in a nuclear age cannot be guaranteed by military measures alone. My major interest today is in religion." Nagai is beginning to add a concern for ecology to his studies, and Kosaka is considering a switch to sociology.

"Up to now, security guarantees have been given particular attention," says Royama, "but it's time that we recognized that typhoons and traffic accidents are as menacing to human life as war. I choose now to think of international politics as but a single element in the human environment."

Since the war, one wave of new American "science" after another has swept across the Japanese academic world: sociology, social psychology, cultural ethnology, and most recently, "realistic" international politics. What is to be next?

Sister Cities

MOTOSHIGE KURIHARA, head of the Foreign Affairs Section of the Yokohama municipal government, gazed in dismay at piles of letters and cards that had deluged his office around Christmas, 1970. Full of thanks for Yokohama's hospitality, messages had poured in from the more than six hundred San Diego residents who had visited their Japanese sister city that year. Of course, they had seen more than just Yokohama. While in Japan, they toured Expo '70 and did the course of Hakone, Kyoto, and Nara. But the real cause of Kurihara's dismay was that five hundred of the visitors wrote that they had enjoyed their stay in Japan so much that they would be back again come summer. Their previous visit had cost Yokohama eight million yen in hospitality, stretching to its limits the city's budget for being nice to foreign visitors. Now the task of finding funds for their second visit would fall to him.

The sister-city affiliation linking Yokohama and San Diego was an offspring of President Eisenhower's appeals for people-to-people ties between American and foreign cities that shared similar historical backgrounds or population sizes. About 130 Japanese cities have formed such affiliations, seventy-eight of them with American cities. Yokohama, with six, has more sisters than any other Japanese city.

Yokohama's ties with San Diego are particularly close. A popular song around the Japanese port city goes something like this:

> San Diego, San Diego, beloved port,
> How I yearn to fly off to you,
> This Yokohama girl,
> Bird of passage with jet-black eyes.

As Christmas approaches every year, San Diego mayor Frank Curran does come flying in to Yokohama, almost like the girl in the song. But some Yokohama citizens suspect that there is more than just international good will bringing him to Japan. He spends much of his time in Japan visiting San Diego boys recovering from Vietnam injuries in U. S. military hospitals in the Tokyo-Yokohama area. These visits, with cameramen in tow, look very much like electioneering. Every time Mayor Curran visits Yokohama he is feted with a luncheon at which he is presented with all sorts of souvenirs. "They're my war trophies!" he roars with laughter as he stuffs them into bulging trunks.

[14]

Recent news dispatches from California report that Mayor Curran is under indictment for alleged bribe-taking. But his friends in Yokohama doubt that this free-wheeling ebullient character will be particularly bothered by such allegations. Curran never tires of repeating that he can remember, with closed eyes, the signature of Mayor Ichio Asukata of Yokohama. Indeed he should: in the past decade more than three hundred Yokohama citizens have paid official visits to San Diego bearing letters of introduction from Mayor Asukata.

Over the same ten years, several thousand citizens of San Diego have traveled in the opposite direction to Japan. Both they and the Japanese visitors to San Diego have been, for the most part, connected with the municipal assemblies or wealthy enough to finance their own trips, giving rise to the criticism that the sister-city program is actually fostering "boss to boss" ties rather than genuine people-to-people contacts. Much the same is true of Yokohama's affiliations with her other sisters. Their mayors visit each other from time to time, as one of the privileges of office, but their citizens do little traveling back and forth. Socialist Mayor Asukata claims to be trying to change this situation. "President Eisenhower envisioned sister-city ties as a sort of spiritual or emotional bulwark to make up for the cuts in numbers of American troops stationed in Japan," says Asukata. "I want to remove such political considerations and promote real people-to-people good will regardless of whether there are American troops here or not. That is why we have organized citizens' committees to attend to relations with each of our sister cities."

The Yokohama committee for relations with San Diego has more than two hundred members, most of them shopkeepers or business executives. "We carry on a varied program," says its chairman, Shinsaburo Yamamoto. "There are exchanges of paintings and drawings by schoolchildren of each city and family visits by high school students. In 1969, we organized a tour to San Diego of 125 people, at their own expense. They were warmly welcomed in California. The welcoming committee took special pains to see that the Japanese and Americans would mix at parties and receptions, but most of the Japanese were shy and embarrassed because they couldn't speak English."

"Language problems, cultural differences, and money difficulties are the three greatest obstacles to smooth functioning of the sister-city programs," points out Reikichi Kojima of the Japan Municipal League for International Fellowship, which serves as go-between in arranging affiliations between Japanese cities and those elsewhere in the world. "We often get requests, from both Japan and abroad, for affiliations with just any city. Some people seem to think of the program as an excuse for foreign junkets at public expense, or as a money-saving means of sightseeing." Kojima is convinced that sister-city ties can be of real benefit if used as a forum for discussing specific problems instead of well-intentioned, but abstract, talk of "world peace" or "international good will." A step in that direction was taken in the spring of 1970, when the U. S. Embassy sponsored a meeting in Tokyo of representatives of American and Japanese sister cities to discuss the problem of pollution. In a speech to that conference, Ambassador Armin Meyer expressed the hope that the sister-city program would serve as a vehicle of regional cooperation between Japan and America.

It looks as though the initiative for furthering Japanese-American cooperation along the lines of the sister-city program is being left almost entirely to the Americans. In contrast to the demonstrated American enthusiasm for the program, the Japanese government is taking the position—unusual for it—of nonintervention in local autonomy.

Direct Communication vs. "Mutual Intuition"

THE TELEPHONE rang in the offices of Simul International in downtown Tokyo. The call was from the Japan Federation of Automobile Dealers Associations, which needed three simultaneous interpreters for a week-long seminar for its members, to be held in Hawaii. There would be two lecturers from a similar American federation of auto dealers, plus ten from among Hawaiian dealers, and simultaneous interpretation would be required, as most of the Japanese dealers knew no English. How soon could they get the interpreters? "We are booked up for the rest of the year," replied the director of Simul International. "Schedule your meeting for late next February and we'll be able to supply the interpreters." The automobile-dealers federation was forced to postpone its seminar, but in the invitational pamphlet it sent out to its members it could say: "The language problem need not worry you; it will be taken care of by simultaneous interpretation."

Simul regularly gets such requests: an economic group wants to send a survey mission to the United States, a science society is planning an international conference in Japan, a television network is arranging a series of lectures by a visiting American specialist. They all need simultaneous interpreters, but they are usually forced to wait until the interpreters are available. In July, 1969, six of Tokyo's television stations vied for interpreters for their telecasting by satellite of the Apollo 11 lunar landing. What was a stiff competition among the networks for their services was for the interpreters—all of whom were employed by Simul—merely a friendly contest staged in the soundproof glass booths that they call "the torture chambers."

Until about fifteen years ago, it was generally believed that simultaneous translation from English to Japanese and vice versa was impossible. The two languages, diametrically opposite in sentence structure, seemed too different to be susceptible to such rapid translation. It was the U. S. Department of State that first began experimenting with making the impossible possible. Around the same time, the Japan Productivity Committee was established and began sending industrial and commercial survey missions to the United States to seek technical assistance in Japan's postwar reconstruction. Few members of the survey missions spoke or understood English, and some method of simultaneous translation was essential if they were to benefit from their tours of America. In 1955, eight Japanese, chosen from a multitude of applicants, were sent to Washington, D. C., for training. Their daily stipend was eight dollars, the minimum wage in the United States at the time. Matsumi Muramatsu, one of the original trainees, asked an American friend how far that paltry amount could be stretched, and received this tip: "Ask American cops or cabbies where you can eat cheaply. They'll know where you can get the best food for the least amount of money. And don't go to a tailor for a suit; get cheap second-hand clothes at Goodwill."

The simultaneous interpreters have no such financial worries any more. Working for Simul International, which was founded in 1965 by the former State Department trainees and graduates of a similar course at International Christian University in Tokyo, they now earn more than eighty dollars a day. Compared with their initial eight dollars a day, their wages have obviously enjoyed a phenomenally high rate of growth.

Simultaneous translation more than halves the time consumed by the slow, old-fashioned method of consecutive interpretation. The new availability of highly trained simultaneous interpreters has increased the opportunities for international interchange. Japan, with her fine reputation for electronic skills and her generally excellent facilities, is now unsurpassed in the world as a site for international

[17]

conferences. In 1970, more than 250 such conferences were held in Japan, meaning that, with weekends and holidays subtracted, a new conference opened nearly every day. Naturally, most of them involved some aspect of Japanese-American relations.

Speedy interpreting does not, however, necessarily bring about deeper understanding. Masao Kunihiro, another of the pioneer simultaneous interpreters, cannot help fearing that Japanese-American relations look much better than they really are. "The United States is a heterogeneous society built of people with widely divergent ethnic backgrounds," he explains. "There, enormous importance is attached to verbal communication and people take pains to make their speech as precise as possible. Japan, on the other hand, is a society of racial homogeneity. Here, social relations depend on *haragei.*" This peculiar Japanese concept, sometimes inadequately translated as "strategic telepathy," is the very opposite of outspokenness; mutual intuition, rather than the actual words uttered, is the main vehicle of *haragei* communication. In concluding his remarks, Kunihiro asks the pertinent question: "Can even the greatest skills in translation be expected to bridge such cultural differences?"

Toshio Shimanouchi, an adviser to the Federation of Economic Organizations and interpreter at numerous Japanese-American conferences since the war, adds: "The accurate transmission of words between two persons is one thing, mutual understanding quite another. Simultaneous interpretation is essentially unnatural and subject to constant strain. It is far from perfect as a medium of communication, and it would be a grave mistake to rely on it for full understanding." As but one example of the difficulty of communicating cultural differences and nuances, one interpreter recalls the jam he found himself in while interpreting for a Japanese cabinet minister visiting Vice-President Richard Nixon in the 1950s. The Japanese minister, when introduced to the vice-president, beamed at Nixon and announced: "We Japanese call your honorable country *Beikoku,* which means 'rice country.' Since we are a rice-eating people, there is no reason why the Japanese and the Americans should not become good friends."

More recently, at a conference of Japanese and American businessmen, Japanese delegates strained to convince the Americans of the reasons for the laggardly Japanese trade liberalization. The Americans regarded their efforts as no more than filibustering. The Japanese were completely misunderstood because each of them had begun with a graciously poetic greeting, quoted from the Chinese classics. Rendered into English as "A friend comes from afar. How happy I am!" it lost all its delicacy of nuance and simply fell flat. Simultaneous interpretation, unable to convey the special flavor of a language, may thus have the opposite effect of disguising or distorting linguistic problems. "Superficial verbal intercourse can give the impression that it has filled unbridgeable cultural gaps," warns Kunihiro from his long experience as an interpreter. "Sometimes I think my work will never amount to more than an abortive effort at communication."

The Press Club

THE FOREIGN Correspondents' Club of Japan (also familiarly called simply the Press Club) celebrated its twenty-first anniversary on November 24, 1970, with a bash. Prime Minister Sato started off the evening with a toast to the club and its members, many of whom went on drinking through most of the night without a thought for the stories they might be filing the next day. On the afternoon of that next day, the clatter of their typewriters must have resounded like bulletfire in their hungover heads as they pounded out one of the biggest news stories of their careers. The first report they sent out over the wires early that afternoon ran: "Internationally famous novelist Yukio Mishima, waving a samurai sword, has invaded the Tokyo headquarters of the Japanese Self-Defense Forces. His motives and the details of what is happening are not clear at this time." Then came the follow-up: "Yukio Mishima, to dramatize his conviction that Japan must rearm, committed ritual suicide by disembowelment after making a frenzied speech to officers of the Ground Self-Defense Force."

Five days later, Yasuhiro Nakasone, director-general of the Defense Agency at the time, addressed members of the club at a special luncheon. The meeting was jammed with foreign reporters, who fired a fusillade of pointed questions at him:

"Mr. Nakasone, the last time you were here you called Mishima's private army, the Tate-no-kai [Shield Society], 'the male version of the Takarazuka all-girl opera group.' Have you changed your mind about it since then?"

"Would you agree that Japan's ruling class shows particular sympathy and tolerance for ultra-rightists?"

"The government recently deceptively described Phantom jets as

[19]

defensive planes. Don't you think that such deceit will serve only to irritate the young and arouse in them a sympathy for appeals like Mishima's for Japan's rearming?"

"The Self-Defense Forces, if their name is to be taken literally, are to provide self-protection for Japan. Why then did they have to call in the riot police to defend them from a middle-aged man waving an old sword?"

Mr. Nakasone, usually outspoken and quick to parry difficult questions, found himself forced onto the defensive. He gave lame answers to these and other questions, and ended apologetically: "The Self-Defense Force is like a boat tossed in a storm. And now with the Diet in session, it also has to be ready for a torpedo to strike it at any moment. I'm sorry if I haven't been able to give you satisfactory answers today. . . ."

With 290 regular members and 1,260 associate members, the Press Club is one of the world's leading journalists' clubs both in size and in the variety of nationalities of its members. There are twenty-five nationalities represented, including the Soviet Union. The club has two bars and an excellent restaurant, but it is not just a place for newspapermen to eat, drink, and relax. Most of its members find its services vital to their work: the switchboard is open around the clock, and its operators will take messages, keep appointment schedules, and trace a reporter all over the city if he is needed urgently for an assignment. The club's library is well stocked with books in English on Japan and Asia. Leading figures in the Japanese government and foreign dignitaries passing through Tokyo frequently appear at the club at special lunches or dinners. A former president, John Rich, sums up the atmosphere of the Correspondents' Club by calling it "an active place."

As the keystone of communications and mass media in the Far East, the Tokyo club has provided a home base for numerous distinguished journalists and writers. When its members won seven Pulitzer Prizes in 1951, the club set a world record that has yet to be broken. Japan, viewed with a mixture of friendship, fear, and hostility by the rest of the world, certainly provides the journalist with an active and exciting setting in which to work. News stories bearing a Tokyo dateline, whether they are about political activity or economic developments, campus crises or women's lib, command the attention of newspapers, magazines, and television networks around the world. The members of the Foreign Correspondents' Club, many of them longtime residents of Tokyo, have played a far greater role in making Japan known to the outside world than any publicity campaign of the Japanese government. The image that Americans have of postwar Japan has been determined largely by the American members of the club.

But the longer the foreign correspondents stay in Japan, the more news coverage they do, and the more Japanese people they interview, the more frustrated they become with the difficulties of understanding the country. The Japanese are known for their friendliness to foreigners, but once aliens try to penetrate their inner feelings and probe their psychology, they are apt to become closed and uncommunicative. Furthermore, to Occidental eyes, the Japanese seem to hang together to an extraordinary degree, acting collectively rather than individually. The single greatest barrier faced by the correspondents is the Japanese language. Only three American members of the club can speak Japanese well enough to use it in their work. Perhaps, then, the very presence of the club and the excellence of the services it provides are illustrations of the fact that foreign newsmen, despite their training in lands of individualism, find it possible to work effectively in Japan only in a group.

Yukio Mishima was a friend of a number of foreign reporters and an occasional visitor to the Press Club. He once delivered a heavily autobiographical speech at a club dinner. Some of the correspondents had been invited to his rococo home, had drunk with him, or traveled with him, and they reacted to his suicide with strong personal feelings. Associated Press correspondent John Roderick, who had rushed in tears to Mishima's house as soon as he heard the news, says he misses profoundly Mishima's particular genius. There are other correspondents, such as Samuel Jameson of the *Los Angeles Times*, who considered Mishima a friend and a man deeply imbued with Western values, and who felt personally betrayed by the manner of his death. Jameson says he felt sick at heart when he heard Mishima's final appeal to the Self-Defense Forces and to the Japanese nation: "The one thing more valuable than human life is neither freedom nor democracy, but Japan." Is this but another example of the feeling of foreigners, confronted with Japan, that they will never penetrate deep enough below the surface for full understanding?

Bluejeans, Cokes, and Tie-Dyes

"DEAR UNCLE ITOI, is it true? Did Jimi Hendrix really die of an overdose of dope? I couldn't believe it when I heard that. I don't care how good a musician he was, taking drugs is wrong. Don't play Jimi's records any more on your program." Similar letters were written to Goro Itoi, a popular Japanese disc jockey, after Janis Joplin died of a heroin overdose not long after. The deaths of these two rock idols, not much written about in the press, were the subject of great controversy and discussion on late-night radio programs. "Japanese kids today," says Itoi, "think of foreign singers and musicians almost as though they were close friends, not strangers thousands of miles away. Jazz and rock have become their own music, not foreign music imported from afar."

"Uncle Itoi" is a pioneer among Japan's disc jockeys. The institution of disc jockeys was first recommended by the Occupation as an effective means of communicating with young people. They have been popular ever since. Nippon Broadcasting Company, which carries Itoi's program, has disc jockeys broadcasting from seven every night to four the next morning. As the night wears on, Japanese popular songs gradually give way to hard rock and other American or European music that is not much played on daytime radio. Itoi carries on what he calls his "postcard dialogue" with his young predawn listeners, who write him five thousand to eight thousand postcards every week requesting particular songs. During examination seasons the number of requests soars even higher.

Bluejeans and *shiborizome* fashions are other illustrations of young Japan's curious relationship with America. *Shiborizome*, or tie-dyeing, is an ancient Japanese technique of dyeing fabrics: the cloth is tied in knots before being immersed in the dye; since the color does not penetrate the knotted sections, an irregular, uncolored pattern appears when the fabric is unknotted. Shirts and pants covered with *shiborizome* designs have been wildly popular in Japan recently, but the modern version bears no direct connection to its traditional Japanese precedents. The fad came to Japan from America, where hippies had begun dyeing their T-shirts using a modified *shiborizome* technique. Shrewd Japanese clothing manufacturers quickly got wind of the new American fad and began mass-producing cloth with printed designs that simulated *shiborizome*. Cotton T-shirts that cost the manufacturer less than three hundred yen to make were avidly snatched up by young people at five or six times that price.

Blue denim jeans, called *G-pan* in Japan, are another popular fashion transmitted from the United States by the more than two hundred fashion watchers that Japanese clothing manufacturers have stationed around the country. Bluejeans, believed to have gotten their start when American cowboys or pioneers cut trousers for themselves out of tent cloth, are as "American" as hamburgers in the popular mind. They have been familiar in Japan since the Occupation, but it is only comparatively recently that they have caught on widely. Department stores used to look contemptuously on them, often refusing to carry them at all. Today, they have special bluejean corners, or "*G-pan* boutiques,*" where jeans can be found, new or faded, plain or in bright colors with all manner of embellishment. Japanese young people wear them not as heavy-duty work clothing but almost as a dressy fashion. Expo '70 was swarming with youths in jeans, contrasting vividly with older people in dark, tailor-made suits. These days even the elegant Imperial Hotel admits men in bluejeans. American manufacturers, currently selling seven to eight million pairs of bluejeans in Japan every year, are already mapping a campaign to boost sales to as many as one hundred million pairs.

Kenneth Boulding, noted American futurologist, predicts increased difficulties for any nation that tries to preserve its unique cultural characteristics amidst the process of global standardization that accompanies exchange of information on a massive scale. Ten years ago he believed that Japan's unique culture would survive far into the future, but viewing today's worldwide youth culture that makes no national distinctions, he is not so sure.

Japanese young people seem less and less able to distinguish, as older generations still do, those elements of the popular culture that are native to Japan and those that are imported from abroad. Jazz and rock are just music to them, bluejeans are just clothes, and pizza is just food. Still, even though they themselves are not much interested in tracing national origins, there is no denying that most of their culture has a strongly American flavor.

At a public antiwar rally in Tokyo's Hibiya Park one windy evening recently, six out of a group of ten high school boys were wearing tight-fitting bluejeans. After linking arms to sing a few songs together and shout some slogans denouncing American imperialism in Southeast Asia, the group moved off toward a sidewalk food stand. There they all bought Cokes and drank deeply from the bottles as sweat poured down their faces.

Blue-eyed Businessmen

FROM THE fourteenth floor of what for Tokyo is a tall building, the city looked dim and gloomy under a blanket of smog. But inside the brightly lit classroom of Sophia University, Robert Ballon was lecturing energetically. He gestured expressively as he talked to his class about the problems of doing business in Japan. "No," he replied to a question as to whether or not a foreigner can succeed as a business administrator in Japan, "put a Japanese at the top. Experience has shown that foreign managers trying to run a company directly generally leads to failure."

Sophia University's international seminar on business administration has long been familiar to foreign executives in Japan. It is offered annually by Professor Ballon, an authority on Japanese labor-management relations and director of the university's Socio-Economic Institute, who frequently invites other members of the faculty, professors from other universities, and prominent businessmen to address the class. James Abegglen, president of the Boston Consulting Group and a leading American student of Japanese business, is an occasional lecturer. In any given year the roll is sure to read like a catalogue of the world's great corporations. On this particular occasion it included representatives of General Electric, Shell, IBM, Dow Chemical, Chase Manhattan Bank, Texas Instruments, and other large companies. Although there are more European businessmen in it each year, Americans still predominate. The students are determined to assimilate themselves into what is for them the totally unfamiliar world of Japanese business.

American enterprises are working hard to remedy their past failure to recognize the potential of the Japanese market. Having once underestimated the almost unlimited purchasing power of a society of one hundred million people, as well as the skyrocketing growth of the Japanese economy as a whole, they seem to be frantically trying to make up for past mistakes. "Americans have realized that by limiting their economic aid to Japan to technological know-how and by holding off participating in the management of Japanese business, they have unwittingly helped Japan become a formidable competitor for them," says Abegglen. "Politically and financially, Japan is stable. Strategically, she is situated close to a densely populated continent. These conditions combine to make her extraordinarily attractive to American business."

Like honeybees catching the scent of a flower garden in full bloom,

American businessmen have swarmed to Japan. They have applied to the Ministry of International Trade and Industry for permission to establish affiliates in Japan at the rate of fifteen or sixteen a month. Branches of foreign firms have opened as rapidly as three a week. No advance permission is required to open a branch, simply a report after the fact. The usual strategy seems to be first to open a branch and only later, at the opportune moment, to apply for permission to establish an affiliate. Many of today's huge affiliates began as mini-branches employing only a manager and a single secretary in a one-room office.

Also increasingly in evidence are the "reconnaissance" men, shuttling between Japan and the United States, constantly on the lookout for the most propitious moment for their employers to open full-fledged business with Japan. Traveling back and forth on brief trips with hardly more than a single suitcase, these men are conspicuous in the hotels and plush apartment houses in the Akasaka area of Tokyo.

Foreigners attempting to do business successfully in Japan usually are forced, to a greater or lesser extent, to alter habits that they have developed from their experience elsewhere in the world. "Foreigners think up here, the Japanese down here," quips Ballon pointing first to his head and then to his stomach. "That is why joint-venture companies have proved so tough to run. For them to go well, the first thing foreigners have to do is to forget about business hours and work schedules and put in three times more work than they would at home." Several books in English have come out of Ballon's long experience with foreign businessmen: a guide to doing business in Japan, a study of joint ventures, and a book on Japanese employment practices; he is now at work on another.

The greatest difficulty faced by an American or European company opening up in Japan is recruiting a staff. There are not many Japanese who possess both the necessary proficiency in English and a talent for business. Those who do are often reluctant to join a foreign firm, whose future in Japan may not be as reliable or promising as that of a comparable Japanese company. Jerome Wattel, of the American public relations firm Hill and Knowlton International, arrived in Tokyo in the fall of 1969 to open a Japan branch. He had been in the State Department for many years and had friends in Japan whom he could call on for help. Even so, it took him more than half a year to get together qualified staff and start business. Learning a lesson from this experience, Hill and Knowlton has since established a training program that sends new Japanese employees to the United States for a year to study public relations at a university there before starting work. The Boston Consulting Group has a similar system, and other companies are beginning to follow suit.

At the same time, the foreign businessmen assigned to branches and joint ventures in Japan are getting younger and younger. Formerly, it was only older company men, about to retire, who had been sent to Japan. Now, with young businessmen arriving for long assignments in Japan, it looks as though foreign business is here to stay.

Japlish

ONE MUGGY summer day in 1945, the late Kikumatsu Ogawa, head of a publishing company, traveled to the farm town of Iwai in Chiba, not far from Tokyo, on an expedition to buy sweet potatoes. With wartime rations at almost starvation level, city people were forced out into the country to purchase additional food. It was August 15, and standing at Iwai station, Ogawa listened to the emperor's personal radio broadcast telling the nation of his decision to accept the Potsdam Declaration's terms for Japan's surrender. The Pacific War was over.

"This is it," thought Ogawa. "The Americans are coming. We're going to need English." He immediately forgot the potatoes and took the next train back to Tokyo. Overnight, he completed the manuscript of a small book titled *Handbook of Japanese-American Conversation.* Next, Ogawa took over the Dai Nippon Printing Company for a solid week to turn out the thirty-two-page manual. It sold four million copies in a month, a record that no subsequent best seller has yet been able to match.

"Until the day before the emperor's broadcast, father had kept five or six shotguns on hand, in case the Americans invaded Japan," laughs Ogawa's son, the present president of the Seibundo Shinkosha publishing firm.

"The end of the war suddenly transformed English from a strictly prohibited enemy language to a license for driving on the highway of life," recalls critic Daizo Kusayanagi. And today, English—or perhaps more correctly Japlish—has overrun the land. What remains of the Japanese language? Amid labels and merchandise wrappers advertising foreign names spelled in roman letters or the *katakana* syllabary (usually reserved for writing foreign words), "only sakè, brand

[26]

names, ancient medicinal herbs, traditional Japanese foods, and a few home electrical appliances retain their Japanese names," observes one expert in the naming of merchandise.

A survey conducted by a language-teaching research institute has revealed that sixty percent of the titles of Japanese TV programs include foreign words and that the *Asahi Shimbun* today uses three times as many foreign words as it did thirty-five years ago. The use of non-Japanese words by both media is predominantly in commercial advertising; more than eighty percent of current advertising copy depends on them. Even Chinese, the oldest foreign language in Japan and certainly the one most thoroughly integrated with the writing of Japanese, is receding before the onrush of English and the "consumer culture" coming from across the Pacific.

English-speaking people often find Japlish quite unintelligible. *Asahi* reporter Junji Kanda smiles as he recalls an American correspondent, hearing the term "running homer" at a baseball game, asking him teasingly: "Does a home run run?" Kanda realizes that the correct English term is "inside-the-park home run." "Base on balls" (BB in American score books) is "four balls" in Japan, and since Japanese lacks a real "f" sound, in "four" it is usually replaced by an "h" sound.

"All this is nothing to get worked up over," insists Professor Keifuku Ueno of Musashino University, who has proved through careful research that the term "nighter," now used even in foreign news dispatches, is of Japanese origin. "It is irrelevant to argue whether such things are misuses of English or whether they pose a threat to Japanese; they are now simply part of the Japanese language."

Occasional Japlish terms are bewildering even to old Japan hands otherwise accustomed to them. "After service" had former U. S. ambassador Edwin O. Reischauer puzzled for half a day before it dawned on him that it meant "after-sales service."

An entomologist avers that Japanese bees, if given an old hive that has previously been inhabited by Occidental bees, will not enter it but instead will thoroughly destroy it and then rebuild it to suit themselves. The analogy to the Japanization of English is not altogether far-fetched.

Other places where examples of Japanized English are flagrantly displayed are department stores and fashion advertising. A popular corner of Isetan Department Store is the so-called, in English, "His-Hers In Shop." What does it mean? "It is where things that will appeal to young men and women alike are sold," explains Hideo Take, sales promotion manager for the store. "Of course it's unintelligible, but it does seem to draw young people. We look to the young as 'market leaders,' and it is in them, rather than in their parents, that we strive to incite an urge to buy. The Japanese language is no longer adequate for that purpose. The parents have the money, to be sure, but—regardless of whether it's clothes or cars—they always seem to follow the advice of their kids as buying consultants. Parents don't trust themselves to pick the right styles or to get their money's worth."

Kyoto University professor Tadao Umezao believes that Japanese young people are no longer conscious of the "nationality" of the many foreign words that they see written in roman letters or in *katakana*. "What they are looking for is something that doesn't smell 'Japanese,' that has no connection with the tradition that they find objectionable. They don't care if that something comes from America. English may serve as a catalyst for 'de-Japanization,' but make no mistake, 'de-Japanization' is a far cry from 'Americanization.' It's like the mannequins standing in department stores. For the most part, they are of mixed blood and unknown nationality."

A recent series of Japan National Railways posters set off a flurry of letters to the *Asahi Shimbun*. One poster shows a herd of cows against a background of blue skies and fleecy white clouds; another pictures a farm family relaxing around the *irori* (hearth) of their old house after a hard day's work. There are no captions, but each poster carries the slogan "Discover Japan" in large, bold roman letters. Many of the letter writers protested the use of English for subjects that seemed so traditionally Japanese. But there is a Japanese title for the benefit of those who read no English at all. Hidden in one corner of the poster and printed in small type is a phrase, which the letter writers have evidently thought was a mistaken translation of "Discover Japan." Word for word, it is almost identical to the title of novelist Yasunari Kawabata's Nobel Prize speech: *Utsukushiki Nippon to Watakushi* ("Beautiful Japan and Myself").

And always the controversy rages. Some protest the use of incorrect English, others object to the very use of English at all. But the phenomenon continues unabated, and we seem to be witnessing the development of an altogether new language.

Fact Finding and Technology Gathering

IN THE FALL of 1970, the Japan Productivity Committee held a reception at a large hotel in Tokyo to celebrate having sent ten thousand men abroad on survey missions. Over the previous fifteen years, 965 separate groups of Japanese businessmen had traveled abroad, to the United States for the most part, to investigate foreign techniques of doing almost everything—from the operation of heavy industries to the management of small shops. Kohei Goshi, managing director of JPC, raising his glass in a toast to the success of those ten thousand men, compared them to the *kentoshi*, the envoys sent to the continent by the Japanese court of the seventh, eighth, and ninth centuries who have been credited with bringing the technology and culture of T'ang China to the Japanese islands. Indeed, the JPC-sponsored modern counterparts of the *kentoshi* had served much the same purpose; they had brought new life to the war-shattered industries and businesses of Japan. Goshi concluded by thanking the American government for its moral and financial assistance in sending the Japanese survey missions abroad.

The mid-1950s found the cold war at its height, the United States in need of a strong Asian ally, and Japan lagging far behind other industrialized nations in modern business management and industrial technology. It was against this background that the United States signed an agreement in April, 1955, to help foster a program to increase Japanese productivity. A month later, a survey mission comprised of men from the steel industry left for America, the first group sent by the JPC. It was soon followed by a top-management team that included Taizo Ishizaka, JPC president at the time and long a prominent business executive. "We were amazed by everything we saw," recalls Nobuo Noda, president of Seikei University, who accompanied the management team. "American technology was so advanced and our own so backward that we wondered whether our observations and reports would be of any use in Japan. . . . Everywhere we went the Americans briefed us with the kind generosity of parents teaching children."

The number of survey groups increased steadily—from 17 in 1955 to 108 in 1959 and 126 in 1960. Although some teams were sent to Europe or other parts of Asia, about seventy percent of them went to the United States. They returned to Japan speaking an exciting new language sprinkled with words like "marketing," "industrial engineering," and "human relations."

The early missions to the United States did not always meet with a friendly reception. One group, touring by car, ran out of water in a small town. When they asked for some water at one house, they were rudely turned away. The family's son had been killed in the Pacific during the war. Another group, waiting to board a plane, saw some of the American passengers refuse to ride on the same plane as Japanese. Today, such signs of hostility have all but disappeared. But in their place there has arisen in American industrial circles a suspicion and sense of caution when dealing with Japanese. In May, 1970, an observation team from small- and medium-sized Japanese industries was refused admittance at twenty-two of the American plants they had asked to see. This is not unusual. More and more American factories have been refusing admittance to Japanese unless they represent firms that have direct technological exchange arrangements with the factory owners. A letter from General Electric, received recently by a Tokyo travel agency, is a good illustration of the feelings of some American companies: "We had made it abundantly clear that we would refuse admittance of your group to our lighting-research laboratories. But when the group arrived, its members insisted on seeing the laboratories anyway. . . . Please be advised that in the future we will not allow Japanese visitors into any of our installations." It is suspected that the offending team included a representative of a Japanese firm that General Electric considered a competitor.

Meanwhile, the Japanese survey teams have gradually ceased to be amazed by what they see in the United States. Exclamations that everything seems to be "up to date," "labor-saving," or "rational" have disappeared from their reports. These days, they are more likely to comment: "We saw factories with backward equipment and limited productivity. . . . American workers are no match for Japanese when it comes to hard work." One group that inspected American department stores in 1968 reported that many of them were "as desolate as Japanese department stores in provincial cities around 1950."

Kiyoshi Nakamura, president of a machinery-manufacturing firm in Kuwana, Mie Prefecture, visited America in 1970 with a team of metalware manufacturers. He was disappointed to find that American small- and medium-sized industries were not as modern as he had expected. He even said as much to a Cleveland industrialist whom he met at one reception. "Japanese industries would go broke if they operated the way you do," Nakamura said, and added half in jest:

"Why don't you come to Japan and see what I mean?" When Nakamura returned to Japan, he found a letter waiting for him: the Cleveland businessman was writing to say that he would be in Japan in a
few months.

It may well be, however, that the real strength of American industry lies beyond the range of vision of the Japanese survey teams.
Their tours are usually rushed affairs, with packed schedules, and
there is probably much that they never see.

"There can be no doubt," says Professor Kazuo Noda of Rikkyo
University, "that the survey teams of the 1950s played a very significant role in spurring the modernization of postwar Japanese industry
and business. To be sure, there have been instances where hasty attempts to adopt American methods without sufficient adaptation has
led to failure. Still, for the most part, personal observation of the
American scene has been enormously beneficial to Japan. But, now
that the gap between Japan and the United States has narrowed, there
seems to be little need for aimless, general survey tours; from now on,
such trips should be made only for more specific purposes."

Legal Hangers-on and
Moonlighting Lawyers

"ADMITTING him would be tantamount to perpetuating the
humiliating legacy of the Occupation," declared one member
of the Tokyo Bar Association in firm opposition to the application for
admission that was being considered. A somewhat more moderate
lawyer counseled: "This matter is deeply rooted in Japanese-American relations; so we must not be hasty in deciding against him. We
must ponder carefully the grounds on which to reject the application."
The matter being debated by the Tokyo lawyers in November, 1970,
was the unprecedented application for admission to the Tokyo bar by
an American lawyer. The applicant was Norman Jensen, an assistant
professor of law at Meiji University. Ordinarily, to practice law in
Japan one must pass a state-administered judicial examination, complete a period of apprenticeship, and be admitted to a local bar association. But a special provision of the Lawyers Law of Japan permits
anyone with more than five years' experience as a professor or assis-

tant professor of the law school of a university to apply for membership in a bar association. Furthermore, the Lawyers Law contains no restrictions as to nationality of lawyers practicing in Japan.

Hope for Jensen's admission to the Tokyo bar has all but faded entirely. More than one Japanese lawyer, when asked his opinion of Jensen's application, replied: "He's acting as the vanguard of Baker and McKenzie, a leading American law firm. No doubt, Japan's economic expansion has made her an attractive market for the American legal profession, and that firm is only one of many that are trying to get a foothold here." Jensen himself says he is more disappointed than angry. "There was a period, after the war, when the Japanese adopted everything American. Now the pendulum seems to be swinging back in the other direction. The Japanese are growing nervous and exclusive. My rejection can readily be understood in that light."

With the entry of more and more foreign firms into Japan, the flourishing of joint ventures, and increasing instances of technological affiliation between Japanese and foreign firms, the demand for English-speaking international lawyers has swelled rapidly. "These developments have also given rise to numerous cases of foreign lawyers, unlicensed to practice in Japan, operating illegally," reveals Kimio Kodama, a member of the special committee in the Japan Federation of Bar Associations charged with investigating just such cases. "Investigation, already a complex task, is made all the more difficult by the fact that certain foreign lawyers are permitted to practice here by an unwritten law that qualifies them as 'associate members' of the bar."

Who are these associate members? When the War Crimes Tribunal completed its business in Tokyo, the Japanese government—at the request of the Occupation—created associate memberships in the bar for those foreign lawyers who had defended Japanese war criminals and who wished to remain in Japan to practice privately. The legal provision recognizing their membership was repealed in 1955, three years after the Occupation ended, but about twenty-eight of the associate members are still practicing. Some Japanese lawyers consider them unwanted "holdovers" from the Occupation and complain that for the legal profession the postwar era will not come to an end until the foreign lawyers are gone. Recalling the absolute powers of the Occupation, these Japanese lawyers relate—with a combination of amusement and resentment—how the American-authorized capital system was incorporated into the Commercial Code of Japan when it was revised in 1950. The system adopted was for all practical purposes a replica of the pertinent provisions in the state laws of Illinois.

One need not look far for the reasons for this odd legal quirk: the American legal-affairs officer responsible for supervising the revision of the Commercial Code happened to be from Illinois.

One of the more prominent foreign law firms in Tokyo is Anderson, Mori, and Rabinowitz; the three partners are all American (Arthur Mori is a Hawaii-born Nisei) and all three are associate members of the Tokyo bar. The firm employs six or seven American trainees and about ten young Japanese lawyers. The latter are among a new breed of Japanese lawyers—protégés of the foreign associate-member lawyers. One of them, Kunio Hamada, who works for Anderson, Mori, and Rabinowitz, does not seem to care a bit about being called an *isoro bengoshi* ("hanger-on lawyer"). "I am well versed in Japanese laws and customs and think of myself as an example of Japanese-American collaboration in the legal profession. The presence of foreign associate members in the bar association is no humiliation to the Japanese," he insists. "Why, there aren't nearly enough Japanese lawyers who can speak English and handle matters of international law. . . . Eventually, however, I am sure that we shall replace the American lawyers practicing here."

Michael Braun is another associate member of the Tokyo bar; he runs a firm jointly with a Japanese lawyer. "We think of ourselves as a stopgap serving a necessary function until Japanese lawyers acquire sufficient ability and experience in international business. I'm sure that they will be more than able to handle international affairs by the time we leave Japan." This prediction is already coming true, for there are Japanese lawyers who are now beginning to move out on their own after working for the foreign associate members.

"We must give the associate members due credit for the part they have played in internationalizing Japanese legal activities," says a spokesman for the Federation of Bar Associations. "Moreover, they are, for the most part, quite law-abiding. What we are more afraid of is that the legal advisers brought here by foreign business enterprises will not be content to limit themselves to working only for their employers, but will begin to operate in Japan as 'moonlighting lawyers.'"

The Elephant Cage

SEVEN kilometers to the north of the U. S. Air Force base at Misawa in Japan's northern Aomori Prefecture, on a narrow spit of land projecting into Lake Ogawa, sits the "elephant cage." Like a huge pen for circus elephants, scores of antennae six and a half feet high are arranged in three concentric circles. At the center of the circles stands a single building, round and windowless. This weird complex, built in the spring of 1965, could only be one thing—an electronic intelligence-collecting center. But, though its function of gathering information on the communist world cannot be disguised, all activities within the center are shrouded in secrecy. The more than one hundred Japanese who work for the U. S. 6921st Security Battalion, which maintains the cage, are denied access to it, and the battalion personnel themselves are prohibited from marrying Japanese citizens, presumably as a precaution against intelligence leakage.

The usual tour of duty for military personnel at Misawa base to the south is one or two years. Cage personnel, however, stay longer: three to six years. They are also much better paid. Shopkeepers in town usually demand cash on delivery from base personnel, but are generous in allowing people at the cage easy credit. But flush as they may be, there are fewer than two thousand people connected with the elephant cage and their spending would not go far toward sustaining the economic well-being of the town of Misawa. That is why townspeople were stunned by the official announcement at the end of December, 1970, that three full air-force units would soon be transferred from Misawa to South Korea. They could visualize their livelihood vanishing almost overnight.

Misawa is perhaps typical of the hundreds of Japanese communities that have depended for economic growth on the presence of an American military base. There are 123 such bases left in Japan today; there used to be more. Until the end of the war, Misawa was hardly more than a fishing village of fewer than ten thousand inhabitants. The arrival of the Occupation forces and the building of the base set off its rapid growth into a township of twenty-seven thousand. In 1958, it was incorporated as a city, and the 1970 census set its population at thirty-six thousand. This figure includes the 4,500 American military and civilian employees of the base, their 4,600 dependents, and 2,500 members of the Japanese Self-Defense Forces and their dependents. When all the nonmilitary Japanese employees of the base and those merchants who trade almost exclusively with base personnel are added in, it becomes quickly apparent that nearly half of the local populace is connected in one way or another with the American military installation.

The spending of base personnel at Misawa amounted to nearly 4.5 million dollars in 1969, one-fifth of the city's income. Although it is just a small rural city, Misawa boasts more than 140 bars and cabarets. English signboards and posters are to be seen everywhere. It is also noteworthy that student-worker "Yankee Go Home!" demonstrations, while not totally absent from the streets of Misawa, have been considerably less fierce or strident than antibase demonstrations elsewhere. It was only fairly recently that Misawa municipal authorities began to measure the noise of American fighter planes, a base-induced public annoyance that has been loudly denounced in other parts of Japan. The average citizen of Misawa, well aware of his dependence on the base for his livelihood, takes a dim view of anti-American agitation, and only four of the thirty men who sit on the city council oppose the presence of the base.

Local American servicemen have shown their friendship for the people of Misawa in a number of ways. They have helped in relief and reconstruction work after fires or earthquakes, and they have used military materials and equipment to repair schools and other public buildings. Col. Edward Aune, commanding officer of the 348th Combat Support Group at Misawa, says that he has made it part of his job to foster friendship and understanding between the people of Misawa and the Americans under him. He cites a number of Japanese-American friendship projects that have been launched under his personal supervision: Operation Eyesight, a fund-raising campaign to benefit people suffering from eye diseases that can be cured by treatment or surgery; visits to orphanages and welfare institutions by officers' wives; donations to the Community Chest Fund amounting to nearly half of the city's total collection; friendly athletic meets between Japanese and American high school boys; free English lessons given by American servicemen and their wives at local schools.

Reassured by the generally friendly mood, the people of Misawa were confident that—regardless of changes in U. S. Asian strategy—the base at Misawa, which even housed nuclear weapons according to some rumors, would be considered vital to Asian security and would not be abandoned outright. It was this former optimism that made the shock all the more intense when the transfer to Korea was announced. Just before the announcement, a poll was taken on the question of what Misawa's future should be. Of the respondents, 22.7% believed that the city's future should depend exclusively on the development of new industries, 28% suggested dependence on both the income from the base and industrial development, 5.4% were satisfied with continued dependence exclusively on the base, and 12.6% advocated total abolition of the military installation. The figures seem to indicate a rising desire to escape from a "base economy" and an increasing interest in attracting other industries to Misawa, but they also testify to the general uneasiness about a future without the support of the base. City fathers, while opposed to any drastic reduction in the size of the base, have been investigating ways to establish steel plants or oil refineries in Misawa as an alternative to total economic dependence on the Americans. Their plans are still at an exploratory stage and there is still no industry to speak of at Misawa.

For the moment, the elephant cage is Misawa's only economic support. Although there is more debate about its presence than ever before, Socialist assemblyman Ko Watanabe represents only a very small minority opinion when he demands that Misawa be purged of "espionage activities." The majority of the city still backs Mayor Tomio Kohirumaki's hopes that the staff of the cage will stay on, even after the personnel of the rest of the base disappear from the streets of Misawa. Present indications are that it will remain—a presence that some find ominous and others reassuring, a symbol of the continuing ambivalence of Japan's relations with the United States.

Oracle of Greatness

" ACCORDING TO Herman Kahn," said the president of the United States, "Japan's GNP will soon be the world's largest. Japan has clearly become a superpower, and we would like to see her live up to her responsibilities as such. Her military power should be increased and she should extend more aid to other Asian countries." President Nixon was talking to Prime Minister Sato at the White House in November, 1969. The prime minister replied: "I cannot agree with Mr. Kahn's theories. Japan, at this moment, simply cannot afford to do all that you are suggesting."

Ever since Herman Kahn announced to the world that it would not be at all surprising if the twenty-first century should prove to be "the Japanese century," he has been riding the crest of a "Kahn boom" in Japan. "The timing was perfect," explains critic Jiro Sakamoto. "Up until he published his book *The Emerging Japanese Superstate*, Japanese writers had been predicting a bleak future for their country. The public, however, had begun traveling abroad in greater numbers and was beginning to feel Japan's remarkable presence in the world. Then Mr. Kahn's rosy view of Japan's future, coming as it did from the distinguished director of the Hudson Institute, known for his analyses and predictions in international relations, had an enormous impact on the Japanese."

Despite his protests in Washington to the contrary, Prime Minister Sato fell for Kahn's pronouncements as much as anyone else. On the campaign trail before the 1968 elections for the Upper House, he quoted Kahn frequently and painted a glowing picture of the future prosperity that Japan would enjoy under a Liberal-Democratic administration. When the American futurologist visited Japan the following year, a beaming Sato acknowledged his party's indebtedness to him for its victory in the election. "The least the government can do," joked Kahn in response, "is to decorate me for giving the Japanese people back their self-confidence."

But if Kahn's oracular pronouncements are inspiring self-confidence in the Japanese, they are having almost the opposite effect in the United States. While in America to attend Congressional subcommittee hearings on foreign economic policy, Saburo Okita, director of the Japan Economic Research Center, found himself besieged wherever he went by the same question: "Was Herman Kahn correct in predicting that Japan would overtake the United States in the twenty-first century?" This much-quoted prophecy has served to intensify the antipathy and anxiety that Japan's incredible economic growth had already inspired in many Americans. It also offers ammunition to those who argue that Japan should spend more on her own defense, or that she should voluntarily reduce her exports to the United States. "Kahn's book has made Americans view Japan with much sharper eyes, and has made my job much tougher," smiles William Tanaka, a Washington lawyer long familiar as a lobbyist for Japanese interests in Congress.

The quickly widening "image gap" in the American opinion of Japan could prove dangerous to Japanese-American relations. Japanese are quick to point out that foreigners place too much emphasis on GNP and consequently tend to overrate Japan. "GNP is but a mirage," say many Japanese, "when the majority of the population is still so poor."

When Kahn visited the Soviet Union in 1969, he warned Russian experts to keep alert or they would find themselves surpassed in GNP by Japan by the end of the 1970s. He went on to astound them by predicting Japan's arming herself with nuclear weaponry by 1975. At a later international conference, a Japanese political scientist, identified only as W, was told of Kahn's predictions by a Soviet military-affairs expert who had heard him. W took great pains to refute Kahn and to explain the actualities of the Japanese situation. Wrapping up his long rebuttal of Kahn's views with the statement that Japan would hardly do anything so stupid as to try to build a nuclear arsenal, he asked: "Well, now do you believe me or Herman Kahn?" The Russian thought for a moment, and then replied: "Kahn was much more convincing."

To be sure, Kahn's analyses, bristling with statistics, seem far more persuasive to Westerners than attempts to explain the complex reality of Japanese society, a reality that defies statistical analysis. Still, many longtime American residents of Japan have little use for Kahn's views and dismiss him, saying that he shows no reluctance to say the most outrageous things. The *New York Times* also criticized him, commenting that a so-called analysis of Japanese national characteristics by someone who does not even speak Japanese could hardly be very credible. Knowledgeable Japanese have also joined in the criticism of Kahn's predictions. Kiichi Saeki, director of the Nomura Research Institute, challenges Kahn's prediction that Japan will develop a nuclear capability: "Once we begin obtaining nuclear weapons, we will throw ourselves into an insane arms race to the death with China. Kahn says that young Japanese will seek the military prestige of a major power for their nation. Can he really think that we have learned nothing from history?"

Eight thousand miles away, at the Hudson Institute, comfortably nestling among the trees in a wooded area thirty miles north of New York City, Herman Kahn lowers his colossal body into a chair in his office. He seems to be enjoying his new role as a Japanologist as he shrugs off the critical reactions to his prophecies: "I predict that Japan's famous allergy to nuclear weaponry will vanish quickly and that she will begin arming herself because China's development of a nuclear potential will make it seem necessary. But don't misunderstand me: I'm not urging Japan to do that. . . . You tell me that I overemphasize GNP and cook up analyses unrelated to the real sentiments of the Japanese people. I know that Japan is not abundantly wealthy and that a majority of her people are dissatisfied with their present life. But wealth is only an accumulation of the past. GNP is an index of present productive capacity. Wealth is actually more equitably distributed in Japan than in the United States or in most other countries. . . . Japan is a 'shame society,' not a 'guilt society.' The Japanese will no doubt continue to be conscious of their defeat in the Pacific War and of the dangers of fighting a war with misguided judgment. But I wonder if they ever consider the Pacific War as being wrong from a moral or ethical point of view as well."

Okinawan New Year

NEW YEAR'S DAY 1971 fell on a Friday. And, as on every Friday, the Tapper Club at an American military base in central Okinawa was open to the local populace for the weekly "American-Ryukyuan Friendship Night." The spacious main room of the club was filled with Okinawan girls in colorful kimono and young men dressed in their best suits. The dance floor was jammed with people dancing to the fast beat of a live band. No clubs or cabarets on Okinawa are as well set up as those on the military bases. They bring talented artists from all over the world to perform, and the entertainment is more up to date than at any private clubs. Anyone who wants to learn the latest go-go steps need only go to a U. S. club.

Okinawa has many military clubs: separate ones for officers, enlisted men, retired military men, American civilians and dependents. For the most part, they offer local people a taste of good, clean, affluent American life. If a young Okinawan is lucky, an American serviceman might even treat him to a "good-will beer." But Okinawans flock to the clubs when they can for another reason: they can buy things there for incredibly low prices. A bottle of American wine, elegantly served in an ice bucket, costs less than two dollars, a glass of scotch and water only thirty-five cents. Wines and liquor are generally cheaper on Okinawa than on the main Japanese islands, but even so, bars off the bases charge at least eighty cents for the same scotch and water and three and a half dollars for a bottle of the same wine. The reason that they can be bought so cheaply on the bases is that there is no tax on them.

The Harbor View Club, located right behind the Ryukyu government buildings, used to be the site of nightly conferences between American administrators and officials of the Ryukyu government. Its membership still includes conservative Okinawan politicians, businessmen, and representatives of the Japanese government or of Japanese firms. But when Chobyo Yara was elected governor of the

Ryukyus, his first order of business was to direct his subordinates to stay away from the Harbor View. His next move was to crack down on the tax-free cigarettes, whisky, food, and beverages from the American clubs that were inundating the local markets. He also forced two military clubs that had been open to local Okinawans every day to close their doors again. Some clubs remain open to Okinawans only on a once-a-week basis. At others, an American doorman will admit local people with a wink and a warning that they are his guests for the evening. But despite such laxity, Yara has succeeded in making tax-free goods harder to obtain by the islanders. What is "tax free" to the American residents is actually "tax evasion" for local citizens. This is but one of many irregularities in the relations between rulers and ruled.

The "affluent America," which Okinawan youths see on or around the bases every day, sharpens their sense of the contrast between the foreigners' wealth and their own poverty, and indirectly lures them into delinquency. American slot machines, for example, have triggered a craze for gambling among the islanders that has resulted in bankruptcies and suicides. Yara, a clean-cut but stubborn former schoolteacher, turned to politics in order to fight "the insidious poison that seeps out through the barbed wire fences of the bases." The thrust of his progressive regime is to foster moral and philosophical resistance to the corruption and decadence that results inevitably from a situation in which occupiers and occupied live together in close proximity. Every youth who stumbles drunkenly out of an American club muttering about the Americans always having their way is exhibiting a psychology common to people living under foreign rule.

The topic on everyone's lips at New Year's parties in January, 1971, was the anti-base riot at Koza. The newspapers had reported it merely as a collective act by a crowd of five thousand people. But each one of the five thousand had his own story to tell about what actually went on. An intriguing question was how such a large crowd could get together so quickly before dawn without any public transportation. Taxis and their obliging drivers were the secret behind the riot. First, the drivers had relayed word of the trouble to surrounding residents. Then they ferried men into Koza from neighboring towns in quick, efficient relays, and charged them nothing for the ride. Other cab drivers parked their cars near the scene of the disturbances in Koza and set about refueling them for the escape. When American MPs began to get the situation under control, the cabbies began ferrying the retreating Okinawans out of Koza, again free of charge.

Why should the taxis be so actively involved in an affair like this?

Since Okinawa has no railways, no streetcars, and a very inadequate network of bus lines, taxis are the major means of transportation for islanders and American servicemen alike. Their drivers have been victimized for years by GIs stealing free rides or robbing them of their fares. Armed robberies of taxi drivers account for ninety percent of the offenses committed by Americans against islanders. Since the offending serviceman is usually shipped home quickly, the murder-robberies of Okinawan taxi drivers are rarely solved. As a primary contact point between the Okinawan people and their American rulers the taxi drivers have been exposed to dangers and have built up a thick residue of distrust and animosity.

Other contact points have been the source of dangerous friction between the United States and Okinawans. The process of removing the stockpile of poison gas from Okinawa and the expected dismissal of numerous Japanese base employees in the near future are sure to bring further turmoil to the island. But Okinawa has always been a tinder-box of turmoil and inflamed passions. It stands today as an illustration of the fact that there can be no true friendship between foreign rulers and a people under subjugation.

PART TWO

From Black Ships
to Atom Bombs

In July, 1853, U. S. Navy Commodore Matthew C. Perry, in command of four warships, sailed into Edo Bay to demand the opening of Japan to Western commerce. Six months later, he returned to sign a treaty forcing open the small island country that had been almost totally closed off from the rest of the world for two and a half centuries. Word of the visits of what the Japanese called the "Black Ships"—not only were they painted black but several of them, though sailing ships, were also equipped with early steam engines that belched black smoke—spread throughout the country, shaking feudal Japan to its foundations: within fifteen years a revolution had occurred in the administration of the country and a program of modernization had been launched that would transform almost every element of traditional Japanese culture beyond recognition. In half a century, the backward nation was hurtled to major-power status, dramatically symbolized by its victory over Russia in 1905. Forty years later, the same nation lay in ruins, shorn of its far-flung empire, its industry demolished, and its people disillusioned and starving.

At every moment during these ninety-two years, America's presence was felt in Japan. Although the period opened with Perry's warships and closed with atomic bombings and military occupation, much of the interim was peaceful. Many of the foreign experts who arrived after 1868 to guide the eager but uncertain first steps of the new Meiji government came from the United States. They were accompanied by American missionaries, diplomats, and businessmen. Japanese also traveled abroad in increasing numbers, as diplomats and businessmen and students, but most of all as cheap labor. These Japanese laborers in America were not greeted with the sort of welcome accorded Americans coming to Japan. Brutalized, under-

paid, and denounced as a "yellow peril," the degradations suffered by Japanese seeking a new life in America culminated in the Exclusion Act of 1924 that was interpreted as a deliberately racist, anti-Japanese affront. During the nineteen-twenties and thirties, the earlier good will enjoyed by the two nations shifted rapidly to mutual suspicion and hostility. Economic tensions and fears of increased military power on both sides of the Pacific contributed to the disharmony then as they do today, and mutual misunderstandings only exacerbated the difficulties. In 1941, suspicion, hostility, and failures to communicate erupted into war.

The articles in this section offer a picture of the enthusiasm and promise of Japanese-American relations with which the century began, of some of the critical difficulties that developed to disrupt the relationship as the century progressed, and of the disaster in which that century ended. The innumerable lessons from the events of the century seem each day more relevant to the tensions plaguing the relations of the two countries today. But have the lessons been learned?

Samurai Seafarers

JAPANESE prime ministers, one after another, have beaten a path to Washington carrying all sorts of policy problems in their satchels. These petitioning missions have been criticized sarcastically by the opposition as *"a modern form of sankin kotai"* (the Tokugawa administrative regulation by which the shoguns required feudal lords to travel to the capital for regular periods of attendance). But not all prime ministers have borne petitions to Washington; more recently they have been carrying national demands from Japan.

The White House was full of people invited for the occasion. As the honor guard stood at attention, the Japanese prime minister walked forward stiffly, his right arm moving with his right foot almost as though they were tied together. He looked extremely tense, and his hand trembled as he held up his prepared message to read. Such is an eyewitness account of Premier Sato's historic meeting with President Johnson in 1968. It was in the course of their talks that the United States agreed to return the Bonin Islands to Japan.

More than a century earlier, on February 13, 1860, another group of Japanese left for the United States. It was the first official mission sent to a Western nation in Japan's history. A cold wind was blowing as the American steamer *Powhatan* pulled out of Yokohama harbor to begin its long, hazardous journey across the Pacific. The samurai on board, each with his hair bound in traditional fashion and wearing two swords at his side, were the envoys sent by the shogunate to exchange ratifications of the Treaty of Amity and Commerce signed two years previously with U. S. Consul Townsend Harris. The party of seventy-seven Japanese aboard the *Powhatan* was led by Niimi Masaoki, Lord of Buzen, the shogunate minister in charge of foreign affairs.

Muragaki Norimasa, Lord of Awaji, was a member of the mission, and he recorded his thoughts as he left Japan in a diary that has been preserved in the home of his great-great-grandson, the composer Raymond Hattori. Muragaki recalled the reaction of the Japanese to the arrival of Commodore Perry's black warships seven years earlier. The inhabitants of the small port of Uraga had lined bronze temple bells along the beach, hoping that the Americans might mistake them for cannons. Later, at a luncheon for the American naval officers, the Japanese hosts had seen to it that the Americans were served sawed-off sticks of bamboo while they themselves ate bamboo shoots cooked the same way, in order to demonstrate the superior strength of Japanese teeth. "What foolishness!" Muragaki had written. "But who can blame the Japanese for that? These were the first foreigners they had ever encountered."

When the United States sent Perry to secure a supply base for American whalers in Japan, he forced open the firmly closed doors of the country by a show of force that the Japanese could not hope to resist. No wonder Niimi and his party of samurai were filled with grim forebodings as they set sail for America. Most of the female members of each man's family had broken down in tears when they heard of his appointment to the mission. Moreover, the party was forced to leave Japan in secret, with only their immediate families informed of their departure. Their fears were no doubt increased by the waves of antiforeignism that were sweeping Japan at the time. While the mission was in America, the shogunate's chief minister Ii Naosuke was assassinated at the gate of Edo Castle by a band of nationalistic extremists because he had encouraged greater inter-course with the outside world.

But contrary to its expectations and fears, the Japanese delegation was royally welcomed in the United States. Wherever it went, Americans were full of curiosity and respect for these rare dignitaries who had come from a distant corner of the world. The samurai, for their part, behaved like samurai: rigid, unbending, and reluctant to display enthusiasm for anything they saw. When they visited the White House and saw the busts of previous presidents lining the hallways, they commented that it reminded them of the heads of executed criminals exposed outside prison gates in Japan. Congress in session seemed "a bedlam like the fishmarket in Edo," and Western vocal music fell on their ears like "the midnight baying of a dog." In time, however, American hospitality converted the Japanese visitors into enthusiastic eulogists of things American. Beyond their immediate experience, it might be said that their conflicting attitudes of praise and disdain were the prototype of Japanese sentiments regarding America that were to prevail over the next hundred years.

The Japanese mission of 1860 received a wonderful press in the United States, far better than the coverage accorded later official visitors. The *New York Times* featured the visit on its front page, calling the Japanese elegant in their behavior and observing that

Americans must seem every bit as odd to them as they appeared to Americans. The climax of the visit was a procession down Broadway escorted by a military band and six thousand honor guards. Even Walt Whitman sang of the mission in *Leaves of Grass:*

> Over the Western sea hither from Niphon come,
> Courteous, the swarth-cheek'd two-sworded envoys,
> Leaning back in their open barouches, bare-headed,
> impassive,
> Ride to-day through Manhattan.

The whole of America was rejoicing over the opening of Japan to the world. For several years after the visit of the samurai, American textbooks described their mission and its significance in international relations. Having opened Japan by flexing her muscle, the United States was determined to appear friendly and make for herself an ally in the Pacific. "This may be viewed as another example of America's traditional impulse to protect the weak," says Takeshi Kimura, a specialist in American affairs. "This sentiment can be detected running continually at the depth of Japanese-American relations; sometimes it was turned to Japan's benefit, sometimes it was used against Japan to protect other, weaker nations."

In contrast to the relative obscurity of the voyage of the Japanese mission on the *Powhatan*, much publicity in Japan has been given to the vessel *Kanrin-maru* which sailed with the *Powhatan*. Its fame is due to the fact that it was the first ship actually built in Japan to cross the Pacific. It was captained by Katsu Kaishu, a high official of the shogunate, whose task it was to witness the mission's safe arrival in America and report back to Japan. "But I wonder if the *Kanrin-maru* would ever have reached San Francisco without the help of Lt. John Mercer Brooke of the American navy and the American sailors on board," says writer Jun Eto. "The Japanese crew was totally unfit, by training and temperament, to sail a modern naval vessel. After the voyage, Katsu told a friend that the samurai on board were always seasick and stayed below in their cabins and that the Japanese crew just sat around smoking. Katsu was apparently deeply impressed by the ability of the American sailors to work on their own initiative, without always requiring orders from above. This helped him realize how the future Japan should be governed."

According to novelist Ryotaro Shiba, Katsu was asked by Sakamoto Ryoma, a leader of the movement to overthrow the shogunate and restore the emperor to sovereignty over the Japanese state, whether

[47]

the descendants of George Washington continued to occupy in America the illustrious position enjoyed in Japan for 250 years by the descendants of the first Tokugawa shogun Ieyasu. "Far from it," replied Katsu. "No one has ever heard of them." It was at that moment, speculates Shiba, that Sakamoto determined to cast his lot with the restoration movement against the shogunate. The image of America communicated to him by Katsu, Sakamoto in turn embodied in the "Eight Articles Conceived on Shipboard," his view of what the new government's policies should be after the shogunate was destroyed. Some of Sakamoto's ideas were later incorporated in the famous "Five Articles Oath" (also called the "Charter Oath") of 1868, which proclaimed the credo of the new government.

After the restoration was accomplished and the new government established, Japanese interest shifted rapidly toward developing closer ties with European nations, particularly France and England. But there is no question that the United States played the leading role in the opening of Japan, and relations with America at that time seem especially significant when viewed in the light of present relations between the two countries.

"A Drop in the Bucket"

A YOUNG American teacher stepped wide-eyed off a boat in Yokohama in December, 1870. William Elliot Griffis had been hired by the lord of Fukui to teach in the clan school. Expecting a savage, primitive land, he was amazed at the sight that greeted his eyes. The Yokohama waterfront was lined with banking houses with stone facades in the Western style; walking through the streets of the city, he saw a hotel that looked like any in a small American city, a photo studio, gaslights, and a shop window with a display of canned milk and a portrait of Abraham Lincoln. Was he really in Japan, had he wandered into some fantastic stage set, or was he seeing a mirage? Before Griffis had left for Japan, he had tried to take out a life insurance policy. The insurance company turned down his application outright, as though the young man were about to venture into some hazardous wilderness.

Both Griffis and the insurance brokers were unaware of the tremendous receptivity of the Japanese to novelty and of the new government's policy of modernization. Ever since Japan had opened her doors to the West and signed the first commercial treaty with the United States twelve years earlier, wave after wave of westernization had swept over sections of the country, transforming them almost beyond recognition.

Griffis first became interested in Japan through two Japanese students whom he met at Rutgers University, in New Jersey, where he had been studying theology. The two were the Yokoi brothers, Tahei and Saheita, the first Japanese students at Rutgers. They were nephews of Yokoi Shonan, an eminent philosopher and a determined advocate of opening Japan to foreign contacts long before the imperial restoration of 1868 made it fashionable to hold such views. The two brothers had studied under Guido Fridolin Verbeck, an American missionary in Nagasaki and later an adviser to the Japanese government; he had sent them to study at Rutgers with a letter of introduction to his mission board in New Jersey. When they escaped from Japan under assumed names, they left behind a letter saying: "One of us may die and never return to our homeland, but the other will live and struggle to be of service to Japan." When the mission board asked them what they wished to study in America, the two young men, one twenty-two and the other only seventeen, declared proudly: "Navigation and military technology, so we can defend Japan against victimization by the West."

More and more young Japanese followed the Yokoi brothers, many of them bearing introductions from Verbeck, and Rutgers soon became a mecca of Japanese students in the United States. The young Japanese worked devotedly at their studies, driven by their consciousness of what they believed to be the impending menace to their country. Some skipped sleep and meals to have more time for their studies. Taro Kusakabe literally worked himself to death from exhaustion; his grave on the Rutgers campus became a small shrine for the Japanese students who studied there.

Griffis, seeing the diligence and patriotic fervor of his Japanese classmates, was stirred by a desire to help them enlighten their countrymen. His missionary zeal and sense of duty to God also impelled him to go to Japan. When he received an invitation from Verbeck and the offer of a teaching position in Fukui, he did not hesitate to accept. Some of his friends warned him of the possible dangers lurking in the unknown land; other missionary friends advised against going to Japan because "among innumerable heathens, you would be no more than a drop in the bucket." With firm religious conviction, Griffis replied: "Then let me be that drop," and set off for Japan.

[49]

Many of the American advisers to the Japanese government or teachers in clan schools during the early years of the Meiji era were missionaries like Griffis. "They were filled with a love of mankind, and felt that they could best accomplish their evangelical mission by first enlightening the Japanese culturally," explains Tadashi Kaneko of the National Institute for Educational Research. "In a Japan whose interest in the West had already been whetted by the earlier Dutch studies, they found an audience highly receptive to their instruction." The missionary-teachers were encouraged at first by the intense eagerness of the Japanese people to learn about the West. The eventual conversion of the country to Christianity would be of little difficulty, they were convinced. But they were wrong. With only rare exceptions, the Japanese, eager as they were to learn Western science and technology, had no use for the gospel. Griffis and his contemporaries of like mind did, indeed, turn out to be no more than drops in the evangelistic bucket. But for Japan the influence of the Western culture, science, and philosophy that they taught was immeasurable.

The list of Americans working in the service of Japan during the first years of Meiji is not long, but it includes names that are still remembered with affection and gratitude by the Japanese. Griffis taught biology, physics, and law at the Fukui clan school. The scientific experiments that he performed in the classroom were a source of fascination and amazement not only to his students, who attended his classes assiduously, but also to officials of the local government, who flocked to the classes in such numbers that many of them were forced to observe through the windows. Verbeck, as supreme adviser to the newly born Meiji government, was instrumental in establishing many of the policies for the modernization of Japan. Henry Willard Denison, serving as legal adviser to the Foreign Ministry from 1880 to 1914, drafted nearly all important diplomatic documents for the Japanese government. David Murray was an adviser to the Education Ministry and the real architect of the reformed educational system. Horace Capron, U. S. Commissioner of Agriculture, was hired along with a staff of American experts to advise the Hokkaido Colonization Office for several years. William Clark taught at the Sapporo School of Agriculture (precursor of Hokkaido University) for eight months and is still remembered for his farewell exhortation to his students: "Boys, be ambitious!" James Curtis Hepburn created the system of romanizing Japanese words that is still in use today. The architect and archaeologist Edward Morse discovered and excavated a prehistoric shell mound in Tokyo; his book *Japanese Houses and Their Surroundings* set off a wave of interest among American architects, who began incorporating Japanese architectural elements in their designs. Lowell Mason, composer of the immortal hymn "Nearer, My God, to Thee," is responsible for developing Japanese interest in Western music.

All these Americans were motivated by benevolence and a sense of mission to transplant Western knowledge to a backward nation that was struggling to modernize itself quickly. They were not soldiers of fortune or idle drifters, but men of professional integrity and superior moral character. It is interesting to note also that the early Americans in Japan came with no financial backing from their government. Japan's good fortune in the quality of her foreign teachers is particularly striking when compared to the colonial experience of other nations in Asia and Latin America.

"Japan's modernization policies were motivated by her sense of resistance to predatory Western invaders," comments Noboru Umetani of Osaka University. "This allowed her to be discriminating in her adoption of Western civilization, culling from it only what seemed best or most useful." The Meiji government sought to inculcate in the Japanese the attitude of *wakon yosai*, "Japanese spirit and Western learning." But despite the Japanese eagerness to learn and the Western willingness to teach, the Americans in the pay of Japanese employers often found themselves confronting exasperating obstacles. "With few exceptions," wrote Griffis in his book *The Mikado's Empire*, "we foreigners were given no authority. . . . The Japanese government was quick to reward loyal and able advisers with trust and cooperation. But should one's usefulness be exhausted or should he try to take charge, he would be removed forthwith."

"Today, Japanese experts abroad suffer from the same dilemma," comments Kazuhiko Nishijima of Tokyo University, who conducted research in America from 1959 to 1966. "Often, imported brains are used to fill important gaps until domestic resources are developed to replace them. Relations between the imported experts and their employers tend to go well at first, but clashes inevitably occur as soon as the foreigners begin to make demands. In this kind of international cooperation, each side must determine precisely what the other wants and establish a clear give-and-take relationship." Be that as it may, William Griffis would probably find it even more amazing than his first view of Japan to learn that, a scant century later, Japan has begun to export her brains to his own country and to the rest of the world.

Treaty Revision Past and Present

SUMMER, 1970. Shariki Village, on the coast of Aomori Prefecture in northern Japan. The occasion was the unveiling of a monument to the memory of the crewmen of an American ore-carrying freighter that had been shipwrecked in a storm off Shariki in 1889. U. S. Ambassador Armin Meyer was on hand, and in his address he recalled with gratitude that those seamen who survived the wreck owed their lives to the local villagers. As the Americans washed ashore, the Japanese villagers stripped naked and managed to revive some of them with their own body warmth. Praising the Shariki spirit as "a human love that knew no national boundaries," Meyer expressed the hope that such sentiments could be kept alive on both sides of the Pacific. His address, and indeed the ceremony itself, was a tribute to a generous and heroic act of direct, impulsive friendship by honest fishermen who had probably never even seen foreigners before.

During the latter part of the nineteenth century, Japanese-American relations were amicable and, for the most part, uneventful. In 1879, former president Ulysses S. Grant visited Japan in the course of a global tour. Emperor Meiji called on him personally at his hotel, and the two leaders talked at length about politics and diplomatic relations. Over the previous several years, demands for the establishment of a parliamentary system of government had been growing louder and had culminated in the "movement for freedom and people's rights." Grant assured the emperor that no form of government was superior to the parliamentary, but he was outspoken in his warning that liberty granted too generously at the outset would be difficult to curb later.

During the Sino-Japanese War of 1894–95, the United States refused to follow the interventionist examples of Britain, Germany, France, and Russia, choosing instead to remain a friendly, uninvolved neutral. So uneventful were Japanese-American relations in those days that Toru Hoshi, Japanese minister in Washington, often delegated diplomatic work to his secretary. Indeed, before Hoshi left for Washington, he had been advised by Foreign Minister Munemitsu Mutsu that, since there were no pressing issues between the two countries, the ambassador might best spend his time in America studying the functioning of the U. S. party-government system. The staff of the legation was very small, consisting only of a secretary, a naval attaché, and one or two American advisers.

While the interests of the United States and Japan coincided and their relations remained friendly, the Meiji government, following its overall policy of "enriching the nation and strengthening the military," directed most of its attention toward Germany and other European nations. The crucial diplomatic task of the government was to obtain the revision of the unequal treaties signed with the Western powers during the last years of the Tokugawa shogunate and the first years of Meiji. The repeal or revision of the unequal treaties required lengthy and arduous diplomatic negotiations, which began to bear fruit only in 1894 with the revised Anglo-Japanese treaty that set the precedent for abolishing the extraterritorial rights of foreign nations in Japan. It was not until Japan regained complete tariff autonomy in 1911 that the process of treaty revision was completed.

Treaty revision was an extremely emotional issue for the Japanese people of the time, and the public clamored, as is its wont, for the best possible deal for the nation. But actual diplomatic negotiation is not so simple. Being a process of compromise and give and take, certain gaps inevitably developed between what the Japanese public demanded and what the government was able to obtain.

"The diplomatic trials of successive Meiji governments offer many interesting parallels with postwar Japanese diplomacy, particularly the problem of the Japan-U. S. Security Treaty," points out Yoshitake Oka, professor emeritus of Japanese political and diplomatic history at Tokyo University. "The campaigners for freedom and people's rights capitalized on the treaty-revision issue in their attack on the clique government of the Meiji oligarchs. This use of a crucial diplomatic issue as ammunition in what was essentially a domestic struggle is directly analogous to the attacks on the government by today's progressive political elements. But there is one distinct difference. In the Meiji era, government and opposition forces shared a common passion for the securing of Japanese sovereignty. Today, however, this passion is lacking, particularly on the part of the government."

A necessary strategy for achieving diplomatic success in the treaty revisions was to convince the Western nations of Japan's modernity and ability to compete on equal terms. This involved rapidly Westernizing Japanese institutions in order to influence foreign opinion in favor of Japan. One noted example of the lengths to which the government went toward this end was the building of the Rokumeikan (Deer Cry Pavilion), an excessively Occidental-style social club in Tokyo, where the Japanese elite, resplendent in the latest European fashions, socialized with foreign residents at fancy-dress balls. Another is the Akasaka Detached Palace in Tokyo, built as a close

[53]

replica of Versailles, but lacking a toilet! "We should not laugh at such frivolity," says Professor Ken'ichi Nakaya of Tokyo University, "for it shows us how pathetically the Meiji governments strained to convince the West of Japan's diplomatic equality."

During the Russo-Japanese War (1904–05), Japan again sought to convince the world of both her strength and her ability to follow the rules of international behavior, finally winning the reputation of being, in the words of one Western observer, "a model belligerent that abides strictly by international law almost all the time." The leaders of the army and navy were well versed in international law, and most of them had had experience abroad. When Navy Minister Gonnohyoe Yamamoto, to the surprise of many, picked Admiral Heihachiro Togo to command the imperial fleet, it was mainly because of Togo's international vision.

In 1960, when huge crowds were swarming around the Diet building in fierce demonstrations against the Japan-U. S. Mutual Security Treaty, which had just been extended by the cabinet of Prime Minister Kishi, Haruhiko Nishi, the former ambassador to London, remarked that he finally understood what the Meiji diplomats must have gone through. "Public pressure and the actualities of diplomatic negotiation forced repeated cabinets to fall or be reshuffled. Nevertheless, successive Meiji governments persevered and eventually won treaty revisions without undue concessions on the part of Japan." Earlier, Nishi had attracted public attention by expressing himself in opposition to the signing of the Security Treaty by the Kishi government.

The mutual-security pact between the United States and Japan has formed the core of Japan's postwar diplomatic relations, just as Meiji diplomatic history revolves around Japan's efforts to obtain treaty revisions. No doubt there are important lessons to be learned from this analogy.

Time Clocks and Black Boxes

ON JULY 17, 1899, a new Japan-U. S. Treaty of Commerce and Navigation went into effect, replacing the earlier Harris Treaty of 1858, and on the same day the first Japanese-American joint-venture firm was established in Tokyo. The articles of incorporation began: "This company shall be known, in Japanese, as Nippon Denki

Kabushiki Kaisha and, in English, as Nippon Electric Company, Ltd."
NEC represented a link-up between the American company Western
Electric, makers of telephone equipment, and Kunihiko Iwadare,
Western Electric's Japan agent. In a speech upon the founding of the
new company, Iwadare recalled: "When the West forced open
Japan's doors with a show of modern armaments, all Japan had was
rifles of a type not used in Europe for two hundred years. Japan is still
backward, but the only way for us to catch up with the West is to
throw open our doors and with a positive attitude import Western
technology and gradually make it our own."

NEC was the forerunner of a number of similar firms established
jointly with American companies. In 1900, Standard Oil arrived in
Japan, took over Zao Oil Company, purchased large oil deposits in
Hokkaido, and established Taihei Oil Company. In 1902, the Annie
N. Brady Company formed a joint venture with Osaka Gas Company.
General Electric formed a capital tie-up with Tokyo Electric Company in 1905, and another with Shibaura Manufacturing Company in
1909 (the two Tokyo firms were merged in 1939 into Tokyo Shibaura Electric Company, Ltd.).

During the early years of the present century, Japan avidly sought
foreign capital and technology. Not only was American technology
adopted in the communication and electrical-appliance industries, but
borrowed U. S. production processes began to appear in paper and
leather manufacture, beer brewing, oil refining, flour milling, and
other industries as well. The country then was certainly far too backward and lacking in resources to limit foreign capital investment in
joint ventures to fifty percent and to insist that management remain
in Japanese hands, as she does today. Takashi Masuda, the Mitsui
executive who arranged the affiliation between Shibaura and General
Electric in 1909, summed up contemporary attitudes when he said:
"It doesn't matter who does it, Japanese or foreigners. All we want
is that Western technology be transplanted to Japanese soil."

According to Keishi Ohara, former professor at Hitotsubashi University, Meiji era Japanese recognized that European industries
tended to be conservative and tradition bound and consequently had
fallen behind American industries in technology. "The United States
still had its pioneer spirit and was progressive in its attitudes toward
technology. No wonder the Japanese set their sights on importing
American technology. Japan always was, and still continues to be, a
good market for technology vendors from the United States."

During the 1955–65 decade, Japan again imported U. S. technology
with great fervor in order to rebuild her war-shattered industries.

The result has been the phenomenal growth of the Japanese economy and, more recently, the demands from the United States and Europe for trade and capital liberalization. When first voiced, some Japanese considered such demands "the second coming of the Black Ships."

Recent technological importation has been rather different from that of the Meiji era. The early joint-venture companies tried to copy techniques, both in manufacturing and in personnel management, as precisely as possible. One example of NEC's determination to do everything "American style" was the time clock it bought in America and installed in its Tokyo plant in 1908. This created a furor because it represented a major change in Japanese employment practices: the strict regulation of working time and the docking of salaries of employees who arrived late or left early was an entirely new concept in Japanese industry. Indeed, NEC probably went too far in adopting American practices. Even worktables and benches were imported from Western Electric's head plant in America. The tables were too high for the Japanese workers, but the American executives refused permission for the legs to be shortened. So the workers had to adjust their stature to the tables by putting platforms under their chairs.

Any quick attempt to adopt radically new techniques creates unavoidable friction. Oki and Company, another Japanese manufacturer of telephone equipment, charged that NEC was going too far in adopting foreign techniques. There followed a price war between the two companies during which the market price of a telephone instrument was forced down from fifty-five yen to ten yen at one point. At about the same time, the Murai Brothers Company was marketing American cigarettes under the brand names Sunrise and Hero. Iwaya and Company declared war on Murai and flooded the market with its own domestic product. The whole city of Tokyo watched as the two companies fought a life-or-death battle in the market.

The reconstruction period following the Great Earthquake of 1923 stimulated Japanese industry to stop its slavish imitation of foreign processes and develop its own. Tokyo Electric and General Electric argued whether their research laboratory or their factory should be rebuilt first. The American firm insisted on priority for the factory, but Tokyo Electric president Kisaburo Yamashita held firm, comparing a factory without a research lab to an insect without antennae. The laboratory was built first, and this incident paved the way for Tokyo Electric's eventual independence from American management.

The destruction in the earthquake of Nippon Electric's newest factory, which had been designed by American engineers, made the NEC management hesitate to continue copying American technology indiscriminately. Koji Kobayashi, who joined the company soon after the earthquake and is now its president, recalls finding a machine in one corner of the factory bearing a seal that read "Do Not Remove." Kobayashi proceeded to remove the seal and investigate the mechanism. "It was so simple that I was certain we could build the same thing ourselves." The newer the industry, the greater the frequency of such seals of secrecy. One recent example is the "black box" attached to IBM's latest-model computer. Hidden in the box is a critical device that converts information into computer language.

Today, the passion for imported technology has clearly subsided. Its mysteries have been mastered by Japanese industries in recent years, and instead of importing advanced technology from the rest of the world the Japanese have begun exporting their own.

The Birth of Women's Education

FERRIS Girls' School in Yokohama celebrated its centenary in the autumn of 1970. The celebration program included a pageant of students dressed in the various kinds of uniforms and clothing worn over the years since Ferris was founded as a small "home school" by an American missionary, Anna H. Kidder. In his address to the three thousand assembled guests, Hidenobu Kuwata, headmaster of the school, emphasized the debt of Japanese education to American missionaries, especially in the area of women's education.

The educational system developed during the Meiji era was molded in large measure by American educational principles. The highest ranking adviser to the Education Ministry was an American, David Murray, and the new education structure established during the 1880s was modeled on the American system. School textbooks were often almost literal translations of American ones.

"No reminiscences of girls' education in those days would be complete without mentioning the American influence on it," says Masumori Hiratsuka, director of the National Institute for Educational Research. Many of the American missionaries who rushed to Japan as soon as the country was opened took a special interest in women's education. It was virtually a new field, for women had traditionally been relegated to a subordinate social position and their formal education had been all but neglected. The missionaries calculated, also, that the best way to spread Christianity was through family education, by initially converting the future mothers of Japan. It was not long before numerous Christian schools for women had sprung up: Ferris and Kyoritsu Gakuen in Yokohama, Aoyama Jogakuin in Tokyo, Kobe College, and Kassui Jogakko in Nagasaki.

If the mission schools mark the first milestone in the history of Japanese women's education, the second is to be seen in the girls' schools founded by Japanese who had studied in the United States. These include: Baika Jogakko founded in Osaka by Paul Sawayama and, in Tokyo, Tsuda College, founded by Umeko Tsuda, and Japan Women's University, established by Jinzo Naruse. Meiji Jogakko, also in Tokyo, was founded by Kumaji Kimura, a former samurai retainer of the Tokugawa shogunate who, together with a band of other loyalists, attempted to resist by force the entry of the emperor into Edo after the shogunate had fallen. After the Restoration, Kimura studied in America for twelve years, attending a theological school for part of that time. In one letter he wrote to his wife from America, he noted: "Japanese women are unlearned, and compared to American women inspire pity." Novelist Yaeko Nogami, remembering her school days at Meiji Jogakko, which Kimura founded after his return from America, says: "There were no examinations and no ethics class. An atmosphere of freedom pervaded the school. It was a good school."

The third milestone of women's education during the Meiji era was the establishment, on David Murray's advice, of the government-sponsored Women's Normal School in Tokyo. It later became a higher normal school for women, and developed further into the present Ochanomizu Women's University. Its first principal was Masanao Nakamura, a contemporary of Yukichi Fukuzawa, who founded Keio University; Nakamura shared Fukuzawa's famous zeal for modernizing Japan. From its earliest days the Women's Normal School was "American" in nearly everything, from curriculum to the students' uniforms. The girls lived in dormitories and slept in Western-style beds. It was considered a modern, fashionable place for daughters of progressive families to study. One of the first students, admitted with high honors, was Chise Aoyama, the mother of Kikue Yamakawa, erstwhile champion of women's rights in Japan. "Mother never told me that I should do this or not do that just because I was a girl," recalls Mrs. Yamakawa.

American influence on education in Japan began to recede after the promulgation of the Imperial Rescript on Education in 1890. "But it was the boys' schools that received the direct impact of the rescript," points out Nao Aoyama, professor at Tokyo Women's University.

"The relative indifference of the authorities to women's education permitted Christian mission schools for girls to continue to thrive."

Toru Haga, an assistant professor at Tokyo University, points out that the influence of Benjamin Franklin on women's education in Japan should not be overlooked. "When Empress Meiji, wise and beautiful, first became acquainted with Franklin's Twelve Moral Resolutions, she was so impressed that she composed twelve odes to them. That was in 1876, when she was twenty-six." One of the odes, to Franklin's resolution for hard work, was rewritten in somewhat simplified language and presented to the Normal School. In 1887, the empress simplified it further and presented it to the Peers Girls' School. Both schools adopted the ode as their school song. The earlier version is still sung at Ochanomizu Women's University. The 1887 version, literally translated, runs:

> A diamond does not glitter
> without polishing.
> Only by the pursuit of learning
> does one become worthy.

This version, set to a simple tune, was sung in primary schools across the nation and should still be familiar to any Japanese woman above middle age. "That bit of information ought to delight Americans," comments Edward Seidensticker, professor at the University of Michigan.

To conclude this brief discussion of the American influence on Japanese women's education, it is interesting to note that every *Asahi Shimbun* survey to date has indicated that more Japanese women than men wish their country to retain close ties of friendship with the United States.

Alternating Sanctions
and Restraints

IT WAS the first President Roosevelt who gave Japan the go-ahead to advance onto the Asian continent, and the second who swept her from it. American historian Charles Tansill offers this as an example of the alternation between encouragement and restraint that characterized U. S. policy toward Japan from the Russo-Japanese War until Pearl Harbor.

In March, 1905, the war with Russia was almost a year old when War Minister General Masatake Terauchi appeared at an imperial conference to announce that Japan had exhausted her armaments, her war budget, and her military manpower as well. The country was rescued from this crisis by a spectacular naval victory in the Japan Sea and by the well-timed good offices of President Theodore Roosevelt in convening the Portsmouth Conference to end the war. The Portsmouth Treaty was favorable to Japan. She was given a lease on Port Arthur and Dairen on the Liaotung Peninsula. In addition, through the Taft-Katsura secret agreement President Roosevelt recognized Japan's "paramount interests" in Korea. This amounted to sanctioning her advance onto the continent.

The Japanese people, however, were dissatisfied with these meager spoils from the war with Russia. On September 5, 1905, their discontent exploded in a huge demonstration in Tokyo's Hibiya Park to protest "the humiliating peace." This initial demonstration set off a rash of riots across the country. Critic Jun Eto says of the anti-Portsmouth riots: "They were the first expression of anti-American sentiment in Japan. The masses instinctively recognized who had won the best deal at Portsmouth."

The Japanese people were not alone in this realization. President Roosevelt himself, in a letter to his son, admitted that Japan had, in effect, fought Russia for the benefit of the United States. American loans of money to support Japan's war effort and America's willingness to sponsor the peace conference bespeak her traditional sympathy for the underdog in any contest. Her real motives, however, were to restrain any significant expansion in Asia by either Russia or Japan and thereby to maintain what has been called a "balance of hostility."

At the height of the September 5 demonstration in Tokyo, a party of foreigners was stoned while riding in a horse-drawn carriage to the home of Finance Minister Arasuke Sone. Among them was the American railroad magnate Edward H. Harriman, in Japan to purchase operating rights over the South Manchurian Railway, which Japan had acquired as a result of the war. Prime Minister Katsura acquiesced to Harriman's request for joint American-Japanese management of the railroad, and the Americans sailed happily for home. However, Foreign Minister Jutaro Komura, arriving back in Japan from the Portsmouth Conference immediately after Harriman had left, was vehemently opposed to the railway agreement and had it nullified. When Harriman disembarked at San Francisco, he was greeted by the Japanese consul-general bearing the news that the deal had fallen through. Although it proved abortive, this proposal that the Manchurian Railway be jointly managed laid bare the actual American designs on China. Having declared the Open Door policy in 1899, America remained as determined to keep hold of her privileges in China as she was vociferous in her insistence on territorial integrity for China.

According to Senator J. W. Fulbright, chairman of the Senate Foreign Relations Committee, the Open Door policy served to apply a brake to the total dismemberment of China by the more advanced nations. But at the same time it allowed the United States to elbow its way, belatedly, into the Chinese market.

"Despite the miscarriage of the Harriman mission, the United States remained conciliatory toward Japan," says Professor Kimitada Miwa of Sophia University. "The fact was that the U. S. Pacific fleet at the time was weaker than the imperial Japanese fleet. President Roosevelt was above all a political realist and he recognized that the Open Door would not amount to much if not backed up by military strength. He saw fit to grant Japan whatever America could without hurting her own interests."

But after the Russian withdrawal from China, Japan quickly stepped in, leaving no room for the United States. It was not long before U. S. policy toward Japan began to shift from gentle restraint through conciliation to outright restraint. Tokyo University professor Sakue Takahashi interprets this shift as a change from relations between senior and junior or elder and younger partners to relations between equals.

In 1907, American military strategists, having taken note of the military might that Japan had demonstrated in the war with Russia, formulated the so-called "Orange Plan," a top-secret scenario envisioning a possible war with Japan. Although Japan was forced by her financial obligations to maintain good relations with the United States, she nevertheless drew up a defense strategy of her own, listing Russia, the United States, and France as hypothetical enemies, in that order. A central feature of this strategy was the launching of the eight-eight naval build-up program to add eight battleships and eight cruisers to the fleet.

General Homer Lea, in a book entitled *The Valor of Ignorance*, warned America of a possible Japanese occupation of California. At about the same time and apparently by coincidence, two Japanese journalists also predicted a major clash between yellow peril and white peril. "Both General Lea and the Japanese journalists predicted defeat for their own countries," comments Professor Shoichi Saeki of Tokyo Municipal University. "Obviously, their warnings were intended for domestic consumption. Public opinion on both sides of the Pacific had perceived the mounting crisis that would eventually force a direct confrontation over territory."

Once the Japanese-American relationship began slipping downhill, it was not to be recovered. Japanese military expansion on the continent proceeded unchecked, while American policy, through the end of World War II, remained committed to protecting weak, helpless China against Japanese aggression and domination. In a book published during the war, Walter Lippmann questioned the value of China to the United States. Doubtless, the lure of her potential market must have been irresistible, and yet American exports to China from 1861 to 1938 never amounted to as much as three percent of her total exports. Exports to Japan, however, rose above five percent. Lippmann stripped away, one after another, all the economic reasons that were supposed to support America's defense of China against Japan, leaving only the more abstract purpose of upholding justice. "Diplomacy that is based on clear-cut principles of national material gain can easily be modified," says Professor Yoshikazu Sakamoto of Tokyo University. "It is the diplomacy based on moral principles or notions of national mission that is usually inflexible."

In the years preceding the war, the United States clearly believed that her mission lay in the protection of China. Perhaps it is in such feelings that the origins of the anti-Communist crusade that followed the war are to be found.

Patriotic Internationalist

IN CONVENING the Portsmouth Conference in 1905 and working out a settlement of the Russo-Japanese hostilities, President Theodore Roosevelt showed himself remarkably well disposed toward Japan. Friendship with Japan was in line with general American interests at the time, to be sure, but it is also believed that a certain book called *Bushido: The Soul of Japan* by Inazo Nitobe did much to foster Roosevelt's admiration for the Japanese people. He is known to have bought sixty copies of the book and to have distributed them to his friends. Later, influenced no doubt by Nitobe's book, he tried to make judo popular in the United States. No other Japanese book written during the Meiji era was so widely read outside of Japan. Nitobe wrote his book in English in 1898. It was born out of his discussions with his American wife Mary, in which he tried to answer her questions about Japanese customs and thinking. He looked hard at himself and at his fellow Japanese, seeking out those qualities that he believed to be hidden in the innermost recesses of the Japanese soul: loyalty, courage, benevolence, courtesy, fidelity. Collecting them under the rubric *bushido*, he was determined to explain them systematically to the Western world. Translated literally, the term *bushido* means "the way of the samurai." Although he was himself the son of a samurai of the Nambu clan (in present-day Iwate Prefecture), Nitobe had nothing of the warrior in him. Professor Shigeo Komatsu of Gakushuin University considers Nitobe's understanding of *bushido* "totally opposite to what Yukio Mishima called by the same name. Mishima rejected all that is rational. Nitobe's *bushido*, although some might consider it an anachronism in the modern world, was really a method of self-discipline." A dedicated internationalist and champion of world peace, Nitobe also remained ever conscious of the legacy of the Japanese tradition. This lent his internationalism a unique coloration and, late in life, brought him severe personal difficulties.

His married life was far from blissful. The slightest breach of Western manners on his part brought a sharp and immediate rebuke from his wife. Wanting only to relax at home, Japanese style, Nitobe must have found this a constant source of tension. "No other Japanese at that time had managed to assimilate himself so thoroughly, or so willingly, to an American way of life as Dr. Nitobe," says Shio Sakanishi, the prominent critic and writer, who was a student of Nitobe's while he was president of Tokyo Women's College. She later lived in America for many years and played a large part in the founding of the excellent Japanese collection at the Library of Congress. "But the long years of marriage must have changed this attitude. His personal difficulties in trying to fuse Japanese and Occidental ideas ultimately drove him back to the Japanese tradition which he had tended to neglect as a younger man. Once, while strolling with several of his students on the campus, he had sighed to them: 'Never marry a foreigner.' "

During his long career of public service, Nitobe held the positions of engineer with the Japanese colonial government of Taiwan, headmaster of the First National Higher School, professor at Tokyo Imperial University, and president of Tokyo Women's College. From 1920 to 1927, he was undersecretary general of the League of Nations. Although his reputation as a great Meiji internationalist is secure, he remained all his life a staunch Japanese patriot. "In his lectures on colonialism, Nitobe limited himself to preaching good government in the colonies," says Kiyoko Takeda of International Christian University, referring to a series of lectures Nitobe delivered at Tokyo Imperial University while acting as an adviser on colonial administration to the government. "He lacked the vision of his student Tadao Yanaihara, who criticized the institution of colonialism itself. But perhaps, as a Meiji liberal and a patriotic Japanese, Nitobe felt that he could not go so far."

Nitobe, devoted to promoting intellectual intercourse between Japan and America, liked to consider himself a "bridge of transpacific understanding." But history was against him, and both Japan and the United States deserted his vision of international harmony. In 1924, when Congress passed the Exclusion Act, which severely restricted Japanese immigration to the United States, Nitobe declared that he would never again set foot on American soil until the law was repealed. But eight years later, when anti-Japanese feeling was running very high following the Manchurian Incident of September 18, 1931, Nitobe felt compelled to try to avert the disastrous clash in Japanese-American relations that he saw rapidly approaching. He broke his vow and traveled to the United States to try to explain Japanese policies. "I left on each of my earlier trips to America full of hope and optimism," he said in a farewell speech. "This time there is little hope. I feel as though I am moving into the dark. I may well be unable to accomplish anything, but still I must go."

Nitobe was seventy, but he traveled tirelessly, trying to explain Japan's belligerent foreign policies. His words fell on deaf ears. The contradiction of a Japanese Quaker preaching war and pan-Asianism inevitably inspired indignation. Many of his old friends rejected him, charging that he was no more than a turncoat acting as spokesman for the Japanese military. When he returned to Japan, he was denounced as a traitor by fanatic patriots infuriated that he had branded both the militarists and the communists as perils to Japan. "Nitobe did not go to America merely to defend the Japanese actions in Manchuria," points out Yasaka Takagi, professor emeritus of Tokyo University. "He did criticize what deserved criticism in Japan. But American feelings about Japan were largely emotional. Nitobe presented the facts and appealed to the American public to consider them rationally. Eventually he came under fire from both sides. The Japanese military accused him of treason and the Americans called him the mouthpiece of the military."

The prayers for peace of the Japanese minority, including Nitobe, were quickly drowned out by the clamor of events. In 1933, Japan withdrew from the League of Nations. This was the saddest event of Nitobe's life. He died not long afterward in Banff, Canada.

"Postwar Japanese-American personal contacts have been immeasurably more extensive than before the war," observes Paul Blum, a scholar of Japan who has lived in Tokyo for twenty-two years. "But by and large, the partners in these contacts have been thinking only of their own countries. Today, more than ever, we need courageous, dedicated internationalists like Nitobe."

Socialism "Made in U.S.A."

AMERICAN democratic ideals have played a major role in inspiring the pioneers of the socialist movement in Japan. Two of the "fathers of Japanese socialism," Sen Katayama and Iso-o Abe, both became interested in socialism while in the United States. Katayama, working his way through Yale as a dishwasher and cook, came to socialism via Christianity. Abe, who attended a theological college in Hartford, Connecticut, followed a similar route. Fusataro Takano, Sentaro Jo, and Hannosuke Sawada, early leaders of the labor movement, all studied in America before establishing the Workers' Comradeship Circle in 1890. The circle expanded gradually as it was joined by Katayama and others interested in socialist thought.

Of somewhat earlier origin was the civil-rights movement, led by Chomin Nakae and others in the late 1870s, which also looked to the United States for inspiration and moral support. One of the rallying songs of this movement ran something like:

Recall the rebellious banner of America's independence!
Now blood must be shed in Japan as well
To make firm the foundations of liberty!

The three separate movements were united into the Social Democratic party—Japan's first socialist party—in 1901. Its platform was equality for all, disarmament, and universal suffrage. Abe, the leading theorist of the movement, drew these objectives largely from his reading in American textbooks. The very day it was formed, the party was outlawed by the Meiji government.

Barred from political activity, Katayama and Abe started the newspaper *Heimin Shimbun* (Commoners' Newspaper); joining in the journalistic venture was the young Shusui Kotoku, who had been converted to socialism under the influence of the two older men. The newspaper took the unpopular position of opposition to the war with Russia then in progress. In its English column it conducted an international antiwar crusade which drew response from around the world. Its editors even went so far as to correspond about pacifism with Tolstoy during the Russo-Japanese War.

It was not long before the government stopped publication of the *Heimin Shimbun*. An angry Kotoku left for the United States in 1905, immediately after the end of the war. After a month there he recorded the following observations: "If Japan ever goes to war again, it will be with the United States, now her closest friend. In the Orient, the clash will come over trade. Here in the United States, it will be over labor; America will seek to drive Japanese labor from her shores. The clashes will gradually grow more hysterical, and will culminate in disaster." No other Japanese at that time was so farsighted.

Kotoku grew more and more radical while in America. After his return to Japan he was implicated in a conspiracy which, according to government charges, aimed at assassinating the emperor Meiji. He was executed on January 23, 1911. On that day in 1971, to mark the hundredth anniversary of Kotoku's birth, and the sixtieth of his death, memorial services were held at his grave in his native Nakamura City in Kochi Prefecture. In their speeches following the services Ichiko Kamichika, former member of the Lower House, and Kazuo Okochi, former president of Tokyo University, traced the history of the socialist movement in Japan and the struggles of its founders.

Severe government repression of socialism in Kotoku's time set off an exodus of Japanese socialists, primarily to the United States, which they considered "the land of the free." Virtually stifled at home, the Japanese socialist movement was kept alive by these exiles in America. Even after the Exclusion Act of 1924 barred Japanese immigration to the United States, Japanese socialists continued to flee to America seeking the liberty they could not find at home. Critic Ayako Ishigaki was one of them. "I was a nonregular student of Waseda University and attended study groups on various social problems. Late one afternoon I stopped to chat on the street with Ikuo, a socialist leader; later I was questioned at a police box for this. I could feel myself suffocating in Japan, so I sold my clothes to pay for passage and fled to the United States in 1926. . . . The Japanese Labor Club in New York had become a factory for turning out socialist literature

[66]

to send to Japan. The beginning of the war with China in 1937 touched off an antiwar demonstration by Japanese socialists in front of the Japanese consulate in New York, and also a fund-raising drive for Chinese victims of the war. Time and time again, we socialists were beaten up by Japanese living in America. Most of them were even more patriotic than people at home in Japan."

Sanzo Nosaka, head of the Japan Communist party, attended the seventh congress of the Comintern in Moscow in 1935, where the united popular-front strategy was adopted. Seeking some way to transmit the policy to Japanese Communists, he devised a scheme which involved going to the United States. In 1936, he sneaked into the country. On the West Coast he managed to obtain Japanese printing type and a supply of cheap newsprint and began publishing messages to Japanese Communists, which were smuggled into Japan by sympathetic Japanese seamen. "I had a forged passport and posed as a Nisei resident," Nosaka reminisces, "but I was always nervous that my poor English would give me away."

Nosaka, fiercely hostile to the United States since the end of World War II, admits that in its infancy the Japanese socialist movement learned much from America and obtained the support that it desperately needed. Even today an affinity can be discerned between Japan's mass movements and anti-establishment struggles and the ideals on which America was founded. These struggles are based upon principles of liberty, equality, peace, and democracy, and question everything in the existing situation that seems contrary to those ideals. Typical are the leadership and beliefs of the Japan "Peace for Vietnam!" Committee (Beheiren). Shunsuke Tsurumi and Makoto Oda, two of its most active leaders, both studied in America. But for them America has changed. "Nowhere," says Tsurumi, "can I recognize the America I knew in the America that has been pursuing this filthy war for more than ten years."

"When Wall Street
Sneezes . . ."

MODERN Japan's industrial development began with silk reeling and cotton spinning. As the survival and expansion of these first modern industries came to depend, inevitably, on the availability of good machines and fuel, the industries of coal mining, iron and steel, and machine tools developed to fill the increasing demand. In turn, rapid, efficient transportation quickly became essential to the operations of the other industries; so railways were built and shipping lines established. . . . The list might go on and on with endless ramifications: such, in capsule form, is the history of the origins of Japanese industry.

Thanks largely to the heavy U. S. demands for silk and to Japan's plentiful supply of labor for sericulture, silk reeling rapidly became the nation's leading industry. Soon after the end of the Russo-Japanese war, in 1905, Japan surpassed China as the world's largest exporter of raw silk. By the mid-1920s, ninety percent of Japan's raw-silk exports were to America; at that time the U. S. accounted for forty-five percent of Japan's total exports, and of that amount sixty percent was raw silk. Other major export items were silk fabrics, tea, and chinaware.

In short, the Japanese economy had quickly become so closely tied to the American market that even farmers deep in the Japanese countryside, depending on sericulture for part of their livelihood, were severely affected by the slightest economic indisposition on the other side of the Pacific. This situation gave rise to the saying, "When America sneezes, Japan comes down with the flu," a state of affairs that is almost as true today as it was then.

"We old-timers in the raw-silk trade were like the cormorants on the Nagara River," reminisces Yujiro Nishimoto, a veteran Yokohama exporter. (His analogy is to the cormorant fishing in Gifu Prefecture, where a fisherman in a boat holds a number of the birds on thin ropes attached to rings around the birds' necks; the ring prevents a bird from swallowing the fish it catches, and after pulling the bird back into the boat, the fisherman forces it to regurgitate its catch.) "The cormorant master was, of course, the Japanese government, which enslaved us, continually urging us on to bigger and bigger catches—catches of the dollars it needed to develop the economic strength and military power of the nation. But our lives were not too bad: like the silkworms we raised, we would eat voraciously for a while and sleep as long as we liked."

For seven years, until about 1927, Nishimoto was the New York branch manager of Hara and Company, leading raw-silk exporters. He was for a time the deputy managing director of the Yokohama Raw Silk Exchange and managing director of the Japan Raw Silk Export Association. "Times have changed and today Japan has to import raw silk," says Nishimoto sadly. He is now the Japan agent for a Swiss raw-silk export company.

Japanese silk cultivators and reelers were acutely sensitive to the movements of the New York Stock Exchange because they usually reflected so sensitively the American political and economic situation. "Everyone paid closest attention to U. S. Steel stock," recalls So Morimoto, editor of the *Yokohama Boeki Shimpo* (Yokohama Trade News), precursor of the present *Kanagawa Shimbun* (Kanagawa Newspaper), and author of several books on raw silk. "U. S. Steel shares, being a speculative commodity, were subject to violent fluctuations in price, and therefore proved to be the most accurate barometer of American business." Even today, in the old silkworm belt in Nagano Prefecture, old men recall their rapidly shifting ups and downs from intense excitement to deep despair as they followed Wall Street news while sitting around the hearths of their thatched farmhouses.

The raw-silk trade was crowded with market speculators. Eighty-year-old Kentaro Kojima, a former broker on the Yokohama Raw Silk Exchange nicknamed "General Lightning" for his sharpness, recalls: "My work day did not end with the close of the exchange in the afternoon. I had to put in many more hours trying to catch the latest news of the activities of the American market before the Yokohama exchange reopened the next morning. In those days, like today, the ones who were best informed about the U. S. economic situation were the big trading companies like Mitsui. I had to spend piles of money trying to get news out of the tight-lipped Mitsui men."

Rural sericulturists and reelers were also given to market speculation. When it was a seller's market they grew careless and skimped on quality, but when business fell off they would swear off such practices and work hard to improve the quality of their silk. Then when business turned good, they would go right back to their old tricks.

"Market speculation went to the heads of many people, and eventually ruined them," says Toshiaki Komura, president of Maruko Industries in Nagano Prefecture. He went to America in 1924, amid a storm of anti-Japanese feeling, and worked in a textile factory on the outskirts of New York for a year, making a close study of how to read market fluctuations and researching improvements in silk production. Returning to Japan, in 1931 he founded the Maruko Silk Reeling Company, precursor of his present company. Many old established reelers have since gone out of business, but Maruko is one of the few to survive. "But we can no longer subsist on silk reeling alone," Komura confesses. "As an alternative to reducing our work force, we decided to dabble in other fields like assembling radio and TV sets. This way we still make use of the manual dexterity acquired from the long experience with silk reeling."

The end of World War I ushered in an era of trial and tribulation for the Japanese silk-reeling industry. First, rayon was developed and gained rapid and wide popularity. Then, the industry was hit by the Depression and the worldwide economic panic. Later, DuPont developed nylon. Japanese silk dealers found themselves unable to adjust to the sudden decline in American demand. They increased production, hoping to compensate for price declines by quantity sales; this only invited further price drops. At one point the price of silk fell from its 1920 peak of 5,600 yen per bale to less than 460 yen. The market never recovered in the years preceding the Pacific War.

The Japanese export situation today is very different from the prewar period. The "silk road" across the Pacific has been replaced by the broader avenue via which Japanese electrical appliances, steel, cars, petrochemicals, and electronic instruments and machines travel to American users. Trade relations with the United States today, if more varied than before the war, are no less close. But the fact that the bulk of Japan's total exports, more than one-third, goes to America masks other notable differences from earlier periods. From the late nineteenth century until the Depression, the United States economy experienced a period of great growth, and the Japanese-American trade complemented it and benefited from it. Expansion of the U. S. silk industry brought prosperity to Japanese silkworm cultivators and silk reelers, for increased American silk manufacture and trade meant increased production in Japan.

This happy symbiosis is now gone. Today, Japan is a great economic power in her own right, and as such presents a menace to American industry. Evidence of this deterioration of trade relations is not hard to find. The American demands that led to voluntary reductions of textile exports from Japan and the charges of dumping leveled against Japanese television manufacturers are only two examples of the intensifying friction.

In short, Japanese-American trade relations have been transformed from conditions of mutual prosperity to competitive coexistence. The need grows stronger day by day for a long-range re-examination of the issues troubling Japanese-American trade relations and for the development of comprehensive political solutions.

The Yellow Peril

O GAI MORI (1862–1922), army surgeon turned novelist and
poet, and one of the foremost figures of modern Japanese literature, wrote a prophetic verse on the battlefield near Liaoyang during
the Russo-Japanese War:

> Win the war,
> And Japan will be denounced as a yellow peril.
> Lose it,
> And she will be branded a barbaric land.

Mori apparently intended "barbaric land" to mean one that had the
temerity to challenge a white nation. He was right. As soon as peace
was restored in 1905, Kaiser Wilhelm II wrote to Theodore Roosevelt that the yellow peril was on the march, and that an invasion of the
American continent by the Japanese was not inconceivable. In such an
event, the kaiser generously offered to send German troops to
America's aid.

The White House laughed off the kaiser's offer, seeing it as a device
of power politics intended to divert the attention of the major powers
toward the East in order to lessen pressures on Germany. But American politicians on the West Coast, where there were large groups of
Oriental immigrants, seized upon the yellow-peril scare for their own
purposes. Anti-Asian statements paid off in votes in an area where
American labor was frightened by the influx of cheap labor from the
Far East. The postwar depression had triggered an exodus of Japanese workers to the United States. In California alone, the average
annual immigration of Japanese shot up from one thousand to twelve
thousand. The California State Legislature passed a resolution
"never to allow the thirty-first star to turn yellow," and in 1906
the San Francisco Board of Education closed the doors of the city's
schools to Japanese children.

Takeshi Haga, former director of the American Affairs Research
Institute, recalls his forty years as a laborer in the United States:
"America had been described to me as a bed of roses. I had been told
that there I could make a dollar a day as a farm worker, more than
four times the maximum I could earn in Japan. A bed of roses! When
I arrived I found that my work would be backbreaking labor, developing cornfields in red soil under a blistering sun. At night I slept in a
hut no better than a chicken coop. In town once, while I was listening

to a Salvation Army sermon in the street, somebody smashed his fist into my back. At a movie theater, a ticket taker yelled at me: 'Hey, Jap! Get up in the back of the gallery!' It didn't take three days in America for me to regret ever having come."

Professor Edward Ross of Stanford University cites three reasons for the agitation against Japanese immigrants during the first decades of the century: their lack of assimilability in American society, their willingness to work for low wages, and their lack of any sense of democracy. This may be partially accurate as a description of many of the Japanese laborers, but Professor Jiro Suzuki of Tokyo Metropolitan University sees the situation somewhat differently: "In the 1880s, West Coast politicians had used denunciations of Chinese immigration as ammunition for successful election campaigns. Then, after World War I, Japanese immigrants provided them with a new target. That, I think, is the basic truth of the matter."

When Japanese children were barred from attending San Francisco public schools, President Roosevelt sent Commerce and Labor Secretary Victor Howard Metcalf to act as a mediator. Metcalf managed to persuade education authorities to reopen the schools to Japanese. The Japanese government reciprocated, in a secret treaty signed in Tokyo by Foreign Minister Gonsuke Hayashi and U. S. Ambassador Thomas O'Brien, by agreeing to impose voluntary quotas on Japanese emigration to America.

But despite the governmental efforts on both sides of the Pacific to ameliorate the increasingly tense situation, anti-Japanese agitation began to shake Japanese-American relations to their foundations. Posters appeared on California streets bearing such messages as: "Ladies, don't spend your husband's hard-earned money on Japanese junk." Japanese were first deprived of the right of naturalization and prohibited from owning land in the United States, and finally, in 1924, the Exclusion Act barred all Japanese immigration to America. "These developments converted the Issei residents, who had virtually forsaken their fatherland, into Japanese superpatriots," says critic Ayako Ishigaki. Money sent home by Japanese immigrants, including contributions for armaments, reached twenty million dollars in a peak year. At one point Tokyo newspapers urged that the entire Japanese fleet be massed around the entrance to San Francisco Bay.

Count Nobuaki Makino, Japanese delegate to the Paris Peace Conference at the end of World War I, sought to ease the tensions of the undeclared Japanese-American war by moving that the principle of racial equality be incorporated in the covenant of the League of Nations. Makino's move was blocked by Anglo-American opposition, but drew strong applause from American blacks and other colored people around the world. For a while, some black people in New York took to inviting home every Japanese person they met on the street. In many homes a large portrait of Count Makino hung on the wall and the Japanese guest would be told by his host, with deep feeling: "We respect him as much as Lincoln. We want you Japanese to stick it out."

In a 1919 issue of the influential monthly magazine *Chuo Koron*, Sakuzo Yoshino, champion of the so-called "Taisho-era democracy," wrote of the necessity of unity among the three major peoples of East Asia—the Chinese, Japanese, and Koreans—against American racial oppression. But he was preaching an impossibility that was quickly contradicted by political and military events. Japan's annexation of Korea and her advance on the Chinese continent had already incurred the hostility of other East Asian peoples.

Yet an idea akin to Yoshino's—that only through power could Japan deal with the United States—took form, in wholly different coloring, in the tripartite Axis alliance of 1940, which linked Japan to Germany and Italy. "Prince Fumimaro Konoe, then prime minister, joined the Axis in the hopes that it would discourage the United States from entering the war in Europe and the Far East," wrote Koichi Kido, keeper of the imperial privy seal, in his diary. Instead, it had the effect of incurring irreparable American distrust of Japan.

Professor Kimitada Miwa of Sophia University believes that Konoe's policies reflected the strong influence of Foreign Minister Yosuke Matsuoka. "After assuming his post, Matsuoka, who had been a labor immigrant in America during his youth, compared the United States to 'a haughty giant approaching along a narrow road from the other direction. Give the giant the impression that you are giving way to him as you face him, and that you will never dare to put yourself on equal footing with him.' This image of America had doubtless been formed in Matsuoka's mind in his immigrant days."

During World War II, 125,000 Japanese residents of the three West Coast states, men and women, young and old, were confined in ten so-called relocation camps. In spite of such treatment, Japanese-Americans proved their loyalty to America by great feats in battle and by the sacrifice of their lives. The dedicated fighting on the Italian front of a Nisei battalion, the famed 442nd Infantry Combat Team, was particularly courageous; casualties among them ran higher than forty percent.

Did the dark years of prejudice directed against Japanese immigrants end with the war? "You might think that the Nisei and Sansei

[73]

are considered one hundred percent American, morally and culturally," says critic Rinjiro Sodei, recently returned from Los Angeles.
"But a yellow-power movement is now on the rise among them. It
seems that at the very heart of American society, there still lingers a
prejudice against yellow skin, a prejudice that might reassert itself at
any moment."

The Washington Conference

"JAPAN was forced to submit to Anglo-American pressures at the
Washington Conference. . . ." "A blood-chilling conspiracy to
topple Japan was hatched in the name of the Washington Naval
Conference. . . ."

Page after page in popular magazines published in the decade prior
to Pearl Harbor bristles with angry phrases like these. The treaty for
reducing naval armaments that came out of the Washington Conference was considered by some to be a noteworthy success, rare in
the annals of the world's attempts at arms limitation. But it also
marked a milestone on the road to disaster in Japanese-American
relations. The Japanese military, rankling with resentment over the
terms of the treaty, gradually seized the initiative in foreign policy
from civilian hands and refused to surrender it.

The Washington Conference, convened by the United States in No-
vember of 1921, was intended to lessen the naval-armaments race that
had been intensifying constantly since the end of the Russo-Japanese
War. In 1908, the American "white fleet" of sixteen ships called at
Yokohama on its round-the-world cruise, dispatched by President
Theodore Roosevelt as an overt display of American naval strength.
"This marked the first significant step in the American attempt to
restrain the expansion of Japanese naval armaments," comments
Shizuo Fukui, a specialist in naval history. "Only a year earlier, Japan
had launched the so-called eight-eight naval construction program
calling for a fleet of eight battleships and eight cruisers." From that
point on, Japan and the United States were engaged in a feverish
naval expansion race. By 1921, nearly half the Japanese budget was going into military spending, much of it for naval construction.

"Regardless of how much she expands her armaments," claimed
statesman Yukio Ozaki in a book calling for arms limitation, "she will
never be a match for the United States. It would be better to strike

an agreement with America and Britain immediately, and to seek conciliation—not competition—with them." The Washington Conference was an attempt at just such limitation. Just before the Japanese delegation, including Navy Minister Tomosaburo Kato and Ambassador to the U. S. Kijuro Shidehara, departed for Washington, Finance Minister Gen Nishino briefed the delegates privately: "The alternative of bankruptcy or financial survival for Japan depends on your decisions." His implication was that they should ignore demands for increases in naval power by military diehards and instead try to reach an international settlement to what seemed to be turning into an endless arms race. The Japanese government in 1921 was not unaware that the real motive behind America's calling the conference was to curb Japanese advances on the Chinese continent. But realizing also that the Japanese economy could no longer afford the arms race, it adopted the realistic posture of avoiding a direct clash with the United States.

Also born of the conference were the Four-Power and Nine-Power treaties, which established the principle of territorial integrity for China and maintained the status quo in the Asia-Pacific area as an attempt to avoid armed conflict. The agreements in Washington replaced the Anglo-Japanese Alliance of 1902, as was desired by the United States, as well as the Lansing-Ishii Agreement of 1917. The latter pact, negotiated in the midst of World War I by Japanese Foreign Minister Kikujiro Ishii and American Secretary of State Robert Lansing, had recognized that Japan had "special interests" in China, just as the Taft-Katsura Agreement of 1905 had recognized her special interests in Korea.

The naval armaments reduction treaty hammered out at Washington limited holdings of capital ships to the ratio of 5:5:3 for the U. S., Britain, and Japan, respectively. This formula was designed to maintain the disparity between the large and secondary powers and also to avoid wastefulness among the major powers due to excessive arms buildups. Since the end of World War II there have been a number of comparable efforts at arms limitation: both the 1963 treaty partially banning nuclear testing and the 1968 treaty against the proliferation of nuclear arms show an intent to maintain the U. S. and Russian cosupremacy in the field of nuclear weaponry. The Strategic Arms Limitation Talks of 1970 and 1971 are no exception. The naval armaments treaty, in that it was a successful Anglo-American attempt to restrain the developing might of Japan, is also analogous to the American and Soviet surveillance of China in recent years.

The merit of the Washington agreements lay in their striking an "organic" balance between political, military, and economic affairs. "Recognizing the value of this, the Japanese government acted properly in signing the treaty, even though it was unfavorable to Japan," comments Sophia University professor Hisashi Maeda, an authority on disarmament and international relations. "But the government then neglected to disseminate its diplomatic policies throughout the country. In failing to gain a national consensus in support of its policies, the government proved unable to hold the military in check. Had it succeeded in doing so, it might well have averted the tragic events of the years following the Washington Conference."

Yet Baron Shidehara, who directed Japan's foreign policy through the years following the conference, continued to act reasonably, even after the blatantly anti-Japanese Exclusion Act was passed in 1924. He conducted an economics-centered foreign policy and remained conciliatory toward the United States and Britain as far as possible. To the military, however, the Shidehara diplomacy was weak-kneed and excessively servile toward the Western powers. In the words of the military cliques, the Washington treaty had marked "Japan's defeat in a bloodless naval battle."

The London Naval Treaty of 1930 was to supplement the Washington pact by limiting the holdings of auxiliary warships. The Japanese naval leadership refused to recognize the treaty, branding it an encroachment upon its own authority. The nation erupted in confused debate, and from this point on Japan's foreign policy changed drastically. It was around this time that denunciations of the terms of the Washington Conference began to appear frequently in the Japanese press.

Professor Yoshitake Oka of Tokyo University has described Japan's aggression in Manchuria, beginning with the Manchurian Incident of September 18, 1931, as "an undisguised counterattack by Japanese imperialism against the terms of the Washington agreements."

Haruhiko Nishi, deputy foreign minister at the time, recalls with some bitterness: "Holding the military in check was as difficult for the Japanese government at that time as it is for the American government today. The Ministry could do nothing but give in gradually to the pressures of the military."

City Lights Along the Ginza

ONCE EVERY month the American Cultural Center in Tokyo presents a showing of old Hollywood silent movies. One month Charlie Chaplin may be featured; the next will bring a program of great old William S. Hart westerns or Douglas Fairbanks classics. When the series began, its sponsors were surprised to find that two-thirds of the audience was made up of young people. Trying to account for the unexpected popularity of the old movies among young Japanese, Sumio Kambayashi, a member of the Cultural Center staff, says: "After all, these silent films were made to attract a mass audience back in the early days. Their mass appeal must still be as strong in Japan today."

From around 1910 to the mid-1930s, American popular culture swept over Japan in successive waves. Movies, music, fashions in clothing and hair styles, dance steps—one after another, they caught on in Japan and penetrated most levels of society. First came the movies, simple in plot, direct, and easy to understand. Young and old Japanese alike became passionate fans of Chaplin, Harold Lloyd, Valentino, and the other Hollywood stars. Signboards, posters, and handbills advertising the movies carried their original English titles, as well as the Japanese versions, for much of their appeal lay in their foreignness. Even children seemed to enjoy calling the movies by their English names, distorted by Japanese pronunciation: *The Broken Coin* became "Burokun Koin" and *The Iron Claw* became "Airon Kuro," and sounded so much more up-to-date than the Japanese equivalents. A survey, conducted by Yasunosuke Gonda of the Ohara Institute of Social Research in 1917, revealed that ninety-eight percent of the pupils in Tokyo's better grammar schools had seen at least one movie, and more than half of them went to the movies as often as once a month. American films were far and away the most popular with them. "I'm sure that it was the movies, far more than books, that had the strongest character-building effect on Japanese men and women of the generation that is now beyond middle age," says Yoshinosuke Masunaga, a fan of old movies with a personal collection of more than one hundred of them.

New fashions that appeared first in the movies caught on and spread like wildfire across Japan. Seeing actresses like Clara Bow, Jean Harlow, and Mary Pickford sent Japanese girls rushing to cut their hair and revamp their wardrobes. Round, horn-rimmed spectacles, almost a trademark of Japanese men before the war, were called "Lloyd glasses," because Harold Lloyd wore them in most of his movies. The up-to-date young set, strolling along the Ginza in their movie fashions, were dubbed *mobo* (short for "modern boys") and *moga* ("modern girls"). *It*, starring Clara Bow, was tremendously popular in Japan for a time, and the word "itto" was instantly added to the vocabulary to indicate feminine sex appeal. Postcard-size portraits of American movie stars sold for ten sen apiece. "You could also get pictures the size of name cards for a twentieth of that," recalls Kyohei Misono, an authority on old movies. "I collected only the small ones, because I was out for quantity." When the Exclusion Act was passed by the U. S. Congress in 1924, a boycott of American movies was launched to protest the law's inherent anti-Japanese bias. But, unable to rally mass support, the boycott petered out almost immediately.

Following movies in popularity was sound—the "American sound" heard on radio, on records, and in the talkies. Keizo Horiuchi was responsible for transplanting much of the "American sound" to Japan. While studying engineering at MIT, he had dabbled in American popular music on the side. When he returned to Japan, he accepted an invitation to join NHK (the Japan Broadcasting Corporation) and take charge of its popular-music programming. He translated such pop tunes as "Desert Song" and "My Blue Heaven," which became hits in Japan as well. Horiuchi attributes the popularity of American music to the general optimism of the period following World War I: "Both the Americans and the Japanese were in high spirits because the war was over. This coincidence of mood is probably why American music caught on so well here."

All older Japanese jazz fans know the name of Kyosuke Kami. While still a law student at Tokyo University, he became passionately enamored of Western classical music and eventually joined the Japan Symphony Orchestra. Then jazz arrived in Japan, and Kami immediately got together his own band. All the while that he was building his reputation as a jazz musician, he continued to perform classical music with the symphony orchestra. "His name fits him perfectly," joked his friends. "*Kami*, meaning paper, has two sides, and so does he." Kami himself recalls, with some amusement, the audiences that came to hear his group play in Tokyo dance halls during the twenties: "They'd fit in fine today, the men in their maxicoats and wide pants, the girls in miniskirts."

Talkies first came to Japan late in 1929. Like audiences everywhere, the Japanese were enthralled at hearing movie stars actually speak on the screen. Hearing them speak English only added to the thrill. It was at this time that Japan was experiencing rapid and intense urbanization. The American movies both reflected the major cultural changes that accompany urbanization and provided inspiration for new changes. Around 1920, for example, movie theaters in the Asakusa entertainment district began rotating films once a week, paralleling the emergence of the concept of a "work week" for Tokyo's citizens. Shortly afterward, weekly magazines began to be published and rapidly became popular.

Sociologist Hidetoshi Kase sees the quick and thorough spread of American mass culture throughout Japanese society as a result of the irresistible appeal its lightness and sense of speed had for Japanese who were eagerly seeking escape from their traditional culture. "But what is light and speedy is also often flashy, garish, and cheap. American mass culture may have created a friendly intimacy with America, but in the long run it did not foster much respect for her people."

"Another attitude created in the Japanese by their experience of American mass culture," adds Tokyo University professor Shoichi Saeki, "was the tendency to think of the United States as a rather feeble giant. There was a slew of war novels that all ended with easy victory for Japan. And after the financial crisis of 1929, there was a rash of books with titles like *S. O. S. America* or *America on the Verge of Collapse*. The general notion that the American giant could be toppled by a quick jab at its 'Achilles' heel' certainly helped pave the way for the Pacific War."

Business Realism, Military Solutions

NEAR NIHOMBASHI in downtown Tokyo, standing between the Mitsukoshi Department Store and the Bank of Japan, is an imposing marble building of five stories and two basements. Today it houses the Mitsui Trust Bank, but before the war it was Mitsui Main Building, the temple of the entire Mitsui financial and industrial empire. It was built early in 1929 by Baron Takuma Dan, top executive of the firm. He had graduated from MIT and had hired an American architect for the building, ordering that it be modeled on the banks that had been built in earlier decades by American financial tycoons and robber barons. Its cost at the time was thirty million yen, roughly equivalent to thirty million dollars today. The first basement still houses a mammoth American-made safe with a door weighing fifty tons. "It took three nights just to haul the safe from Nihombashi to this building, a distance of only about two hundred yards. The work was done only at night," recalls Haruo Nagaoka, adviser to the Mitsui Real Estate Company.

Three years to the month after his great building was completed, Baron Dan was assassinated outside its front entrance. This assault was only one incident in a nationwide eruption of hatred directed against *zaibatsu* during the early thirties. The *zaibatsu*, as the Japanese industrial giants were called, had invited such sentiments by their self-serving manipulations of the economy. An example of their practices was the dollar-buying incident of 1931. There had been in-dications that the gold export embargo which had been lifted the previous year would soon be reimposed. This would serve to force down the exchange value of the yen. *Zaibatsu* banks anticipated this by buying dollars heavily on speculation, intending to make a killing by selling the accumulated dollars for yen when the embargo was reimposed. The scheme succeeded, but served also to intensify the fury of the general populace.

Anti-*zaibatsu* sentiment was expressed eloquently by one of the defendants in the trial following the assassination of Prime Minister Tsuyoshi Inukai on May 11, 1932. "*Zaibatsu* are devoted only to furthering their own selfish interests, with callous disregard for the misery of the farmers." Similar feelings were voiced by the young army officers charged with murdering Finance Minister Korekiyo Takahashi and other government and business leaders in the February 26 Incident of 1936.

The cumulative effect of the Great Kanto Earthquake of 1923, the financial crisis of 1927, and finally the worldwide depression begin-ning in 1929 had cast the Japanese economy into a profound slump by the early thirties. Unemployment was rife, and strikes and struggles of tenants against landlords were almost daily occurrences. Govern-ment financial policies seemed only to exacerbate the crisis. In 1930, the government lifted its ban on gold export, hoping to facilitate trade and the flow of capital. The measure produced the opposite effect of a calamitous outflow of gold with few returns, plunging the economy even deeper into depression.

Farmers were impoverished by the collapse of the raw-silk market. Then in 1931 and 1934 disastrous crop failures made their lives even more wretched. Many farm daughters were sold as prostitutes by families that could not afford to feed them or to marry them off. Countless children in farm villages went without lunch at school.

Franklin Roosevelt, assuming the American presidency in 1933, began to pull his country out of the depression with his New Deal measures. Japan, however, was steered by the military down a different path, one that led to fascist dictatorship. Disgusted with government inaction, corruption of political parties, and the greedy corpulence of the *zaibatsu* while the masses starved, the military solution for the nation's ills required territorial aggression on the Chinese continent.

Fascism gained momentum during the early thirties. The Manchurian Incident of September 18, 1931, had developed into full-scale war with China by 1937, and the international censure incurred by Japan's actions served only to intensify the nationalistic spirit within the country and to whip up further antiforeign feeling, directed primarily against the United States. Still, big business in Japan tried to evade the attention of the military and to keep open channels of intercourse with private American business interests. Around 1940, a plan arose to get a billion-dollar loan from America for the economic development of Manchuria and to induce U. S. recognition of the Japanese interests that had been acquired by aggression in Manchuria and China. John Francis O'Ryan, a former army officer and currently a New York lawyer with extensive contacts and considerable influence with American business leaders, was invited to Japan. He also toured Manchuria and China before leaving for home in August, 1940. Hardly was he back on American soil, however, when Japan signed the treaty linking her with Germany and Italy. The United States responded in October by banning the export of scrap iron to Japan. These and subsequent developments reduced the former plans for attracting American capital to hardly more than an idle daydream.

"Japan's business leaders were more realistic than the military in their estimation of American strength, the world situation, and the China problem," says Professor Yukio Cho of Tokyo University of Foreign Languages. "Until the last possible moment, they continued to seek American cooperation in solving the China problem."

When the Pacific War began, Koyata Iwasaki, president of Mitsubishi, announced to his staff that it was their moral obligation to protect the lives and interests of Mitsubishi's British and American business associates. No doubt he was already contemplating the end of the war, when the cooperation of foreign businessmen would again be essential. "It must have taken great courage for Iwasaki to have made statements like that in those times," muses Jun Usami, former governor of the Bank of Japan, who was then the acting manager of Mitsubishi Bank's Shinjuku branch.

With the war in full swing, the *zaibatsu* were forced to shed whatever pro-American sentiment they still had. By then they had found better sources of profit in the militarization of the Japanese economy and militarist advances overseas. Arm in arm with the military they went off together, like twins, to their mutual doom.

Two Who "Understood" America

ONE DAY in 1893, a small Japanese boy of thirteen landed in Portland, Oregon. He had made the crossing in the company of an elder cousin, who left him in Portland, encouraging him to make his own way in the world. Taken into the home of a kindly Christian lady, he was raised with her own son as though the two were brothers. With various odd jobs as a newsboy or waiter, he managed to work his way through college. Unlike most Japanese students in America, who generally studied at famous, name schools, he attended a small obscure college in Oregon.

When he returned to Portland in 1933, his name was known around the world. As chief delegate of the Japanese mission, Yosuke Matsuoka had just led Japan out of the League of Nations because her aggressive actions in Manchuria had been attacked in international debates. Japan's withdrawal from the league hastened the disintegration of the international body and provoked intense censure from the other member nations. Nevertheless, Matsuoka's alma mater welcomed him magnanimously as the school's most distinguished alumnus. While in Portland, Matsuoka ordered a fine marble monument for the grave of his former "American mother."

Seven years later, in 1940, Matsuoka was foreign minister of Japan. Straightforward and outspoken, yet considerate of trifles, he had made a great many American friends. Joseph Grew, U. S. ambassador to Japan until the outbreak of the Pacific War, wrote in his diary that Matsuoka was the first Japanese foreign minister with whom he could communicate in perfect candor. Whenever the two parted in disagreement, Matsuoka would later send flowers to Mrs. Grew by a messenger who would explain the minister's "real intentions" to the ambassador.

"Japanese don't know how to behave with Americans," Matsuoka

[82]

used to tell Japanese visitors to his office. "They either fawn on them and act excessively humble or they get angry and offensive. There probably isn't a single other Japanese who can sit like this talking to Americans," he added breezily, stretching out his legs on top of his desk.

Japanese military leaders were well disposed toward Matsuoka, as long as they were confident that he would be able to smooth over any problems in Japanese-American relations, thus facilitating their territorial ambitions elsewhere in Asia. But one of Matsuoka's first major actions after taking office was hardly a step in adjusting relations with the United States. He joined Germany and Italy in the Axis alliance and was hotly denounced for it in America. The following year, 1941, he visited Europe to confer with Hitler and Mussolini. On his way home, he stopped in Moscow to sign a Japan-Soviet neutrality pact with Stalin. Hailed at home as a national hero, Matsuoka continued on to Manchuria, where he announced that his next flight would be to America.

He longed to meet President Roosevelt for a close, heart-to-heart talk. Matsuoka's boyhood days in America created in him the image of America as a powerful giant who would ignore the problems of the powerless. But he also saw this giant as abandoning a dispute if convinced by direct and sincere talk of its opponent's difficulties. He was making overtures toward a meeting with Roosevelt, but sought first to put Japan in a powerful position from which to negotiate. His plan was to invite American mediation in Japan's war with China, which was already four years old; in return, he would offer to mediate a settlement of the European war. But when he returned to Tokyo from his European tour, he was surprised to learn that talks with the United States on the China issue had already begun through another unexpected channel and that he was not to take part in the negotiations. His vociferous and persistent opposition to the talks brought down the Konoe cabinet of which he was a part. The next cabinet formed by Prime Minister Fumimaro Konoe retained all the ministers of the previous administration except Matsuoka.

Perhaps a more direct reason for his ouster from the cabinet was that the military no longer needed him to serve as a buffer between their actions on the continent and reprisals from Washington. The generals and admirals had also lost patience with his outspoken objections to their more extreme moves, notably his opposition to the Japanese armed advance into French Indochina.

Matsuoka had been idolized by the masses for his decisiveness in pulling Japan out of the League of Nations. But mass support, in

[83]

Japanese politics, was no guarantee of longevity in office, and Matsuoka had to go. A recent gathering of veteran Foreign Ministry men debated for half a day the question of whether Japan would have joined Germany and Italy in the Axis if Matsuoka had not been foreign minister. The consensus they reached was that the tripartite Axis would have been formed even with a different man in office. Until it was too late, there was simply no resisting the militarists' insistence that Japan make common cause with Nazi Germany, whose star seemed to be in the ascendancy. Matsuoka's motivation for taking this crucial step seems to have been that once having ingratiated himself thus with the military it would be easier to wrest back control of foreign policy initiative from them. But Matsuoka's scheme failed, and he was denounced in the United States as a "friend of totalitarianism."

On December 8, 1941, all Japan thrilled to the news of the successful bombardment of Pearl Harbor. But Matsuoka, ill in bed, greeted the news with tears streaming down his face. "The Triple Alliance was the greatest mistake of my life. I shall not die happy with its memory haunting me." Matsuoka was an emotional man who wept easily, but this time his tears were those of genuine and profound regret.

Admiral Isoroku Yamamoto, fleet commander of the Imperial Japanese Navy and originator of the plan to bomb Pearl Harbor, had attended Harvard University and had been naval attaché at the Japanese Embassy in Washington. He knew America to be a valorous and powerful nation, despite attempts of the military to paint the opposite image at home. He also branded Japan's alliance with Germany and Italy as an act of madness. But still he suggested the attack on Pearl Harbor in order "to depress the morale of the American navy and people beyond recovery." "Admiral Yamamoto apparently hoped that the attack would make Americans think of the Japanese as a crazed and reckless people against whom it would not pay to fight," says Minoru Genda, Upper House member who planned and carried out the assault on Pearl Harbor. Actually, it had the effect of uniting a divided America in a long and bitter fight against Japan.

There were few men better informed than Matsuoka and Yamamoto on the situation in the United States or the American national character. Yet the fact that their predictions of America's response to Japan's belligerent actions were so far off the mark illustrates the difficulty in international relations for one nation thoroughly to understand another.

Yesterday's Enemies
Today's Friends

"CLIMB MOUNT NIITAKA. 1208." So read the telegram from Tokyo that was handed to First Lieutenant Ryuichi Itaya, duty officer on December 2, 1941, aboard the *Nagato*, flagship of the imperial Japanese fleet. He took it to the captain, who glanced at it and thrust it immediately into his pocket. "It's not important," he remarked calmly, as if to forestall any questions from his subordinate. Itaya was puzzled by the message, which made no sense to him. To the captain, it signaled the go-ahead for the attack on Pearl Harbor.

Vice Admiral Itaya is now chairman of the Council of the Chiefs of Staff, top military officer in the Defense Agency. Last year he played golf in Washington with Admiral Thomas Moorer, his American conterpart as chairman of the U. S. Joint Chiefs of Staff.

During the game, Admiral Moorer's lieutenant whispered jokingly to Itaya: "Win, and you'll have licked him for a third time." During the Pacific War, Moorer, then a young officer, had been shot down in a seaplane by the Japanese. He was rescued by a U. S. transport ship that was subsequently sunk. His defeat in the golf game would be his third loss to Japan. "Military men bear no grudges against their former enemies," Itaya quotes Moorer as having told him. "Both sides fought well, and in fact, Japan is responsible for having made the American navy strong."

Naraichi Fujiyama, former director of the Public Information and Cultural Affairs Bureau in the Foreign Ministry, was popular with foreign correspondents when he acted as a spokesman for the government. They consider him to have been the most straight-talking chief of the bureau. On Pearl Harbor day he had been in Washington, the youngest member of the Japanese Embassy staff. He recalls that the embassy was surrounded by an angry crowd screaming vituperations against Japan's treacherous attack. With nightfall the crowd swelled, and police and FBI men had to surround the embassy building to protect the staff inside. Fujiyama had been confined temporarily as an enemy national, then sent on a prisoner-exchange ship to his next post in Berlin. When Germany fell he was captured by U. S. forces and shipped back to America for confinement again. Disembarking, he was met by some of the FBI men he had known earlier in Washington. "Hey, how'd you get caught again?" they kidded him.

Yesterday's enemies are today's friends. Itaya and Fujiyama and numerous others, who, like them, were once in the van of the conflict with the United States, are now serving as points of friendly contact between the two nations. Perhaps the most prominent is Nobusuke Kishi, a member of the cabinet at the time of Pearl Harbor, defendant at the War Crimes Tribunal, prime minister at the time of the controversial Security Treaty renewal in 1960, and now president of the Japan-America Society.

How is it that two former enemies can be such close partners today? The Pacific War might be roughly defined as a clash of the Asia policies of the two nations, particularly their China policies. Its origins can be traced back to the Manchurian Incident of September 18, 1931. As Japan engaged in out and out war with China in 1937, the United States responded with aid to China and economic sanctions against Japan.

Why did the United States engage in such fierce conflict with Japan over China, where it had no economic rights or interests to speak of? Ideologically, the war was a showdown between democracy and totalitarianism. Furthermore, traditional American policy was opposed to allowing Asia to come under the control of any single power. But these are obviously only surface reasons. The American people must have had deeper motives for rallying behind the simple moral principle that was the basis of Secretary of State Cordell Hull's foreign policy: that the world is divided between honest, law-abiding, peace-loving nations and nations which set no special value on law and order but seek supremacy by force.

Perhaps something of a clue may be found in the following anecdotes. Tamon Maeda, education minister after the war, struggled to achieve greater Japanese-American understanding while serving as director of the Japanese Cultural Center in New York until the outbreak of the war in 1941. Strangers frequently came up to him on the street to express their great sympathy for his country, but as soon as they learned he was not Chinese but Japanese, they would abruptly turn away and stomp off indignantly. Similarly, any Japanese-sponsored essay contest on Japan, offering Americans a free trip to Japan as first prize, was certain to inspire a Chinese organization to advertise a contest offering more attractive prizes. Upon investigation it turned out the "Chinese" sponsoring organization was always a front for some pro-Chinese American group.

If the United States did not have major economic interests in China, she did have important "cultural" attachments and interests there. Churches, hospitals, schools, and the like had been built by American missionaries who had penetrated deep into the interior of

China. These missionaries, ousted from China by the Japanese army, assiduously built up an image of Japan as aggressor. It was against this background that the U. S. Asian policy evolved. The concept, as enunciated by Stanley Hornbeck, adviser to the State Department on Far Eastern affairs, was that the United States had "a moral responsibility for the future security of China." Until the Communist takeover, U. S. policy toward China was consistently sympathetic and supportive, while toward Japan it alternated between restraint and conciliation.

"In the annals of international diplomatic relations, rarely have two countries been so closely linked as the United States and China from the declaration of the Open Door in 1899 until the Communist revolution fifty years later," says Shigeharu Matsumoto, director of International House of Japan in Tokyo. George McGovern, U. S. senator and Democratic presidential contender, has described the reopening of relations with the People's Republic of China as the single most important task facing the next American president, adding that the myths and fears about China that have been built up in the last several decades may prove to be the costliest fiction in American foreign policy.

Just as yesterday's foe can be today's friend, today's friend may just as quickly turn into tomorrow's foe unless careful attention is paid to the lessons of history.

The ABCDs of Oil

HAD LENIN lived to witness the Pacific War he might well have smiled with malicious delight at the accuracy of his predictions and at his own contribution to the armed clash of two imperialist powers. In the days following the revolution, Lenin reasoned that the survival of Soviet Russia—surrounded by hostile neighbors—lay in playing one enemy off against another. On the eastern front, it was his goal to encourage armed conflict between Japan and the United States.

In 1918, the Allied Powers sent an international expeditionary force, consisting largely of Japanese and American troops, to Siberia, which was then torn by internal strife. To hasten the withdrawal of the international force, Lenin established the Far Eastern Siberian Republic, modeled along the lines of American democracy, and sent emissaries to the U. S. to win American sympathy for the new republic. Whether out of such sympathy or not, the U. S. withdrew her troops from Siberia ahead of the Japanese. The continued presence of the Japanese troops bred misgivings and distrust among Americans. Then, in a surprise tactic, Lenin granted oil rights in the Japanese-held regions of Siberia to American interests. He was probably acting on the advice of an unidentified soldier of fortune that it would be in Russia's best interests to deprive Japan of this source of oil. Since modern warfare could not be waged without oil supplies, Japan and the United States were bound eventually to come to blows over the Siberian oil rights.

When Japan protested his favoring the United States with oil rights, Lenin is alleged to have replied: "All right, you go ahead and kick out the Americans. We won't object." When American economic pressures finally forced the Japanese out of Siberia, Lenin proceeded to incorporate the republic into the Soviet Union. He had no further use for it.

Whatever the underlying causes of the war between the U. S. and Japan, it is generally agreed that the issue that finally precipitated hostilities was oil. In 1939, the United States registered its disapproval of Japan's two-year war with China by scrapping the forty-year-old Treaty of Commerce and Navigation. The advance of Japanese troops into northern Indochina the following year invited a U. S. ban on the export of iron ore, scrap, and steel to Japan. When Japan continued into southern Indochina in July, 1941, Washington reacted by freezing Japanese assets in the United States and finally played its trump card: an embargo on oil exports to Japan. America, Britain, China, and the Netherlands joined in imposing the oil embargo, unofficially referred to as the "ABCD encirclement of Japan."

In thus escalating economic sanctions against Japan, President Roosevelt and his top aides were most likely following the line of reasoning of Secretary of War Henry Stimson. Earlier, Stimson had advised that the only way to deal with Japan was to give her nothing. "A two-month embargo on U. S. raw-cotton exports and raw-silk imports had brought Japan to her knees and had forced her troops to withdraw from Siberia like so many whipped dogs," Stimson had told the administration. "Since Japan depended on imports for practically all her needs, including strategic materials, hardly anyone ever doubted that economic sanctions would quickly put an end to her belligerence," recalls Professor Norman Graebner of the University of Virginia.

A minority group was convinced, however, that economic sanctions would have the opposite effect of inducing further Japanese armed advances southward and would increase the possibility of war between Japan and America. Among those subscribing to this view were the ambassador in Tokyo Joseph Grew and a number of American naval officers.

The oil embargo came as a bolt out of the blue to the Japanese military. The country's oil supplies were believed to be sufficient for a war with America lasting at most two years. Thus, Japan had two alternatives open to her: to push further south until she took control of the Indonesian oil fields, or to negotiate with the ABCD powers for an easing of the embargo. The decision of which route to take was an urgent one, for already her oil supplies were being consumed without replenishment.

Japanese military and government leaders met in anguished council in Tokyo on November 1, 1941, deliberating for seventeen consecutive hours the proper course of action for their nation. According to Kenryo Sato, director of the Military Affairs Bureau in the War Ministry at the time: "The Japanese offer to withdraw all troops from Saigon northward amounted to a plea, made on bended knees, for oil and for a loosening of the noose around her neck. But the United States refused to listen. Americans today, seeing their country mired in the war in Vietnam, should be able to appreciate what the Japanese concession meant for us then." Nevertheless, the fact remains that the military, especially officers of middle rank, were still determined to go to war.

Foreign Minister Shigenori Togo believed that there was no more than a ten percent chance for peace, but he persisted in seeking an accord with the United States until the military threatened to force his removal from office unless he subscribed to their hawkish policies.

"There is a time in every man's life when he must gamble everything and make a sink-or-swim plunge," announced War Minister General Hideki Tojo to the third Konoe cabinet. The cabinet resigned shortly afterward, to be replaced by one with Tojo himself as prime minister. It was his new government that, with no guarantees of future oil supply, decided on war. Japan attacked the U. S. Pacific fleet at Pearl Harbor, simultaneously moving into the Indonesian oil fields. Eventually, however, she lost control of the oil fields, and her oil stock fell so low that the superbattleship *Yamato* had to operate with insufficient fuel. It was a war begun as a fight for oil and ended by the lack of it.

Today a global oil war has been set off by recent demands for higher prices from the oil-producing countries of the Middle East. Japan is the world's largest importer of crude oil; Japan's total oil stocks before Pearl Harbor would not even cover a single year's demand for kerosene to heat Japanese homes today.

"In the old days," recalls Yoshitaro Wakimura, professor emeritus of Tokyo University, "Japan needed oil primarily for military purposes. The economy as a whole could be run without much of it. But not today. Japan's economic survival depends on oil." This explains why Japan is so sensitive to today's oil war, why the issue of ownership of Okinawa and the Senkaku Islands is so important, why Japanese oil interests are calling for autonomous development of oil resources independent of the restrictions involved in using international oil capital, and why some groups are urging active defense of the Straits of Malacca by Japan.

"For whom should we defend Malacca, and how?" wonders Wakimura. "Such a notion is really nonsensical when one considers that Japan has to import all the materials she needs, not just oil. The idea is amateurish and seems to be a relapse into the prewar mentality. If Malacca is impassable, use some other route. The moral of the Pacific War is that Japan must remain a peace-abiding nation, through and through. The need for oil and other imported resources must absolutely preclude her from engaging in another war."

Eight Corners Under One Roof

SECRETARY of State Cordell Hull handed three notes to Kichisaburo Nomura, Japanese ambassador in Washington, remarking at the same time that he was compelled to deliver the notes by public opinion in the United States and by the continued belligerence of the leadership of Japan. The date was November 26, 1941, and the notes were stern and ominous. They ignored all previous negotiations between the two countries and demanded, among other things, the complete withdrawal of Japanese forces from China and Indochina and Japan's renunciation of her alliance with Germany and Italy. After delivering the notes Hull reportedly sighed to the secretary of the army that the matter was out of his hands and that from then on it was up to the military.

News of the Hull notes worried Kazushige Hirasawa, the Japanese consul in New York, so much that he flew to Washington to meet an old friend in the State Department. "Those notes mean war, you know," commented Hirasawa anxiously to his friend over dinner.

"Well, they are a complete statement of our principles," answered his friend. Each paid for his own meal that evening, and they parted gloomily.

In Tokyo, Foreign Minister Shigenori Togo ordered that a "wind signal" be flashed by radio to overseas weather forecasters. "Easterly wind, rain," was flashed repeatedly, this being the prearranged code to indicate to the Washington embassy that a rupture of diplomatic relations was imminent.

Professor James Thomson of Harvard University defines the clash between the United States and Japan as one between American "principle" and Japanese "program." U. S. doctrine refused to recognize any change in the status quo in Asia, particularly a change imposed by force of arms. The Japanese program projected the development—by military means if necessary—of a new order in Asia, namely, the Greater East Asia Co-Prosperity Sphere. Mistaken evaluations of the enemy by each party to the conflict and lack of mutual understanding and tolerance served to intensify the clash when it came.

"Throughout the negotiations there was absolutely no sense of give and take on the part of the United States," recalls former ambassador Nomura. Not only did the United States adamantly refuse to recognize Japan's program, it was also determined that totalitarianism and militarism should be destroyed. There are still lingering suspicions in some quarters that President Roosevelt provoked Japan into striking the first blow so that he could unite the American nation to rise in arms against her. Whether or not such notions have any basis in fact, nearly all of America had decided that Japan was totally in the wrong and refused to listen to her. Tamon Maeda, director of the Japanese Cultural Center in New York during the years immediately preceding Pearl Harbor, described discussion of Japan at that time as "a closed debate." America-Japan societies found themselves unable to collect dues from their American members or even to hold meetings. Even Americans friendly to Japan had to hide that fact and asked not to be invited to parties at the Japanese Embassy.

American organizations and influential citizens opposing U. S. involvement in the European war strongly supported Roosevelt's rigid policies toward Japan. Generally, the American populace feared Nazi Germany as much as they misunderstood or underrated Japan. Curious myths regarding the Japanese were rife and often accepted at face value. One held that Japanese have peculiarly constructed eyes which make them unfit for flying; another was that Japanese lack any sense of equilibrium because of an odd defect of their inner ears.

[91]

It must be admitted that Japan, at the time, was as self-righteous as the United States. Her population was nearly half that of America and yet it was crammed into a tiny land bereft of important natural resources; moreover, that population was expanding at the rate of one million a year. Despite that, the United States had locked her doors to Japanese immigration. Most of Asia was divided up under colonial rule by Western nations and, consequently, closed to the Japanese. What, then, was wrong in her seeking room on the nearby Chinese continent? Hadn't the European powers done the same, with far less justification? Had not each nation the obligation to its own people of self-preservation and self-defense? So went the Japanese arguments.

Japanese opinions on the China issue were certainly not altogether unified, but the divisions lay largely over whether breathing space on the continent should be obtained by military or diplomatic means. But the tough policies of the "have" countries, led by the United States, toward "have not" Japan frustrated her diplomatic efforts and re-assured the military that they were justified in their actions.

Japan's actions in Asia, seemingly motivated by selfish purposes of self-aggrandizement, failed to win understanding from the rest of the world. The high-flown and altruistic slogan *Hakko Ichiu*, literally "eight corners of the world under a single roof," simply did not convince non-Japanese observers. It is rumored that shortly before Pearl Harbor the Japanese government asked a group of Tokyo University professors to provide a new slogan to improve its image. The professors refused, asking the government to look elsewhere. Turning to Kyoto University with the same request, the slogan *Minzoku Kaiho* ("racial emancipation") was offered to the government and was accepted. When novelist Mitsuharu Kaneko had earlier pointed out to the government that *Hakko Ichiu* might well be unintelligible to Westerners, his objections were dismissed. "The 'one roof' makes no distinction between Japanese and foreigners," he was told. "It will house all people of the Co-Prosperity Sphere gathering together under the august virtue of the emperor." But Japan's arbitrarily appointing herself the leader of the Co-Prosperity Sphere and reserving to herself the rights of prior claim to natural resources tended to render the slogan of "racial emancipation" nonsensical or hypocritical.

Without any intention of condoning actions by the Japanese military in China, it should still be pointed out that parallel events have been witnessed more recently.

—A rikisha puller is beaten to a pulp by his passenger for demanding the fare for the ride. The poor fellow goes to a police box seeking redress, but is rebuffed and told that the passenger was right.

—It is always the innocent harmless ones who are injured most in guerrilla warfare. Noncombatant villagers, remaining in their homes after the guerrillas have fled, are summarily fired upon and bombarded, and the casualties are invariably reported as guerrillas killed. The worst case has been the rounding up and massacre of inhabitants of a small hamlet that formerly served as a guerrilla base.

These happen to be reports of atrocities which came out of Manchuria under Japanese military control—but the first might just as well have occurred more recently on Okinawa and the latter at Song My in Vietnam.

Diplomatic Fumbling

THE JAPANESE would rather commit national hara-kiri than yield to foreign pressure. Judging by their traits and temperament, it is dangerous to assume that American economic pressure on Japan will avert war. This was the substance of a telegram that U. S. Ambassador Joseph Grew sent to Washington in November, 1941. Earlier, in January of the same year, he cabled a warning that Japan might launch a major surprise attack on Pearl Harbor should war with the United States break out. Grew's warnings went unheeded. Shortly before the actual attack on Pearl Harbor, he sent another similar cable to Washington. Fearing that this one might be ignored as well, he sent his young assistant John Emmerson to Washington to insist that greater attention be paid. Stanley Hornbeck, a special State Department adviser on Far Eastern affairs, contemptuously challenged Emmerson to name a single country in the history of the world that had been driven to launch a war by its sense of despair. The young diplomat could not come up with one and withdrew in silence.

Hornbeck was the most hawkish of advocates of rigid U. S. policies toward Japan. He kept a detailed list of the economic sanctions of Japan that he had recommended to the administration. Underlined in blue were those that had been enacted; he underlined in red those that had yet to be adopted, as a reminder to himself to lobby for them further.

Lack of coordination in both the Japanese and American governments was partly responsible for misunderstandings between them; some in the Japanese Foreign Ministry feel that this was even a remote cause of the Pacific War. "Dispatches from the Tokyo embassy were like pebbles tossed into a lake," Grew once said. "They barely even rippled the surface." There was a notable lack of coordination between the personnel manning the Far Eastern desk at the State Department, Secretary of State Hull, and President Roosevelt. The Far Eastern desk, consisting of two percent of the State Department staff, as much as made policy toward Japan.

Kazushige Hirasawa, Japanese consul in New York prior to Pearl Harbor, has likened Japanese-American lines of communication at the time to a very thin thread, and has also observed that communication has not been much improved since.

One probable reason why Washington paid such scant attention to dispatches coming from its Tokyo embassy was that the State Department had been able to break the Japanese code and read every communication reaching the Japanese Embassy from Tokyo. In fact, every time that Secretary Hull met Ambassador Nomura, he had to take great care not to betray by word or facial expression that he had prior knowledge of something that Nomura was telling him. But State Department translations of Japanese dispatches contained many mistakes and misinterpretations—some of them serious. In the early postwar years, Haruhiko Nishi, deputy foreign minister at the time of Pearl Harbor, discovered to his horror that an important Japanese dispatch, containing the decisions made after a heated dispute between the Japanese government and military staffs, had been mistranslated at the State Department to read like an insincere proposition. "I shudder to think that a small mistake like that might cause a war."

While the U. S. State Department could claim at least continuity, in that Hornbeck had been in charge of Japan policy since 1928, in Japan there were thirteen changes of the cabinet and twenty-one different foreign ministers during the decade between the Manchurian Incident and Pearl Harbor. Furthermore, since the Foreign Ministry had traditionally attached first importance to European affairs, no America Bureau even existed until as late as 1934. Frequent cabinet reshufflings, the increasing ascendancy of the military, the quick rise of highly vocal "activist" factions in the army, navy, and bureaucracy, the influence of persons close to the emperor—such complex power relations in top decision-making circles made it difficult for the outside world to fathom what was really going on in Japan. Small wonder that the United States was careful to judge Japan only by her behavior rather than her statements. Since the most visible behavior was increased reliance on armed force, American distrust of Japan mounted.

The second Konoe cabinet, after joining the Axis, abruptly opened new negotiations with the United States, at the risk of invalidating the Axis pact. But a dark cloud hung over these negotiations from the outset. The United States was represented by two Catholic priests, Japan by civilians and army intelligence officers. Toshikazu Kase and many other diplomats think the attempted negotiations were an unwise and unsound diplomatic move. Even after the talks were properly returned to the hands of Ambassador Nomura and Secretary of State Hull, they made little headway. One reason for the difficulties was that Nomura was often in trouble with Tokyo. He was known to withhold Japanese government communications from the American State Department or change their wording before delivering them; likewise, he also withheld U. S. proposals from his own government or advanced his own proposals to the Americans in an attempt at personal, independent diplomacy.

"Nomura's naval background unquestionably influenced his diplomacy," observes Professor Chihiro Hosoya of Hitotsubashi University. "A commander who defies orders from above on the battlefield is forgiven and even commended if he later proves victorious."

Hull trusted Nomura's good intentions but doubted his diplomatic caliber and had difficulty understanding his heavily accented English. Nomura was equally troubled by the southern accent of the "Tennessee preacher." The Japanese ambassador was bothered by his own less than perfect understanding of English; one day he returned from a meeting with President Roosevelt particularly elated because, for once, he had understood every word of their conversation.

Nomura was unquestionably an amateur at diplomacy. But the Foreign Ministry, which should have educated and guided him, was also headed by an amateur. The third Konoe cabinet had not retained the rather controversial Yosuke Matsuoka as foreign minister, but had replaced him with Admiral Teijiro Toyoda. The foreign minister in the succeeding Tojo cabinet was Shigenori Togo, a career diplomat, but by the time he assumed the post and began putting in order the records of the Japanese-American negotiations, he realized that "the time bomb I held in my hands had already been ignited."

The Japanese Embassy staff in Washington was a loosely organized, uncoordinated group of men who had, in standard bureaucratic fashion, been kicked upstairs from lower positions in the Foreign Ministry. Its incompetence is clearly illustrated by its failure to decode and type out for delivery the final Japanese ultimatum before the attack on Pearl Harbor—a blunder unmatched in the history of international diplomatic relations.

"Communication between the United States and Japan immediately before Pearl Harbor was as much a mess as transpacific Japanese-Japanese or American-American contacts," observes Shigeharu Matsumoto, director of International House of Japan and head of the Domei Agency at the time. About an hour before the Japanese ultimatum was finally delivered in Washington, Commander Mitsuo Fuchida was already in the air, his armada of Zero fighters and bombers streaking toward Hawaii. When he ordered the radio operator seated behind him to flash "Tora! Tora! Tora!" the prearranged code signal indicating success in surprise attack, it was premature: Japanese bombs did not hit the water for another nine minutes. But Fuchida, knowing that the entire Imperial Japanese Navy was anxiously awaiting the signal, was impatient to send it and confident that the attack would go well. "At that moment, it never occurred to me that this might be the first step on the road to defeat, or that it was a tactical or political mistake," recalls Fuchida, now a Christian missionary. "All I knew then was that I was on the stage of history, bearing the future of my country on my shoulders. It was exhilarating to feel that all the rigorous training I had been through was about to be crowned with glorious success!"

Bombs and Baseball

IT WAS a perfect day for a ball game: sunny, clear, not a cloud in the sky. Shortly after noon on April 18, 1942, the annual Big-Six University League Baseball Tournament was due to open with a march of all the teams out onto the field of the Jingu Stadium near Meiji Shrine in Tokyo. The stands were packed with an excited crowd of baseball fans and student cheering squads.

Suddenly, air-raid signals rang out. Antiaircraft guns began spewing fire, and U. S. warplanes dropped the first American bombs on Tokyo. The black specks of the planes were visible from the stadium, but at first no one could believe that it was a genuine attack. There was hardly any commotion at all in the grandstands. The game was called off that day, but it was played a week later. These are the reminiscences of Shozo Fujita, manager at the time of the Hosei University baseball team and now director of the Konan Electric Com-

From Black Ships to Atom Bombs

1. *The* Powhatan, *Commodore Perry's flagship on his second visit to Japan, as depicted by a Japanese eyewitness. Six years later, in 1860, the ship carried the first official Japanese mission to the United States. Inscription: "A True Picture. Steamship Hohattan. Such ships are called in English* sutomu furekatto *(steam frigate). Fleet Commander Hiri (Perry) on board. Crew of 350. 21 medium cannon, 8 large cannon."*

2–3. *Two portraits of Commodore Matthew C. Perry, one by an American painter, the other by a contemporary Japanese artist.*

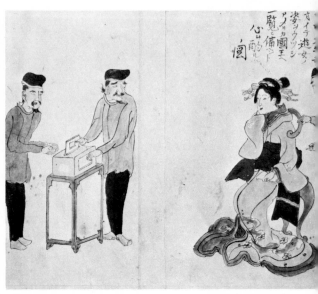

4. *Townsend Harris, the first American consul in Japan.*

5. *A contemporary sketch showing American seamen photographing a Japanese geisha. Inscription: "This picture shows how at Daian-ji, a temple in Shimoda, they took great pains to record the appearance of a courtesan to show the American king."*

6. *Front page of the* New York Times *for June 18, 1860, reporting the arrival in New York of the first official Japanese mission to visit the United States. Superimposed is a page of a letter, containing pressed leaves and flowers, sent by Muragaki Norimasa, one of the samurai envoys, to his family in Japan.*

7. *A group of Japanese scholars, visiting the United States in 1965, stops at the grave of Taro Kusakabe on the campus of Rutgers University in New Jersey. Kusakabe, one of the earliest Japanese students sent to America, died of overwork and exhaustion while at Rutgers. Inset shows William Griffis, a Rutgers graduate, who went to Japan in 1870 to teach at the Fukui clan school.*

8. *Sketch by George Mathis of Japanese immigrant farmers in California. Inscription: "Wakamatsu Colonists Planting Mulberry Trees, 1870."*

9. *Japanese officers photographed at the Manchurian front during the Russo-Japanese War.*

10. *Yosuke Matsuoka (left), Japan's representative at the League of Nations and later her foreign minister. Here he is seen arriving at Yokohama in 1933, after leading Japan's walkout from the League.*

11. February 26, 1936. Young officers of the Imperial Army move through the snowy streets of Tokyo from their headquarters at Sanno-shita, in the first steps of their bloody coup that was to prove abortive.

12. American press coverage of the dramatic February 26 Incident.

13. *November 2, 1934. Babe Ruth, visiting Japan as part of a team of American baseball all-stars, responds exuberantly to an enthusiastic welcome at Tokyo Station.*

14. *Hollywood's silent movies found many fans in Japan during the twenties. Pictured here are programs and handbills for several of the most popular films, including Charlie Chaplin's* The Gold Rush, *Rudolph Valentino's* Blood and Sand, *and Douglas Fairbanks'* The Thief of Baghdad.

15. *The arrival in Japan of American ambassador Joseph C. Grew and his wife. At Mrs. Grew's left, wearing a top hat, is Yukio Ozaki, ardent advocate of friendly relations with the U.S. and known as "the father of Japanese democracy."*

16. *Ambassador and Mrs. Grew visiting the graves of American seamen at Shimoda.*

17. *The famous cherry trees that line Washington's Tidal Basin were a 1912 gift to the United States from Yukio Ozaki, then the mayor of Tokyo.*

18–19. *December 7, 1941. The attack on Pearl Harbor. Above, Japanese dive-bomber planes, taking off at 5:45* A.M. *from the carrier* Soryu *for their flight to Hawaii. Below, the scene on the ground two hours later, after the waves of Japanese attackers had passed.*

20–21. *December 8, 1941. Japan and the Allied Powers declare war upon each other. Above, President Roosevelt, in a furious address to both houses of Congress, demands a declaration of war on Japan. Right, high ranking Japanese officers broadcast reports of Pearl Harbor and the Imperial Army's advance into the Malay Peninsula to the Japanese nation. Behind them is the front page of the* Asahi Shimbun *for December 9, carrying news of the military successes of the previous day and of the declaration of war on England and the U.S.*

帝國・米英に宣戰を布

西太平洋に戰鬪開始
布哇米艦隊航空兵力を痛爆

宣戰の大詔渙發さる

詔書

22. *April, 1943. The Imperial Conference of the Japanese Supreme Command, meeting at the palace in Tokyo in the presence of Emperor Hirohito.*

23. *A private meeting of retired prime minister Fumimaro Konoe (left) and General Hideki Tojo (right), who was both prime minister and army chief of staff. To Tojo's immediate right is Navy Minister Mitsumasa Yonai, and to his right an unidentified naval officer.*

24. *February, 1945. Churchill, Roosevelt, and Stalin, meeting at the Crimean resort of Yalta to determine the postwar disposition of Europe and to arrange the entrance of the Soviet Union into the war against Japan.*

25. *July, 1945. Five months after Yalta, Truman had become president upon Roosevelt's death and Atlee was the newly elected British premier. Here, they meet with Stalin at Potsdam to determine the terms for Japan's surrender. Superimposed is a leaflet dropped by U.S. planes over Japan, announcing the surrender terms contained in the Potsdam Declaration.*

. August 6, 1945, 8:15 A.M. The atomic bomb dropped on Hiroshima (and the second e dropped on Nagasaki three days later) rendered all further Japanese resistance imposle. Together, the two bombs killed at least three hundred thousand Japanese and brought ending agony from radiation diseases to hundreds of thousands of survivors.

27–28. The city of Hiroshima was reduced in an instant to a plain of rubble. Bottom, the Hiroshima Prefectural Production Bureau, located near the epicenter of the blast area, as it looked in August, 1945. As the rest of the city was rebuilt into a thriving industrial metropolis, this building—rechristened the "Peace Dome"—has been preserved as an eternal reminder of the horror of nuclear destruction.

29. *August 14, 1945. The final Imperial Conference. In a bomb shelter far below the palace, Prime Minister Kantaro Suzuki (foreground, black suit) informed the emperor that his ministers were unable to reach a unanimous decision on whether to surrender or continue to fight. Emperor Hirohito, wiping the tears from his eyes, then asked the assembled ministers and military leaders to "endure the unendurable" and to lay down their arms. He offered also to make the same request by radio to the entire nation. (Courtesy of the painter, Ichiro Shirakawa)*

30. *August 15, 1945. After the emperor's historic broadcast informing his people of the surrender, crowds gathered in the plaza in front of the palace and gave vent both to their despair and to their relief that the long war was finally over.*

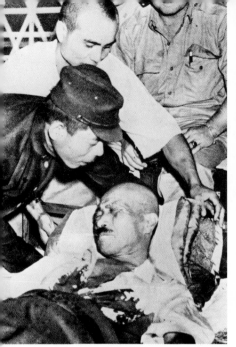
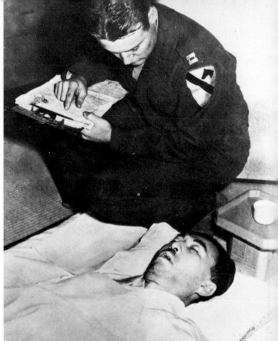

31–32. *The fall of Japan's leaders. General Tojo (left) and Prince Konoe, two of Japan's wartime premiers, tried to kill themselves rather than be tried as war criminals. Tojo shot himself in the chest, but recovered to stand trial and was finally executed. Konoe took poison and died on December 12, 1945.*

33. *Preparations for the Occupation began even before any American forces arrived in Tokyo. Here, former soldiers erect street signs in English in central Tokyo.*

34. *August 18, 1945. Douglas MacArthur, supreme commander for the Allied Powers, arrives at Atsugi Air Base. According to one observer, the general's words upon starting down the ladder were, "This is the payoff."*

35. *September 2, 1945. In the presence of General MacArthur, Admiral Nimitz, and representatives of the Allied Powers, Foreign Minister Mamoru Shigemitsu signs the surrender instrument on board the* Missouri *at anchor in Tokyo Bay.*

pany. It was Hosei's turn that year to organize the baseball tournament.

In 1942, government authorities were trying to discourage the playing of baseball on the grounds that it was a sport of foreign origin. They had taken upon themselves a difficult task, for baseball was extremely popular among the Japanese. In the fall of that year, the universities managed to prevail once again over government objections, and the tournament was held one more time; but the following spring, the sport was officially banned in Japan. A single exception to the ban was granted, however, on October 16, 1943. A special send-off game was played that day by the teams of Keio and Waseda universities in honor of all the students who had been called up for military service. The two teams met at Totsuka Stadium, from which all steel in the grandstands had already been scrapped for the war effort.

The War Ministry had at first been unwilling to permit the game; aware of the emotional circumstances surrounding it, however, the Ministry finally gave its grudging permission. Keio-Waseda games had always been the central feature of the six-university-league tournament, and had attracted enthusiastic attention from more than just the alumni of the two schools. The Keio-Waseda competition occupies today, as it did then, roughly the same position in the popular mind as the Harvard-Yale football game in America and the Oxford-Cambridge boat races in England. All of Tokyo, and much of Japan, is annually divided in supporting one or the other of the two teams.

The send-off match in 1943 ended in a 10-1 victory for Waseda. But neither players nor cheering sections were much interested in the score. More important was the farewell to fellow students about to go off to war. "There was one lusty chorus after another of school songs and cheering songs as deafening as the roar of waves. Keio boys and Waseda boys reciprocated in singing each others' school songs," reported the *Asahi Shimbun*. "Tears glistened in the eyes of the young soldiers-to-be and of those bidding them farewell. Finally the deafening choruses of school songs gave way to the solemn, subdued singing by twenty thousand young people of a patriotic song then sweeping the nation:

Umi yukaba	Going out to sea,
Mizuku kabane	A waterlogged corpse I'll be.
Yama yukaba	Going up the mountains,
Koke musu kabane	A moss-covered corpse I'll be.
Ogimi no	Beside my Sovereign do I wish to die.

[97]

Heni koso shiname   Never will I
Kaerimi wa seji   From my duty turn.

This last send-off tournament had been the idea of Arata Hirai, then head of the Keio baseball club and now an emeritus professor. He trudged repeatedly to the War Ministry pleading for permission to hold the game as an emotion-laden farewell gift to the departing boys. At Waseda, likewise, Suishu Tobita, an early advocate of student baseball, and Monjuro Tonooka, manager of the Waseda team, both worked tirelessly to persuade university authorities to support plans for the game. Earlier the same year, the Waseda administration, after conferring for three days, declined an invitation from Keio to play in a tournament. Their answer was that baseball seemed inappropriate in the present circumstances.

Kaoru Betto, fourth batter in the Keio lineup for that memorable game and today manager of the professional Taiyo Whales team, recalls that most of the young players had left Tokyo to return to their native places. "Some had obeyed their parents' wishes that they get married in case they were ordered to the front. We recruited them by telegraph, and they all showed up. But it was clear that they were all out of training. Still, they were overjoyed to get together and play baseball one last time. I think that many had been feeling rejected because they were players of an 'enemy sport.' "

"The night before the game, the teams swept the entire stadium so clean that there wasn't a speck of dust. I can still see them working at it," recalls Tonooka.

Professional players may have felt even more guilty about playing the enemy sport. They improvised curious Japanese words to avoid using the English baseball jargon that had become common. That was the least of their efforts to make baseball seem a bit more respectable. Before a game began they often dressed themselves in military uniforms and hurled mock hand grenades at a target set up in the stadium, yelling: "Down with America and Britain!" They played in regular baseball uniforms but wore caps modeled after those worn by soldiers, with straps under their chins. Baseball critic Kyushi Yamato credits such efforts as these with the success in keeping professional baseball alive in Japan until the end of the war, when it underwent another terrific upsurge in popularity.

Baseball had been played widely in Japan for years before the war and had become part of Japanese life. It was even played sometimes in army barracks during the war. Tetsuharu Kawakami, present manager of the Tokyo Giants, claims that as a soldier he always gripped

[98]

his sword like a baseball bat, and former pitcher Shin'ichi Ishimaru apparently played catch to his heart's content right up until he boarded his plane for a kamikaze attack. Indeed, in 1944, Tobita wrote in a sports magazine that baseball had taken far too firm a hold in Japan over the past fifty years to be suddenly swept aside by official repression.

How had this American transplant managed to put down such deep roots in Japan? Sociologist Chie Nakane believes that it is because of the similarity of America and Japan as mass societies, unlike European societies. Toshihide Kato, also a sociologist, attributes baseball's popularity in Japan to the fact that "it is a management game and both America and Japan are management societies."

"Baseball is governed by rules more complicated than in any other sport," observes Junji Kanda, former manager of the Tokyo University team and today a sportswriter for the *Asahi.* "The Japanese, being passionate lovers of rules, find it very appealing."

Another explanation comes from Osamu Miura, manager of the Yakult Atoms. "Sports, in general, should be honest and pure. But subterfuge and 'stealing' play as important a part in baseball success as they do in the battles of daily life. The kick that one gets out of baseball is that it takes a lot of deception and trickery to win a game. This appeals to Japanese and Americans alike, because both are the world's poorest cheaters and greatest losers at fraudulent tactics."

Whatever the explanation, not even the long and bloody Pacific War could kill the enthusiasm in Japan for baseball, more than any other "the American sport."

Hundred to One

TWO OFFICERS sat deep in conversation on September 16, 1944, in the paymaster's office aboard the aircraft carrier *Kumotaka,* cruising in waters off Taiwan. "I'm sure," said 1st Lt. Tadao Aiura, "that the U. S. will crush Japan, simply by the sheer strength of its resources and technology. In less than a year, the Americans will have taken the Philippines, invaded the home islands, and there will be GIs in the streets of Tokyo." His listener, 2d Lt. Kuniyasu Tsuchida, now director of the Police Affairs Division of the Tokyo Metropolitan Police Board, was only half convinced. Both had won positions in the civil service, Aiura in the Ministry of Commerce and Industry and

Tsuchida in the Home Affairs Ministry, but neither had been able to assume his post because he had entered the navy directly out of school. Aiura, a graduate of the Musashi Higher School, had studied in the United States for several years as one of the last Japanese exchange students to go to America before the war. The bookshelf in his shipboard cabin was laden incongruously with English books.

Tsuchida thought hard to come up with a rebuttal for Aiura's pessimism. To him the Japanese Imperial Navy still seemed strong. He had served on the mighty battleship *Musashi* until his transfer to the *Kumotaka* only a month before. Aiura's predictions were ominous but unconvincing.

A few hours before dawn the next day, the *Kumotaka* was sunk by American torpedoes. Aiura went down with it; Tsuchida was rescued by a Japanese frigate after being lost at sea for several hours.

Earlier that year, in July, Japanese forces on Saipan fought down to the last man. Three months later, American troops landed in the Philippines, and the battleship *Musashi* was sunk on October 24 in a battle off the Philippines. With sea and air power around the Philippines in enemy hands, Japan was effectively cut off from her oil supply in the Dutch East Indies. In 1942, about 240 tons of the vital oil had reached Japan from Indonesia; by 1944, she was getting less than a third of that amount. The beginning of 1945 saw the Japanese forces begin using a mixture of gasoline and pine-root oil as aircraft fuel. Junior high school students and members of women's organizations were recruited to dig pine roots from which the oil would be extracted. "The mixture was so sticky that it was almost impossible to start airplane engines on it," recalls Soshitsu Sen, who was in training in a naval air force unit in Tokushima late in 1944. He is now headmaster of the Urasenke school of tea ceremony in Kyoto.

There was an appalling shortage of steel as well. Production dwindled from 4.9 million tons in 1938 to less than 4 million tons only two years later. Reasons for the abrupt drop in steel production are not hard to find. In 1938, the steel industry was still backed by 1.7 million tons of American scrap iron, which was then abruptly cut off. U. S. steel production at the same time was nearing 100 million tons a year, and some members of the industry were even beginning to urge a production cut to avoid a postwar surplus.

"U. S. and Japanese production rates, as well as rates of war consumption, fall into a ratio of one hundred to less than one," revealed Shigeyoshi Matsumae, director of the Engineering Bureau in the Ministry of Communications, in an official report compiled early in

[100]

1943. "At our present rate of production, continuing the war will reduce Japan to a miserable ruin, however strong our faith in ultimate Japanese triumph may be." Matsumae reached these conclusions after a disheartening conference in Hakone with technical experts of the Planning Board and the ministries of Commerce and Industry, Agriculture and Forestry, and Railways. He hoped that his report, supported by indisputable logic and statistics, would convince the military powers of the futility of pursuing the hostilities. Instead, Prime Minister Tojo was infuriated to learn of the report and had Matsumae drafted as a buck private and shipped to Manila when the U. S. invasion of the Philippines was imminent. Matsumae is now president of Tokai University in Nagoya.

Early in 1944, 2nd Lt. Ichiro Koda, assigned to a naval unit on Iwojima, was startled one day to find the island encircled by a dark swarm of American naval craft. Their continuous bombardment shattered the island almost beyond recognition. The Japanese forces there were reportedly annihilated, but Koda miraculously survived and was taken to a U. S. military installation. There, to his great surprise, he was given plenty of water to wash himself, and he still has not forgotten the sensation of that first shower. The Japanese forces on the island had suffered an extreme shortage of drinking water, but the Americans were well supplied by their fleet offshore. Koda is now a department manager of Toyota Motor Company.

"We felt directly the pinch of that 100:1 ratio between American and Japanese productive capacities," recalls Tokusaburo Kosaka, then a naval paymaster and now a member of the Upper House. He and 1st Lt. Yasushi Morishita were assigned to the Fleet Administration Headquarters of the Navy Ministry as collectors of building materials for warships. They would go to a steel mill at five in the morning to snap up all available steel—ahead of the army procurers. They were even ordered to devise means for converting steel from automobile springs into bayonets. Morishita is now president of Morishita Pharmaceutical Company.

Early on the morning of July 14, 1945, President Truman received War Secretary Henry Stimson's report of the success of the atomic-bomb tests. In less than ten days the War Department ordered that the first such "special bomb" be dropped on Hiroshima, Kokura, Niigata, or Nagasaki as soon as weather permitted. The bombs dropped on Hiroshima and Nagasaki on August 6 and 9, respectively, stifled the possibility of any further war effort by Japan. The Manhattan Project that had required more than thirty months' steady work by a force of more than one hundred thousand men and had cost two and a half billion dollars had achieved the success envisioned for it.

Far from the Battlefield

THE PACIFIC WAR inspired numerous instances of cooperation between Japanese and Americans, personal friendships which survived the war, and unexpectedly touching or humorous incidents involving citizens of the two hostile nations. The few anecdotes recorded here will serve to prove anew that individual human beings can often find responsive chords in others and can establish fulfilling relationships despite the fact that their countries are at war.

"Sensei." The outbreak of the Pacific War set the U. S. government casting about in search of Japanese residents qualified to teach the Japanese language professionally. One such man, Ryusaku Tsunoda, seemed ideally suited for such employment, but Washington authorities were taken aback when he turned down their offer and refused to help them. This aroused suspicion against him and he was charged briefly with organizing a conspiracy to blow up the George Washington Bridge, which was not far from his apartment house in New York City. Summoned for questioning, Tsunoda said: "I refuse to cooperate in any way in a fight against my fatherland. However, I am aware of my obligations and the etiquette I should observe as a foreigner in this country." Tsunoda spoke such beautifully dignified English that the investigating officer asked if he were a poet.

When he was released, Tsunoda accepted a teaching position at Columbia University, where he established an institute of Japanese studies. His students affectionately called him *sensei* ("master"), and soon the title became synonymous with Professor Tsunoda on the Columbia campus. At Columbia, he taught Japanese language, history, and civilization, and among his students were such distinguished scholars as Donald Keene, John Embree, and E. H. Norman.

American Liberal. "It is possible to test the loyalty of American citizens of Caucasian origin, but not the loyalty of Japanese-Americans. I believe that we are faced by the menace of sabotage by citizens of Japanese origin on the Pacific Coast." In testimony to this effect at a House subcommittee hearing, California Governor Earl Warren urged the relocation of the Japanese-American residents of the West Coast states during the war. His opinion was accepted and acted upon. Ten years later, as Supreme Court chief justice, Warren won the commendation of American liberals for his strong stand on the unconstitutionality of segregated education in southern schools.

Low-grade paper. Soon after the beginning of the war, the American government took over the type fonts owned by the three Japanese-language newspapers in New York. The publishers of these newspapers, many of them Socialists who had been influenced by Sen Katayama, decided to help the Office of War Information in its propaganda work directed toward Japan, feeling that they would thus be joining the fight against Japanese militarism. "In producing propaganda materials we were aided in the choice of paper and ink by seeing the popular Japanese magazines like *King* and *Kodan Zasshi* seized by American forces at the front," muses Takeshi Haga, one of the publishers. "We had a hard time getting low-grade paper equaling the Japanese product in affluent America," he laughs.

Rotarians. Dr. Hachiro Yuasa, former president of Doshisha University, was in New York during the war, working for a relief committee for Japanese residents organized by the Methodist church. One day a State Department official came to show him a photo of about forty Japanese people. Yuasa recognized them at once: members of the Kyoto Rotary Club. "Who of these people do you think will cooperate with Americans when the U. S. Occupation sets about the rebuilding of Japan?" he was asked long before the outcome of the war was clear.

Jewel box. A few days before Joseph Grew, U. S. ambassador to Japan, was to leave for home on the exchange ship *Asama-maru,* Imperial Household Minister Tsuneo Matsudaira summoned to his office Toshikazu Kase, chief of the North American Section of the Foreign Ministry. The imperial family wished to present a farewell gift to the Grews. Would Kase try to deliver it to them one way or another?

Evading the hawk-eyed vigilance of the secret police, Kase called on the Grews at their embassy residence. "Let me first deliver a message from Princess Chichibu," he began. The Grews rose from their chairs and stood at attention. "Unfortunate events have set our two nations against each other, but I am sure that it will not be long before peace returns," Kase read aloud, and then handed them a small package. Tears came to the eyes of the ambassador and his wife.

Mrs. Grew would have broken down but for her husband's support.

"The hardships the Grews had suffered together since the beginning of the war must have made them feel all the more grateful for the princess's warmth and generosity," Kase reminisces. While in Washington after the war, he visited the Grews and found the gift prominently displayed in their guest room. It was a small jewel box. As a State Department official during the closing days of the war, Grew had struggled to insure the perpetuation of the emperor system in Japan after the war.

Yoroshiku. The scene was the Opera House in Kuybyshev, wartime seat of the foreign diplomatic corps in the Soviet Union; the date, spring of 1943. Saburo Ota, a Foreign Ministry official, was surprised to meet a close American friend, Eugene Dooman, former counselor at the prewar U. S. Embassy in Tokyo. Being enemies, they merely exchanged glances of recognition. Later, at a luncheon given by the Swedish ambassador, Dooman slipped a piece of paper into Ota's hand. The message on it, written in Japanese, moved him almost to tears: *"Mina-san ni yoroshiku. Genki de ne."* (Regards to everybody. Keep well.) Dooman, a graduate of Gyosei Gakuen in Tokyo, later joined with Ambassador Grew at the State Department in working for the preservation of the emperor system.

Yenan Americans. From 1943 on, a group of fifteen Americans was stationed as a military mission in Yenan, wartime stronghold of the Chinese Communist party. "They seemed to be collecting intelligence on Japanese military activities in North China," recalls Sanzo Nosaka, chairman of the Japan Communist party; he was then based in Yenan, engaged in the anti-Japanese struggle under the alias Susumu Okano. "John Emmerson, who later served as U. S. embassy minister in Tokyo after the war, was in the group. We Japanese were cave dwellers. The Americans lived in a one-story brick house. From time to time, they displayed the latest American weapons for the men of the Chinese Eighth Route Army, who all looked wistfully at them."

Kinuyo and Kazuo. During the war, actress Kinuyo Tanaka was the best-known Japanese woman among American students of Japanese. The U. S. government encouraged the showing of Japanese domestic drama and melodrama movies as part of a crash education program in Japanese language and culture. Miss Tanaka, who appeared in many such films at the time, soon became as popular with American students as she was with audiences in Japan.

[104]

Otis Carey, now a professor at Doshisha University in Kyoto, recalls that while he was the commanding officer of a POW camp in Hawaii he was puzzled to come upon one prisoner after another with the same name. He grew suspicious and investigated further. The name was Kazuo Hasegawa. It turned out that many Japanese soldiers, in surrendering to the enemy, picked the name of this celebrated movie star to use as an alias.

Holocaust of Patriotism and Prejudice

ON THE COLD windy evening of December 4, 1942, only days before the first anniversary of Pearl Harbor, a car tore through the streets of Tokyo and pulled up in front of the main offices of the Japan Broadcasting Corporation (NHK). A stern-looking army officer got out and disappeared into the building. Minutes later, Lt. Col. Kunio Akiyama, information officer for Imperial Army Headquarters, stood before a microphone ready for the seven-thirty broadcast. When he received the signal to speak, his words poured forth so furiously that he did not even bother to turn the pages of the prepared text that he clutched in his fist.

"The other day I overheard something that horrified me and which should scandalize every one of you," he began. "An upper-class Tokyo lady, seeing American prisoners of war from Wake Island, spoke tender words of compassion on their behalf. Compassion from a Japanese woman toward American prisoners of war, at a moment when our soldiers are shedding their blood at the front! Shame! Every shred of friendship for the enemy must be obliterated! If any such sentiments remain on the home front, they must be stamped out!"

Akiyama's broadcast set off a flood of telephone calls to NHK from listeners asking the name of the unpatriotic woman. Letters asking the same question poured into the Information Bureau of the War Ministry from members of youth corps and reservists' associations across the country.

The outbreak of war with the United States had come as a great surprise to large segments of the Japanese populace. With all news strictly controlled by the military, it was impossible for the Japanese people at large to grasp the particulars of the international situation with any understanding or to size up the enemy strength accurately. As a result, the nation was swept along on a wave of blind patriotism. Even intellectuals were intoxicated by the news of the initial victories and crowed with belligerent enthusiasm.

Novelist Osamu Dazai wrote: "Japan has changed this morning. I am itching to beat the bestial, insensitive Americans to a pulp!" Poet Kotaro Takamura echoed: "With eyes closed in meditation, I can still hear the tremors of the Anglo-American way of life as it was crushed and destroyed!"

Nevertheless, the fact remained that Anglo-Saxon civilization had become too deeply rooted in the Japanese mind and in all aspects of Japanese life to be obliterated so quickly. Hatred of the United States and Britain did not flame so intensely as had the anti-Russian sentiment during the Russo-Japanese War.

"The news of Pearl Harbor made my father-in-law shout: 'That idiot Tojo!' and stamp his feet with helpless rage and chagrin," recalls Upper House member Hisatsune Sakomizu. His father-in-law was Admiral Keisuke Okada, prime minister from 1934 to 1936. "Sensible men could not have turned passionately anti-American or anti-British overnight."

Akiyama, now a Tokyo business executive, explains in a tone considerably more sober than that of his 1942 broadcast: "With the fortunes of war on our side, it seemed to us at Imperial Army Headquarters that there was not enough hatred for the enemy across the land. I thought it necessary to broadcast a speech like that to incite more passionate feelings directed against the enemy." After this broadcast condemning the unidentified woman's compassion for American prisoners, anti-American propaganda distributed by the army grew increasingly strident and lurid.

One propaganda story charged that U. S. forces on Guadalcanal had laid wounded Japanese soldiers side by side in rows and run over them with steamrollers. Another piece accused an American girl of using the skull of a fallen Japanese soldier as a paperweight. At no moment in the eighty-year history of relations between the United States and Japan had the American image been so low.

But the time came when the need for anti-American propaganda tapered off. The fortunes of war had turned against Japan and her islands were exposed to indiscriminate bombings that brought widespread destruction and death to thousands and thousands of Japanese citizens. The nighttime air raids on Tokyo by American B-29 bombers on March 10, 1945, dropped 48,000 bombs in only four hours, leaving

124,000 Japanese dead or maimed and an estimated one million homeless. These figures are taken from a survey conducted by the Metropolitan Police Board. Military propaganda was no longer necessary to foment rage against the Americans. One bomb could accomplish far more toward this end than the screech of propaganda.

The incident in which a downed American pilot was ripped apart alive at Kyushu University is an illustration of the intensity of anti-American feeling toward the end of the war. "A hysterical crowd dragged the pilot about, beating and kicking him so savagely that troops had to be called in to restrain them," wrote Shusaku Endo, whose postwar retelling of the case appeared in one of his novels.

In addition to hatred, the bombs also bred fear of the United States. The tremendous destruction and widespread hunger after the air raids were intensified created a desire for an early surrender, the objective that American strategists had hoped for. More than six thousand people, most of them over fifty, were arrested by the police or the military for expressing in one way or another their desire for a Japanese surrender. Most of them said that immediate surrender was far preferable to continued suffering and privation. An arrested Nagasaki radio dealer had predicted a Japanese defeat, and said that if he were drafted he would desert and surrender to the Americans to be taken prisoner.

In July, 1945, a month before the end of the war, the military distributed, throughout their native Miyagi Prefecture, photos of all 2,400 members of a Sendai infantry regiment killed on Guadalcanal. Propaganda officers expected that this would enhance the morale of the Miyagi populace. But instead of feeling admiration for the bravery of the young men, the people were only cast into deeper despair by seeing their pictures.

The nation's youth, pure and innocent, had been raised on a steady diet of government propaganda and undying faith in the myth of Japan, "the divine land." It responded selflessly to the call of the military to "fight on until the last American and Britisher is destroyed." Grammar-school children in the Tohoku region of northeastern Japan, assembling on the school grounds, would chant spiritedly: "Cursed America is on the wrong side of the earth we walk on," and then stamp their feet furiously, as though to trample all Americans to death.

"I hated the Americans and the British because I had been taught how they had bullied Asians. I wanted to hurl them back and free all of Asia as Yamada Nagamasa had done," recalls novelist Hyozo Kashiwara, remembering childhood sentiments.

[107]

Toward the end of the war, countless Japanese youths—students of the military academies, teen-age airmen, student soldiers, and kamikaze pilots—sacrificed their lives for their country, burning with hatred for Americans whom they had never met face to face. Let it be recorded here that they were far less happy to fly off to the certain death awaiting them than the military would have had the Japanese people believe. Tsugio Iida, now publicity director for NHK, who broadcast on-the-spot reports of kamikaze pilots leaving on their final missions, tells his story: "Behind the flames of anti-American hatred burning within the kamikaze pilots, I sensed the human feelings of anguish, yearning, and regret. I offered to record their last messages and to transmit them to the beloved ones the young men were leaving behind. Most shouted tearfully the name of a wife or sweetheart onto the disc before climbing into the cockpit of their planes. They all cried: 'I don't want to die!' I couldn't hold back my own tears."

The Pacific War revealed the intensity of prejudice and national hatred that can be developed by governments unable to communicate with each other, by feeding propaganda to the people, and by indiscriminate bombings of innocent citizens. It is an important lesson, but the sacrifice in learning it was staggering.

PART THREE

The Occupation
and Its Legacy

In 1945, Japan lay in ruins. Her people had listened for eight bloody years of war to their leaders' glorification of the Japanese spirit, only to witness the nation's collapse in atomic holocaust, fire-bombings, and military surrender. At this moment of extreme agony, a proud people that had never before been defeated, and indeed had never even fought a war on its home territory, was finally asked by its divine ruler to "endure the unendurable." Exhausted, starving, shelterless, and spiritually shattered, the Japanese had to face subjugation under the occupation of a feared enemy nation.

The American occupiers, arriving under the leadership of General Douglas MacArthur in August of that terrible year, were wary of the reception they would receive from the defeated Japanese. There were widely believed rumors of Japanese women protecting their homes with bamboo spears, of mass suicides, of children clutching mines in their arms and throwing their small bodies beneath advancing American tanks. The Japanese, for their part, feared murder and rape by barbaric American soldiers bent on plunder and further destruction. Both sides were surprised. The Japanese accepted defeat with dignity and resignation, laying aside their arms, if not all their hostility. And the Occupation showed far more of benevolence than of the harsh vindictiveness that the Japanese had expected. Its policies, although many of them were conceived with an eye to the securing of American power or the furthering of long-range American interests in Asia, were immediately beneficial to the rebuilding of Japan.

The Occupation set out to "democratize" a nation that had experimented, briefly and idealistically, with democratic institutions twenty years earlier, but that was still feudal and militaristic in many ways. The

American democratization policies were written in the rough in Washington; actual implementation was left to the authorities in Tokyo, who, despite their energy and idealism, were inadequately prepared for their enormous task. Of course, there could be no real training for a task like this. The fact that the Occupation proved to be as successful as it did in accomplishing its myriad functions, ranging from writing a new constitution for Japan to censoring public information and feeding hungry people, speaks well for the diligence and good will of most of its members. Working with only the loosest of guidelines, limited experience, and the most superficial understanding of Japanese society, Occupation reformers managed, with Japanese cooperation, to effect a social revolution that has been the foundation of postwar Japan.

But all was not so positive. Midway through the Occupation's seven years, cold-war tensions, erupting in the war in Korea, forced American concern away from Japan to the larger picture of Asian security and the containment of the communist world. It was this later mood that colored the background of the peace treaty that ended the Occupation in 1952 but left the Japanese uncertain whether they had regained genuine independence or not. Hindsight has also revealed that many presumably well-intentioned Occupation reforms led to later complications which could not have been predicted at the time they were made but which are now proving far more troublesome than the ills originally cured. To the Occupation can be traced many of the critical issues now confronting Japan, a quarter-century after the war's end, as she begins to assert her full independence.

Should the Occupation be praised as the source of Japan's present stability, affluence, and power? Or should it be blamed for Japan's difficulties in establishing for herself an autonomous identity? This is a question for scholars and historians to grapple with, and the final resolution must be left to them. Viewed here in kaleidoscopic fashion and without the benefit of their comprehensive analyses, the separate events of this cathartic period reveal the Japanese nation struggling to reconstruct its flattened cities and restore its soul, creating—sometimes with American help and sometimes without full American realization—a new existence on which to build its future.

To Uproot the Chrysanthemum?

EARLY in 1942, the "divine troops" of the Japanese army descended out of the sky by parachute onto oil-rich Palembang on Sumatra Island. Japanese at home ecstatically celebrated the event, convinced that victory was not far off. Few would have dreamed that, even at that moment, the American State Department was already planning the occupation of Japan. A special research office within the State Department, headed by George Blakeslee and Hugh Borton, had been assigned to draw up the initial blueprints for postwar policies.

No sooner had the war begun than the United States launched an extensive program of research on Japan. College and university students who showed particular talent or promise were recruited for intensive language study and research in special fields of Japanese studies. At the instigation of the government, sociologists organized themselves into peace research groups to develop a model of what postwar Japan should be like.

One well-known product of the Japan study program was the book *The Chrysanthemum and the Sword*, written by cultural anthropologist Ruth Benedict for the Office of War Information. It was an attempt to elucidate, if not explain, the mind of the "most inscrutable" enemy that the United States had ever fought. The book's title was intended to represent the Japanese polity: the chrysanthemum was the emblem of the imperial family, and the sword symbolic of Japan's military might. For General MacArthur's staff during the early days of the Occupation, this book was the most authoritative guide to Japanese society and individual personality.

The central debate among the men who were charged with preparing for the occupation of Japan was whether to uproot the chrysanthemum, i.e., the imperial institution, or to let it live. In January, 1943, President Roosevelt issued his demand for the unconditional surrender of the Axis nations so that the Allied powers might control and rebuild them arbitrarily. "Roosevelt not only suggested a formula on how to end the war," observed Waseda University professor Keishiro Irie, "he went further and made it clear that the ultimate aim of the Allies was to change the fundamental structures of the enemy nations after the cessation of hostilities." Harry Lloyd Hopkins, then a presidential assistant, explained Roosevelt's announcement as ex-

[111]

pressing his resolve not to permit a repetition of the mistakes of the Versailles Treaty that ended World War I, mistakes which he believed facilitated Hitler's rise to power. In Japan, Roosevelt was determined to secure the total elimination of the authority of both chrysanthemum and sword. To quote Saburo Ota, former chief of the War Termination Central Liaison Office: "This preoccupation of Roosevelt's was bred by his almost physical abhorrence of hereditary monarchical systems."

Meanwhile, the special research office in the State Department evolved into the Committee on Far Eastern Affairs. This, in turn, expanded into a three-department State-War-Navy Coordinating Committee. Still, coordination between Roosevelt and this committee was often inadequate, and the State Department suffered as a consequence. Borton once complained that his office learned the contents of the Casablanca Conference and Cairo Declaration only over the ticker tape from the wire agencies.

In May, 1944, the Committee on Far Eastern Affairs submitted to the administration an unpublicized list of "postwar objectives for Japan." It moderated Roosevelt's intentions by proposing indirect rule and retention of the emperor system. This recommendation was based largely on the practical consideration that the United States had no ready substitute for a disintegrated Japanese government.

Public opinion was considerably more hostile toward Japan. A 1944 Gallup poll showed that thirty-three percent of the respondents demanded death by hanging for the emperor and thirty-seven percent that he should be tried as a war criminal. American intellectuals, many of them with long emotional ties to China, were equally hostile. Owen Lattimore, then director of the Far Eastern division in the Office of War Information, demanded the exile to China of the emperor and the male members of the imperial family.

As if ignoring public opinion, Joseph Grew, former ambassador to Japan, surrounded himself with "old Japan hands" when he assumed office as undersecretary of state. His staff, among whom were Eugene Dooman and Joseph Ballantine, proceeded to formulate a policy of indirect rule by the Occupation government with the aid of the existing system of government in Japan. Grew succinctly explained his stand on Japan in a statement before the Senate Foreign Relations Committee. Citing the example of a queen bee, he said: "Take her away, and you destroy the whole swarm under her rule. . . . [Remove] the emperor and the United States will have to nurse forever a crumbling society of seventy million people."

Grew's opinion, although shared initially by only a small minority,

[112]

eventually won out for several reasons. First of all, Roosevelt's sudden death in April, 1945, weakened the authority of his top aide, Treasury Secretary Henry Morgenthau; the "old China hands" who advocated eliminating the emperor system and establishing military rule over Japan likewise became less influential within the administration. Another reason was the advent of the cold war. It was on May 12, 1945, only days after Germany's surrender, that Winston Churchill warned President Truman of the iron curtain that the Soviet Union was beginning to lower over the occupied territories of eastern Europe. Churchill's report alarmed Grew so much that he was unable to sleep. He was well aware that, under the terms of the secret agreement reached by Roosevelt, Churchill, and Stalin at Yalta in February of that year, the Soviet Union would soon declare war on Japan. At the time Grew was virtual head of the State Department because Secretary Stettinus was often away attending international conferences, and his anticommunist sentiments were sharpened by increasing cold-war rivalries. Diplomatic historian Waldo Heinrichs believes that it was Grew's strong antipathy to communism that induced him to include in the Potsdam Declaration an indirect promise that the emperor system would be retained, as well as the demand for an unconditional surrender of Japan and sole U. S. occupation of the country. Six years later, at the signing of the peace treaty in San Francisco in 1951, Grew mentioned to his old friend Toshikazu Kase his conviction that the American abstention from a punitive occupation policy and the refusal to abolish the emperor system won her Japan as an important ally.

The postwar reform of Japan under the Occupation was a far cry from what Roosevelt had envisioned and was criticized as a "soft reform" by the Soviet Union, Australia, and other Allied powers. But Chie Nakane, like Ruth Benedict a cultural anthropologist, agrees that the retention of the emperor system was justified. "The emperor has no authority and no rival. He is a symbol of authority," she explains, "but the presence of this symbol at the top of a layered society seems to lend stability as well as structural and psychological coherence to Japanese society." Thus, the emperor, shorn of all real political power, does still perform a political function as a buttress of social equilibrium.

Yalta and Beyond

O NE JUNE DAY in 1945, two months before the end of the war, a Japanese correspondent in Madrid was consoling a German newspaperman as he had been doing almost daily since Germany's surrender in May. He thought to himself that he was really trying to buck up his own spirits too. *Asahi Shimbun* correspondent Noboru Ito had also been feeding the German journalist and giving him money ever since his remittances from home had been cut off. "Day in and out I kept my ears glued to the radio for war news, my heart heavy with fear for the fate of my country," recalls Ito, now a professor at Tsuda College, as he thumbs through his old wartime diary.

During those dark days the Allies were busy establishing the occupation of Germany, and preparing for the occupation of Japan. The blueprint for the Japanese occupation was based largely on the Cairo Conference statement of 1943, following the surrender of the German forces in Stalingrad and the withdrawal of Japanese forces from Guadalcanal, and the secret Yalta pact of February, 1945. The Cairo Declaration established the basic American policy toward Japan: to stop and punish Japanese aggression and oust her from the territories she had acquired by violence and greed. An earlier expression of this policy was a radio speech by Joseph Grew in August, 1943. The former American ambassador to Japan had urged severe measures to prevent Japan's ever again menacing international peace, and had also called for a reform of Japanese thought and life reaching to the most fundamental levels. A still earlier expression was in the notes that Secretary of State Cordell Hull had sent the Japanese government immediately before Pearl Harbor. Hull had demanded security for the Pacific nations and for Japan's neighbors against the threat of Japanese armed aggression.

The Potsdam Declaration of July, 1945, was the final expression of U. S. policy toward Japan. In it can be discerned the American impulse to remodel the political systems of other nations after her own for the purpose of facilitating the establishment of an international setting harmonious with American foreign-policy objectives. This attitude has consistently characterized American foreign policy since the war as well.

"American leaders held high hopes that the end of World War II would bring about the birth of one world of peace," comments Professor Tadashi Ariga of Seikei University. Obviously, the quest for one world would require forming a new world order around an American

[114]

axis. There is reason to believe that President Roosevelt recognized that American-Soviet cooperation would be an essential ingredient not only for victory in war but also for building a stable peace later.

At the Yalta Conference, the United States, Britain, and the Soviet Union decided among themselves—without the participation of the other Allied powers—the postwar disposition of the war theaters. Even Chiang Kai-shek's Nationalist Chinese government, considered by some to be entitled to a voice in the planning of postwar Asia, was kept ignorant of the contents of the agreements reached at Yalta. The conference acquiesced to Soviet territorial ambitions and thus was to touch off the long, bitter postwar competition. The secret six-point Yalta Agreement ceded, among other things, southern Sakhalin and the Kurile Islands to the Soviet Union. This was the bait used by the United States to lure Russia into the war against Japan; today Moscow continues to use the Yalta Agreement as the basis for its repeated rejections of Japan's claims to her former northern territories. The Yalta Agreement has been interpreted by some historians as proof that, in American eyes, any means to reduce the death and bloodshed of Yankee boys was considered fair, regardless of the consequent sacrifices of other nations. Some have branded it a blanket justification for territorial expansion.

In the final analysis, the Yalta pact provides the model for the American-Soviet domination of international politics that has lurked behind all postwar disputes—a tyranny that has been challenged determinedly by France and the People's Republic of China. The seeds that have grown into the complex and tension-ridden international situation of the present day were sown at that Russian resort in February, 1945.

Wholly unaware of the decisions reached at Yalta, Japan requested Soviet intercession in concluding peace with the United States shortly before the Russians shocked her by entering the war on the American side. "Japan, at this point, is like the proverbial drowning man clutching at straws," remarked Chief Cabinet Secretary Hisatsune Sakomizu to his friend, correspondent Kazushige Hirasawa. American historian Robert Butow has described the dilemma as Japan standing at Russia's back door, bearing the gifts of a supplicant but still confident that Russia would remain neutral and agree to act as mediator, while the United States was lining up trophies for the Soviet Union at her front door.

Instead of helping create the new international order that America was supposedly seeking, cooperation with the Soviet Union—for which the United States paid dearly—grew more and more tenuous as the two nations were besieged by conflicts of interest in Europe. The Yalta Conference was hardly over when questions regarding further American-Soviet cooperation began to be voiced in various sectors of the American government. "How thoroughly need we crush Japan? Won't we need a force to counter Soviet influence in the Far East? Shouldn't we re-examine the Yalta Agreement and reconsider our request for Russia's entering the war against Japan?" Viewed with the hindsight of postwar developments, these questions seem to be premonitions of the cold war.

Japanese Minister of War General Korechika Anami predicted as much in conferring with Japanese war leaders: "The Soviet Union is bound to come into conflict with the United States soon after this war. I don't believe that Moscow will want to weaken Japan too much." Anami kept insisting that Japan request Soviet intercession in drawing up a peace with the United States. He committed hara-kiri soon after the war ended.

On August 6, 1945, the first atomic bomb was dropped on Hiroshima; two days later Russia declared war on Japan. On August 9, the second atomic bomb was dropped on Nagasaki and Russian troops moved into Manchuria and Korea. On August 14, in conference with the emperor, the Japanese government formally accepted the terms of the Potsdam Declaration, and the following day the emperor announced the nation's defeat to the nation in his historic radio broadcast.

It cannot be denied that Japan's defeat brought certain benefits—freedom and democracy. Out of these have grown the present economic prosperity and love of peace. But a fact that must not be overlooked is that the American policies of democratization changed gradually with the progress of the cold war that began almost simultaneously with the Occupation. Thus, the final question that we are left with is: "What is the meaning of democracy established under military occupation?"

The Second Opening of Japan

PUFFING on a corncob pipe, he kept pacing up and down the aisle of the plane carrying him toward Japan. From time to time, he would say something which his adjutant dutifully jotted down. Finally

[116]

the man sank into a seat and fell asleep. As the plane neared its destination, the adjutant wondered whether he should wake him. He hesitated for a moment, then cleared his throat and said: "Sir, you can see Mount Fuji." The man opened his eyes, glanced out the window, and remarked: "Always good to look at." Then he closed his eyes again.

At 2:05 P.M., August 30, 1945, the *Bataan* set down at Atsugi Naval Air Base. The forward door was thrown open. After a short interval, Gen. Douglas MacArthur, supreme commander for the Allied Powers, appeared, gazed deliberately to the right and the left, and then slowly descended to the tarmac.

"Melbourne to Tokyo—it was a long way," came the five-star general's first words in Japan.

"Perhaps it would have been more grammatical to say: 'It was a long way from Melbourne to Tokyo,' " comments Lower House member Hirohide Ishida who covered MacArthur's landing as a reporter for the *Nihon Keizai Shimbun*. "I'm not very good at English, but I knew, or I thought I knew, the difference.... There was no ceremony, no pageantry, no troops for him to review. But the general's personal bearing seemed to include all the pomp and ceremony demanded by the occasion. His demeanor seemed affected to me, but he was a far greater actor than most Japanese commanders." Winston Churchill, seeing photographs of MacArthur's landing in the midst of the enemy, unarmed and wearing only shirt sleeves, called it "the most extraordinary bearing of a military commander in time of war." As later events showed, this was but the first expression of the great self-confidence and assertiveness which were to characterize the following years as "Mac's Occupation."

Three days later, on September 2, the instrument of surrender was signed in a solemn ceremony on the deck of the U. S. S. *Missouri* in Tokyo Bay. The atmosphere was charged with tension. "The gaze of the victors fell on us like a hail of fire-tipped arrows," reminisces diplomat Toshikazu Kase, who was a member of the Japanese delegation. Adm. William Halsey, a survivor of Pearl Harbor, was irritated by the slowness of the chief Japanese delegate Mamoru Shigemitsu in limping forward to sign the surrender document (Shigemitsu had a false leg and used a crutch). To one unidentified observer, Halsey looked as though he "itched to smash a fist into Shigemitsu's face and shout 'Hurry up and get on with your signing!' " The only ornament of the ceremony was the Stars and Stripes standing to one side. It was the same flag that, ninety-two years earlier, had fluttered on the mast of Perry's flagship when he arrived to force open Japan's doors and end her policy of isolation. The second opening of Japan was about to begin.

What this "second opening" would mean for the Japanese, no one knew. The occupiers settled down in Yokohama and remained silent for a time, giving no inkling whatever of the form their occupation would take. More than two weeks after the signing of the surrender on September 2, Prime Minister Naruhiko Higashikuni, a member of the imperial family, paid a call on MacArthur to try to break the American silence. Higashikuni came dressed in a white-linen business suit, apologizing that the shortage of goods prevented his wearing more formal attire. "You are lucky to have that," replied MacArthur curtly. He meant no doubt that Higashikuni should consider himself lucky to have even as much as that one suit, but the prime minister's interpreter was tactful enough to translate the words a bit more gently.

"For a conquering general receiving his vanquished foe, MacArthur was more polite than I had expected," recalls Higashikuni. "Later, he began sending out so many directives and orders that I got exasperated and resigned. Looking back now, I think I may have been too hasty in doing so."

When directives began to issue from MacArthur, they came on a wide variety of subjects: democratizing the government, granting voting rights to women, liberating farmers and reforming land tenure, unshackling the labor movement, eliminating all vestiges of police repression, establishing freedom of speech, educational reforms, local self-government, and an endless succession of others. Many of these directives had first received expression in the notes taken down by MacArthur's adjutant during the flight to Japan aboard the *Bataan*. Later they took form as actual Occupation policies.

MacArthur's seven years in Japan were unique in the history of military occupations. The Occupation's object was neither to disarm the country nor to impose punitive measures in retaliation for the war. Instead of binding and whipping the defeated enemy, the victor sought to reach deep into his heart and reform him. This was clear from the democratization plans that were announced one after the other in rapid-fire succession.

Democratization was an obsession of MacArthur and his aides. Efforts in that direction were so determined that legend attributes such conversations as the following to members of the Occupation staff:

[118]

"How many women's organizations did you democratize this week?"

"Three, how about you?"

In the last analysis, the Occupation must be viewed as a further extension of the U. S. policy—the same as that which led to the Pacific War—to dismantle the Japanese government and military machine, rendering the nation unable ever again to menace the United States or world peace. It was obvious that the spirit of the founding of the United States, and the missionary zeal and pioneer vigor that had developed from the American experience, underlay the attitudes of the Occupation.

"The end of the war was not really the beginning of occupation for the Japanese people at large. They had previously been under an occupation by their own military that had penetrated every thought and action of Japanese life. The United States had simply replaced the Japanese military as occupier," remarks novelist Ryotaro Shiba. "But the new American occupation possessed a splendor that had been lacking in that of the Japanese military." To be sure, it was not as despotic; it even imparted a certain sense of emancipation to many people. But, ultimately, U. S. Occupation policy had a built-in inconsistency in that it imposed freedom on Japan.

Occupation policy was neither fully established in advance nor rigidly applied. Indeed, it was a "personal" occupation in that it reflected the idiosyncracies and individual styles of MacArthur and his aides. Later, it was to undergo basic changes as a consequence of the explosion of the cold war into a hot war in Korea. Many Japanese feel that these and other circumstances cast shadows over the Occupation, shadows that have still not faded. Whether these lingering shadows are to be considered the legacy of the Occupation or whether they are reactions to it is not the crucial question. In a sense, Japan has yet to emerge from the Occupation. The Occupation itself may not have been despotic, but its aftermath is, for Japan continues to be limited in autonomy and freedom of choice.

MacArthur's Two Caps

IN THE FIRST postwar spring, on April 5, 1946, the Allied Council for Japan sat for the first time, in the Meiji Life Insurance

Building, across the moat from the emperor's palace in Tokyo. The council, comprised of representatives of the United States, the Soviet Union, China, and Australia, was the organ through which the Allied Powers were to implement Occupation policy. Delegates from all the member nations attended: the Soviet Union's Lt. Gen. Kuzma Derevyanko in his uniform adorned with red epaulettes, British Commonwealth delegate Macmahon Ball looking like a university professor, and China's Shang Chen, with an unchanging, expressionless face. Japan was under solely U. S. occupation, but the Meiji Life Insurance Building was the only place in the country that was under joint Allied occupation in the full sense of the words.

When MacArthur rose as chairman to address the council, he announced that it was but an advisory organ to the supreme commander for the Allied Powers and did not share his administrative responsibilities. In plain words, MacArthur was saying that he was the boss and would not stand for meddling by any of the others. Derevyanko's shoulders shook with rage and Ball's mouth twisted as though he were about to deliver a biting remark.

To the Japanese, MacArthur represented absolute authority. But, technically, "Absolute Emperor" MacArthur was not vested with supreme authority. Occupation policies were fixed by the Far Eastern Commission, headquartered in Washington and consisting of delegates from eleven nations that had fought Japan in the Pacific War. MacArthur, as supreme commander for the Allied Powers, was to execute those policies with the advice of the Allied Council, as defined by the decision of the Four-Power Foreign Ministers Conference in Moscow in December, 1945. But despite MacArthur's position below the Far Eastern Commission (which at the time was housed in the former Japanese Embassy in Washington), his strong character would tolerate no interference by other council nations in the implementation of Occupation policies.

On March 29, 1946, the council addressed a long series of questions to MacArthur. The council feared that if he permitted the constitution-revision issue to be debated in the campaign for the first general election under the Occupation, reactionary parties might make political fodder out of it. Would MacArthur consent to order that the election be postponed?

MacArthur shot back a single word in reply: "No."

He had initially promised to pass on to the council copies of the directives issued by GHQ (General Headquarters) and SCAP (Supreme Commander for the Allied Powers). He kept his word for a time, then stopped sending the copies. "SCAP directives came in writing in the early days, then they began to come verbally, and later not at all," recalls Hisanari Yamada, Liberal-Democratic member of the Lower House who acted as liaison between the Japanese government and GHQ/SCAP. MacArthur issued the directives as "informal directives" without feeling it necessary to give their texts to the council. In a sense, the council was kicked upstairs.

One explanation of the supreme commander's authoritarian attitudes was his sensitivity to the increasing tensions of the cold war and his distrust of and antipathy for the Soviet Union. The other was his pride in the sole U. S. occupation of Japan, except for a very limited stationing of some British Commonwealth forces. Thanks to this exclusive U. S. presence, Japan was spared the tragedy of Berlin. But, as Tokyo University professor Yu Ishida points out in his book *Catastrophe and Peace*, the only "democracy" allowed in Japan was the American armed forces' interpretation. The notion of democracy imposed under military occupation seems in itself an anomaly, and the unilateral U. S. occupation allowed Japan no choice among different democratic forms.

U. S. eagerness to set an example of democracy in Japan often took on the rather maternal quality of wishing to protect Japan against interference by the other Allied Powers, particularly the Soviet Union. The American struggle to protect Japan was staged, ironically, at the meetings of the Allied Council, which MacArthur all but ignored.

Between 1946 and the end of the Occupation in 1952, the council sat 162 times to debate a wide range of problems: farmland reform, dismantling of the *zaibatsu*, food shortages, repatriation of Japanese soldiers. . . .

"The U. S. stood by Japan as a mother by her child," reminisces Koichiro Asakai, director of the War Termination Central Liaison Council and a regular observer of meetings of the Allied Council for Japan. "How often I felt an urge to rush over and grab the hands of the American delegates in gratitude."

Obviously, the main motive behind America's treating Japan as a favored protégé was its desire to make Occupation policies look mild to the Japanese. This bred in the Japanese a certain pauperlike dependence on the United States, a feeling which has yet to disappear completely. Occasional anti-American outbursts by some segments of the population have made some Americans regard the Japanese as ungrateful, "after we did so much for them." Japan is also charged with enjoying a free ride on the U. S. defense bus.

It was through the Allied Council that the Japanese first glimpsed the depth of the cold war. Against this cold-war background, MacArthur's two caps—head of the Occupation and Commander-in-Chief, U. S. Forces Far East—symbolized the true nature of Japanese-American relations. The Japanese view of these relations was purely bi-national, but MacArthur thought of Japan in the larger context of Asia. The end of U. S. military government in Japan is a case in point. After the Korean War began, Japanese Foreign Minister Katsuo Okazaki talked with MacArthur and persuaded him to suspend the U. S. military government. Japan interpreted this as her own success in Japanese-American diplomatic relations. Apparently Mac-Arthur thought differently, still regarding Japan as just another Asian country to be protected from communism. Eiji Takesaki, lecturer at Tokyo Metropolitan University, explains: "Security in South Korea had grown so shaky by that time that MacArthur had no choice but to transfer the main American forces in Japan to Korea. He was too short-handed to carry on the military government simultaneously even had he wanted to."

The United States considered the Japanese islands and the Korean peninsula together as a single security problem. This seems clear from the transfer of the bulk of American forces to Korea and the creation, by SCAP directive, of the Japanese Police Reserve Force.

The Sato-Nixon joint communiqué of November, 1969, states that the security of the Korean peninsula is vital to Japan's security. "That shows," according to some political observers, "that young Japan is trying now to don the cap that her big brother has been wearing."

Candy Bars and Corn Meal

IN THE early postwar days, leftover food from the American naval base at Yokosuka—bits of bread, salad, slices of meat, small quantitities of milk and butter—was being rationed in the town. The food had been brought home by local women who took turns working in the base kitchens in groups of about ten. "The food saved our lives in those days," says Mrs. Toshiko Tanaka, then president of the Yokosuka New Life Women's Association. "Of course, we wouldn't touch it today, though."

The commander of the naval base, Capt. B. W. Decker, was a little MacArthur. He called himself "the law in Yokosuka." He had little use for Japanese men, but devoted great energy to helping women's organizations. He allowed one group to use certain buildings for their activities. He gave another group a large supply of chocolate from the base stock to be distributed in a membership-expansion campaign. Accepting kitchen help from the women and giving them scraps of food in return was intended as an act of charity. He also recruited Yokosuka women to attend to trash disposal on the base and allowed them to take home whatever odds and ends they sorted out from the litter. More than one hundred women did this work and carried home useful or remunerative materials. "We made toys out of empty beer cans, tested and ate discarded food. . . . There was hardly anything to throw away after we were finished with it," recalls one of the women.

Today, a splendid statue of Decker stands in the center of the park that faces the Yokosuka Municipal Government Building.

All Japan was hungry in 1946. The previous year's rice crop was the poorest in forty years, and there were countless unexpected mouths to feed as demobilized servicemen returned from overseas and Japanese immigrant families began drifting back from Manchuria and Korea. There were grim predictions that ten million Japanese would starve to death. One Diet member screamed in the parliament chambers: "Rice before a new constitution!"

"How are you keeping body and soul together?" was the theme of the first "Man on the Street" interviews conducted by the Japan Broadcasting Corporation (NHK) in May, 1946. People disclosed over the radio, for the benefit of listeners all over the country, tricks and devices for survival: buying food from farmers on the sly, thinning out already thin rice gruel to make it last longer, mixing various vegetables with rice, cooking potato vines, and other techniques. It was not easy to get people to speak up before a microphone. Japanese hadn't had any experience, and many passersby shied away from the sidewalk interviewer with a skittery "not me."

The interviewer often chased after them, promising them a gift of chocolate or a ticket to an American movie in return for speaking. One young girl was thanked for her interview with: "Here's a pack of chocolate for you."

"What's chocolate?" she asked in bewilderment.

"I can still see her earnest, questioning eyes," says Shuichi Fujikura, the first NHK broadcaster to conduct the sidewalk interviews.

Japan was barely saved from starvation by American food, food from GARIOA (Government and Relief in Occupied Areas), food releases from the military forces, and food gifts from Japanese residents of America sent through LARA (Licensed Agencies for Relief of Asia). The food was mainly corn meal, de-oiled soy beans, and skim milk—hardly better than cattle feed. Occupied Germany declined to accept such food shipments. But Japan was too hungry to pick and choose.

When the Diet passed a resolution of thanks to the Occupation forces, GHQ and SCAP were deluged with letters of thanks from hungry schoolchildren. Any intention that the United States may have had to win the hearts of the Japanese people through food succeeded beyond all expectations. Japan considered the GARIOA food an outright gift and was amazed when GARIOA sent her a bill for $490 million. She agreed to pay off the bill over a fifteen-year period.

Japan's dependence upon American relief during the postwar period served to affect later relations between the two countries in subtle ways. First, it imprinted on the Japanese mind an image of great American affluence. The image was rendered almost indelible by the huge amounts of chocolate and chewing gum which GIs gave away or sold illegally, by PX goods flowing through the black markets of Tokyo's Ameya-yokocho district and Kobe's Sannomiya, by the occasional glimpses of the easy life on the military bases, by American radio programs, and by the enormous, sumptuous sandwiches pictured in the *Blondie* comic strips. This image of American affluence bred in the Japanese a certain servility, a beggarly sense of dependence on the United States. Signs that this attitude still lingers on are to be seen at Japanese-American government conferences and in economic negotiations.

As further evidence of Japan's postwar pauperlike mentality, Tokyo University professor Yoshikazu Sakamoto mentions the collection of letters from Prime Minister Shigeru Yoshida to Secretary of State John Foster Dulles that is now preserved in Princeton University's Dulles Library. "Most of them recount tales of Japan's suffering and read like letters from a son begging his father for money."

Many Americans, recalling their help to Japan, now complain that she no longer reciprocates with unquestioning friendship or that she is stingy about offering aid to other nations. Be that as it may, it has no doubt been a combination of a fear of hunger and a yearning after an American-type affluence that has been the strongest motivation behind Japan's postwar economic miracle.

"But, now that Japan has attained that American-type prosperity, a new type of hunger is evident," observes novelist Akiyuki Nozaka. He himself lost both his parents in an air raid on Kobe, was hungry throughout the postwar period, and calls himself a "former waif and prowler among the black markets that sprang up on wartime ruins."

Nozaka finds curious similarity between the waifs of those days and today's young kids. The tentlike roofs of the pavilions at EXPO '70 looked to him like a colossal black market: "The long lines of spectators, waiting with grim, wistful expressions, seemed like hungry people lining up for food handouts. And the participants in EXPO— purveyors of new American technology and prophets of a rosy future for Japan—looked just like the black-market merchants when I was a kid, drumming up trade for goods that were stolen or released by the U. S. Army."

Japan's Postwar Women

ONE DAY, near the war's end, a shower of propaganda leaflets came fluttering down on Tokyo from U. S. B-29s flying overhead. Mrs. Fusae Ichikawa, former Socialist member of the Upper House and well known as a campaigner for women's rights, happened to pick one up. On it was printed the Potsdam Declaration. "The Japanese government shall remove all obstacles to the revival and strengthening of democratic tendencies among the Japanese people. . . ." it read in part. To Mrs. Ichikawa this meant suffrage for Japanese women. She and her associates acted quickly. Ten days after the end of the war, they organized a Women's Committee on Postwar Countermeasures.

They were not the only ones concerned with rights for women. On the plane carrying him from Manila to Japan, General MacArthur had mentioned to his adjutant that Japanese women, gentle, cultured, and self-sacrificing, had been treated unfairly. One of his first items of business would be to see that they received the right to vote. Women participating in government would never permit the revival of militarism.

"MacArthur was deeply concerned with women's suffrage," recalls Prince Higashikuni, the Japanese prime minister who met MacArthur fifteen days after the end of the war. "He mentioned it again and again in our conversation." But the Higashikuni cabinet quit without tackling the issue. At the first meeting of the succeeding cabinet on October 10, 1945, Home Affairs Minister Zenjiro Horikiri raised the question of women's suffrage. Prime Minister Shidehara reacted favorably: "The other day when my car fell into a ditch,

[125]

neighborhood women gathered and helped pull it out. . . . Japanese women deserve the vote in return for their suffering during the war and since."

The next day, MacArthur issued a five-point directive on democratization. The very first item insisted that the Japanese woman be given the vote. Emancipated by it, they would become part of the body politic and bring new ideals and a new direction to Japanese government. This would be directly beneficial to the welfare of the Japanese family.

On April 10, 1946, Japanese women voted for the first time. Many of them admitted that they were afraid they would be scolded by MacArthur personally if they neglected to go to the polls. The general election produced thirty-nine female members of the Lower House in one fell swoop, surprising even the campaigners themselves with their own success. The rate of voter turnout in that election was 78.52 percent for men and 66.97 for women. The difference narrowed in subsequent elections until female votes exceeded those of males in elections in 1968 and 1969.

One of the prime arguments of opponents of women's suffrage had been that wives would meekly vote for the candidates of their husbands' choice. But surveys have proved that this was not the case and that women followed their own minds in voting. Another criticism, voiced more recently by novelist Tatsuzo Ishikawa, is that female voting spawned the so-called "celebrity legislators," people elected purely on the basis of their popularity in the entertainment or literary worlds. Provoking some controversy, Ishikawa has wondered aloud whether women are not more subject to the influences of mass psychology. Yoko Morosawa, a critic concerned with women's problems, rebuts this by saying: "It's altogether wrong to interpret the election of TV celebrities as a matter of female versus male voting habits. It is rather a reflection of the dissatisfaction of the public, especially the silent masses, with the deterioration of conventional politics."

Although, legally, Japanese women are now politically liberated, for many young women today much still seems to be lacking. They are flocking to the cause of Women's Lib, and many housewives have begun protesting skyrocketing prices, pollution, and myriad other problems of daily life through consumer boycotts and other campaigns. Whether "influenced by mass psychology" or not, Japanese women are continuing to increase and extend their strength and influence.

A single American woman stands out conspicuously in the history of the postwar emancipation of Japanese womanhood. 1st Lt. Ethel Weed, a member of the Civil Information and Education Section of GHQ, looked much younger than her thirty-nine years in her petite, skirted army uniform. Typically American in her cheerfulness and her plain, direct speech, she was also an extremely energetic advocate of increased rights and privileges for Japanese women. She lectured from Hokkaido in the north to southernmost Kyushu, meeting women from all walks of life, sharing their tubs in rural hotspring bathhouses, and listening to their problems.

"Lieutenant Weed devoted herself to the democratizing of Japan with a passion," recalls Upper House member Shizue Kato, who was a close friend of hers. "Her fairness and modesty won for her the cooperation of Japanese women as she went about her difficult tasks," says Nobuko Takahashi, a former colleague who is now director of the Women's and Minors' Bureau of the Labor Ministry (the bureau was created by Lieutenant Weed). But if she was fair and modest, the American woman was also tough enough to order the disbanding of any women's organizations which she considered undesirable. "Japan was for her a piece of white cloth on which she was free to paint to her heart's content," says Toshiko Momijima, a public relations consultant who was Lieutenant Weed's assistant.

Today Miss Weed is the proprietor of the East and West Bookshop in a small town in rural Connecticut; the shop is known to universities and public libraries in the area as a source of books on Japan and Asia. "I haven't forgotten Japan for a second," she told an *Asahi* correspondent who visited her recently. "I often get letters from Japanese friends keeping me up to date on the women's movement in Japan. Japan's women have finally won for themselves a position as advanced as any in the world, and I'm sure they are now strong enough to unite in fights against pollution and other urban ills." She laughed merrily when she heard for the first time the popular joke that "stockings and women have gotten strong in Japan."

Although she mothered and nursed the postwar Japanese women's movement during her seven busy years in Japan, Miss Weed is all but unknown in her own country. She moved to Connecticut from New York in December, 1970. "As soon as I'm settled here, I'm going to start fighting air and water pollution," she exclaimed with the fervor of a much younger woman.

Power to the People

SEPTEMBER 27, 1945. The emperor was attired in morning dress when he went to call on General MacArthur at his residence in the compound of the American Embassy. MacArthur greeted him at the door dressed in khakis, his shirt open at the neck. Although the weather had not yet turned cold, a fire burned in the fireplace.

"Tell the emperor . . ." began MacArthur, addressing Katsuzo Okumura, who had accompanied the emperor as interpreter. There followed a long oration, sounding almost as though the general had been up all night preparing it.

"MacArthur's face was lusterless, like leather, and still bore signs of fatigue from heavy fighting. He didn't have his corncob pipe, and he looked tense," recalls Okumura, now an adviser to the Foreign Ministry. As a member of the Political Affairs Bureau, he was the only interpreter present at that historic meeting between the emperor and the supreme commander for the Allied Powers.

Five months later, the Japanese government was handed MacArthur's plan for the emperor's future status and for the form the new constitution would take. In February, 1946, irritated by attempts by the Japanese government to retain the emperor's status almost unchanged from what it had been under the Meiji constitution, MacArthur and his subordinates quickly drew up a draft plan for a new constitution. It is now generally accepted that the draft, which provided for the emperor's status to be reduced to that of a mere symbol of the Japanese nation, was abruptly thrust on Japan in order to thwart the opposition of the Far Eastern Commission in Washington to the retention of the emperor system in any form.

The United States government had decided to rule Japan indirectly, through the Japanese government, with consideration given to Japan's wishes about the status of the emperor. MacArthur's impression, formed after that first meeting in September, 1945, was that as a private individual the emperor was the foremost gentleman in Japan and that his position should not be eliminated.

The Japanese government presented a draft constitution to the Diet in June, 1946, for debate. One night, during the debate, Col. Charles Kades, deputy chief of the Civil Government Section of GHQ, summoned the groups concerned with constitutional revision to a conference the following day. In this conference, held at the prime minister's official residence at eight the next morning, Kades informed

Tokujiro Kanamori, state minister in charge of constitutional revision, of a change that would have to be made in the draft. The draft had defined the emperor as the symbol of the unity of the people and stated: "He derives his position from the will of the Japanese people." Kades wished the phrase revised to read: "He derives his position from the people, in whom resides sovereign power." The Japanese government complied, and thus the emperor relinquished his sovereign power to the people. In this way MacArthur's headquarters played the historic role of guaranteeing the security of the emperor system by limiting it to a symbolic role.

"It was definitely an act of interference by SCAP," says Toyoji Shinada, then Kanamori's secretary and today dean of the Department of Economics at Sophia University.

"I was sorry to see the emperor system fixed in that way, and I felt as much guilt as sadness," recalls Tatsuo Sato, director of the first division of the cabinet's Legislative Bureau at the time and now president of the National Personnel Authority. Now he finds the present emperor system completely stabilized. Professor Ko Sato, dean of the Faculty of Law at Sophia University, believes that seventy percent of the people support the present system, including those who consider it harmless and, therefore, acceptable. Professor Toshiyoshi Miyazawa, professor emeritus at Tokyo University, also believes the newly defined emperor system has taken and stuck.

As the new Japanese constitution was being debated, the Soviet Union and Britain asked the Far Eastern Commission in Washington for safeguards against former service officers obtaining cabinet posts. GHQ and SCAP acted quickly, proposing that the clause "the prime minister and other ministers of state shall be civilians" be inserted in the constitution. There was no precise Japanese equivalent for the word "civilian," however, and members of the Upper House Special Committee on Constitutional Revision were hard pressed to provide a suitable translation. They came up with hundreds of possible terms, some quite farfetched. Some of their suggestions: *heijin* ("commoner"), *minjin* ("man of the people"), *bunjin* ("man of letters"), *bunchijin* ("man who rules by the pen"), *heiwa gyomusha* ("person in the peace business"), *sekaijin* ("man of the world"). Eventually *bunmin* was adopted; literally, it means "literatus" or "man of letters," but it also has ancient connotations of one who rules through philosophy, learning, and the arts, rather than by the sword.

In the years since the new constitution, written with the close consultation of American Occupation authorities, was promulgated in

1947, important contradictions, unforeseen at the time, have arisen from its application to Japanese society. Who in those days could have conceived of the Self-Defense Forces that exist today, for example? Are SDF officers military personnel or *bunmin*? The government's official interpretation today is that they are *bunmin* when out of uniform.

When Tokyo governor Ryokichi Minobe approved a financial grant to a nursery school that was not an officially recognized institution, the Metropolitan Assembly accused him of violating Article 89 of the constitution. This bans the appropriation of public money or property for the use, benefit, or support of any charitable, educational, or benevolent institution not under the control of the state. Minobe retorted that the accusation was based on a twisted interpretation of the constitution. He was acting, he claimed, under the constitutional guarantee of basic human rights and of the minimum standard of living. The grant was approved as "an expenditure in trust."

It is interesting to note that Article 89 is a precise copy of a provision in the Montana state constitution. Similar provisions are also to be found in the constitutions of Alabama and Colorado. Interpreted literally, Article 89 virtually prohibits state grants to private schools and welfare institutions. This is a leaf borrowed directly from the American book, where private educational and welfare projects must rely on donations from religious bodies, corporations, foundations, or wealthy individuals. But Japan's law governing private schools makes them eligible for grants from the state treasury on the ground that state control extends to them as well as to public schools. Here is an attempt to fit the constitution to actualities by means of labored interpretations.

Since 1947, the Japanese people have been continually debating whether the constitution was imposed by the Occupation or whether it was born of the free will of the people. In 1961, a special commission was established to investigate this question. It concluded that both interpretations were valid, adding ambiguously: "We must accept fact as fact."

No doubt the majority of the people would agree with Professor Hideo Wada of Waseda University when he says: "It is a fact that the new constitution was imposed on us. But we must not fail to recognize that we were unable at the time to make a constitution ourselves. Democracy in postwar Japan has taken the new constitution as its standard and tried to live up to it."

Masami Takatsuji, director of the cabinet's Legislative Bureau, says privately: "So long as the present constitution survives, its identity as the product of a foreign country will cling to it like a shadow. People who object to it on these grounds might try submitting the same document to the National Diet and have it passed there again."

Turmoil over Article Nine

"MY COUNTRY'S peace constitution was born out of the devastation of World War II. It was an expression of our resolve never to repeat the tragedy. . . ." Such was Prime Minister Sato's statement in his address to the General Assembly of the United Nations in October, 1970. His voice rising, he emphatically denied any intention on Japan's part to appropriate a greater part of her national budget for military purposes.

On the same day, Japan's Fourth Defense Program, involving a total expenditure of over fifteen billion dollars, was announced in Tokyo. Among other armaments, this so-called "defense capability consolidation" program allocated over one-sixth of its budget to antinaval missiles and numerous new-model fighter planes.

Is a more glaring inconsistency conceivable? While professing firm adherence to the pacifist constitution before a global audience halfway around the globe, at home the Japanese government was forging ahead with a program to boost the nation's defense capability by interpreting that same constitution in a less altruistic fashion.

A month later, the novelist Yukio Mishima galvanized public opinion and shocked the world with his dramatic hara-kiri. He left behind a terrible indictment: "Defense, the basic issue for the nation, has been wrapped deliberately in a cloak of ambiguity through opportunistic interpretations. The presence of an army in fact but not in name has been the root cause of the spiritual corruption and moral decay of the Japanese people."

The democratization measures handed down by the Occupation have caused various controversies, but none has provoked more soul-searching and national turmoil than the so-called "war renunciation clause" contained in Article 9 of the 1947 constitution.

Both the Occupation authorities and the Japanese government of the time regarded Article 9 as being of "epochal significance" because it required the full and complete disarmament of Japan. During the 1946 session of the Lower House, which promulgated the new constitution, Communist party representative Sanzo Nosaka, recognizing

[131]

that the term "war" could apply equally to military activity for purposes of self-defense as well as aggression, urged that the constitution specifically renounce wars of aggression only. Prime Minister Yoshida replied: "Japan will fight no wars of any kind. But to recognize defensive war would be to invite war. Therefore, limiting war renunciation specifically to aggression could do more harm than good."

Has the no-war clause amounted, in fact, to the disintegration of Japanese militarism along the lines proposed in the Potsdam Declaration? "Article 9 is all but a farce in the political actualities of today. But we must not forget that there was another meaning to this provision when it was first established," points out Professor Yasusaburo Hoshino of Tokyo University of Arts and Sciences. "Article 9 was used as justification for the retention of the emperor system. MacArthur said that the emperor system, as a force unifying anticommunist ideologies, was equal in strength to twenty army divisions." Wataru Narahashi, chief cabinet secretary when the new constitution was promulgated, agrees: "The Allied ax was to have fallen on the emperor, but it was diverted onto the military by Article 9."

The official American reasoning doubtless must have been that American interests would be better served by retaining and using the emperor system as a safeguard against communism than by permitting the survival of the military machine of the former enemy country. It must not be forgotten that when the new constitution was promulgated in 1947, the Soviet Union was the new enemy and tensions with the communist world were intensifying. But with China still in the hands of Chiang Kai-shek, the need for a Japanese rear base in the anticommunist struggle was not so urgent.

If such was the U. S. reasoning, it collapsed with the victory of the Chinese Communists in October, 1949. This change in the background to Article 9 compelled a change in its interpretation by the United States government and also by the Japanese government, which took its lead from the United States. No sooner had the Korean War begun than a Japanese Police Reserve Force was created. It was organized with lightning speed, on orders of MacArthur. This was the first step on the road to expanding Japan's defensive strength and to the building and strengthening of the Japanese-American security arrangement that has prevailed since Japan regained her independence with the end of the Occupation in 1952. Japanese governments have continually increased national-defense allocations, with a sort of automatic guilt reaction caused by the shadow of the constitution.

At times feelings against constitutional restrictions have been made explicit. Early in 1970, for instance, Agriculture and Forestry Minister Tadao Kuraishi made headlines when he declared: "The constitution is no good because, under it, we must depend on a foreign nation for our own defense." Although it was widely held that Kuraishi was acting as a spokesman for the government, the government has since changed its line, insisting that it is better to continue the status quo and preserve the peace constitution.

One possible reason behind this shift is that the Supreme Court decisions on the controversial Sunagawa and Eniwa cases have absolved the government of charges of violating the constitution by maintaining the Security Treaty and the Self-Defense Forces. Another reason is the current trend of public opinion in Japan. There is strong opposition to any constitutional revision which would permit Japan to develop an armed force in name as well as in fact. But an equally large body of opinion recognizes the need for "some degree" of armed strength for national defense. In a recent *Asahi Shimbun* poll on the question of Japan's defense, twenty-six percent (the greatest single bloc of opinion) favored "Japanese-American cooperation through the increase of self-defense strength."

The question may well be asked: How long does the government propose to continue building defensive capability while maintaining the constitutional guise of an "unarmed nation"?

"It does not require a Mishima incident to make us realize that Article 9, the seed of a political fiction, cannot be left alone forever," says Osamu Inaba, chairman of the cabinet's Commission on the Constitution.

Meanwhile, the steady increase of nationalistic sentiment has reinforced and inspired new demands for a constitution that Japan can consider thoroughly her own. "The existence of such opinion is all the more reason for us to remember and reconsider the circumstances in which the no-war clause was established," says Professor Tadao Sakuma of Meiji Gakuin University, an authority on constitutional law. "Even granting that Article 9 was imposed on us by the United States, we must never forget that it symbolizes our resolve to reject war and support peace. I am not worried. I am confident that that resolve remains firmly fixed in the Japanese mind. Otherwise, Mishima would not have had reason to despair of ever seeing a revision of the constitution."

Education at the Movies

D EANNA DURBIN'S *Spring Parade* and Greer Garson's *Madame Curie* opened in Japanese movie theaters affiliated with the Shochiku, Toho, and Nikkatsu chains on February 28, 1946, the first American films shown in Japan in nearly six years. The long lines that immediately formed outside of theaters were evidence of the hunger of Japanese moviegoers for this sort of entertainment. Soon, thirty-eight percent of the two thousand movie houses in Japan were showing only American productions and every one of them was packed to capacity day in and day out, even without the benefit of advertising.

"Seeing American movies again was like meeting long-lost friends," says critic Choji Yodogawa. "America may have been the enemy until only the day before, but still we had missed the movies. After all, it really hadn't been the masses who wanted to fight the war."

"When the American movies started playing again, I felt keenly that the war was truly over and that I had survived," recalls novelist Hitomi Yamaguchi. "I had been in the army, but only for two months."

Critic Tadao Sato was only a boy when the war ended, but he had nevertheless held strong militaristic convictions. He had been led to believe that Japan had suffered defeat simply because the fortunes of war had turned against her. "The American movies were a revelation to me," he recalls today. "I was dumbfounded at their picture of America's affluence. Could such a way of life really exist in this world? I felt all my values suddenly crumbling under the impact of those first movies."

In encouraging the showing of American movies, had Occupation authorities intended so drastic an effect on Japanese values? The Civil Information and Education Section (CIE) deliberately made use of movies to show the Japanese people democratic life. Critic Akira Iwasaki, a former staff member of the Nichiei movie-production company, reveals that CIE confided in him its intention to publicize Occupation policies through a combination of edification and entertainment. In fact, CIE took such pains in selecting appropriate films that Japanese audiences had to wait six months after the war ended to see the movies they were so eagerly awaiting.

Many people still cherish memories of seeing such films as *Rhapsody in Blue* and *The Best Years of Our Lives* at the Subaru-za, a movie

[134]

theater near Yuraku-cho Station in downtown Tokyo. "Customers would start lining up around four in the morning," recalls Taro Oshima, an executive of the company that operated the Subaru-za. "The Occupation authorities insisted that the entire audience be seated and that no one be allowed to stand. This gave rise to three things—reserved seats, roadshows, and ticket scalpers—all unknown in the Japanese entertainment world before the war. The first theater to have all three was the Subaru-za."

"Japan was swept by a wave of Hollywood productions made during the war, and many of them were good," says critic Masahiro Ogi. "These American movies were based on simple but irrefutable truths: 'Crime doesn't pay,' 'Right always wins out in the end,' 'There's happiness in being poor,' and the like. Hollywood had an infallible instinct for mass sentiment, and it cranked out productions which had served as primers on democracy and the American war aims for the heterogeneous immigrant groups that made up the American population." If such was the nature of American wartime movies, they also served perfectly the purpose of disseminating the ideas that the Occupation sought to instill in the Japanese mind.

"In those movies we saw the refrigerators, cars, modern houses, highways, and all the other accouterments of the 'Good Life' that we take for granted these days," says Sato. "American movies and the *Blondie* comic strips that were also so popular right after the war created a certain image of Americans in our minds. Except for occasionally selfish tendencies, they seemed to be basically good people."

CIE was careful, however, to prevent the showing of any films that contained even the slightest criticism of democracy or dissatisfaction with the American way of life. In *Citizen Kane* Orson Welles exposed the corruption of the mass-communication industry, and *The Grapes of Wrath* was a powerful description of American rural poverty during the Depression; both were hailed as cinematic masterpieces in the United States and in Europe, but their screening in Japan was prohibited until after the peace treaty had been signed and the Occupation ended. Similar precautions were taken with Japanese movies. *Chushingura* and other films on the vendetta theme were banned; so were the samurai movies full of swordplay, on the grounds that they contained an implied approval of "the feudalistic way of thinking that condoned violence."

A Japanese movie that was approved was *Aoi Sammyaku* (Blue Mountains), directed by Tadashi Imai and hailed as an "exemplary statement on democracy" by the Japanese movie world. In one scene, Shinko, the young heroine, is surrounded by a bunch of young toughs

[135]

on a deserted street. Tominaga, a high school boy, happens along just in time. He rescues her by driving away the ruffians without using any violence, merely by giving out gorillalike grunts. The climax of the movie is a meeting of the PTA council of the girl's school. There, a group of virtuous young people come to a showdown with the local bosses, and prevail by dialogue alone. "The story was about the clash of new and old values at a provincial girls' high school," says Yojiro Ishizaka, on whose novel the movie was based. "I tried to show the sort of democratic ideals that Japanese people should develop in their lives."

At about the same time that this movie was made, the American stock of wartime movies began to run out. Edifying films began to be replaced by those that were merely entertaining. Soon European films were also allowed into Japan for the first time since the war's end, and intellectuals immediately shifted their interest to French and Italian films. Baseball was also making its comeback, and television was beginning to catch on. These attractions all drew popular interest away from American movies.

"Nowadays, students go for tough movie dramas and cartoon magazines that glorify violence. This is the legacy of violence inherited from American westerns," comments critic Yukio Akatsuka. "The darker side of American culture is filtering its way into Japan through the gaps and chinks that are opening in the postwar democracy as it grows more and more rickety. You might say that American movies sowed the seeds both of democracy and of a passion for violence."

Trust Busting

" "THE LEADERS of the postwar Mitsubishi firms are imbued with loyalty to their companies and have taken business principles solidly to heart. With speed and determination they have rebuilt the collapsed businesses using rational economic theory. They rallied to the Mitsubishi banner and soon displayed their vitality and enterprise." Thus reads one part of the Mitsubishi Group White Paper, published in 1970 on the hundredth anniversary of the founding of the Mitsubishi house. Change the name of the company, and a similar report might be made for the Mitsui, Sumitomo, and Fuji (formerly Yasuda) firms. These former *zaibatsu*, branded as "war potentials" by the Occupation and forced to disband, are now making determined efforts to recombine and rise again, like phoenixes, from the ashes of the postwar period.

One month after the end of the war, on September 22, 1945, the Initial Post-Surrender Policy for Japan announced that Washington favored "a program for the dissolution of the large industrial and banking combinations which have exercised control over a great part of Japan's trade and industry." In plain English, this meant that Mitsubishi, Mitsui, Sumitomo, Yasuda, and all the other *zaibatsu* would have to go.

This news came as a bolt out of the blue to all the *zaibatsu* and their executive staffs. "Even in our worst nightmares, it never occurred to us that the United States would attempt to crush us after we had been kicked about so roughly by the militarists and the ultra-rightists during the war." This was the reaction of Hideo Edo, a manager in the General Affairs Department of the Mitsui main office at the time and now president of the Mitsui Real Estate Company. He was not alone in his bitter surprise that the United States should consider their past activities sinful and worthy of such extreme punishment. At the time Koyata Iwasaki, president of the main Mitsubishi office, complained: "We obeyed national policy and have done our duty as good Japanese. We have done nothing to be ashamed of."

For a brief while, the *zaibatsu* clung to the faint hope that their friendly cooperation with American business and industry and their record of ill-treatment at the hands of the Japanese militarists might serve to soften GHQ's attitude toward them and stave off total dissolution. But these hopes came to nought. General MacArthur's headquarters issued one harsh directive after another. Eighty-three holding companies, including four *zaibatsu*, were dissolved and their assets disposed of; the assets of fifty-six members of *zaibatsu* families were frozen, and many individuals associated with such firms were purged.

In August, 1946, a Holding Companies Liquidation Commission was created. Tadao Sasayama, its chairman, intimated to one rightist politician that he would rather reform the *zaibatsu* than dismantle them. Aware of the hatred for them on the far right, Sasayama felt that, apart from the MacArthur directives, the time had come for self-examination and self-criticism by the *zaibatsu*. But he was too busy pleading with GHQ for relaxation of its program calling for total dissolution to do much toward reforming them.

The Japanese government did not sit back and look on in silence. Finance Minister Tanzan Ishibashi advised Prime Minister Yoshida

[137]

that a distinction should be made between good *zaibatsu* and bad, depending on the degree of their cooperation in the war effort. Yoshida said as much to MacArthur but did not get far with him. There ensued a Yoshida-MacArthur contest of non-cooperation on this issue. "It was my job to ferret out and report on what Yoshida was only pretending to do but actually not doing," laughs Miss Eleanor Hadley, at the time a member of the GHQ staff charged with overseeing the dissolution of the *zaibatsu* and now employed by the U. S. Federal Customs Tariff Commission in Washington.

The *zaibatsu* dissolution program increased in severity with time. When Mitsui's Edo met Col. Raymond Kramer, an officer of GHQ's Economic and Scientific Section, early in 1947, his gaze was directed out the window at a crowd of shabbily dressed people below, knapsacks on their backs, on their way out to the country to scavenge for food. Kramer told him that the Mitsui family had no right to live better than those people.

"SCAP's reasoning was understandable in theory, but even I thought it ignored the actualities of the Japanese economy," recalls Yoshitaro Wakimura, professor emeritus at Tokyo University. He had been appointed a member of the Holding Companies Liquidation Commission because of the moderate anti-*zaibatsu* views the public attributed to him. He struggled to convince SCAP that a nation with so small a domestic market as Japan's needed large-capital firms for economic growth. "But the Americans stuck to their guns. SCAP continued to insist that the economy should grow only through free enterprise and free competition, and that the *zaibatsu* would only obstruct it. That they were right has been proved by Japan's extraordinary economic expansion since then," admits Wakimura with a strained smile.

In 1948, the *zaibatsu* dissolution program underwent abrupt, radical changes. Miss Hadley explains: "The intensifying cold war induced the U. S. to treat Japan as a partner, rather than as an enemy still to be punished or weakened. The dissolution of the *zaibatsu* was abruptly called off." To Sasayama's delight, U. S. policy shifted away from punishment toward reform of the *zaibatsu*.

With the policy shift, investigation into the issue of *zaibatsu* responsibility for the war was terminated inconclusively, and purged members of *zaibatsu* firms returned to public life in increasing numbers. The total number of firms affected by the Economic Power Decentralization Law had by then reached 325; but now, one after another, they were released from the terms of the law until only eighteen remained affected. One of the eighteen was the Nippon Iron and Steel Manufacturing Company, which had been split into the Yawata and Fuji steel companies. Then, in 1970, even these two recombined, forming the Shin Nihon Iron and Steel Manufacturing Company, one of the world's greatest producers of steel.

"I cannot imagine that the family-controlled *zaibatsu* firms of old will return fully to life," says Wakimura. "But I am worried that the banks, the prop of the new *zaibatsu*-type concerns, are becoming decidedly cliquish." This fear is shared by Tokyo governor Ryokichi Minobe, a former member of the Holding Companies Liquidation Commission, who still believes today, as he did then, that reversing the policy of dissolving the *zaibatsu* banks in particular was a major U. S. blunder.

The question of what form future groupings of Japanese enterprises will take is still open to speculation, but it is clear that a close review of the history of the *zaibatsu* and the abortive attempt at dissolving them after the war will be essential to understanding the peculiarities of Japanese industrial organization.

The Enduring Mandarins

THE JAPANESE bureaucracy found itself in an extremely difficult position during the years immediately following the end of the war. The performance of its duties was complicated by the fact that it was expected to serve both the Japanese nation and the American Occupation government. In the unsettled circumstances of the postwar period, it was often unsure of just what those duties were, unsure of the extent of its authority, and unsure of how far it might be held accountable for some earlier war crime. The bureaucracy was forced to tread lightly and to deal with individual personalities far more carefully than might have been necessary in a less complicated situation. Perhaps the dilemma of the bureaucracy is best illustrated through the recounting of several episodes involving individual officials.

It was a young, low-ranking interpreter connected with the War Termination Central Liaison Office who caught the first inkling of the imminent collapse of Japan's initial postwar cabinet. Genshichi Akatani received a memorandum from SCAP on the evening of October 4, 1945, which he read while riding back to his office. Strictly speaking, he was exceeding his authority by reading the message before delivering it to his superiors, but he knew that he would have to read it anyway in order to translate it for them. Entitled "Political and Religious Liberties," it was a directive ordering, among other things, the immediate abolition of the special security police (the dreaded wartime force often called the "thought police" in the West) and the removal from office of the minister of home affairs and other high officials of the ministry. Akatani guessed instinctively that this would bring down the cabinet.

He was right. Prime Minister Higashikuni, unable or unwilling to deal with such fundamental changes, stepped down the following day, after only fifty days in office. Kijuro Shidehara was picked to form a new cabinet. He had served as foreign minister in the early 1930s but had been forced out of office by the military's rejection of his concilia-tory policies toward the United States and Great Britain and had been in retirement ever since. Shigeru Yoshida, foreign minister in the new cabinet, was sent to call on General MacArthur to request ap-proval of Shidehara's appointment. MacArthur asked him only two questions before granting it: "How old is Shidehara?" and "Does the man speak English?" Yoshida smiled to himself as he assured the general that Shidehara did, indeed, speak English. He was wondering how Shidehara, who prided himself on being the most fluent speaker of English in the entire Foreign Ministry, would have responded to the question.

At one point, early in the Occupation, Toshikazu Kase, chief of the Information Department of the Foreign Ministry, was asked by an American correspondent what he thought of the atomic bombings. Kase replied simply: "They were inhuman. President Truman boarded a train for hell when he ordered that the bombs be dropped." Almost immediately afterward, Kase was summoned to the head-quarters of the U. S. military police, where the following exchange took place:

"You criticized Occupation policy."

"The atomic bombs were dropped before the Occupation."

"A diplomat should not go around making statements like that."

"Excuse me, but I am not a diplomat. Not now. Japan has no right to conduct her own diplomacy. You know whom to ask if I'm telling the truth."

The MPs, furious at Kase's insolence, insisted that action be taken against him, but eventually they had to let him off. It was rumored that MacArthur himself had interceded in Kase's defense, commenting that it was a lucky thing that there was at least one man like him in the government. Before being taken to MP headquarters, the Harvard-educated former diplomat, with perfect English at his command, had not neglected to warn SCAP officials: "Without me, your work would be most difficult indeed."

Japan's defeat and the Occupation that followed had shaken to their foundations the makeup of Japanese society and the values of the Japanese people. The emperor system was altered from its age-old sanctity, the Imperial Japanese Army and Navy were abolished, the *zaibatsu* were being dismantled, and most familiar politicians were being purged from public life. Somehow, the bureaucracy survived all these upheavals. Top-level officials were purged, to be sure, but as an institution the bureaucracy pulled through. To make the transition to democracy, however, its members were forced to abandon their label of "officers on high" and become "public servants" instead.

The bureaucracy was preserved by the Occupation's policy of indirect rule of Japan, i.e., ruling through the existing administrative apparatus. Its new function was to act as the administrative agent of SCAP. For this purpose it was necessary to discover what MacArthur and the officials of the American General Headquarters were thinking and what they intended to do in Japan. It was equally important to communicate to the Occupation what Japan wished done or did not wish done to her or for her. The job was delegated, largely as a matter of course, to the diplomatic branch of the bureaucracy, the career diplomats in the Foreign Ministry who knew English and had some understanding of the customs and personality makeup of Americans.

The War Termination Central Liaison Office (CLO)—the primary channel of communication with the Occupation offices—was the only place where career diplomats could really function while their country was barred from all diplomatic activities. One member of the CLO, Koichiro Asakai, who would later become ambassador to the United States, often got wind of new SCAP policies before they were announced and would divulge them at cabinet meetings. Despite his rather low rank, his intelligence value enabled him to sit in on cabinet meetings. One day, he brought in the scoop that SCAP had officially decided to limit Japan's steel production to 1.2 million tons. The cabinet heaved a collective sigh of relief because this figure was well above what had been expected.

Eight successive cabinets, headed by five different prime ministers, served under the Occupation. Three of the prime ministers were former diplomats: Shidehara, Yoshida, and Hitoshi Ashida. They had been the presidents of the Democratic party, the Liberal party, and the Progressive party, respectively. Of the three it was Yoshida who developed the strongest relationship with MacArthur. Men who served under him have evolved into politicians of distinctly bureau-cratic nature, and today they comprise the "mainstream" of the con-servative Liberal-Democratic party.

The entry of bureaucrats into politics began most conspicuously in the second postwar general election, held in April, 1947. Thereafter their numbers increased, as if to fill the vacancies created by the purge of former politicians.

Despite the pains taken by the Occupation to foster a democratic parliamentary system in Japan, under the system that actually de-veloped the government could easily silence any opposition in the Diet with the magic words: "That is how 'competent authorities' want it." A cabinet minister could decline an opposition demand for his appearance on the grounds of unavoidable business with Occupation headquarters and get away with it.

The democratization of Japan was enthusiastically advocated by the Occupation, but the actual implementation of this highly touted goal was largely left up to the Japanese government. Hence the com-plaints of "democratization from above" or "democracy in name only" that are still to be heard today. There was, however, one branch of the Japanese bureaucracy that refused to delegate liaison with GHQ to the Foreign Ministry men in the CLO. Staffed by men proficient in English and expert in their field, the Finance Ministry carried on its own liaison with the Occupation authorities. It managed to fight off an Occupation plan to create a bureau of the budget under direct cabinet control, and thus retained the right to make the annual budget.

The rivalry of the Finance Ministry and the Foreign Ministry (most of the officers of which were in the CLO) has had long-lasting consequences. With the end of the Occupation and the so-called "era of abnormal diplomacy," the power of Foreign Ministry bureaucrats gave way to the rising influence of Finance Ministry men. In the present Sato cabinet, eight major posts—Justice, Foreign, Finance, Health and Welfare, International Trade and Industry, and Economic Planning—are held by former officials of the Finance Ministry.

The Media Democratized

IN NOVEMBER, 1968, the Liberal-Democratic party lost the elec-tion for governor of Okinawa to a progressive-party candidate for the first time. Conservative leaders moaned that the defeat was due to the press and the merciless spotlight it had turned on government corruption, particularly cases of bribery of officials by taxi companies trying to secure licenses. It is true that local newspapers had exposed the corruption of the ruling conservative power, and numerous officials had been arrested as the election neared. The American military powers on Okinawa were no less dismayed by the vigorous press crusade, but there was little they could do about it, for what they were witnessing was the direct effect of an Occupation policy to encourage the development of an active and responsible press.

The first press campaign in Japan was begun with the help of Occupation authorities; it too had resulted in more than they had bargained for. One summer day in 1948, an *Asahi Shimbun* reporter was beaten up on the street by hoodlums in the pay of an assemblyman of the town of Honjo in Saitama Prefecture. The journalist had apparently blown the lid off a complicated racket involving local politicians and even police, in which the profits on black-market silk were being funneled to various gangs. He refused to be cowed into silence but knew he was powerless against the politicians and the bosses backing them. He turned for help to a *Washington Post* correspondent who happened to be visiting the Saitama branch of the U. S. military government. The American journalist asked for three days in which to act.

In a strictly confidential letter to *Asahi* executives, SCAP offered assistance in staging a press crusade in Honjo. No news could have been more invigorating to the contingent of *Asahi* reporters that had already entered the town at considerable personal risk. Impressed that a word from a single American newsman carried so much weight with SCAP, they eagerly set about their campaign. The endeavors of the press inspired the local populace to rise at last against their corrupt government. A mass rally quickly passed a resolution calling for the resignation of the chief of police and deputy procurator and the recall of the local Public Safety Commission.

The Occupation authorities, while favoring the anticorruption struggle, began to worry that it might come under Communist leadership. Lt. Col. Daniel Imboden, chief of the press section of SCAP, was noticeably disturbed when he found red union flags unfurled at one of the local mass rallies. He had come to deliver a pep talk to the rally but left his speech half finished. Housewife Noriko Nakamura, a participant in the rally, recalled the scene in a short verse:

> Mistaking union banners
> For red flags,

[143]

Lt. Col. Imboden shrank
From taking the rostrum.

It was through such vicissitudes that the press campaign came to be institutionalized in postwar Japan. Three years earlier, during the first days of the Occupation, SCAP had stated its basic policy toward the Japanese press in a conference between Brigadier General Phelps, MacArthur's special adviser on public information, and Chief Cabinet Secretary Taketora Ogata. Japanese newspapers would be permitted to continue operations with the conditions that they cooperate in disseminating Occupation policies and that they refrain from commenting on American-Soviet differences.

"I was overjoyed to learn that the Japanese papers would not be dismantled as the German press had been," says Shogo Nakamura, then secretary to Ogata and now an *Asahi Shimbun* director. "Of course, the ban on writing about the American-Soviet entanglement brought home to me the fact that the discord between the two powers was reaching serious proportions."

Soon after that initial conference, the famous ten-point Press Code was announced. Among other stipulations, it banned all criticism of the atomic bombings and also required that only any American soldiers involved in crimes against Japanese citizens be referred to simply as "big men."

Japanese reporters were brought to GHQ for briefings on the rudiments of objective reporting, the so-called "five Ws"—when, who, where, what, and why. "We already knew all about them," recalls Kyozo Mori, editorial adviser to the *Asahi*. "But when the educators in democracy eventually took to restricting freedom of speech in order to repress communism, then we really began to learn something."

Critic Sozo Matsuura adds: "The policy on free speech and the press was reduced to an absurdity by the mixing of democratic ideals with repressive techniques. The only lasting good was that the communication media learned to transmit the voices of the little men below to the power elite above. Before the Occupation, the media limited themselves to handing down commands from above."

Occupation authorities also took great pains to democratize—or Americanize—radio as a means of transmitting desires and opinions from the bottom up. New programs such as "Man on the Street" interviews and "Twenty Questions" ("Twenty Doors" in its Japanese version) were initiated by the Japan Broadcasting Corporation (NHK). These led to other "audience participation" programs, including amateur-talent shows and radio debates between ordinary citizens. According to NHK's Public Information Office, between thirty-five and forty percent of its general TV and radio programs today are of the "audience participation" type, and the percentage is even higher with the commercial networks.

A unique NHK program, free of any particular American coloration and not of the "audience participation" type, was the "Joke Music, Humor Theater" program hosted by Toriro Miki. It featured biting but funny satire of political or social evils. During the sensational shipbuilding scandal of 1954, when one high government official after another was arrested for accepting bribes from shipyards, Eisaku Sato was almost arrested. He was then secretary general of the Liberal party and is now prime minister. He narrowly escaped apprehension and political disgrace only through the intervention of the justice minister. Miki, making a pun on "sato," which also means sugar in Japanese, cracked: "Stirring turned black sugar into white." The ruling party and the government immediately flew into a rage and demanded suspension of the program. Miki claims that he was spared because an Occupation adviser managed to persuade the Japanese government that he was "a safety valve against revolution."

For all the highly touted democratization of speech after the war, it seems that the Japanese have yet to learn the art of democratic debate. Late in 1970, NHK sponsored a TV debate on environmental pollution with the participation of Dennis Hayes, a young American leader of the antipollution movement, and a thousand Japanese from across the country. The Japanese debaters tended to stray far from the issues at hand, taking the opportunity to air long-held but often irrelevant views. Hayes struggled to keep to the subject, and as a result the debate simply failed to materialize. Kenji Suzuki, moderator of the debate, recalls with embarrassment that Hayes told him afterward that the Japanese, while learning how to overcome pollution, could stand to learn something of the art of democratic discussion in the process.

The Land Reform

VISITING Tokyo several years ago, a highly placed Philippine government official who had been grappling at home with the complex problems of land reform asked an acquaintance in the

Ministry of Agriculture and Forestry whether Japan's postwar land reform could have been carried off without the prodding and assistance of the Occupation.

"Probably," answered Keiki Owada, the ministry's Agricultural Economic Bureau director, who had worked on the land-reform program. "But it would have been a lot harder and would have taken much longer."

The Occupation demands for land reform had not taken Japan quite so unawares as had other SCAP directives. Indeed, a program to weaken landlordism had been instigated even before the war; among other things, it had offered financial incentives to landed and tenant farmers alike and had attempted to curb farm-rent rates. Again, late in 1945, before the Occupation directive on land reform was handed down, Kenzo Matsumura, Agriculture-Forestry minister in the Shide-hara cabinet, presented a farmland-reform bill to the Diet. Its immediate object was to alleviate the terrible food shortage, but the intention underlying the proposed legislation was the eventual creation of an agricultural system based on landed farmers; this was a goal long cherished by both Matsumura and the ministry as a whole.

While this bill was being buffeted about by the powerful landlord influence in the Diet, SCAP presented its first directive on land reform. This was called the "Fearey Document," and it was based on a report written even before the war ended by R. A. Fearey, a State Department official, and Wolf Ladejinsky, an Agriculture Department expert. It denounced the Japanese system of land tenure as "a cancer" in the Japanese political and economic body, and described the farm population as supporting the military. "The low income of farm families limits the domestic market. Without thorough reform of the agricultural system, there is little hope that the Japanese economy can be stabilized and redirected toward a peaceful direction."

The SCAP directive undercut the opposition that had been building in the Diet to Matsumura's bill, and it was passed. It reduced the amount of land that a single landlord could rent out to tenants to five *chobu* (slightly less than five hectares). But SCAP, dissatisfied with the fact that this new law freed only about one-third of the tenant-farmer population, had it shelved and demanded more radical measures. The government then framed a second bill, based on a new SCAP directive that, in turn, had been based on a British plan submitted to the Allied Council for Japan. The British proposal had been offered in order to block a Soviet plan that called for the confiscation of all tenanted farmlands without compensation.

Land reform, as carried out under the second bill, was completed by 1950, and resulted in the resale of 1,933,000 hectares, formerly held by 2,341,000 landlords, to 4,748,000 tenant cultivators. Farmland commissions to oversee the land-reform program were to be elected in cities, towns, and villages. On election day, a group of officers from the Natural Resources Section of SCAP traveled by jeep to every village in the rural Nishi-Tama area on the outskirts of Tokyo. They were dismayed to find no election in progress. According to Katsumasa Tanabe, who was director of the Agricultural Land Department of the Agriculture-Forestry Ministry at the time and acting as guide for the Americans, the village officials were quick to explain: "We don't need an election here because the landlords and tenants already came to terms by discussion. That's as good as an election."

SCAP kept landlords under close surveillance during the early stages of land reform. Watchdog officers of the local military governments made regular jeep tours through farms and villages in order to ferret out any attempts by landlords to bribe the commission members or to get back land from tenants by other means. The entire reform commission in a village in Ibaraki Prefecture was removed from office for proceeding too slowly in transferring land ownership. Detailed monthly progress reports were sent by the local military governments to SCAP, where they were studied carefully and transformed into maps and statistical charts to use in prodding the Japanese government whenever the land-reform program seemed to be slowing down.

There is no question that the land reform unburdened tenants of onerous rents and stimulated their will to produce more. Increased incentive, together with notable advances in agricultural technology, has resulted in the enormous rice surplus that Japan has built up in recent years. But even with improved insecticides, better fertilizers, the development of new strains of seed, and rice-price policies, the current overabundance of rice would never have been achieved without the land reform.

One unexpected consequence of the reform program has been the high degree of fractionalization of farmlands into small patches, separately owned and farmed. "This was permitted to happen because at the time of the land reform no one conceived of the spectacular Japanese economic growth that would occur," says Takekazu Ogura, former deputy minister of the Agriculture and Forestry Ministry and currently a member of the Institute of Developing Economies. "Hindsight suggests that enterprise and productivity might have expanded even further, if not for the extreme fractionalization of land."

Postwar inflation has rendered the land redistribution under the reform program excessively unfair to landlords. Under the reform, landlords were compelled to sell their land for no more than ¥2.60 per 3.3 square-meter plot. Today the same amount of land easily fetches more than ¥100,000 in some places. Small wonder, then, that the government came under heavy fire from the Diet and the public for its recent move, later withdrawn, to sell back the land purchased under compulsion to its former owners for the purchase price of ¥2.60. During the early days of the reform, there occurred a torrent of lawsuits by landlords protesting that the government purchase price was too low. But in 1953, the Supreme Court ruled that the price was reasonable compensation. In an amusing incident that recently came to light, a former tenant farmer who made a fortune from selling the land he had acquired through the reform offered part of his new wealth to his impoverished former landlord as a gift.

When MacArthur addressed Congress upon his return to the United States, he called the Japanese land reform a magnificent achievement, adding that he knew of no more successful attempt at land reform since the days of the Roman Empire. It would be wrong to brush this aside as yet another example of the vainglorious self-adulation that MacArthur frequently indulged in. Many Japanese also share the general's high regard for the Occupation's land reform. Former Agriculture-Forestry vice-minister Shiro Tohata, has called it "a success unequaled in the history of the world." And Takeo Miki, a leading conservative politician, has said: "If I had to choose only one thing that could not have been accomplished without the Occupation, it would have to be the land reform."

Having succeeded with the Japanese land reform, the United States tried similar reforms in Southeast Asia in the 1950s, achieving moderately satisfying results only in Taiwan. The record elsewhere—in the Philippines, Korea, Vietnam—has been poor. This tends to reinforce the credit due the agricultural experts of the Occupation for the success of their land-reform program in Japan.

Law and Order

A T A POLICE station in the rough Senju district of Tokyo, a man had his hands handcuffed behind his back and was knocked over and trampled on by policemen. Three of his ribs were broken. And in Kurume City two young boys, one in high school, the other in junior high school, were stopped on the street by a policeman and taken to a police box, where they were beaten so severely that their molars came loose. Are these prewar incidents involving the feared security police? They occurred within the past two years but were bitter reminders of the virtually unlimited powers and the brutality of the Japanese police before the war.

Today, the police are often described as displaying two images. One is that of the tireless local cop patrolling his deserted beat in icy cold late at night or patiently trying to unravel impossible rush-hour traffic jams. He inspires universal respect and gratitude. But the other image is that illustrated by the two incidents outlined above: the harsh law-enforcer swaggering about as the representative of state power, and occasionally exceeding his authority.

General MacArthur and the Occupation tried to efface the latter, fearsome image of the Japanese police in one fell swoop. In a letter to Prime Minister Tetsu Katayama dated September 16, 1947, MacArthur ordered "a fundamental reform of the abuse of police power by the state . . . through decentralization of the police system in accordance with the principle of local autonomy as embodied in the constitution." The Home Ministry was abolished and the police system was decentralized under the radically new Police Service Law enacted in December, 1947. Under the new law, each city, town, or village with a population of more than five thousand was required to create its own Public Safety Commission and "municipal" police force. Only smaller communities were put under the jurisdiction of the National Rural Police.

Police decentralization was at first hailed by the Occupation as a major step toward bringing democracy to local communities. Even before the Occupation ended, however, the police decentralization began to lose momentum; it has since disappeared entirely. Toji Nakagawa, former criminal investigation chief in both the National Rural Police and the National Police Agency that followed it, accounts for the shift as largely a problem of financing. "The decentralized police system of the United States functions well because the municipal and state police and the FBI all are backed by funds adequate to efficient law enforcement. Japan's decentralized police were simply too strapped for money to operate." Take, for example, Yoshiwara Village, located between Higashi Tagonoura and Yoshiwara stations on the Tokaido railway line. Having a population of somewhat more than five thousand, the village had its own municipal police force. But the village could not afford a force of even ten men. The few who were hired had to work twenty-four-hour shifts every other day. Two men were assigned to the policebox in front of the village offices and two to the box at Yoshiwara station. That left none for Tagonoura, which, as a result, became a haven for black marketeers. And Yoshiwara was only one of hundreds of communities unable to finance their own forces.

When the Police Service Law was revised in 1951 to permit local governing bodies to relinquish police powers to the state by local plebiscite, 1,214 of 1,605 communities leaped at the opportunity to remove the police from the local budget. Their police forces came under the jurisdiction of the National Rural Police. Meanwhile the decentralization program had bred such evils as alliances between police and corrupt local politicians and police involvement in election offenses.

Even while the Police Service Law of 1947 was being drawn up, the situation was already complicated by factionalism within the Occupation government. G-2, the military staff section of SCAP, began voicing opposition to the plans of GS, the civil government section, to weaken the Japanese police machinery through drastic measures. With the Communist victory in China and the onset of the cold war, the more conservative voice of G-2 steadily gained power within the Occupation.

Almost as if they were intended to reinforce G-2's position, three shocking criminal cases, with political overtones, occurred in 1949: the Shimoyama case (the mysterious death, under circumstances that have yet to be fully explained, of Sadanori Shimoyama, president of the Japanese National Railways); the runaway train case in Mitaka, in which ten people were killed; and the Matsukawa case, in which a passenger train was derailed by the deliberate removal of a section of track. In the aftermath of these incidents, SCAP expressed itself in favor of strengthening Japanese police instead of pursuing the decentralization policy, which appeared only to weaken them. MacArthur's memoirs refer only obliquely to the police policy as a baffling issue on which there was more than one school of thought.

In 1954, two years after the Occupation ended, a new Police Service Law was passed amid a physical clash of legislators in the Diet so violent that police had to be called into the assembly chamber. This was only the first of a number of rough-and-tumble melees within the Diet that tended to inspire further public contempt and distrust of politicians. A 1959 revision of the police law, passed by the Diet over strong nationwide protest, expanded the power and authority of the police. Today, as anyone who has witnessed the special riot police in action will readily attest, their equipment and techniques have been considerably modernized. " 'Modernization' and 'administrative labor saving' have served as excuses for watering down noticeably the postwar democratization of the police," comments Professor Hideo Wada of Meiji University.

Although democratic trial proceedings with due respect for the personal rights of the accused have been thoroughly institutionalized in the Criminal Procedure Code, written after the war, there are few restraints on an individual policeman's exceeding his authority. "Excesses in criminal investigation and police brutality still continue, and each incident should signal us to remain constantly on the alert," warns Yasusaburo Hoshino of Tokyo University of Arts and Sciences.

The public-safety commissions are supposed to insure that the police treat members of all political beliefs impartially, but recent critics complain that they are ineffective because the men picked as members do not represent the entire social or political spectrum. "The real hurdle to the democratization of the police is not the police themselves but the longevity of the conservative party," says Joji Tagami, professor emeritus at Hitotsubashi University and an authority on constitutional law. "When a party remains in power too long, the executive branch, particularly its law-enforcement arm, begins to look 'tinged' in the public view. Once the police get that sort of reputation, nothing can efface the taint, no matter how much charm and public relations effort they pour on. It may be jumping to a conclusion, but it would seem to me that the basic prerequisite to the democratization of the police is a replacement of the party in power."

Poolside Nationalism

JAPAN'S re-emergence in international athletic competition after the war came in August, 1949, when a swimming team was sent to a championship meet in Los Angeles. The team, which included such famous swimmers as Hironoshin Furuhashi, Shiro Hashizume, and Yoshihiro Hamaguchi, was summoned to meet General MacArthur before it left for America. Addressing the swimmers in his stark office, corncob pipe clenched between his teeth, the ordinarily austere supreme commander smiled and joked throughout the interview. One of the swimmers recalls MacArthur's saying something like: "You mustn't feel ashamed of Japan's defeat in the war. This time I want you to beat every American you swim against. Don't hesitate for a second to fight as hard as you can. That's what sports are all about, and that's how you'll win the respect of Americans. If anything happens, I'm responsible, and I'm on your side. But remember, if you lose, I won't let you back into Japan."

"I had always despised MacArthur for his arrogance, but I changed my opinion then and there," says Masaji Tabata, former president of the Japan Swimmers Federation. "I remembered that he had headed the American team at the Amsterdam Olympics, and admired him as a truly great man," says Furuhashi, now a professor at Nihon University.

The Japanese swimmers thrilled their entire nation with their performance in Los Angeles. They totally demolished their American opponents and set nine new world records. All Japan had remained in a state of dazed bewilderment since the defeat in 1945. In a nation that had lost its self-confidence, along with all pride or sense of national endeavor, the news of the swimmers' triumphs in Los Angeles shocked the Japanese like a wave of icy water breaking over them. People went wild with glee and, according to Professor Hiroshi Minami of Hitotsubashi University: "The news awoke Japanese nationalism from its hibernation."

Prewar Olympics had seen exciting swimming contests between American and Japanese teams, with Japan emerging victorious from many of them. But, just one year before the swimming meet at Los Angeles, Japan had been barred from participation in the London Olympics. Feeling slighted by this, Japanese swimming circles had staged a national-championship tournament in Tokyo with a slate of events that corresponded exactly to those in London. The Japanese participants compared their times with the records set in London and consoled themselves that they would have won gold medals had they been allowed to go. The news of these unofficial world records set in Tokyo reached London and brought a cable of congratulation from the manager of the U. S. swimming team. The Japanese swimmers read the telegram with mixed feelings but remained eager to get back into direct competition with American swimmers.

Japanese pole vaulters, leading rivals of the Americans at Olympic games before the war, were equally chagrined at being prevented from competing in London. They consoled themselves somewhat by sending Japanese bamboo poles to the American track team. This had been suggested by Kan Ito, a retired *Asahi Shimbun* writer, who recalled the great demand for Japanese bamboo poles at every past international track meet and thought that pole vaulters in London would miss them. The task of collecting and choosing the right poles fell to Shuhei Nishida, now a Hitachi executive. "I was picked for the job," he says, "because I had made the rounds of bamboo-pole dealers with every foreign team that had visited Japan in the past." At the London Olympics, the U. S. pole vaulters used their Japanese poles and won.

The Japanese swimming victories in Los Angeles in 1949 cheered more than General MacArthur and the swimmers' compatriots at home. Local Japanese-American residents were every bit as jubilant watching the Japanese team rack up one triumph after another. They filled the bleachers every day and waved small Rising Sun flags. The successes of the Japanese swimmers were the first cheering news to them in more than twenty-five years. They had suffered from the discriminatory Exclusion Act of 1924, anti-Japanese prejudice and propaganda, the Pacific War and internment and Japan's defeat, and most recently, the horrifying possibility that ten million of their relatives in Japan might die of starvation.

Japanese-American citizens of California extended an extraordinary welcome to the young swimmers. Isamu Wada threw open his home to lodge the entire team. "Our life in Mr. Wada's home was like paradise," recalls Furuhashi. "Back home we had to divide our time between practicing for the tournament and scrounging for food to supplement our rations. In America, we got enough to eat for the first time in nearly ten years. We all ate so much that we got diarrhea, but we could feel the nutrition seeping through every inch of our bodies." Other Nisei residents across the United States responded generously when Katsumi Yonetani, living in Hawaii, launched a fund-raising campaign to cover the team's travel expenses.

The response of the American public to the Japanese team's success was perhaps the greatest surprise of all. The team's sponsors had feared verbal attacks, at the very least, and Shoji Kiyokawa, the team manager (now a member of the International Olympic Committee), went to Los Angeles two months early to take necessary precautions. Fearing that the team members might have rocks thrown at them, he had requested police protection. But all these fears proved unfounded. After they began setting new world records, the Japanese swimmers were congratulated warmly all over Los Angeles. Flowers and other gifts flowed in a steady stream into Wada's house, where they were staying. After the Tokyo national championship meet of the year before, American sportswriters had been skeptical of the unofficial records, even voicing suspicions that the timekeepers' watches were inaccurate. But the press now responded enthusiastically to seeing the

Japanese perform, nicknaming them "flying fish of Mount Fuji." Takizo Matsumoto, one of the team's managers, asked an American reporter, with a sly grin: "Are you sure your American stopwatches are working all right?"

On the day the Los Angeles meet closed, General MacArthur issued a special statement: "Nothing reveals national character in its true colors like the actions of champions in international competition. The new Japan has passed its first character test with flying colors!" Tabata and Kiyokawa speculate that MacArthur's motives for sending the swimming champions to America were not simply to cheer the Japanese nation, but also to impress upon the American public the success of his Occupation policies.

In the autumn of the same year, the San Francisco Seals professional baseball team arrived in Japan to play Japanese teams. Japan was roundly defeated on the baseball diamond, but this time no one seemed to mind. Spectators were thrilled when, by special permission, the Rising Sun flag was flown at the stadium and the national anthem was played. Many say they were moved to tears. "I realized for the first time," says writer Yoriyoshi Arima, "that national emblems and anthems were not necessarily to be associated only with war, but could be used for clean purposes too. I felt as if the scales had suddenly fallen from my eyes."

During the Occupation, Japanese nationalism was thus awakened by sports. It was strengthened by the Tokyo Olympics of 1964, and now has reached the point where it seems to be making some Americans uneasy.

Social Studies at the Post Office

" "THE POSTWAR educational reforms were made in haste under the abnormal circumstance of occupation. To insist on retaining them as the only desirable educational system is to refuse to consider education as a growing and changing part of the entire social environment." Thus reads one paragraph in the *Basic Plan for the Reform of Elementary and Secondary Education* issued by the Central Council for Education in November, 1970. The chairman of the government-backed council, Dr. Tatsuo Morito, goes further in explaining that statement. "The educational reform accomplished in Japan by the Americans after the war was excellent in an ideal sense, but it is out of harmony with the 'Japanese climate' in many ways and has experienced serious problems of assimilation. It puts such great emphasis on democratization, in particular, that educational planning and efficiency are subordinated to secondary positions. This really must be corrected."

To counter the report of the government council, the Japan Teachers' Union established an Education System Investigating Committee in 1970. Pending the publication of an official report of its findings, committee chairman Satoru Umene, who is also president of Wako University, has stated: "The 6-3 system (six years of primary school followed by three years of junior high or lower secondary school) was not forced upon Japan. It was decided upon following a thorough re-examination of the prewar and wartime educational systems and put into effect by Japanese and American joint efforts as a conscientious embodiment of what were then the most up-to-date educational principles in the world. Instead of nurturing the system with adequate financial support, the government has destroyed it deliberately. I think we should urge in our report a return to the original spirit of the postwar reforms."

These diametrically opposed positions reveal that the Japanese government is trying to forsake, while the teachers' union is struggling to preserve, what the Americans did for Japanese education. Ironically, in matters of educational policy the conservative government comes off looking anti-American and the progressive teachers' union strongly pro-American.

It is often said that the spirit of the postwar reforms has been better preserved in Kyoto Prefecture than anywhere else in Japan. There, for example, the three basic principles governing secondary schools are most rigidly followed. These three principles are coeducation, one school per school district, and a curriculum which embraces both a regular (liberal arts) course and a commercial (vocational) course. "The postwar educational system is unquestionably a legacy of the Occupation," admits Hideo Nakashima, Kyoto superintendant of education. "But we are dedicated to keeping it alive, because we believe it to be the best."

Two American officers—the chief of the Civil Education Division of the First Army Corps and the director of the Civil Education Section of the Kyoto military government—figure importantly in the history of educational reform in Kyoto. Stating baldly that they intended to accomplish in Kyoto what educators had been unable to do in America, they advocated educational reforms with impressive determination throughout Kyoto Prefecture. They soon earned the reputation of being zealous to a fault. Kyoto was one of the few major Japanese cities that had escaped bombing, and the plants of the prewar schools were still intact. One of the first moves of the two American reformers was to order that the buildings formerly occupied by the old middle (secondary) schools be used to house the junior high schools that had been created under the new educational system. Parents' associations and graduates of the schools that would be affected rose in arms, and prefectural authorities asked the two Americans to reconsider their directive. The parents and alumni also appealed directly to higher Occupation authorities. They wished the school buildings to continue to be used for the senior high schools which had been created out of the former middle schools. But their campaign was unsuccessful, and the buildings of Kyoto's famous middle schools, like Kyoto First and Kyoto Second, were transformed into junior high schools.

"Even so, there was a severe shortage of space for the newly established junior high schools," recalls Toshitake Amano, then Educational Affairs Section chief of the Kyoto prefectural government and now president of Otemongakuin University. "I was caught between the fire of the zealous Americans and the angry parents and graduates of the affected middle schools."

The shortage of school buildings was not the only problem plaguing the new education system as it was applied across the nation; the question of what to teach, what to include in the curriculum, was an even more serious issue. The teaching of ethics, Japanese history, and geography was prohibited by Occupation order, to be replaced in the curriculum for primary and junior high schools by something called "social studies." Education Ministry officials and local teachers alike had to grapple with the question of just what this new subject should include. The Education Ministry received from the Occupation authorities a copy of a social-studies textbook used in Virginia schools, had it translated, and distributed it to a number of teachers to examine. Both the ministry and teachers found it impossible to understand what the book was about.

After pondering deeply what might be covered by a course called "social studies," Miss Shige Kusakabe, an elementary school teacher in Tokyo, developed her own unique approach to the subject. It was based upon the many processes involved in writing and sending a letter. In the letter-writing stage, she taught Japanese language and calligraphy. The letter-weighing and stamp-buying stage was used to teach arithmetic. The mailing and delivery stage was used to illustrate the social makeup of a community. Word of this ingenious method spread across Japan, attracting hordes of curious observers to Miss Kusakabe's school; she was also invited to travel about the country demonstrating the simple but effective method of teaching the previously unknown subject, social studies.

Miss Kusakabe's example is but one illustration of the great zeal with which teachers and school administrators went about their tasks under the new education system. "My former pupils all tell me that those were their happiest school days," says Miss Kusakabe, who is now a counselor on domestic relations for the Tokyo metropolitan government. "Classes were held amid the devastation of burned-out school buildings, but teachers, Education Ministry officials, and Occupation authorities were all determined to make the new system work well. I don't see that sort of zeal anywhere in Japanese education today."

Why has that zeal disappeared? "Mainly because democratic education failed to take root in Japan," explains Noboru Ito, professor at Tsuda College and also a member of the Tokyo Metropolitan Education Board. "For one thing, the Occupation authorities changed their policies too soon, and for another, parents too frequently blamed their children's lack of courtesy or traditional etiquette on the new education system. Most important of all is the fact that politicians capitalized on such criticisms by parents in order to regain government control of education."

It was the U. S. Education Mission, which visited Japan early in 1946, that paved the way for the initial reforms. In its report to General MacArthur, the commission emphasized that it is in an atmosphere of freedom that a teacher functions most effectively, adding that it is the duty of administrators to create that atmosphere. Twenty-four years later, in 1970, an education survey mission for the Organization of Economic Cooperation and Development wrote in its report to the Japanese government that nowhere else in the world has a government intervened in the selection of textbooks and the conducting of education so much as in Japan. The Japanese insistence on centralizing the administration of education and on standardizing teaching methods serves only to discourage experimentation and to impede the development of a form of education suited to modern society.

"Wet" and "Dry" Economics

AFTER the war, the United States first demanded $670 million in
reparations from Japan, then reduced the figure to $450 million,
reduced it again to $180 million, and finally canceled it altogether.
Meanwhile, U. S. economic aid to Japan, beginning at around $350
million, swelled first to $470 million, then to $550 million, and
finally reached a total of $2.1 billion.

The Japanese had a mixed reaction to this replacement of reparations by aid. Some still gratefully regard it as generosity. Others, like
Kihachiro Kimura, Socialist member of the Upper House, think that
it was motivated only by U. S. self-interest. "The price for the withdrawal of the reparations demands was the dangerous Security
Treaty," says Kimura. "We are paying for the economic aid, and
we may yet get a bigger bill for it." (He was speaking before President Nixon started his save-the-dollar program; today he would
doubtless say the new bill has now been presented.)

One cold December morning in 1945, an Occupation train bound
for Nikko pulled out of the Tobu Railway station in the almost totally devastated Asakusa section of Tokyo. Just as it began to move,
a Japanese man leaped nimbly aboard and, entering a coach, approached a tall American gentlemen who was relaxing in a special
reserved seat.

"Mr. Ambassador," the Japanese ventured, "I am a representative
of the Japanese government. May I—"

The American—Ambassador Edwin W. Pauley, head of the U. S.
Mission on Japanese Reparations—cut him short with an annoyed
glance. Then, as if realizing he could hardly have the intruder thrown
off the moving train, even though he was one of the defeated enemy,
he smiled coolly and made room for the other to sit beside him. In excited haste, the Japanese fired off a series of question and hastily
scribbled the ambassador's replies:

"No, the United States will not demand indemnities and reparations of a retaliatory nature from Japan. . . . Yes, the Soviet Union,
having removed so much equipment from Japanese factories in Manchuria and southern Sakhalin, has been refused the right to claim further reparations. . . . No, the United States will not collect reparations in money. . . ."

The Japanese man was Koichi Asakai, who would later become
ambassador to the United States. In 1945, he was the director of the
General Affairs Department of the War Termination Central Liaison

Office. The following day he reported his feat and all that he had learned to the cabinet. His information was greeted with considerable relief, because there had been rumors that America was determined to reduce Japan to economic impotency. Though Pauley had made it clear that the Japanese would not be allowed a higher standard of living than that of the people of any Allied nation, even this was much better than the rumors had it.

As things developed, the American policy on Japanese reparations was to transfer the industrial equipment made surplus by the demilitarization program to those Allied nations that most needed it, especially to China, where it would be used to bolster the Nationalist government. Should the China situation shift in a direction unfavorable to the United States, Washington's policy on Japanese reparations for China would also, it was expected, change as a matter of course. All in all, the reparations policy would accord with the general policy for Japan as enunciated by Secretary of the Army Kenneth C. Royall in 1948: "We hold to . . . the purpose of building in Japan a self-sufficient democracy strong enough . . . to serve as a deterrent against any other totalitarian threats which might hereafter arise in the Far East."

When the Communists won control of China the following year, factories that had been impounded for reparations were released one by one. The first was the Japan Steel Company plant at Hirohata in Hyogo Prefecture. Its blast furnace was refired for the first time in 1950. "The firing of the Hirohata blast furnace marked the starting point of Japan's economic miracle," observes Kikuichiro Yamaguchi, former director-general of the Reparations Agency and speaker of the Lower House. "Until that time we weren't allowed even to turn a screw on a lathe in the steel industry."

Gradually increasing economic aid accompanied the relaxation of demands for reparations. Early in the Occupation, MacArthur had been able to remark nonchalantly that the problem of Japan's economic rehabilitation was outside his province; but the cold war soon changed that attitude and hastened the flow of aid to Japan. Initially, economic assistance to Japan was aimed at preventing mass starvation but, as factories began reopening, the emphasis shifted toward industrial rehabilitation. The source of aid shifted from GARIOA (Government and Relief in Occupied Areas) to EROA (Economic Rehabilitation in Occupied Areas).

American economic aid to Japan in those years came to about $27 per capita, as compared with $122 to Britain, $103 to France, and $77 to West Germany. The figure seems relatively miserly but, according to Kyoto University professor Yasukichi Yasuba: "The aid to Japan was not small considering the size of the Japanese GNP in those days. Later, Japan was asked to repay the aid, and we are now doing so—easily. We are like a successful man repaying an old debt incurred when he was a struggling student. And in those days the aid meant as much to Japan as a loan would mean to a young, hard-up student."

As might have been expected, the sweeping shift in American policy from demanding reparations to offering economic assistance was not accomplished without opposition from the American public. "We were hard put to appease a public demanding to know why we should repay the attack on Pearl Harbor with economic help," observed Maj. Gen. Frank McCoy, U. S. delegate to the Far Eastern Commission in charge of the Advance Transfer Program (for reparations). Outright aid tapered off gradually, being replaced by measures to speed Japan's economic self-help. Examples are the removal of restrictions on shipbuilding and permission to expand the Japanese mercantile fleet.

"The foremost preoccupation of the American government was to manage somehow to keep Japan in the American camp with a minimum of inducement in the form of economic aid," says Takeshi Watanabe, president of the Asian Development Bank, who was in charge of the Finance Ministry's liaison with the Occupation authorities. "There was, after all, always the American taxpayer to worry about."

The relinquishing of reparations demands, the granting of economic aid, and the implementation of self-help measures all breathed new life into Japanese capitalism. Then war in Korea brought a windfall for the economy in the form of massive American procurement orders for Japanese goods. That war laid the groundwork for Japan's subsequent economic growth.

"Japanese heavy industries and chemical industries benefited immeasurably from the changes in American reparations policy," says Tokyo University economic historian Yoshio Ando. "Specifically, the release to Japanese big businesses of such huge military installations as those at Yokkaichi and Iwakuni served as a 'traction engine' pulling Japan's rate of growth higher and higher." Ando also compares the release of those installations to the sale of government-owned factories to private Japanese companies during the Meiji era, a policy that did much to spur the growth of such *zaibatsu* houses as Mitsubishi and Furukawa. He also points out that the United States subsequently proceeded to incorporate Japan in the security and defense program and economically "to put her under the dollar umbrella."

The relinquishing of reparations and the extending of economic aid had so salutary an effect on Japanese public opinion that many people believed naively that the umbrella was held over Japan purely out of motives of kindness and good will. The Diet regarded the economic aid as an outright gift and passed a resolution of thanks. Little wonder then that government, Diet, and the people at large were taken aback when the United States, finding it necessary to defend the dollar, suddenly turned business minded and demanded repayment of the GARIOA and EROA aid. These apparently contradictory qualities, which the Japanese call "wet" and "dry"—sentimental attachment contrasted with hard-headed business sense—can still be seen today in the economic relations between America and Japan.

Collapse of the Family System

IN THE SUMMER of 1946, the Office of Civil Affairs Research within the Justice Ministry set about the task of revising the civil code to bring it into accord with the new constitution. The constitution had not yet been promulgated, but an outline of it was already circulating within the government.

The OCAR set out by abolishing the *ie*—the "house" or family system—which had formed, in effect, an unwritten code of domestic relations and had served as the keystone of the old civil code. Absolute authority over the family members of the *ie* had rested with the "house head." His permission was required if a family member wished to live apart from the house. If his son was killed in war, it was his privilege to prohibit his widowed daughter-in-law from returning to her parental home. If she chose to force the issue and return to her home against his will, he could have her name removed from the family register and claim for himself the pension due the next of kin of the deceased. By the law of succession under the old code, the status and estate of the family head were normally transferable only to his eldest son; the wife of the family head was legally an "incompetent."

Japanese families had long chafed under this feudalistic system, and criticism of it had smoldered for years before the war. This discontent flared up dramatically when the war ended, compelling the revision of the civil code. There was also pressure from SCAP, but it remained quiet and subtle. "Japan moved to abolish the family system of her own volition. Abolition was not forced on us by General Mac-Arthur," states Ken'ichi Okuno emphatically. He was director of the Civil Affairs Bureau at the time, was later a Supreme Court justice, and is now a practicing lawyer.

"The new civil code was one of the postwar legal revisions least, influenced by SCAP," agrees Sakae Wagatsuma, a member of the commission that drafted the outline for the new code and now a professor emeritus of Tokyo University. "SCAP or MacArthur himself might have stepped in and ordered it had Japan herself shown no inclination toward abolishing the family system. Fortunately, both the Americans and the Japanese were of the same mind on this particular issue. After all, abolition of the *ie* only conformed with the general legal evolution from the concept of status to one of contract. All of us on the commission considered it the logical step to bring the civil code into conformity with the new constitution's emphasis on the dignity of the individual and the equality of the sexes."

For all that, when the outline of the new code was submitted to a legislative committee of the Diet it was attacked vehemently. "The conservatism of the opposition was so strong as to be virtually unimaginable today," recalls Zennosuke Nakagawa, a member of the revision commission and now president of Kanazawa University. "In attacking the revision, the old family system was extolled as 'a praiseworthy tradition of Japan,' 'the very root of Oriental morality,' and 'the glory of the Japanese spirit.' But, ultimately, silent pressure from SCAP decided the issue in favor of revision." While carefully refraining from issuing any formal directives or statements of its position on the matter, SCAP expressed its wishes indirectly, through personal contacts and other channels. The bill for the new code was approved by SCAP even before it was presented to the Diet.

"The provision recognizing serious mental disability beyond hope of cure in a spouse as justifiable cause for divorce was included in the new civil code because of 'the strong desire' of SCAP," reveals Fumio Ozawa, former head of the Office of Civil Affairs Research and now chairman of the Central Investigating Commission on Pollution.

Thomas Blakemore, a lawyer now practicing in Tokyo, who studied law at Tokyo University before the war and served in the legislative division of SCAP, recalls the circumspect attitude adopted by his office in regard to this delicate issue. "Unlike the antitrust law, the civil-code revision was not forced on Japan. It was our basic policy to respect Japan's own intentions in the matter. It was an affair of a nature that prohibited interference by foreigners. But we were confident that the code would be revised; it had to be if the spirit of the new constitution were to be respected."

If the older generation felt uneasy over the collapse of the Japanese *ie*, the new order was hailed by the nation's youth and its women. Immediate misunderstandings of the new code arose because of the irresponsible or self-serving interpretations by younger people and the unfounded misgivings of the old. Some children interpreted the code as freeing them from any obligation to support their parents, despite the code's general exhortation to persons of direct blood relationship to support each other. There were occasional cases of a young man showing up at a home for the aged and requesting in all seriousness that his mother be taken in and cared for. "She was sixty yesterday, and they tell me that the new law obligates the state to care for people of sixty or older." Another drastic effect of the revision of the code was the divorce rate, which soared temporarily; no doubt, long pent-up grievances of Japanese women were seeking a sudden outlet.

Nuclear families, consisting only of married couples and their children, were a product of the new code, for grown children were no longer required to remain under the roof of the family head. As the housing situation began to improve after about 1955, such families began springing up like mushrooms.

The disintegration of old family relations that had been so rigidly cemented in the *ie* weakened family unity and bred serious difficulties between husbands and wives and parents and children, often over trifles. The disciplining of children was frequently neglected and old people felt increasingly isolated, lonely, and helpless. "A mother and her daughter-in-law have exchanged places," sighs a mother in a book by Kazuhiro Oikawa. "Today a mother must stand in awe of her daughter-in-law. Maybe we old folks are unlucky to have lived so long as to be caught up in the changes going on right now."

It would be a mistake to blame all such problems on democratization. The major social upheavals inevitably touched off by Japan's fantastic economic growth are largely the cause of what many consider the domestic chaos that prevails today. "No average man or woman can keep pace with rapid changes in value systems, particularly in those values directly affecting family relations and everyday life," says Professor Seiichi Isono of Tokyo University of Education. "The authors of the reforms in the family system failed to take adequate steps to prepare people who might be hurt by convulsive changes in their daily lives induced by the new code. I suspect that they considered their job finished as soon as the democratization of the Japanese family had been written into law."

[163]

In April, 1971, the Justice Ministry's Legislative Council created a subcommittee to re-examine the twenty-five-year-old civil code. "A review of the experience of a quarter of a century will suggest what to retain and what to eliminate," says Wagatsuma, special adviser to the committee. "I hope that our study of the code will give us a hint of the form future domestic relations should take."

The Purge

KEITA GENJI, winner of the 1971 Yoshikawa Eiji Literary Prize, struck it rich twenty years ago with his first novel, *Santo Juyaku* (Third-Rank Executives). The novel, a satirical exposé of the careers of white-collar workers, was a runaway best seller when it first appeared and has since become established as a modern classic that still sells more than twenty thousand copies a year. "It never would have been written if not for the purge," says Genji today.

"First-rank executives," as defined in the novel, were the real capitalists, men born to wealth and power or else self-made business tycoons; "second-rank executives" were also men of elite family background. But the "third-rank executives" of the title were upstarts—men who in normal times would never have risen higher than a minor department directorship, at best, but who suddenly found themselves company presidents, sitting on boards, because their superiors had been purged. Genji himself had worked for the Sumitomo Real Estate Company, and had conceived of the theme of the book when he overheard an executive of the firm grumbling about being a "third-rank board director."

What was this purge that had such a sweeping effect on the Japanese business world? Perhaps it is best described by the *Asahi* headlines of the time that proclaimed it "a bloodless revolution." Early in January, 1946, SCAP suddenly decreed the removal from public life of all men of power during the prewar and wartime periods. The ax fell on former military officers, right-wingers, bureaucrats, politicians, business leaders, influential journalists—more than 210,000 men in all. Several million more of their relatives were prohibited from succeeding the purgees in their positions.

An unending variety of tragicomedies ensued from the purge. One man, a member of the Reservists' Association (the Japanese equivalent of the American Legion) happened to be a rice dealer. Since rice was under rigid government control and was rationed to consumers through authorized distribution stations manned by rice dealers, he was considered a public servant and as such was purged. He tried to have his wife or son succeed him in the dealership, but was prevented because they were too closely related to him. Only after filing complicated petitions with Occupation authorities did he succeed in having an exception made.

Although the name Budo-kai literally means "Martial Arts Association," the organization was actually only a club of men interested in judo and fencing as sports. Nevertheless, the directors of the Budo-kai were purged when an Occupation censor intercepted a letter written from one member to another. The correspondents had both lost their jobs as instructors when the Occupation banned the teaching of the so-called martial arts in schools, and the letter-writer was attempting to console his friend with these incriminating words: "Let's not lose heart. We'll see better days." The censor who noticed this was all the more frightened when the name Budo-kai was translated for him as "Military Virtues Association." His alarmed imagination concluded that a dangerous military organization was plotting to revive. Hence the Budo-kai was added to the purge list, despite the protest of its members that they were interested only in athletics.

The actual execution of the purge—the screening of so-called undesirables and the compiling of a purge list—was delegated by SCAP to the Japanese government. As a result, the bureaucracy was least hard hit. Only 145 ranking bureaucrats were purged (less than one percent of all purgees), and sixty-seven of these men were police administrators who would have been spared had they not also been members of the Budo-kai.

In the business world, however, one out of every four top-level executives was purged. Considering SCAP's relentless denunciation of the *zaibatsu* as bearing major responsibility for the war, many were surprised that the number of business purgees was not even larger. For this the Japanese business world could thank Hisanari Yamada, chief of the Political Affairs Department in the War Termination Central Liaison Office, for a daring trick he played on SCAP. A check list drawn up by SCAP included the title of "standing director" as the category of businessmen to be screened. Yamada knew that the term referred to all full-time directors, but chose to interpret it as including only managing directors and executive directors, thereby letting off the hook all ordinary directors, even though they too occupied full-time positions. The scheme was successful, and men of ordinary-director rank went unpurged. Today, it is they who are the top business leaders, the "third-rank executives" of Genji's novel.

"I really deserve fatter political donations from the business community," jokes Yamada, who is now a member of the Lower House. He later fell out of favor with Prime Minister Yoshida and became one of the "Y-purgees," men ousted from office by Yoshida.

Wataru Narahashi, chief cabinet secretary during the purges, was in charge of screening. In his office he sometimes shouted: "Look out! Watch it!" and made an elaborate pretense of ducking bullets whizzing above his head. He fully expected to be himself shot down from office by the purge, and eventually he was. Other influential politicians who were removed from office—Tanzan Ishibashi, Rikizo Hirano, Jiichiro Matsumoto—have been considered by some people to have been victims of political intrigue. Perhaps the most prominent political purgee of all was Ichiro Hatoyama, president of the Liberal party (precursor of today's Liberal-Democratic party). He was on the point of forming a cabinet when he was suddenly purged. He was replaced as prime minister by Shigeru Yoshida, who proceeded to become the foremost statesman of postwar Japan.

As soon as the purges were initiated, GHQ was inundated by a flood of anonymous tips exposing the sins, real or fancied, of established men of influence. Japanese purveyors of "purge intelligence" began haunting the halls and offices of GHQ to nose out bits of information and to warn people that they were being considered for screening or that the purge verdict had been decided. GHQ tried to gag its personnel, but information inevitably leaked from time to time.

The shift in the purge policy came as the cold war increased in intensity and the Occupation found itself needing the cooperation of Japanese conservatives. One by one they were depurged and returned to public life. Then, in 1950, came the notorious "red purge," in which Japanese Communists, who had earlier been cheered by the purge of rightists and conservatives, were themselves struck down.

When the San Francisco peace treaty took effect in 1952, all purge orders were withdrawn and any remaining purgee was free to return to public life. Like many other Occupation policies, the "bloodless revolution" also ended inconclusively. But in spite of stopping halfway and reversing itself, it produced some serious repercussions. For one thing, the purge of politicians opened the gates for bureaucrats to enter politics and easily replace the purgees. Although many purged politicians later returned to political influence, they had to compete with the bureaucrats-turned-politicians. The reins of government for the past ten years have been in the hands of Hayato Ikeda and Eisaku Sato, both of them ex-bureaucrats and close disciples of Yoshida.

Purged business leaders had a far harder time returning to power than their political counterparts. The number of "first-rank executives" who accomplished successful comebacks after the signing of the peace treaty can almost be counted on one hand. Ichizo Kobayashi, head of the Toho entertainment empire, and Keita Goto, president of the Tokyu Railway and associated companies, were two who did manage to fight off the "upstarts" and regain their former positions, but they were the exceptions rather than the rule. Toughened by their experience with labor offensives and financial maneuverings unknown to the oldtime executives, the "third-rank executives" had quickly and shrewdly consolidated their positions in the business world and could no longer be dislodged. "Although scorned as upstarts, adversity has made capable business leaders of them," comments novelist Genji. These leaders are proud to take credit for the incredible Japanese reconstruction and industrial and commercial expansion since the end of the Occupation.

"A reappraisal of postwar Japanese business leaders shows their merits clearly outweighing their failings," agrees economic analyst Mitsuo Suzuki. "But the reverse may prove true if they are reluctant to relinquish their powers or delegate them to others as they grow older. Rapid advances in technology and environmental pollution are signals warning them to make way for younger men. If today's business leaders persist in outliving their usefulness, pleading that there are no suitable successors, it will amount to an admission that they are, in fact, 'third-rank executives' incapable even of training men to follow them."

The New Look

" A MARRIED woman falling in love with a younger man? What if Japanese women began imitating her? What terrible consequences might result! That novel must not be used for the program." This was the worried reaction of a certain Miss Lindsey, employed in the radio section of the Occupation's Civil Information and Education Department, to an NHK plan in 1946 to adapt Balzac's novel *Lys dans la Valée* for use as a Japanese radio drama. NHK directors asked immediately, with some annoyance, whether her criticism amounted merely to advice or to an order. She said that it was not an order, but emphasized her opinion of the theme's unsuitability. Finally, after further argument, Miss Lindsey gave in and the dramatized French novel went on the air in a nationwide broadcast.

This minor incident serves to illustrate the close, and rather nervous, attention that Occupation authorities paid to the image of women in a modern democratic society. The attention was not directed only at radio programs. Magazine editors were frequently urged to publish articles explaining or describing American democracy and the equality of the sexes in the United States. "Perhaps SCAP felt that Japanese women needed re-education from scratch," comments Saeko Saegusa, who was then an editor of *Fujin Koron* (Women's Review) and later a managing editor of *Chuo Koron* (Central Review), both prestigious monthly magazines.

While Occupation authorities went about liberating and democratizing Japanese women through education, the most basic and direct form of relationship developed between Japanese women and American soldiers. It was the traditional relationship that springs up inevitably between soldiers of an occupying army and the women of the occupied country. The relationship flowered first between the "comfort" girls furnished by the Special Comfort Service Society established by Japan for the benefit of the Americans. Other girls were soon swarming to the entertainment districts that sprang up around the U. S. bases.

In March, 1946, Occupation authorities issued an order banning public displays of affection between Americans and Japanese women. The order may have been motivated by a sense of the impropriety of displays of affection for members of what had so recently been an enemy nation, but it also recognized the fact that Japanese people were unused to showing affection between men and women in public. The edict did not, however, prohibit "ordinary fraternization" of military personnel with Japanese women, revealing clearly the discrepancy between the proclaimed cause of liberating Japanese women and the realities of Occupation policy.

Mixed-blood children born of GI fathers and Japanese mothers have now reached maturity. More than twelve hundred of them, orphaned or abandoned, were raised in the Elizabeth Saunders Home run by Mrs. Miki Sawada. A recent news story reported that four of Mrs. Sawada's former charges, who had been adopted into American families, were killed fighting in Vietnam. Two of the four had been abandoned by their Japanese mothers after their fathers were killed in the Korean War. Mrs. Sawada weeps at the thought of fathers and sons being killed in wars only twenty years apart, and when the adoptive parents of one of the youths wrote from America offering to adopt another boy from the home, Mrs. Sawada replied that she would not consider the offer until she could be sure that the United States would never go to war again.

On the whole, Japanese women were more interested in American fashions than in democracy. Long skirts—then called the New Look —and nylon stockings were eagerly sought by Japanese women. Critic Fuyuko Kamisaka recalls that attractive clothes were so scarce that, when she began working in 1949, she attended the ceremony marking the first day on the job wearing *mompe* (thick, bloomerlike pants worn by farm women working in the fields). "I did have a skirt, but no stockings to wear with it."

It was only years later that Japanese women learned that the long skirts that they had called "American" were actually of French origin. Previously, all new fashions had come to Japan from the United States. "Long skirts represented for us our liberation from the privations of war, just as maxiskirts today are a return to human grace and elegance from a period of fascination with absurdly erotic or grotesque fashions," says dress designer Hanae Mori.

In 1950, a group of twelve Japanese women visited the United States as guests of the State Department. They sailed from Yokohama wearing overcoats donated by the wives of American officers, but returned four months later clad in nylon blouses thin and transparent as a cicada's wing, fascinating every woman who saw them. One member of the group, Mrs. Fuji Egami, a former researcher for NHK, brought back a dozen of the blouses as gifts for friends. They were snapped up joyfully. "On my last trip to America I went shopping and found a sweater that I especially liked," says Mrs. Egami. "When I looked at the label, I was surprised to see that it said 'Made in Japan.' That really made me realize that Japan now produces all the clothing she needs and exports so much surplus that the Americans are furious."

One surviving part of the legacy of the Occupation's determination to liberate Japanese women is a series of provisions written into the Labor Standards Law for the protection of women. They prohibit employing women for dangerous, harmful, or excessively heavy labor, limit the amount of overtime work women can do, and grant them maternity and menstruation holidays. "Only South Korea and Indonesia follow the Japanese example of legally allowing women menstruation holidays," comments Nobuko Takahashi, director of the

Women's and Minors' Bureau in the Labor Ministry. "I believe our Labor Standards Law to be the best in the world."

Do Japanese women still need the protection of such laws? An excerpt from a document entitled *An Opinion on the Labor Standards Law*, published in 1970 by the Tokyo Chamber of Commerce and Industry, reads: "The physical strength of Japanese women has increased measurably in recent years, and modern technology has produced many new types of work which are neither hazardous nor harmful. Yet the law unfairly equates women with minors. This amounts to discrimination against women. . . . The menstruation leave is a typical example of the unnecessary pampering of women."

Hiroko Kagayama, a director of the National Telegraph and Telephone Bureau and an ardent advocate of women's rights, tends to agree. "The times have changed and so have social conditions. The protective clauses certainly benefited women when they were written, but today they serve only to prevent women from making full use of their abilities. There is little sense in limiting overtime for women in managerial positions." This raises the final question of whether women have grown so strong as to find unnecessary the special privileges that they once fought for.

The Grammar School
of Democracy

ONE DAY in 1947 a directive from SCAP was delivered to the Ministry of Home Affairs. It required the ministry to submit complete career resumés of its entire staff. "It has finally begun," thought the official who received the directive. He was Shun'ichi Suzuki, then personnel director of the ministry and later secretary general of the EXPO '70 Association.

He was right. The order was the first step in SCAP's action to break up the Home Ministry and end the bureaucratic centralization of government authority. No other Japanese ministry had been ordered to submit career statements on its entire staff, ranging from the minister himself down to the clerical workers. The Home Ministry's personnel numbered more than five hundred. The Ministry had managed local-government affairs through prefectural governors, whom it appointed. Local administrative bodies in cities, towns, and villages were but myrmidons of the few men in power at the top of the structure. To the Americans the system must have seemed tailor-made for totalitarianism, and they were determined to replace it with strong, autonomous local authority.

Home Ministry bureaucrats struggled desperately against the harsh orders that they disband. Tamotsu Ogita, chief of the ministry's Archives Section, pleaded: "Redistribution of administrative authority and the establishment of local government are all to the good, but to thrive, the local governments need a stable Home Ministry to co-ordinate their activities and act as a spokesman for them to the central government." In requesting that at least the ministry's headquarters be retained, Ogita offered to have its name changed from Naimu-sho to Naisei-sho. SCAP was unimpressed, pointing out that the new name, translated into English as Home Administration Ministry, was virtually the same as that of the old Home Affairs Ministry.

Thus, the Home Affairs Ministry was no more as of December 31, 1947. It was divided into a National Public Election Management Commission and a Local Fiscal Administration Commission, and its police functions were distributed among a National Rural Police and many autonomous municipal forces. Nevertheless, early the following spring Suzuki could recruit Tokyo University students for local-government jobs with the following speech: "We need able men for local government. With the Ministry gone, these jobs may seem to lack any future and may have no appeal for you. But don't worry: there will soon be opportunities for power again."

Suzuki was right. As the Occupation policies shifted in emphasis midway in its history, moves toward recentralization of government authority were initiated with such plausible motives as "labor-saving in government and modernization of government machinery" and "clarifying the measure of state responsibility." This tendency gained in momentum as the peace treaty neared. In 1949, the commissions and other organizations into which the Home Affairs Ministry had been split were reunited into something called the Local Autonomy Agency. This was elevated three years later to the Autonomy Agency, and finally, in 1960, became the Autonomy Ministry (Jichi-sho), which some English-language newspapers in Tokyo still call the Home Affairs Ministry.

"The Americans were more concerned with breaking up the Home Ministry than actually nurturing local self-government," comments Suzuki. "Even after the ministry was abolished, we were ordered to announce publicly the whereabouts of each of its former members. No doubt Occupation authorities, being public servants of the

U. S. government, wanted to be able to report home to Washington the successful breaking up of the Home Ministry as proof of their thoroughness in executing Occupation policies."

Ogita observes: "I have always felt that the territory consciousness of the ministries and the excessive powers they hold are what really stand in the way of strong local self-government. Seeing the way recent antipollution measures have been administered only reaffirms my opinion."

Ryuichi Arai, professor of public administration at Waseda University, takes a different tack from Suzuki and Ogita, and takes the central government to task for "merely criticizing the local-government system as ordered by the Occupation and failing to strengthen it, to say nothing of giving it enough money to function independently. The central government has perpetuated its authority over local bodies through a policy of subsidizing them."

Acting on the recommendations of Dr. Carl S. Shoup, who surveyed the Japanese tax system for SCAP, the Local Government Research Commission in 1950–51 decided to put local finances on firm ground through "a redistribution of local-government business." But the recommendations of the commission failed to materialize in the form of adequate legislation. Instead, poor local finances were capitalized upon to perpetuate the central government's authority.

Over the years, ex-bureaucrats—officials from all the ministries—have gradually worked their way into local-government posts while maintaining connections with the ministries from which they came. They provide the central government and the ruling party with the perfect instrument for avoiding "needless friction" with local administrative bodies. And the local-government institutions, generally pressed for funds, often prefer "material gains" from the central government despite the cost to their prestige and to complete autonomy. For these reasons, the slogan for "local government linked directly to the central government" goes unchallenged and indeed unquestioned in local election campaigns.

In the United States, state governors have greater powers than cabinet secretaries and command more public prestige. This attitude is extended to the representatives of other governments as well. When Ichiro Kono visited Washington as head of the Japanese Construction Ministry and sought an appointment with President Kennedy, Kennedy had no time for him. A group of Japanese prefectural governors was cordially welcomed at the White House, however. American governors would be amazed to see their counterparts in Japan kowtowing to cabinet ministers and begging for funds.

The Local Fiscal Program announced by the government exceeds the national budget, but Dr. Takeo Fujita, professor emeritus of Rikkyo University and a specialist in local-government financing, nevertheless sees imminent threats to local autonomy: "While grants by the central government to local bodies are increasing, local tax revenue is rapidly decreasing. The pollution issue has served to re-orient local governments back to protecting the well-being of the local populace, but the state of local finances makes me worry that they may soon have to depend entirely on the central government. I wish every Japanese were as deeply interested in local government as in national defense and foreign relations. Local government occupies a central place in our lives from the cradle to the grave. I dread most of all the possibility of local government succumbing entirely to control from above. Now that we are finding ourselves engulfed by all the harmful effects of our rapid economic expansion, local government may be more important to our day-to-day well-being than ever before."

Meanwhile a process undreamed of by the Occupation and the old Home Ministry is having far-reaching effects on the relationship of central and local governments. The economic expansion which has brought Japan the third highest GNP in the world has also caused excessive urban concentrations of population and a drastic drain of people from farming and fishing communities. A survey taken recently at a grammar school in Sayama in rural Saitama Prefecture measured the percentage of pupils whose parents had also attended the same school. It turned out to be only about ten percent.

With the drain of population from the countryside to the cities, all the ill-effects of excessive urbanization are to be seen in every important Japanese city. Moreover, local culture and patriotism and local person-to-person ties—the foundations of effective local government —have been eroded. The problem seems all the more serious when we think of local government as "the guardian of democracy" and "the grammar school of democratic government," as it has been called. This is because the local political situation is in fact a mirror reflecting the political system of the country and, hence, the political consciousness of the nation. Now is the time that we should look at ourselves in this mirror.

One Step Backward,
Two Forward

A LMOST immediately after the war ended, Japanese Communist leaders were released from prison. Among them were Kyuichi Tokuda and Yoshio Shiga, emerging to freedom after eighteen years' imprisonment. The Occupation initially thought that the Communists could be used in developing antimilitarist public sentiment. Soon, however, mutual disenchantment set in, producing important repercussions, particularly for the future of the labor movement in Japan.

Eager haste marked Occupation efforts to unionize Japanese labor. American officials made rounds of factories by jeep, often accompanied by Communist leaders, in order to organize unions rapidly. Shiga, newly released from prison, toured ports in an American LST while working to organize the Japan Seamen's Union.

When the war ended in August, 1945, there were no unions in Japan. A year later there were 12,000 of them with a total membership of 3,700,000. Thrown together in great haste, many were company-based, unaffiliated unions, reminiscent of the wartime Patriotic Production Associations. In their close familylike ties with management, they are unique to Japan and are the envy of foreign managers. Conversely, they are criticized by Japanese labor leaders as the fundamental cause of the weakness of the Japanese union movement.

Through various labor legislation—the Labor Union Law, the Labor Relations Adjustment Law, the Labor Standards Law—the Occupation gave to Japanese labor guarantees that, according to Goro Yamasaki, former member of the Labor Policy Bureau in the Ministry of Health and Welfare and now a member of the Upper House, "were so strong as to be unparalleled even in the Allied countries." Some of the provisions contained in those laws came directly from the pen of labor experts in the Occupation.

After the war, Japanese labor revolted throughout the country, believing that it had the backing of the "Army of Liberation," as the Communists had called the Occupation forces. But labor was soon disillusioned by the Occupation's reluctance to follow through with unquestioning support.

A speech by Prime Minister Yoshida in the Diet in January, 1947, branding unionists as "recalcitrant," touched off the threat of a general strike by workers in the Japanese National Railways and postal services. Scheduled for February 1, the strike was called off at the eleventh hour, by personal order of General MacArthur. Yoshiro Ii, chairman of the National Labor Struggle Committee, made a moving radio speech in which he said that abandoning the strike was "one step backward in preparation for moving two steps forward." Today a member of the Central Committee of the Japan Communist party, Ii still defends the last-minute cancellation of the strike as the proper move. "There were more than six million unionists and only thirty thousand policemen to oppose them. We could have defied the government and gone on with the strike, but we could not have defied the Occupation forces without serious consequences, including the possible disbanding of the unions, chaos, and an irretrievable loss of unity within the movement. But I still can't understand why MacArthur's headquarters suddenly blocked the strike at the last minute. Until then, SCAP had been sympathetic to labor."

"Ii misunderstood Occupation policy," explains Theodore Cohen, chief of the Labor Division of SCAP at the time and now an executive of a Tokyo trading firm. "We could never have let the railway and communications industries go out on strike because that would have interfered with the functioning of the Occupation. Our problem was not whether or not to permit the general strike but how to avoid it. About two weeks before the strike was scheduled, I recommended that MacArthur issue a statement against it. He chose to wait until the last minute to avert the strike."

The later shift to the right of MacArthur's labor policy has also presented a riddle to historians and concerned parties. There is no easy answer to the question, and Cohen's explanation is three-pronged: "First, in the United States the Democratic party, backed by American labor, lost the national election of November, 1946, and the Republicans became the majority party. MacArthur, who had been out of the United States since the height of the New Deal and who believed that labor held great political weight, began to revise his thinking as a result of the election. (In fact, the next year MacArthur's own candidacy for the Republican presidential nomination was announced.) Second, from his experience with the threatened Japanese strike in February, 1947, he decided that he should deal more conservatively with the Japanese unions. Third, U. S. foreign policy changed dramatically in 1947 and 1948. As American-Soviet antagonisms intensified, the emphasis of the policies for the Japanese and German occupations shifted away from political reform to economic rehabilitation."

Occupation policies also turned nakedly anticommunist in intent and Japan began to be converted into an arsenal in the Far East. In July, 1948, General MacArthur sent a letter to the Japanese government indicating that he was removing the right of collective bargaining from the Japan Council of National and Local Government Workers Unions. That group was the most combative in Japan, and its membership amounted to forty percent of Japanese organized labor.

Soon after the outbreak of the Korean War, Robert T. Amis, fifth chief of the Labor Division of SCAP, showed Saijiro Kaku, director of the Labor Policy Bureau in the Labor Ministry and currently a professor at Rikkyo University, a mimeographed document, saying: "This is what we want you to do." It was, in effect, an order for a red purge. Kaku protested that he could not act on an unofficial document like that and requested the proper directive that he would need to defend the action against opposition in the Diet. Amis refused to comply. Nevertheless, the red purge was accomplished, ousting an estimated fourteen thousand Communists and so-called "radical elements" from government offices, key industries, and the press.

"In no other country has the labor movement been divided and unified so frequently under pressures from above," comments Meiji University professor Saburo Matsuoka. "The main reason for this is that the labor movement got under way in Japan before working-class people really awakened to the spirit of independence."

Matsuta Hosoya, adviser to the National Federation of Industrial Organizations, says much the same thing in different words. "The frequent divisions and reunifications of the labor movement illustrate the general subservience of the Japanese people; it is not in their nature to stand up against their patrons or powerful superiors. Lacking this autonomy, they are swayed as well by trends coming from abroad, such as the Cultural Revolution in China. Riding the crest of the rapid economic expansion, Japanese labor has remained comfortably within the system. But now, the problems of environmental pollution that have quietly developed alongside the expansion leave the unions bewildered. They have, in a sense, cooperated with management in the creation of the pollution problem, but now lack the initiative to make it an object of resistance."

The most durable product of the Occupation's labor policies is Sohyo, the General Council of Trade Unions of Japan. Determined to develop, before the Occupation ended, a labor front matching the American ideal, SCAP played so intimate a role in the creation of Sohyo that it has been called "a child of the Occupation." "Labor officials from SCAP went so far afield in making such fervent campaigns recruiting members for Sohyo that I was finally forced to warn them against direct meddling," recalls Shingo Kaite, former head of the Labor Union Section of the Labor Policy Bureau and now Tokyo bureau chief of the International Labor Organization. Minoru Takano, former secretary general of Sohyo adds: "SCAP was extremely friendly to Sohyo, but we always held the initiative."

In 1951, when Secretary of State Dulles attempted to force Japan to rearm, Sohyo took a firm stand against rearmament and has been sharply critical of American policies ever since. Quoting an old Japanese adage, Takano compares the drastic shift in American policy to "trying to transform a hen into a duck."

The Dodge Plan

SURVEYING black-market price fluctuations for the period between September, 1945, and January, 1947, the Bank of Japan came up with the following rough figures: sugar, soy sauce, and cooking oil had doubled in price; beer, meat, eggs, salt, bean paste, hand towels, wooden clogs, and charcoal had tripled; socks and firewood had increased sixfold. Japan had never before experienced an inflation so extreme as that which raged out of control immediately following the war. Production was at a standstill because nearly all major factories had been destroyed and left unrepaired. Food was so scarce that mass starvation threatened the nation. Prices rose with the speed of a thermometer dipped into boiling water.

The more money the government poured into industry to promote production, the worse the inflation grew. Likewise, all measures to curb consumer buying—the freezing of bank deposits, issuance of new banknotes, suspension of compensation to former munitions industries—were of no avail.

SCAP at first found it impossible to fight the inflation and was as frustrated as the Japanese government in its attempts to control it. Maj. Gen. William F. Marquat, chief of the Economic and Scientific Section of SCAP, suggested taxing new issues of Bank of Japan notes as a means to increase revenue and check new note issues, but this was found impracticable.

Takeshi Watanabe, chief secretary of the Finance Ministry and today president of the Asian Development Bank, requested repeatedly that SCAP put someone better versed in economics in charge of monetary policy for Japan. One day, an adjutant of General MacArthur's whispered to Watanabe that the sort of person he wanted was on the way. On February 1, 1949, Joseph M. Dodge, president of the Bank of Detroit, took over as senior economic adviser to SCAP.

Dodge was to cure Japan's economic ills in short order. He was convinced that inflation benefits only a small minority and should be quickly stopped. He was also determined to put Japan on her feet in order to make her a bulwark against communism. At his very first meeting with Finance Minister Shinzo Oya (now president of Teijin Textile Manufacturing Company), Dodge hinted that he would perform whatever drastic surgery on the Japanese economy that seemed necessary to restore it to health. "Before anything else, the Japanese budget must be balanced," Dodge insisted. "Forget your dreams and start with the most realistic, as well as the most merciless, measures."

"Everyone on the Japanese side at that meeting stared at Dodge in amazed disbelief, and must have wondered: 'What kind of character is this old man?'" recalls Kiichi Miyazawa, minister of Trade and Industry, who was then serving as Oya's interpreter. Hayato Ikeda, who replaced Oya as finance minister and who was later to become prime minister, also realized that Dodge meant business.

Comparing the Japanese economy to a pair of stilts of which one stilt was U. S. aid and the other the practice of paying special grants to encourage domestic industries, Dodge warned: "If you walk on stilts with the steps set too high, you'll fall and break your neck." He proceeded to readjust U. S. aid and ordered the grants to enterprises reduced. Before the budget was established, the government asked Dodge to allow it to honor the election pledges the ruling Democratic-Liberal party had made—tax cuts and increased spending for public utilities. Dodge refused. The result of his strict measures was a balanced budget for 1949, with figures showing in the black. The drastic emergency budget which Dodge had forced on the government touched off heated controversy within the party, and Ikeda was ridiculed as "a phonograph playing a record of Dodge's voice."

"Mr. Dodge felt he had a historic mission: to stop the expansion of government spending which had increased for nearly twenty years since the Manchurian Incident of September, 1931, and to conquer the terrible inflation that was rooted in that expansion," muses Toshihiko Yoshino, director of the Bank of Japan.

Not only did Dodge take command of producing a perfectly balanced budget, he also policed the execution of that budget with constant vigilance. He ordered the Finance Ministry to submit monthly statements of government revenues and spending, scrutinizing the statements carefully to make sure that spending did not exceed income. "We called the statement 'the scroll,' and it was my job to compile it every month," recalls Gengo Suzuki, a former member of the Finance Ministry who is now president of the International Union Bank. He was a frequent visitor to Dodge's office in the Nokyo Building in Otemachi, Tokyo, where he delivered the monthly "scroll" and discussed other economic matters.

The unflinching execution of the Dodge policies brought the raging inflation, at its fiercest early in 1949, somewhat under control. But the drastic credit squeeze that resulted caused a great number of bankruptcies among small- and medium-sized industries. To keep the credit squeeze within tolerable bounds, Japanese industries resorted to a variety of palliatives. "One," recalled Naoto Ichimada, then governor of the Bank of Japan, "was to release central-bank funds from time to time on my own responsibility." Unrest of a new type, different from that caused by the inflation, began to appear in the streets.

Just in the nick of time, a new windfall blew Japan's way in the form of procurement orders to supply the U. S. forces fighting the Korean War. Japanese business picked up at once, but even today Japanese businessmen shudder at the thought of what might have happened if there had been no war in Korea at that time.

Dodge visited Japan three times to continue urging on hesitant government leaders the necessity of a balanced budget and sound fiscal planning. He never wearied of telling the Finance Ministry that it was the responsibility of the government to turn off or on the tap of inflation as necessary. It is clear that the Dodge program proved successful only because it carried MacArthur's authority behind it. And it should not be forgotten that the plan was put into effect without consideration for the small businessmen, who were unable to keep pace with it. Nevertheless, it enabled Japan to steer clear of an economic catastrophe like that suffered by Germany after World War I. Suzuki speaks of Dodge as "a doctor who taught Japan what medicine to take for her economic ailments and how to swallow it regardless of its bitterness."

Today, Japan is plagued by a "stagflation," an illness with the concurrent symptoms of depression and rising prices that is exceedingly hard to fight. To be sure, today's price rises are incomparably milder than those of the years immediately following the war, but housewives and consumers are uneasy nonetheless.

"Return to the Dodge spirit," urges Professor Takeo Suzuki of

Musashi University. "Price stabilization will never come so long as the government shrinks from taking drastic steps out of fear of a mild depression."

Military Justice

TWENTY-FIVE-ODD years have elapsed since the end of the Pacific War, and two famous sites of Japanese war crimes have been transformed into tourist spots. At Santiago Fortress in Manila, guides point through a dark hole to the prison cells below and describe to their fascinated audience how prisoners of war of the Japanese were tortured twice every day by the tide rising in their cells. In a place flooded with strong tropical sunlight, the sight of that dark hole casts a fearful gloom over the hearts of all sensitive observers. The other spot is Pearl Harbor, where the Japanese Imperial Navy assaulted the proud American fleet and ignited the Pacific War on December 7, 1941.

Four years later, December 7 was the day chosen by the judges for sentencing Gen. Tomoyuki Yamashita to death by hanging. As commander of the Japanese forces in the Philippines, Yamashita had been found guilty of the massacre of Philippine citizens in Manila. During his trial before the International Military Tribunal of the Far East at Manila, the prosecution had failed to prove that he had ordered, condoned, or had knowledge of the atrocities carried out by men under him. The remaining issue was whether or not Yamashita had had sufficient control of the unit blamed for the massacre to have prevented it from running amok. Yamashita's American defense lawyer made it clear that the Japanese forces in the Philippines had broken discipline and were stampeding at the time of the Manila atrocities, and that Yamashita had lacked the means of communication by which to control his units. He had been transferred to the Philippines shortly before the Pacific War ended, and the naval unit blamed for the massacre had come under his command only one month earlier. The charge finally brought by the prosecution corresponded, in Japanese legal terminology, to "criminal negligence resulting in death (involuntary manslaughter)."

The prosecution cited the case of a fire on a Connecticut circus ground several years earlier. Flames had spread to the circus tents and spectators had been killed. The circus managers were convicted of negligence for failing to take adequate fire-prevention measures. In the Manila case, Yamashita was to be held accountable on the same grounds.

The tribunal, in explaining its verdict of guilty, said that the arguments of the defense would lead to the inescapable conclusion that Japanese commanders acted in a world holding different standards from those which American generals took for granted. It pointed out that the broad measure of authority vested in commanders "by all armies in history" was accompanied by heavy responsibilities, and that a commander who neglected to make effective efforts to detect and control criminal or unlawful acts committed by his subordinates must hold himself responsible and accept punishment for such acts.

The verdict meant that a commander could be held accountable for failure to prevent units under him from committing atrocities—apart from whether such prevention was in fact possible. It set a precedent in international law for measuring the extent of command responsibility. Before the verdict was announced, twelve reporters of various nationalities covering the War Crimes Tribunal had voted among themselves whether or not Yamashita should be executed. They voted unanimously against the death sentence.

A quarter of a century passed before Japanese could question the real meaning of the verdict passed on Yamashita by the War Crimes Tribunal. The news of the mass murder of Vietnamese villagers at My Lai by U. S. soldiers immediately set Japanese asking the question: "Is not General Westmoreland guilty of the same crime for which Yamashita paid with his life?" In light of standards invoked as those which American generals "took for granted," how can Westmoreland, commander of U. S. forces in Vietnam and a general of the U. S. army, unquestionably one of "all armies in history," be considered free from accountability for the crime?

Professor Telford Taylor of Columbia University argues that Westmoreland had such means of communication as helicopters and radio equipment at his disposal, which Yamashita did not. The U. S. Department of the Army, however, credits Westmoreland with having taken appropriate steps to prevent cruel acts by men under him. Capt. Adolf Reel, the defense lawyer provided for Yamashita, recalls that the court found the Japanese general guilty without considering whether or not the anticruelty orders he had issued were effectual. With such a precedent, Reel believes that Westmoreland is unquestionably guilty.

The troubled soul of General Yamashita is not the only one that is now returning to haunt the American victors over Japan. The defense arguments presented by other Japanese convicted war criminals often sound remarkably similar to more recent pleas by American military men.

1st Lt. William Calley, the first defendant brought to trial in the My Lai case, has protested his innocence on the grounds that he had only obeyed orders. In his memoirs he has accused the U. S. Army of degenerating into an uncontrollable monster of destruction, and has defended himself as no more than a tiny part of it. This is virtually the same defense as that voiced by the 920 Japanese soldiers tried for war crimes and sentenced to death and the 5,472 more who were sentenced to prison terms by the military courts of the seven victor nations in the Pacific War. These numbers do not include the top-level Japanese officers tried and sentenced by the War Crimes Tribunal in Tokyo; most of them were noncommissioned officers or privates who had only obeyed the orders of the monster that was the Japanese army, which had imposed on them absolute obedience to orders of superiors.

One such soldier was tried, convicted, and sentenced to death for making enemy prisoners work at building the Thailand-Burma railroad, made famous by the novel and film, *The Bridge on the River Kwai*. Before he went to the gallows, he spoke with tears streaming down his face: "I am prepared to die, but listen to my last appeal: never start so hideous a war again."

In his memoirs, Calley wrote that he and his fellow soldiers had grown deeply frustrated long before they entered My Lai. Innocent-looking villagers in the area had frequently ambushed his platoon until it was reduced from forty-four men to twenty-four. But My Lai is not the first case to call attention to the terrible frustrations of guerrilla warfare. When an army in uniform tries to fight an enemy disguised as innocent civilians, can criminal acts still be defined by the traditional rules of war? In 1947, Col. Shoichi Yamaguchi, former commander of the Japanese forces defending Negros Island, spoke his final defense in a U. S. military court in Manila. "Fighting guerrillas is like fighting ghosts. I lost most of my beloved men to enemy guerrillas. For three years I fought powerful guerrillas, all the while taking meticulous care not to kill innocent local inhabitants. . . . I appeal to the court to consider, with total fairness, my conscience and my difficulties." Yamaguchi was found guilty and hanged.

Tadao Inoue, a member of the Judiciary and Legislative Department of the Justice Ministry, has spent most of the years following the war in research on the issues raised at the war-crime trials. He comments: "Acts of cruelty in time of war are, to the victims, violations of their rights as human beings. Similarly, what the victor did to his defeated enemy after the war to satisfy, under the guise of justice, his hunger for retaliation was, to the defendants, as great a violation of their human rights."

Are the People Heard?

"I'M SORRY," apologized Prime Minister Sato in lame embarrassment, "that the ministry has given the impression of collusion with industry." He was addressing a special session of the Lower House Budget Committee in January, 1971. Shortly before, Masashi Ishibashi, secretary general of the Japan Socialist party, had made a startling exposure of collusion between the Ministry of International Trade and Industry and a private industrial firm, and the government had been unable to deny the charge. Ishibashi had accused the ministry of assisting the Ishihara Sangyo Company to falsify official records of the date when new facilities—a major pollution source which would have been liable under subsequent legislation—at Ishihara's chemical plant in Yokkaichi near Nagoya first went into operation. Ishibashi's accusation extended beyond this single violation. He kept insisting: "Public officials should fight pollution for the sake of the people. Instead, they are more apt to defend industry every time the pollution issue arises."

It goes without saying that Ishibashi is correct in his insistence upon the responsibilities of public officials. He is only echoing Article 15 of the constitution, which clearly states: "All public officials are servants of the entire community and not of any single group therein."

Soon after the new constitution was written in the autumn of 1946, an American administrative reform mission headed by Blaine Hoover was invited to Japan by SCAP and set to work democratizing the Japanese civil service. After studying the system for half a year, the mission diagnosed the civil service as being in an advanced state of illness. SCAP acted on the diagnosis, and in June, 1947, thrust upon the government an English draft of a Law on National Public Service Workers, ordering that the Diet pass it without altering a word or phrase. This law listed the emperor, prime minister, and ministers of state, in that order, as national public-service workers.

"We were shocked," recalls Kiyoshi Asai, then chairman of the Temporary National Personnel Commission and later president of the

National Personnel Authority. "We pleaded with GHQ until it relented and removed the emperor from the list." The law, drafted by Hoover, stressed that civil-service workers, being servants of the people, should be politically neutral. This gave birth to the National Personnel Authority, an organ independent of the government, designed specifically to guarantee the neutrality of public servants. It was to prevent any repetition of the prewar situation in which the bureaucracy became intimately linked to the military and the *zaibatsu*.

"But in spite of this, the only question about public service that really interests both the government and the opposition is the right of government servants to strike. They argue passionately about it, and forget all about real public service," laments National Personnel Authority president Tatsuo Sato.

To break the Japanese habit of placing government above the people, SCAP tried one device after another. One was the Merit Examination for Higher Officials, conducted in the autumn of 1949. All higher civil servants were required to take the examination; it was also open to nongovernment men. Its purpose was to open the doors of the bureaucracy to a wider variety of applicants; Tokyo University graduates had long held a monopoly of the higher positions in the bureaucracy, but they would now have to compete with men from private universities in an equitably administered examination. The questions included in the exam were deliberately unconventional. An example of one of them: "What would you do if an office boy accidentally spilled tea on the section chief's desk?"

A section chief who passed the exam could replace a bureau director who failed it. A career diplomat with a Tokyo University diploma failed the exam, and Kiichi Aichi, then director of the Banking Bureau in the Finance Ministry, quit in protest over "the disgusting atmosphere that has taken over government offices." He was foreign minister until the cabinet reshuffle of 1971. Other prominent government men also abandoned the bureaucracy for politics or business at about the same time.

The determination to allow the will of the people to be reflected in government led to the importation of numerous American institutions intact or in slightly modified form. Among them were the "deliberative councils" that sprang up like mushrooms after a rain: various commissions like the Fair Trade Commission, and such investigating boards as the People's Examination of Supreme Court Justices. Alfred Oppler, chief of the Legal Section of SCAP, wanted to add another: he ordered Tosuke Sato, vice-minister of justice at the time, to create an American-style grand jury system that would

[184]

examine accusations filed against people charged with serious crimes and hand down indictments if the evidence warranted them. But Japan could not afford the enormous expenditure that would be necessary to maintain permanent grand juries. After much deliberation between American and Japanese legal authorities, a compromise system was worked out: a Board of Review of Procuratorial Actions for each district court. If the prosecutor for a district court drops his case against an accused person before bringing him to trial, a citizen dissatisfied with that action may request the board to review the case. If the board considers that the evidence warrants a trial, it can advise the prosecutor to reopen the case. Board members are picked at random from voter-registration lists. A recent Supreme Court survey shows that cases reopened on the recommendations of the boards amount to only 18.5 percent of the total number of dropped cases. Many Japanese doubt whether the boards, made up of laymen with no particular knowledge of the law, are qualified to act as watchdogs over procuratorial justice.

The institution of public hearings was another import from America during the Occupation. Today, however, the institution has grown so ineffective that it seems no more than a stage where the government can cynically make a pretense of listening to the demands or opinions of the people.

The democratization of public administration has not been standardized in the central and local governments. Perhaps this is only natural, since the central government, as the maker of policy, deals primarily with the Diet and the political parties, while local governments are in constant communication with the public at the grassroots level.

In 1970, Mayor Kiyoshi Matsumoto of Matsudo, Chiba Prefecture, made headlines when he created a "Do-It-Now Section" in his municipal government. This was to bring more efficient service to the people, and Matsumoto claims to have gotten the idea from American government offices where "the man at the counter does things on his own judgment and authority, and most papers require only his signature." Matsumoto went on to explain: "But in most government offices in Japan, the man at the counter puts his seal on a paper, then passes it to his immediate superior, who does the same thing and then passes it on. On and on it goes in this fashion until it finally reaches the man at the top. But if anyone along the way up happens to be away from his desk, the paper will sit there until he gets back. That only makes for delay and the citizen suffers needlessly." At Matsudo's new "Do-It-Now Section," the man at the counter efficiently handles the matter on his own responsibility, and later reports to his superiors.

The Matsudo "Do-It-Now Section" is an example of how the local elections that occur every four years have made local governments more attentive to the wishes of the constituency, more polite and more obliging than in the era before democratization. But relations between the national bureaucracy and the people is a continuing problem. How are high-ranking officers, unelected and governing on a plane far removed from the common people, to remain responsive and responsible? "They feign political neutrality but ally themselves totally with the ruling party because there is no risk of a change in regime in the foreseeable future," charges Tokyo University professor Kiyoaki Tsuji. The Diet and the parties are supposed to keep their eyes on the bureaucracy, but actually they often find themselves manipulated by it. And there is no question that today the bureaucracy is an important reservoir of manpower of the ruling conservatives.

It seems, then, that the Occupation's radical program of democratization of public administration has barely affected the Japanese bureaucracy at its highest levels.

The Socialists in Power

IN APRIL, 1947, on the day after Japan's first general election under the new constitution, the secretary general of the Japan Socialist party was traveling from Osaka, the constituency where he had stood for election, to the party headquarters in Tokyo. Sitting in the train, Suehiro Nishio worried about his own election and how the party as a whole had fared; he had predicted that the Socialists would finish second, at best. Upon arriving at Tokyo Station, his first question to party members waiting to meet him was: "Did I get in?"

"Better than that," they replied. "The Socialists have won the election." Nishio was amazed at the party's success and at his own miscalculation. He had already drawn up the party's official postelection statement, but he certainly had no regrets about the necessity for changing it to accord with the unexpected victory.

On May 25, 1947, Tetsu Katayama, the chairman of the Socialist party, became prime minister. He took the reins of government confused and unprepared. "But I had the purity, naiveté, and straightforwardness of youth to guide me," recalls Katayama, who was sixty years old when he became prime minister. His coalition cabinet began its life with an impressive mandate—the support of nearly sixty-nine percent of the people. It preached austerity to a nation struggling to recover from defeat, and the cabinet ministers, for once, practiced what they preached. They all came to work carrying lunch boxes. One brought his lunch in a beautiful antique tea-ceremony carrying case, but the food was as coarse and scanty as that of his colleagues.

It is amusing to recall that, in 1947, the Occupation authorities greeted the new Socialist cabinet with open arms, leading political scientists to speculate on how the United States would react to the election of a Socialist government in Japan today. "The reaction probably would not be as hostile as to the Castro regime in Cuba, but at least as hostile as it has been to Chile's Marxist president Salvador Allende," guesses Gerald Curtis, a specialist in Japanese politics and associate professor at Columbia University.

In 1947, General MacArthur congratulated Prime Minister Katayama on his election, noting that the three great nations of Asia—Japan, China, and the Philippines—were all now headed by Christians. The response of SCAP to the new Katayama cabinet was no doubt much warmer than it would be today, but one need not seek far for reasons. The Occupation had already purged nearly all prewar and wartime political and military leaders, and had encouraged labor to unionize. Organized labor had already grown so strong that a general strike scheduled for February 1, 1947, could be stopped only by MacArthur's personal order. The labor offensive remained strong, and SCAP hoped to find a cushion against it in the new cabinet, a middle-of-the-road regime that made a careful distinction between socialism and communism. Thus, the development was well suited to the Occupation's democratization programs. An analogy may be drawn between SCAP's attitude toward the Katayama cabinet and that of U. S. military authorities in Okinawa, who have sought to use Chobyo Yara's moderately progressive government for their purposes ever since agitation for the return of Okinawa to Japan began gaining momentum.

As chief cabinet secretary of the new government, Suehiro Nishio experienced considerable difficulties in steering the Katayama regime, which was actually a three-party coalition of the Socialist, Democratic, and People's Cooperative parties. Whenever he entered the prime minister's official residence for a cabinet meeting, he would find ministers lost in the corridors and searching for the meeting room. This is perhaps only symbolic of their inadequacies. The cabinet ministers had been skilled fighters in the proletarian movement, but few had the

[187]

necessary administrative experience for running the bureaucratic machinery.

The cabinet needed most urgently a deputy cabinet secretary who could handle the complicated liaison duties with SCAP, but such a man was apparently not to be found. Assistance finally came from SCAP itself: the Occupation headquarters knew of an unusual man in the Foreign Ministry who had the guts and the stubbornness, as well as the mental and verbal acumen, that the position seemed to require. Still another point in his favor was the fact that Shigeru Yoshida, the former conservative prime minister, did not much like him and had "banished" him to a comparatively obscure post in Kyushu. The man was Eki Sone, and he was appointed deputy secretary of the cabinet on SCAP's recommendation. He and Nishio soon became fast comrades.

SCAP helped bail the Katayama cabinet out of other difficulties, as well. Once, when a government bill was experiencing rough sailing in the Diet and seemed about to run aground, Justin Williams, chief of the Diet Division in SCAP's Government Section, gave Nishio some shrewd advice: "Stop the clock in the plenary session chamber until the bill goes through." Ever since then the conservative governments have frequently resorted to the same tactic in fighting opposition to their bills.

The Katayama cabinet, on which high hopes had been pinned initially, soon began to exhibit the usual weaknesses of coalition governments, and its public support declined rapidly. It was forced out of office after only eight months, the direct cause of its downfall being a revolt by the leader of the Socialist party's leftist faction, who also headed the Budget Committee in the Lower House. Mosaburo Suzuki brought down the coalition regime by rejecting its budget. He had earlier warned SCAP, guardian of the cabinet, that if it wanted to keep the government in office it should order that the budget be revised. SCAP did not act on the warning.

When Katayama reported his resignation to SCAP, MacArthur asked the fallen prime minister whether he would not carry on a while longer. Katayama declined. He had once been excited by MacArthur's advice that Japan should try to remake herself into a thoroughly neutral nation, "the Switzerland of the Orient." But almost before that phrase became widely known, it ceased to issue from the Occupation policy-makers. Perceiving the subtle changes that were taking place within the Occupation as the cold war progressed, Katayama decided he had better not stay too long in office. "I had been looking for a chance to quit," he reveals today, "because I was afraid that the Occupation was about to reverse its stand and order Japan to rearm."

Following the fall of the Katayama cabinet, SCAP needed another middle-of-the-road government and helped the succeeding Ashida cabinet into being.

Since the downfall of that first short-lived Socialist government, the Japan Socialist party has been kept out of power. Many of its members agree that the party came to power prematurely, and that that initial blunder has prevented any great resurgence of strength. The party has also been fragmented by factionalism. Its leftist faction subscribes wholeheartedly to the view expressed in the booklet *The Twenty-Year Record of the Japan Socialist Party*: "The party deviated from its doctrine and platform to the disillusionment of the people. This has contributed in large measure to the perpetuation of the conservative regime, which only later came to real power."

But Katayama, well into his eighties, has no regrets as he looks back over his career in politics. The only way the Socialist party can return to power, he advises today, is by submerging its minor differences for the greater common purpose.

SCAP at Odds with Itself

AT BOOKSTORES across the country recently, a book called *Dilemma in Japan*, written by Andrew Roth and published in Japanese translation by the Shinko Publishing Company, went on sale. It was written twenty-five years ago. During the Occupation, Iwanami, another publishing firm, kept listing it as "a forthcoming book," but it never appeared. It joined the long list of speeches and publications suppressed by SCAP on the grounds that they were harmful to, or critical of, Occupation policy. This particular book was banned, not because it was critical of Occupation policy, but because it *was* Occupation policy condensed into book form. The prosecution and punishment of war criminals, abolition of the special security police, dissolution of the *zaibatsu*, encouragement of rights for labor, educational reform, land reform—these and other details of the Occupation administration were included in the book. It has been rumored that even the members of the Government Section of SCAP, originators of the American policies, pored over the book as though it were a handbook of what they were trying to achieve. It seems obvious, then, that SCAP felt it would be showing too much of its hand if it allowed the book to be published.

Roth, a progressive critic, was twenty-eight years old when he wrote the book immediately after Japan's surrender in 1945. The "dilemma" of the title was the choice the United States would have to make in occupying Japan. Roth saw two possible courses for Occupation policy: either to delegate the governing of the nation to the leaders of the "moderate factions," who were believed to have opposed the militarists before the war, or to allow the "democratic minority" (the progressive factions) to take control of Japan's government. Roth explained that the former was the easy course, but it would bring only immediate gain. It could not democratize Japan permanently or make a peaceful nation of her. He doubted that the "moderates" were truly against the imperialistic expansion of Japan; sharing the objectives of the military, they were opposed only to the use of "rough methods" in the expansion. Thus, Roth advocated the latter alternative. Although parliamentary democrats, social democrats, agricultural reformers, Socialists, and Communists were minorities, he believed that they could be united into a "majority faction" based on medium- and small-scale entrepreneurs, technicians, industrial laborers, and farmers.

An account of the formation of the Ashida cabinet and its collapse only seven months later will illustrate how closely the Occupation's Government Section adhered to Roth's "manual," and how it came to grief for it.

The Katayama coalition cabinet fell in February, 1948, due to internal dissension over the national budget. In the period of uncertainty and indecision that followed, it took Hitoshi Ashida a month to organize a new cabinet. Like its predecessor, the new government was a three-party coalition linking the Socialist party, the People's Cooperative party, and Ashida's own Democratic party; in fact, critics dubbed it "a prearranged switch among the partners of the previous coalition." Whether or not Ashida himself would have qualified for membership in Roth's "progressive faction" is questionable, but he could answer critics of this relaylike rearrangement of the coalition by claiming that he had received the blessing of SCAP. Indeed, shortly after the formation of the new cabinet, the Government Section reaffirmed that the transfer of power to Ashida was fully in accord with democratic principles.

Ashida's regime was toppled, after barely more than half a year in office, by the Showa Denko case, an infamous scandal that exposed corruption at all levels of the Japanese political, bureaucratic, and business worlds. For the first time in Japanese history, cabinet members were implicated for accepting bribes from the huge Showa Denko chemical manufacturing firm, and some went to prison. The Ashida cabinet was nicknamed "the Kosuge cabinet," after the site of one of Tokyo's prisons. The scandal also spawned the adage: "Politics costs money."

"Implicating Ashida as it did, the scandal dealt a crushing blow to the middle-of-the-road progressives," says Eki Sone, deputy cabinet secretary in the Katayama cabinet and today a Democratic Socialist member of the Lower House. A number of other graft cases came to light at about the same time, and by the end of 1948 thirty more members of the Diet had landed in Kosuge Prison.

After a trial that stretched on for four years, nearly all defendants in the Showa Denko case, including Ashida, were acquitted. But questions remained as to how the scandal had started and how it had spread so far, implicating so many people in high places. Rumors of scandal had begun to be whispered about even while the Katayama cabinet was still in office, and informed sources suspected that the Ashida cabinet would be toppled by it even before it had been installed.

They were right. Anonymous tips made public the government ties with Showa Denko. Still, many observers would agree with Takeo Miki, president of the People's Cooperative party at the time, that many crucial facts did not emerge during the trials and that the case remains shrouded in mystery. The consensus is that the story that was never told has something to do with dissension within the Occupation and the campaign of the G-2 Section (intelligence) against the "pinkos" in the Government Section. The two offices had constantly been at odds over how Occupation policies should be executed, and G-2 had begun implying that communist infection was spreading through the Government Section. These accusations, as well as other major shifts in Occupation policies for Japan, must be read in the cold-war context in which they were occurring. Initially urging demilitarization and neutrality—encouraging Japan to become "the Switzerland of the Orient"—American policy had gradually shifted to economic rehabilitation and finally to rearmament, whereby Japan might serve as a bulwark against the communist world. The outbreak of the Korean War in June, 1950, provided the most dramatic shove, but tendencies in that direction had been gaining momentum for several years.

It is suspected by many that some Japanese tipped off G-2 to the involvement of the Ashida cabinet and other members of the government with Showa Denko, and that this inspired the probe that erupted into scandal. If G-2's assertiveness within SCAP was behind the case, it also forced what Roth called the "progressive faction" (including those members not directly involved in the scandal) off the political scene and permitted the rise to power of the "moderates," who had been close to G-2.

When Ashida's government fell, many expected that Shigeru Yoshida, president of the "moderate" Liberal party, would be picked to form the next cabinet. But to the Government Section, Yoshida symbolized resistance to Occupation policies, and it had little taste for him. It first approached Takeo Miki, but he was uninterested in the premiership at that time. The Government Section next asked Takeshi Yamasaki, secretary general of the Liberal party. He attempted to form a cabinet, but was generally ridiculed for his bungling, unsuccessful efforts. Frustrated in its efforts to find an alternative, the Government Section reluctantly approved Yoshida. His second cabinet, which replaced Ashida's on October 15, 1948, established the power of the conservatives (Roth's "moderates"). They have maintained their supremacy until the present. Yoshida's own political longevity lasted through five cabinets, until he resigned in 1954; until his death thirteen years later, he played the role of "elder statesman," with continuing influence over the more active participants of successive Japanese governments.

Once in office, Yoshida took upon himself the task of "correcting the excesses of the Occupation policies." When MacArthur was relieved of his command in April, 1951, and replaced by General Matthew Ridgway, Yoshida's first request of the new supreme commander was the withdrawal of the purge directive of 1946, which had removed from office all men whom SCAP had considered undesirable. Yoshida went about his work assiduously, and was charged by the progressives with following an undemocratic "reverse course."

Today, Yoshida's direct political descendants are entrenched in the Liberal-Democratic party and proudly call themselves the "conservative main current." They are led by Prime Minister Sato. In the autumn of 1970, Takeo Miki, a "side current" man, challenged Sato by running for the party presidency but was defeated. It has not been forgotten, however, that the present "main current" was not always just that. Had the background situation been different, others might well be riding the "main current" today.

"Merchants of Death"

SHOTARO KAMIYA, president of Toyota Motor Sales Company, was greeted by a great commotion when he landed at Los Angeles Airport on the evening of June 24, 1950. News of the outbreak of war in Korea had just been announced. For a second, Kamiya wondered whether he would ever get home safely. One thing that never occurred to him was that this war would bring a new lease on life to Toyota, not to mention the enormous effect it would have on the entire Japanese economy.

Toyota was then saddled with a large unsold stock created by the balanced-budget and credit-squeeze policies of Joseph Dodge, General MacArthur's economic adviser. It had been trying to lay off its surplus labor force but was being beleaguered by resistance from labor unions. Kamiya was seeking a way out of the crisis and had come to America to negotiate a possible tie-up with the Ford Motor Company. He was disappointed by Ford's lukewarm response. Ford had picked five men to send to Toyota, but the Department of Defense had abruptly refused them permission to go to Japan because they would be needed at home for the war effort.

When Kamiya returned home two months later, he was amazed to find Toyota plants swamped with work. What had happened in so short a time? Order upon order had been received from the Defense Department for trucks for U. S. forces in Korea. In July, 1950, the second month of the war, Toyota received the first order for 1,000 trucks. By March of the following year the orders totaled 4,679 trucks. When Kamiya had left Japan in June, Toyota's production of trucks was a mere 304 a month; in March, 1951, production jumped to 1,542, an all-time high. Toyota declared a twenty percent dividend for its shareholders, the first paid since the end of World War II.

"Those orders were Toyota's salvation," Kamiya reminisces. "I felt a mingling of joy for my company and a sense of guilt that I was rejoicing over another country's war." At that time production was limited largely to trucks, but, saving sufficient reserve funds from the American orders, the Japanese automobile industry returned to passenger-car production, and its history since then has been one of unparalleled expansion.

In 1970, without the benefit of any link with Ford, Toyota's exports to the United States rose to about eighteen thousand vehicles a month, eighty percent of them passenger cars. In the same year, Ford began negotiations for a tie-up with Toyo Kogyo Company, another Japanese automaker.

The procurement orders—as orders to supply American forces in Korea were called—for goods and services in the first year of the war totaled $329 million in value, roughly forty percent of Japan's total exports for 1950. Orders over the next five years, reaching an estimated $1.62 billion in total value, ranged from ordnance, coal, automobiles, communications equipment, textiles, and other manufactured products, to services for building-construction, warehousing, and installation of telegraph and telephone equipment. The procurement orders enriched big Japanese industries, subcontractors, and back-street cottage industries alike.

In one representative incident, soon after the Korean War began, five Japanese manufacturers of gunny sacks were asked to come to the U. S. Army Procurement Office in Yokohama. The officer in charge announced: "We need all the gunny sacks you have, and we need them urgently for making combat sandbags. It doesn't even matter if they're used. Name your price and we'll pay it." The makers jumped at the offer, feeling as though they were living through a fantastic dream. Until then they had barely eked out a subsistence by making sacks for rice at a small price. They would have made a profit selling the bags for ten cents each, but the U. S. Army paid them twice that for the first few lots, and then went on to order more than 200 million sacks. One-fourth of the orders were taken by Nippon Matai Company; the following year the company was able to increase its work force from thirty people to five times that number and its equipment from thirty to one hundred sewing machines. With the profits from the continued procurement orders, Nippon Matai diversified its business, and today it is a well-established medium-sized company employing more than one thousand people.

The Tokyo yards of Higashi Nippon Heavy Industries, now Mitsubishi Heavy Industries, repaired and rebuilt U. S. military vehicles under the direct supervision of the military. Its shops were the first to obtain American conveyers and forklifts, as well as the benefit of careful guidance in integrated operations and plant maintenance by more than one hundred military men and army civilians regularly stationed there. "Everyone in the plant, from the foreman down, was given a chance to learn a mechanized, integrated process," recalls Toshio Miyahara gratefully. He was then production manager of Higashi Nippon Heavy Industries and is now an executive director of Mitsubishi Motors Corporation.

Of all the procurement orders pouring into Japan for the war effort in Korea, about ten percent were for ordance, the largest single item. The Japanese arms industry, demolished by the defeat in the Pacific War, was quickly restored to healthy activity. "We were branded 'merchants of death' for manufacturing arms for the Americans," says Minoru Yamada, vice-president of Daikin Kogyo Company, "but there was no other means to insure the survival of the enterprise." In addition to manufacturing arms, new standards and maintenance techniques were learned and proved useful in repairing the used American weapons with which the Japanese Self-Defense Forces were equipped during their early days. The Korean War served, thus, to provide vocational re-education for Japan's arms industry.

With the exception of the Pacific War, the economy of modern Japan has grown fat on each war that followed the Sino-Japanese War of 1894–95. The war in Vietnam has also brought business to Japan, although such business today is not so desperately needed as it was in the early 1950s. Still, each step toward peace in Vietnam today sends the New York stock market up and brings the market down in Tokyo. "Paradoxical though it may seem, it was under the postwar pacifist constitution that the tradition that war brings economic prosperity to Japan and a better life for her people was revived by the Korean War," says Yoshio Ando, professor of Japanese economic history at Tokyo University. "Japan's deliverance from destitution by war in a neighboring country, just at the moment when the Japanese were turning pacifist, has subtly influenced her later attitude toward peace."

There can be no question that the procurement orders of the Korean War were exactly what the Japanese economy needed to tide it over depression and direct its course away from the "stabilization panic" that was expected. The procurement orders led to the biggest economic boom in the nation's history and paved the way for the later high economic growth rate. "Divine aid" was what Naoto Ichimada, governor of the Bank of Japan, called the procurement orders.

But Hiromi Arisawa, professor emeritus of Tokyo University, sees them as "a drastic, quick-working medicine" that produced only the immediate result of a rapid, but temporary, economic recovery. From a long-range point of view, the orders may prove to have been poison. Restored to health by this speedy palliative, Japan was spared the rigors of a "stabilization panic," which perhaps it ought to have suffered to insure its lasting economic health. That is why, despite the high growth rate, individual Japanese enterprises still have little capital and suffer heavy losses in profits whenever bank loans are cut down or slowed. This has become a chronic ill. Rooted in it, among

[195]

many other things, are the pollution problems and the fact that Japan is lagging in the developing of social capital.

Birth of the Self-Defense Forces

TWO WEEKS after the outbreak of the Korean War, Katsuo Okazaki, secretary of the cabinet, and Takeo Ohashi, minister of justice, tried in vain to puzzle out the meaning of a phrase in a note from General MacArthur that had just been delivered to them. What was the meaning of the "police reserve" that the supreme commander was writing about? The two men finally went to GHQ for an explanation, and as they were leaving the Occupation headquarters they whispered to each other: "It sounds like an army that can't be sent overseas." It was at this moment that the Japanese Self-Defense Forces—bastard offspring of the Korean War—were born.

Although both were creations of Occupation policy, the land and sea branches of the Self-Defense Forces were born through very different processes. "There is no real break between the old Imperial Japanese Navy and the postwar Maritime Self-Defense Force," asserts James Auer of the Fletcher School of Law and Diplomacy, who is currently writing a doctoral dissertation on the establishment of the Maritime Self-Defense Force. Extensive interviewing in Japan revealed to him the continuity with the old navy. "About the only difference between the Imperial Navy and the MSDF is that the MSDF bans drinking on board ship."

Immediately after disarming the Japanese army and navy, the Occupation ordered the creation of a special minesweeping unit of about 15,000 former navy men and 350 vessels that had survived the war. The unit was to clear Japanese waters of the estimated 12,000 live mines that had been dropped around Japan by B-29 bombers in the closing days of the war. Clearing the mines was a long and arduous process, one requiring infinite care and patience and involving risks that occasionally proved fatal. The mines first had to be located by small wooden ships dragging magnetized electric wires. Then they were hauled away on cables by larger "sacrifice ships." The operation continued until the end of the Occupation, taking a toll of seventy-seven lives from mines that exploded accidentally.

The minesweeping operation was carried on as secretly as possible. Ever conscious of a provision in the Hague Treaty banning the use of lethal weapons by combatants after the cessation of hostilities, the Occupation suppressed all news of the casualties. Kyuzo Tamura, now a vice-president of Ishikawa Manufacturing Company, directed the difficult and dangerous operation that is still unsung and largely unknown. "Despite all the difficulties, the morale of the men never waned," he recalls. "They knew that Japan would never be able to resume trade with the rest of the world if her waters remained mine infested. They carried on in fine, traditional navy spirit. Not a single mine was ever discovered in any area after they finished their work there and it was officially declared mine free."

Full of admiration for the techniques and diligence of this Japanese minesweeping unit, the U. S. Navy later ordered it to clear the waters off Korea immediately before the landings at Inchon and Wonsan. About twenty of the Japanese minesweepers took part in this vital operation in Korean waters, and there was some loss of life, but details were again suppressed by the Occupation.

When the Maritime Safety Agency was created in May, 1948, on orders from SCAP, acting on the recommendation of an adviser from the U. S. Coast Guard, it received special permission to employ a maximum of ten thousand former naval men. This is revealed by Takeo Okubo, its first director and today a member of the Lower House. MSA patrol ships would also have been armed if SCAP's initial plans had not been quashed by strong opposition from the Soviet Union and Australia voiced in the Allied Council for Japan. "Without guns, the only way we could catch smugglers was to go alongside with a patrol boat and send our men jumping over into the other boat carrying clubs," recalls Okubo. "Remembering that the U. S. Navy had been born out of the Coast Guard reassured me that a new Japanese navy would someday be born by a similar process."

He was right. The Maritime Self-Defense Force developed as an offshoot of the Maritime Safety Agency. But it also owes its birth to the energetic efforts of a group of ex-naval officers soon after the Korean War began. In January, 1951, the group, headed by former Vice Admiral Zenshiro Hoshina (now president of the Japan National Defense Society) presented to the U. S. Far East Naval Command, and later to John Foster Dulles, a plan to rebuild the Japanese navy that the group had been quietly nurturing since the days immediately following the defeat. The United States responded with an offer of sixty-eight naval craft, including frigates. The Japanese government then asked former Rear Admiral Yoshio Yamamoto, now chairman of the board of Ito Iron Works, to arrange for acceptance of the ships. Yamamoto accepted the duty on the provision that the ships be considered "a small navy." The next step was the recruitment of officers for this "small navy." A group of thirty former commanders and lieutenant commanders was recruited and billeted in a warehouse on the site of the prewar Naval Torpedo School at Taura; they commuted daily to the American naval base at Yokosuka for study and training. Out of this initial group have come today's top officers of the Maritime Self-Defense Force. Prominent among them are Vice Admiral Sugaichi Itaya, chairman of the Joint Chiefs of Staff; Vice Admiral Suteo Ishida, deputy chief of the MSDF General Staff; Rear Admiral Tatsuo Tsukudo, head of the MSDF Cadet Academy; and Vice Admiral Tatsuhiko Ishikawa, Commander of the Fleet.

Compared to the gradual, well-prepared birth of the Maritime Self-Defense Force, the Ground Self-Defense Force, which began as the Police Reserve, sprang suddenly into being: as a result, its infancy was full of confusion. Although the Police Reserve could attract enough men for the rank and file—largely because of the attraction of a retirement offer of sixty thousand yen that is said to have been the brainchild of Prime Minister Yoshida—it had a hard time finding officers. One of the first officers was Tsutomu Sakamoto, who resigned as a reporter for NHK to join the Police Reserve. Recalling the early days of the reserve, he says: "Men who knew English were picked to command battalions because one of their main functions was to translate the drill commands of the U. S. military instructors to the men. 'Rightabout-face' was a two-motion turn, American-style. The drill manual was a verbatim translation of the U. S. text. 'Eyes right!' was translated literally as *'manako migi!'* In the old army it had been *'kashira migi!'* [head right]."

For a long time a curious anomaly was to be seen in the GSDF's system of appointing officers. Its origins lay in SCAP's purge order of January 4, 1946, removing from public life large numbers of men considered "undesirable," including former military officers. Later these men were depurged. In the case of former servicemen, depurging began with the lowest ranks and worked up. The GSDF officer corps was filled by former officers of the Imperial Army, and certain regulations permitted the old ranks to survive intact. Thus, as the officers were depurged from the bottom upward, GSDF officers often found themselves suddenly outranked by newcomers who had been of higher rank in the old army. Sakamoto was demoted successively from corps commander to division commander to regiment commander to regiment staff officer in order to make way for newly depurged officers who had outranked him in the Imperial Army.

The Maritime Self-Defense Force claims emphatically that it is a continuation of the old navy. The Ground Self-Defense Force disclaims just as emphatically any link to the old army. Both, however, were brought into being on orders from SCAP and owe their growth to American help and guidance. The GSDF refers, with a certain measure of self-contempt, to its establishment by American command as "the secret of our birth." It resents the haste with which it was brought into being, contrasting it with the West German army, created only after thorough advance preparation. It is further troubled by identity conflicts: its role as a "link in the chain of U. S. military strategy in the Far East" has an unpleasant ring in the ears of many of its members. That characterization of the force is being challenged by the naive nationalism now on the increase among young GSDF men.

Ironies of Occupation

THE OCCUPATION era—aside from the special character of the relations of victor and vanquished—was a time of broad, as well as intimate, contact between two entirely different cultures. From the personal encounters between various individuals of both nations emerge numerous incidents of lasting interest. The following are a few such moments in the vast drama of the period:

The View from the Rooftop. "To see the suffering they brought upon their fellow countrymen, one need only walk a few steps to the roof of this building." This statement is drawn from the opening address of Joseph B. Keenan, the chief prosecutor for the War Crimes Tribunal, as the trial of General Hideki Tojo began. The building where the trials were being held now houses the headquarters of the Ground Self-Defense Force.

Later that same day, the defendant Tojo wrote this rebuttal from his prison cell: "To see what the victor, professing dedication to the cause of justice, did to innocent noncombatants one need only walk to that same rooftop and look down at the total devastation wrought by the indiscriminate air raids on Tokyo."

Twenty-four years later, the surrounding ruins long since transformed into a dense forest of skyscrapers, a famous Japanese novelist shouted from a balcony high on the very same building at Ichigaya in Tokyo: "Deluded by economic prosperity . . . Japan has entrusted her national defense to foreign hands. We have never been cleansed of the shame of defeat, but merely deceived." Yukio Mishima's harangue was drowned out by heckling from the GSDF men who had gathered below. Their laughter ceased abruptly when they heard that Mishima, immediately after stepping back into the building, had killed himself in a solemnly executed hara-kiri.

Consultant Service.   Soon after the end of the war, a group of men who were well versed in American affairs and had access to GHQ got together to form a "service agency." Among them were Kazushige Hirasawa, now a news commentator for NHK; Takizo Matsumoto, late member of the Lower House; and Shintaro Fukushima, now president of the Kyodo News Service. Their agency's primary business was advising people which office in GHQ to visit to discuss specific problems, or whom to contact. Matsumoto's wife recalls that the agency was used most by people wondering how to go about applying for depurging. Her husband, who had free entry to GHQ, busied himself on behalf of the purgees day after day. They never paid for the service, and financial difficulties eventually forced the agency to close. At a time when our present "information-oriented society" was yet to be born, this short-lived company was Japan's first information agency, not to mention her first postwar bankruptcy.

The Three Freedoms.   Robert B. Textor was only in his twenties when he was appointed chief of the Education Division of the U. S. military government in Wakayama Prefecture. Calling himself "walking democracy," he was committed to President Roosevelt's Four Freedoms, and dedicated himself to making them understood by the Wakayama public. He hit upon the device of distributing handsome posters illustrating the freedoms. He managed to design appropriate pictorial images of Freedom of Speech, Freedom of Faith, and Freedom from Fear. The last, Freedom from Want, had him stumped. What point was there in preaching freedom from want when there was never enough food to go around? He abandoned the last and settled for posters of only the first three freedoms.

After he returned to America, Occupation policies shifted in emphasis and intent. Textor wrote a book entitled *Failures in Japan* criticizing the Occupation for abandoning most of its reforms half-completed.

Reunion.   Miss Eleanor Hadley kept a relentless watch over the dissolution of the *zaibatsu* from her office in the Economic Section of

GHQ. One of her toughest opponents was Hideo Edo, General Affairs Department deputy manager of the Mitsui Main Office (now president of the Mitsui Real Estate Company). In trying to defend Mitsui from forced dissolution, Edo engaged in frequent, intense arguments with Miss Hadley. Several years ago, they met again at the Mitsui Club in Tokyo, and the following conversation took place:

"The Japanese *zaibatsu* have been completely broken up, just as you wished," began Edo.

"That's just not true," replied Miss Hadley. "Look at Mitsui Real Estate, which you head. Its majority shareholder is Mitsui Bank and its board chairman a Mitsui Bank man. Right?"

"That's true, but the bank has no control of how we run our business."

The argument went on in this fashion for several hours, but Miss Hadley left unconvinced. She had obtained a doctorate with a dissertation on trustbusting in Japan, and was apparently still conducting research on the subject.

Momentary Pause. SCAP officials from the Civil Information and Education Section acted as advisers and radio program directors for NHK during the Occupation. With their experience in commercial broadcasting in America, where every second of radio time means money, they grew terribly impatient with the momentary pauses taken by NHK announcers in mid-sentence or between sentences. They were constantly urging the announcers to speed up their speech and to stop making the pauses. The general impatience was fully shared by 2d Lt. Ralph Hunter, a handsome young radio man who originated the Japanese versions of the "Man in the Street" public opinion program and "Twenty Questions."

Every time announcer Shuichi Fujikura took a short pause while broadcasting, Hunter would jab a finger in his back and shout: "Dead air again!"

"I always felt pushed by a sense of driving urgency," recalls Fujikura. "I would almost guess that Japanese radio announcers got their habit of talking so fast from the Americans."

Sazae-san. The beginning of the Occupation saw MacArthur replace the emperor as supreme ruler of Japan. His headquarters in the Dai Ichi Life Insurance Building was located just across the moat from the Imperial Palace. Americans were surprised at how little resistance the change provoked among Japanese people.

"The Japanese had grown accustomed to the phenomenon of dual

[201]

authority," explains Chie Nakane, a cultural anthropologist at Tokyo University. "During the long Tokugawa period, and earlier, they witnessed dictatorial military governments, with the emperor relegated to a background role." Whenever MacArthur and Emperor Hirohito met, it was the emperor who had to travel out to the interview.

When MacArthur was abruptly relieved of his position in April, 1951, many Japanese were shocked to learn that there was a power higher than the general. Others looked with a certain wonder at a country that could fire summarily a commander so highly decorated with military honors. "I realized with admiration how firmly established was civilian control of the armed forces in the American system of government," recalls critic Michio Takeyama. "I could not help contrasting this with the Japanese government before and during the war."

"After MacArthur was relieved of his command, I expected that he would come to see the emperor once before he left for home," says Takeshi Usami, director of the Imperial Household Agency. "I gazed expectantly over the pine groves in the palace grounds at the Dai Ichi Building across the moat. But he never came. It was just like MacArthur not to do what was expected."

On the very day the American five-star general left Japan, the serial cartoon *Blondie*, which had run for years in the *Asahi Shimbun*, was replaced by *Sazae-san*.

The Price of Peace

JAPAN is a seagirt land, and one favored with abundant rainfall— two facts which inspired in the Japanese the confidence that "security and water cost nothing." This curious point is made by Isaiah Ben-Dasan in his best-selling book, *The Japanese and the Jews*.

Since the war, Japan has insured her national security with the United States and has sought to have the "premiums" kept small. It is time that we look once again at the circumstances of this arrangement and the background against which the insurance policy was drawn up.

The San Francisco peace treaty was signed "uneventfully" on September 8, 1951. Immediately after the signatures had been affixed to the historic document, U. S. Senator John Sparkman congratulated

John Foster Dulles, the architect of the treaty, and asked: "Just when did you first receive Truman's orders to arrange this peace with Japan?"

"A year ago to the day," answered Dulles. "I told the president that it would take me a year to get it done."

"About what time of day was it?" was the senator's next question.

"Exactly at noon."

Sparkman took out his pocket watch and announced with some wonder: "It's now eight minutes to noon."

A year earlier, at the beginning of September, 1950, soon after the United States had launched a full-scale counteroffensive in the cold war, including the landing at Inchon in Korea, President Truman unified divided opinion within his administration and announced the decision for an early peace with Japan. With a detailed timetable in hand, Dulles set out on his labors to accomplish independence for Japan "within the framework of the larger U. S. strategy in the Far East." It was not to be a peace signed by all the former belligerents, only a sort of semipeace designed to permit Japan to restore diplomatic relations only with the nations of the free world. The thought of arranging a preliminary international conference, attended by the Soviet Union and other communist nations, to discuss a peace treaty with Japan never occurred to Dulles. Carrying his briefcase, he traveled from Europe to Asia, from Asia to Oceania, visiting Japan's former enemies in the noncommunist world and diligently peddling his formula for peace.

From the outset of the Occupation, the United States had been sending up trial balloons to test a variety of plans for peace with Japan. The State Department had taken to heart General MacArthur's warning that "any policy for occupation will collapse under its own weight in three years' time."

But the problem of guaranteeing the security of an independent but unarmed Japan was Washington's greatest obstacle to effecting a peace treaty. In February, 1950, when Finance Minister Hayato Ikeda went to Washington to plead for an early peace, high officials of the State Department are understood to have indicated to him that, with the Soviet blockade of Berlin and other critical problems, the United States had her hands full defending Europe and was in no position to devote particular attention to Japan's security. This seemed to imply that the end of the Occupation and Japan's independence were still far off.

At home, the Occupation-weary Japanese public was divided into two schools on the type of peace treaty considered most desirable:

[203]

those advocating a total peace and those favoring separate treaties between Japan and each of her former enemies. The total-peace school urged peace with all former belligerents—the United States, the Soviet Union, and China included—as the best guarantee of Japan's future security. Leading this opinion was the Conference on Peace Issues, comprised of well-known intellectuals who criticized the militarism that had led to World War II and strongly supported the pacifism of the new constitution. The concept of a separate peace would, they were convinced, result in binding Japan to one of the two parties of the cold war, and thereby intensify that war.

The opposition to this view was led by the conservatives under Prime Minister Yoshida, who held that the actualities of the cold war ruled out all possibility of total peace, at least for the time being. Separate peace, or "majority peace" in the conservative terminology, was the only route to Japan's early independence.

While visiting Japan in June, 1950, immediately before the outbreak of the Korean War, Dulles pressed Yoshida to agree to Japan's rearming. Yoshida rejected the idea, pointing out the economic impossibility of rearming, the intense distaste of the Japanese people for the very thought of bearing arms again, and the easily predictable reaction of the rest of Asia to Japan's reassuming any military capacity. "For the time being, at least, Japan can hardly consider rearming," concluded Yoshida.

It was in these circumstances that the framework of the present security system was constructed. Japan would provide bases to the United States in return for continued protection even after she had been granted her independence. Under this U. S. defense shield, Japan would be progressing toward a piecemeal rearmament. Yoshida had previously reached an understanding with MacArthur on this plan, which later came to be called the "Yoshida-Dulles formula." When the guns began to roar across the thirty-eighth parallel in Korea, Truman decided to conclude peace with Japan on the basis of this formula.

One of the basic principles underlying the San Francisco peace treaty was that Japan would maintain her security through cooperation with the United States. Article 5 reads in part: "The Allied Powers for their part recognize that Japan as a sovereign nation possesses the inherent right of individual or collective self-defense . . . and that Japan may voluntarily enter into collective security arrangements." Article 6 continues: "Nothing in this provision shall . . . prevent the stationing or retention of foreign armed forces in Japanese territory under or in consequence of any bilateral or multilateral agreements which have been or may be made between one or more of the Allied Powers, on the one hand, and Japan on the other."

What the United States was driving at was "security" rather than "peace." Nevertheless, Yoshida was convinced that popular support could be rallied to the idea of an early peace, despite its price of the continued presence of U. S. armed forces, as preferable to an interminable continuation of the Occupation.

" 'We haven't got a minute to lose,' Yoshida told me gruffly in the car immediately after the peace treaty was signed," recalls Kenji Fukunaga, a Liberal-Democratic member of the Lower House who accompanied Yoshida to San Francisco. "We rushed back to where we were staying, ate a light lunch, and then dashed right out again to an army installation in the city. There the prime minister signed the security pact." It had been agreed earlier that the Japanese-American Mutual Security Treaty would be signed in either Washington or Tokyo at an opportune occasion sometime after the peace had been concluded. But both peace treaty and security pact were signed on the same day in San Francisco.

Normal international practice usually requires that an occupation force withdraw from the occupied country within ninety days of the signing of a peace treaty. But, with the immediate signing of the security pact, Dulles had accomplished what he needed for his Pacific policy: the privilege to continue, without any hiatus, the stationing of American forces in Japan under the new name of "Security Garrison Force."

This virtual continuation of the Occupation, despite Japan's newly gained independence, has cast a dark psychological shadow over the Japanese people. It has also divided, and continues to divide, the nation into two camps on the issue of renewing the security arrangements. It is this inability to achieve national consensus on critical diplomatic issues that remains the basic determinant of the political chart in Japan today.

"The best peace treaty is the one most quickly forgotten," goes an often-quoted saying. But the San Francisco peace treaty has never been forgotten. It is an unfortunate fact of Japanese political life that the treaty is remembered on almost every occasion involving Japan's relations with the rest of the world.

No Chinese in San Francisco

PRIME MINISTER Sato, on a state visit to Washington in November, 1969, obtained President Nixon's pledge to return Okinawa to Japan. His long-cherished objective accomplished, he then began a round of sites historically associated with the destiny of postwar Japan.

Sato first visited Arlington National Cemetery to stop at the tomb of John Foster Dulles, architect of the peace treaty which had ended the Occupation and which had defined Okinawa's legal status during the post-Occupation years. Next, he went to the San Francisco Opera House, where the peace treaty had been signed eighteen years earlier. To the prime minister, this sentimental journey undoubtedly symbolized the end of Japan's postwar period. On numerous occasions he had defined the period and what would end it. Not long before, he had stated in the Diet: "The postwar era will not end for Japan until we have achieved the reversion of Okinawa."

But in that much-quoted statement he was overlooking his country's greatest postwar problem: China. The country most aggrieved by Japan in World War II had not been invited to join the San Francisco Peace Conference, and as a result, normal ties between Japan and continental China had yet to be restored.

In preparing for the peace conference, the United States intended first to invite the Nationalist Chinese government to attend. Britain objected, insisting that the Peking regime, which she had recognized, be invited instead to represent the Chinese people. Dulles probably would not have heeded an objection of this sort coming from the Soviet Union, but he could not ignore the stand taken by Britain, America's staunchest ally. He flew to London to try to settle the dispute and managed to work out a compromise formula acceptable to Downing Street. Neither the Taiwan government of Chiang Kai-shek nor Mao Tse-tung's Peking regime would be invited to the conference, and Japan would have to arrange later a formal peace with one regime or the other of her own choosing. The Anglo-American disagreement caused Prime Minister Shigeru Yoshida, a dyed-in-the-wool Anglophile, to sigh to his aides: "How difficult it is to serve two masters at once."

Yoshida was a career diplomat with strong views of his own on the China question. When he learned of the compromise formula worked out by Dulles in London, he argued strongly against the American secretary of state's firm determination to "contain" China. But Dulles was too conscious of the blood then being shed by American boys in a fight against Communist Chinese volunteer forces on the Korean peninsula to be swayed. He brushed aside all Yoshida's protests, and Yoshida—always the "realist politician"—remonstrated no further. Thus, in September, 1951, the Chinese flag was notably absent from the banners of fifty-one nations adorning the stage of the San Francisco Opera House as the peace treaty was signed.

After the conference, Yoshida returned to Japan to confront vigorous debate in the Diet. "Which Chinese government will Japan choose to make peace with, Taiwan or the mainland?" repeated the opposition parties insistently, demanding an answer from Yoshida on the "homework" he had temporarily put aside. At first, with his conversations with Dulles on the containment of the communists strong in his memory, Yoshida deliberately kept his replies ambiguous. Gradually, however, his vague answers began to change into statements that might be taken to indicate that Japan was considering a rapprochement with Peking. On October 29, 1951, for example, Yoshida announced to the Upper House Special Committee on the Peace Treaty: "Japan will have to decide, from a position of realistic diplomacy, whether or not to recognize the People's Republic of China. At the moment, the government is thinking of opening trade relations with that country and of establishing a commercial office in Shanghai."

This statement agitated the pro-Taiwan segment of the American Congress. A shocked Dulles rushed immediately to Tokyo together with several senators, including John Sparkman of Alabama. "If you make any overtures toward recognizing Peking," Dulles threatened Yoshida, "I can promise you that the peace treaty will never be ratified by the Senate." Yoshida apologized for having created any misunderstanding, to which Dulles replied, like the lawyer he was: "That's all right, but please put it in writing." The Japanese prime minister was thus railroaded into writing a letter to the effect that Japan was prepared to open normal relations with Nationalist China.

"If Mr. Yoshida had never made that statement in the Diet, Dulles would not have rushed to Tokyo, and the peace treaty would have been ratified without a hitch," muses Kumao Nishimura, then director of the Treaty Bureau of the Foreign Ministry and later ambassador to France. He had been charged with drafting the letter that Yoshida sent to Dulles. "The choice of which China to recognize could then have been decided independently, after the peace treaty went into effect."

The Yoshida letter was publicly announced by Senator Sparkman at the opening of Senate deliberations on the peace treaty in January,

1952, and it was favorably received by American politicians. However, its publication immediately impelled Peking to accuse both Washington and Tokyo of a naked provocation of war against China. It was against this background that, on April 28, 1952—the very day that the peace treaty went into effect—Japan signed a peace pact with the Nationalist government on Taiwan that has forced later Japanese governments to regard the communist mainland as a "remote neighbor."

While the Japanese and American governments have adhered stubbornly to the Dulles principle that China must be contained, the actual world situation has changed so drastically that the inevitable question is now being asked in Japan: "Did Japan really consider the Taiwan regime the official representative of China, as prime ministers from Yoshida to Sato have said she did, when she signed the Sino-Japanese pact?"

It is at this point in the critical international drama that another Yoshida draft letter emerges from the safe in the Foreign Ministry where it has hibernated for more than twenty years. After his arguments with Dulles over the peace-treaty formula in April, 1951, a disgruntled Yoshida had apparently written a letter intended "to educate Americans on the China problem." This document refers to the Nationalist government in unmistakable terms as a "mere local regime with authority over no more than Taiwan and the Pescadores." It continued: "Temperamentally, the Chinese people will not be converted to communism. Rather than attempt to contain China, the United States would do far better to maintain regular contacts with the mainland in order to sell democracy to her." The draft letter also mentions the possibility of an armed uprising occurring on the mainland.

In 1951, the Foreign Ministry had advised against sending the letter, fearing that it might touch off further international difficulties. This advice was heeded, and the letter was consigned to a safe. "Had Japan not been still under occupation at the time, Mr. Yoshida, with his characteristic stubbornness, would no doubt have made the same points in his arguments with Dulles as he later wrote in that letter," say high officials of the Foreign Ministry who have seen that the letter was safely preserved.

In view of his present stand on China, how does Sato, who considers himself one of Yoshida's favorite disciples, reply to this? Early in 1971, Aiichiro Fujiyama, a Liberal-Democratic member of the Lower House and former foreign minister, was dispatched to Peking, where he conferred with Premier Chou En-lai and other Chinese leaders. In a press conference upon his return to Japan, Fujiyama was asked: "We recall that as foreign minister you worked for renewal of the Japanese-American Security Treaty in 1960. Don't you consider it contradictory that you should now be urging formal ties between Japan and China?"

"I have inherited the conviction of my father Raita," Fujiyama countered adroitly, "that Japan should live amicably with both the United States and China. The Chinese government is not opposed, in principle, to Japan's participation in a collective-security system."

The Pacific War grew out of a struggle between Japan, on the one hand, and the U. S. and China, on the other. Can we believe, then, that the postwar era has ended with the reversion of Okinawa? Or must we wait for genuine, peaceful coexistence to be achieved among Japan, the United States, and China before we can emerge from the postwar era into a new age?

PART FOUR

Postwar Diplomacy

Prime Minister Shigeru Yoshida was known to recount, with some glee, how one day, early in the Occupation, his official car had been flagged down by a young GI demanding a ride into Tokyo. Amused, and unable to refuse a request from a member of the occupying army, Yoshida opened the car door and invited the American to sit beside him. In return for the lift, the GI offered him a candy bar and some chewing gum.

The relationship of occupier and occupied illustrated by this incident was officially terminated in April, 1952, when the peace treaty that had been signed in San Francisco the previous September went into effect. "Whereas the Allied Powers and Japan are resolved that henceforth their relations shall be those of nations which, as sovereign equals, cooperate in friendly association . . ." the peace treaty had stated, but whether or not Japan could, in fact, act independently was a very different matter. The articles collected here reveal the complex reasons for her hesitation, during the years immediately following the peace treaty, to emerge from the unbalanced master-servant relationship of the Occupation and to lay claim to her newly gained autonomy. They also trace, through glimpses of the activities of diplomats, scholars, and businessmen, the increasing confidence of Japan's movements vis-à-vis the United States during the late 1950s and the 1960s.

The American ambassadors sent to Japan during this period were men of very different personalities and backgrounds, and each was confronted with very different problems. Robert Murphy, the first of them, was charged with overseeing the delicate transition from military occupation to nominal autonomy, and had to do so while a war was being fought in Korea with rear support from Japan. Armin Meyer, serving as ambassador at this writing, nearly twenty years later, has had to negotiate the return of Okinawa to a far more self-assured Japan and also to oversee Japanese-

American relations amid intensified economic competition. Between the ambassadorships of these two men occurred the long build-up of tensions that erupted in the 1960 riots over the Security Treaty, the difficult aftermath of those events and the adjustments they necessitated, and the speedy industrial and social rehabilitation that has sustained Japan's "economic miracle."

The Japanese side of the relationship has been borne by men of equally diverse character, the behavior of each influenced by his unique memories of the war and the Occupation years. The earliest Japanese ambassadors to the United States took up their posts with Prime Minister Yoshida's "suicide theory" in the back of their minds: at least the first three of them would have to struggle so hard to convince the Americans of Japan's desire for autonomy that they might have to commit suicide in Washington to underline their determination. Fortunately, no such drastic act proved necessary. Still, the consecutive conservative Japanese governments—while seeking full independence of action—felt themselves constrained, on the one hand, by a fear of offending the United States and, on the other, by a rising tide of popular Japanese nationalism.

The United States government, deluded by the obsequiousness of Japanese politicians and diplomats and insensitive to the pulse of the Japanese people at large, was astounded at the outcry greeting the renewal of the Security Treaty in 1960. Nothing had prepared America for the intensity of popular opposition; indeed, many Americans were hardly even aware of the existence of an opposition in Japan. Aside from the immediate issues of the security arrangements, the more important implication of these events was that the official channels of communication had failed so thoroughly to carry the dialogue that was their function.

Conflicts of interest and differences of opinion are to be expected between two nations as ambitious and self-centered as Japan and the United States. But, in trying to deal with the serious problems that plague their relationship, each country has been remarkably unable to achieve a balanced, reasoned perception of the other. Too often, Japanese-American attempts at dialogue have been characterized by hysterical overreaction or unpardonable ignorance and insensitivity. Are the cultural differences that are usually blamed truly so great as to be fully responsible for the deep abysses in mutual understanding? Who is to blame? The diplomats of both countries for working so hard—with sophisticated devices and highly trained staffs at their disposal—to listen to each other and yet somehow failing to understand what is being said, or their home governments for disregarding the advice of their appointed representatives?

The "Lawrence of Africa"

WHEN ASKED which year in the history of modern Japan was the most important politically, one observer answered without hesitation that it could only be 1952. The man answering the question, Robert D. Murphy, was himself a protagonist in the history of that year and the years following.

On April 28, 1952, the San Francisco peace treaty went into effect, and Japan began life anew as an independent nation. At 11:55 P.M., with only five minutes of that historic day remaining, Murphy arrived at Haneda Airport to take up his post as the first American ambassador accredited to the Japanese government since the beginning of the war, his immediate predecessors having served as chiefs of SCAP's Diplomatic Section. At the airport to meet his plane was Gen. Matthew B. Ridgway, whose title had changed that day from Supreme Commander for the Allied Powers to Commander of U. S. Forces in Japan. The Occupation had officially ended, and Ridgway's new position was head of the American "Security Garrison Force," which would remain in Japan under the provisions of the Security Treaty signed in San Francisco by Japan and the United States on the same day as the formal peace treaty. The peace treaty had brought Japan independence, but an independence in which she remained under virtual occupation, for there was no change in the fact that foreign troops remained on Japanese soil.

His choice as ambassador to Japan surprised Murphy as much as it did the Japanese, who were expecting someone well versed in Japanese affairs. Although a diplomat of long standing, he had not distinguished himself by any particular experience or knowledge of the Far East. His last post had been in Brussels. During the war, he had made a name for himself by his daring intelligence maneuvers preceding Allied landing operations in North Africa. So outstanding had been his contributions there that he had won the nickname "Lawrence of Africa," after T. E. Lawrence, whose exploits as an intelligence officer for the British in Arabia during World War I are legendary.

Japan had emerged from military occupation when Murphy took

up his post in Tokyo, but she was still far from free of the American
military presence. Her situation made her critical to the prosecution
of the war in Korea, and Murphy notes in his book, *A Diplomat
Among Soldiers*, that he was probably selected as ambassador because
he was known to get along well with the military. Just before
Murphy's appointment, Assistant Undersecretary of State John M.
Allison, later to serve as his successor at the Tokyo embassy, had told
Congress: "Japan holds the key to victory or defeat in the fight
against communism in the Far East."

Murphy had a record of vigorous anticommunist work in Europe,
and it was obvious that Washington expected him to be instrumental
in guiding Japan's rebirth as an anticommunist stronghold. During
his term in Tokyo, he was reunited with an old friend, Gen. Mark
Clark, who replaced General Ridgway as commander of the U. S.
forces in Japan. Earlier in their careers, Murphy had saved Clark from
capture by German military police in Algiers by hiding him in a
basement just before the Allied landing in North Africa. The general's
Tokyo headquarters were located very near the U. S. Embassy, and
the former soldier-diplomat team from North Africa was "in business" again, this time for an anticommunist offensive in the Far East.

In Murphy's personal library, alongside books on the American
Occupation of Japan and kabuki, were works on the operating methods
of the communists. To Japanese businessmen and political leaders
alike, Murphy preached a total and uncompromising anticommunist
doctrine. A typical example might be the sentiments regarding trade
with China that he expressed in a speech to a group of business leaders
at the Tokyo Chamber of Commerce and Industry: "I can hardly
comprehend why Japanese business seeks to trade with continental
China, a trade which would serve only to strengthen the fighting
potential of communism. Would it not be a far better policy to cooperate in the effort to check communist aggression?"

Bearing secret State Department orders to prepare for the reopening of normal relations between Japan and the Republic of Korea,
Murphy flew to South Korea. "Although my official functions are
restricted to Japan, Washington strongly wishes me to rove farther
afield, beyond the actual framework of my duties." Relations between
Japan and South Korea were re-established later, but obviously preparations were begun during Murphy's Tokyo days for the building
of the sort of anticommunist bulwark as that described as late as 1969
in the Sato-Nixon communiqué on the return of Okinawa: "The
President and the Prime Minister specifically noted the continuing

tension over the Korean peninsula. . . . The Prime Minister stated that the security of . . . Korea was essential to Japan's own security."

"There could hardly have been a better choice than Mr. Murphy for a role in the building of an anticommunist bulwark in Japan," comments Shigeharu Matsumoto, director of International House of Japan. "However, it was also Mr. Murphy who first began talking about 'equal partnership' with Japan—a term which became fashionable only much later when Professor Reischauer was ambassador." Yasusaburo Hoshino, professor at Tokyo University of Arts and Sciences, takes exception to this view and claims that "equal partnership" was no more than an empty phrase at that time. "During the Murphy era there was nothing that could be called Japanese-American diplomacy in the true sense of the word. Everything proceeded under Pentagon control, as part of the general Far Eastern policy of the United States."

Under Murphy's ambassadorship, the size of the Tokyo embassy grew dramatically. Embassy buildings contained a staff of five hundred American employees, eight hundred Japanese, and a host of military attachés. "U. S. foreign policy invariably sets priorities in the following order: military, political, economic; Japan was no exception to the rule," says Kazushige Hirasawa, a news commentator for NHK. "However, since the war Japan's own foreign policy has been precisely the reverse. It is this difference of priority that seems to be at the heart of all tensions in Japanese-American relations." The choice of Murphy for the Tokyo post, by his own admission because of his good relations with the military, was thus but another illustration of this pattern in U. S. foreign policy.

Murphy eventually handed over his stewardship of the anticommunist setup that dominated Japanese-American relations to John M. Allison. During Allison's tenure as ambassador, the joint security arrangements were improved and strengthened by such new provisions as the Mutual Security Assistance Pact. But meanwhile, a clear anti-American sentiment had sprung up among the Japanese people. Its first dramatic appearance came only three days after Murphy's arrival, in the violent May Day riot in the Imperial Palace Plaza in 1952.

MacArthur II

TWO AMBITIOUS diplomats arrived in Tokyo in quick succession in 1957 and 1958. First came Douglas MacArthur II, the third postwar American ambassador to Japan; he was soon followed by Nikolai T. Fedorenko, the Soviet ambassador. For a time, Tokyo diplomatic circles hummed with gossip of the two ambitious career men, both rapidly on the way up. But events later in MacArthur's stay in Japan, particularly those surrounding the 1960 revision of the Japanese-American Security Treaty, probably did more harm than good to the advance of his diplomatic career.

Washington's choice of the nephew and namesake of Gen. Douglas MacArthur for the Tokyo post was carefully calculated to take advantage of the lingering personality cult that had developed around the former supreme commander during the Occupation. But the nephew was forced to grapple with the problem-ridden legacy of his uncle's Occupation, and it was a far from easy task. Japanese nationalism, rising rapidly as a reaction to the Occupation, was focusing pressure on the Security Treaty, viewed by many as an "unequal treaty," the likes of which Japan had not been subjected to since the Meiji era.

There are many in Japanese diplomatic circles who, even in retrospect, rate highly Ambassador MacArthur's abilities in negotiating the revision of the Security Treaty and handling other diplomatic issues. "Mr. MacArthur transmitted Japan's wishes and claims ably and obligingly to Washington through his own well-laid pipeline," recalls former foreign minister Zentaro Kosaka. "If I were to characterize him in a word or two, I would call him a single-minded individual," says Hisanari Yamada, former deputy foreign minister. "When the Defense Department was objecting to the 'prior consultation' clause in the revised treaty on the grounds that it gave Japan what amounted to a veto power, it was MacArthur who managed to ram the clause down the Pentagon's throat." Perhaps the greatest approval of all, at least on the Japanese side, came from former prime minister Yoshida himself when he described MacArthur as "more a Japanese ambassador than an American one."

But regardless of the appraisal of his abilities, it is clear that Ambassador MacArthur was consistently striving to instill ever more vitality into the pro-American regime in Japan. As a result, the meaning of the mass movement gradually rising in opposition to the Japan-America defense arrangements proved utterly beyond his comprehension until it exploded into bloody riots when the revision of the security pact was forced through the Diet by the ruling Liberal-Democratic party in 1960.

President Eisenhower was scheduled to make a state visit to Japan in June, 1960, the occasion being designed to add the final touches to the process of bolstering the pro-American image of the conservative government. But with the mounting popular agitation against the treaty revision, a presidential visit began to seem inadvisable, and later even dangerous. Nevertheless, Ambassador MacArthur continued to fire off message after message to Washington urging that the president not cancel or reschedule his visit. Eisenhower's trip was essential, argued MacArthur, to save Japanese democracy from threats to its very existence: if he did not come, the Kishi cabinet would collapse and radicals would come to power.

Early in the development of the popular rising against the treaty revision, Shigeharu Matsumoto, well known as an internationalist, had urged the Japanese government to send an invitation to the American president. He had been worried about the deteriorating relations between the two countries and believed that a state visit could do much to repair them. Matsumoto's advice was qualified, however, by a particular condition: President Eisenhower should be invited only if he would visit Japan on his way home from a visit to the Soviet Union, scheduled to follow the Soviet-U. S. summit talks in Paris. Matsumoto had every reason to expect that the American president would be hailed in Russia as an apostle of peace, and hence that his visit to Japan could hardly be criticized by Japanese leftists. The general public seemed to react favorably to the welcome-for-Eisenhower program that got under way at the time.

But these well-laid plans were suddenly demolished by an event which almost no one could have foreseen. An American U-2 plane was shot down on a reconnaissance mission over Soviet territory and its pilot captured. This spy incident wrecked the summit talks, as well as the peace-loving image that the United States was trying to project. "If not for that U-2 incident, the history of recent Japanese-American relations might well have been very different," sighs Matsumoto.

With the summit talks called off, an alternative plan was arranged to include Japan in an enlarged itinerary which would take Eisenhower on a round of visits to anticommunist countries in Southeast Asia. When the visit to Japan was imminent, Matsumoto came to the American Embassy together with Yasaka Takagi, a noted American-ologist, and Shinzo Koizumi, former president of Keio University. The three influential Japanese intellectuals strongly advised that the presidential visit be canceled due to both the intensifying mass protests and the fact that the visit would be interpreted simply as a gesture of support for the Kishi government, thus causing further difficulties. But Ambassador MacArthur turned a deaf ear to their arguments and outtalked them until the three left angrily. As the pitch of the protests against Eisenhower's visit rose higher, with even Christian groups and scholars who had studied in America joining in the opposition, MacArthur was reduced to impotent anger, asking: "Where are the pro-American intellectuals at a critical moment like this? What are our so-called friends doing now?"

The waves of demonstrations increased daily, but the Kishi cabinet, still anxious for an Eisenhower visit, summarily dismissed the disturbances as "an international communist plot." The American ambassador echoed the Japanese government until the Hagarty incident on June 10, 1960.

When U. S. Presidential Press Secretary James C. Hagarty arrived in Japan to finalize preparations for Eisenhower's visit, his limousine was swarmed at the airport by angry students and he was trapped in it until rescued by police. This extreme incident finally caused the Kishi cabinet to request that President Eisenhower not come to Japan until the mass demonstrations subsided.

What especially angered some Americans involved in the planning for the presidential visit was the attitude of their own ambassador. A Secret Service agent recalls that MacArthur did no more than give vague assurances, such as advising that the student demonstrations not be taken too seriously. According to the agent, when MacArthur continued to insist on the Eisenhower trip, even on the day the bloodiest riot occurred, his opinion ceased to be regarded as that of an expert.

There is no doubt that the Tokyo riots and the cancellation of President Eisenhower's visit shocked Americans. But, by and large, they heard only about the "communist plot" and the "anti-American struggle." They knew little, if anything, about the threat to democratic government posed by Prime Minister Kishi's political tactics. They were not told that many of the Japanese who joined the demonstrations were impelled to do so not by any anti-American sentiments, but out of fears for the future of parliamentary democracy in Japan.

Few Americans could grasp the meaning of one tiny incident that occurred in the midst of the demonstrations swirling through Tokyo streets. A crowd of demonstrators noticed blond amateur actress Linda Beech, who was starring in a popular television series, standing on a street corner in Kasumigaseki, near the government buildings.

The demonstrators' grim faces loosened into friendly smiles of recognition as they passed, and they waved and called out: "Hi, Linda-san!"

But failure to understand the real meaning of such a moment is not necessarily due to misinformation from an American ambassador and his staff unable to read the Japanese mind. It is perhaps better seen as part of the McCarthyism that conditioned Americans to view anyone not an anticommunist as an enemy of the United States. Or it may have been an illustration of the "demon theory" in action, what Columbia University professor Richard Hofstadter has called "the narrow-minded American trait of taking a decisive incident not as part of the march of history, but as the result of some plot."

Soon after the end of the struggle against the security-pact revision, a young army man arrived in Japan on a military assignment. It quickly became clear to him that the image of the Tokyo riots painted for him at home was very different from the Japanese realities that he was witnessing firsthand. After his discharge from the army, he returned to Japan as a journalist, determined to transmit his image of the country to Americans. Samuel Jameson, now Tokyo bureau chief of the *Los Angeles Times*, is one of the few foreign newsmen in Japan fluent in Japanese.

It was a professor of Japanese studies at Harvard University who described the Tokyo riots as a "broken dialogue" between the United States and Japan. His comments on the deep seriousness of the break caught the notice of the newly elected president, John F. Kennedy, and led to his choice of the man to replace MacArthur as ambassador to Japan. The professor-diplomat, Edwin O. Reischauer, proved to be an extraordinary ambassador indeed.

The "Kennedy-Reischauer Offensive"

"I SHOULD like to perform the ordinary functions of an American ambassador to Japan. At the same time, I hope to have heart-to-heart talks with Japanese people all over the country and be able to inform my home government what the Japanese are actually thinking and feeling." These were the words of Harvard professor Edwin O. Reischauer as he was about to leave his academic duties in the spring

[219]

of 1961 to take up his new position as American ambassador to Japan.

A year earlier, the mass demonstrations against the revision of the security pact—the Tokyo riots, as they were known in America—had created the most severe strain in relations between the two countries since World War II. President Kennedy, in his campaign, branded the U-2 incident and the cancellation of President Eisenhower's Japan visit as the two greatest diplomatic blunders of the Republican party. To recover the enormous diplomatic losses of 1960 in Tokyo, Kennedy was determined to select as ambassador the person best qualified to speak the American half of the Japan-America dialogue. The State Department, sensing this, announced that it would oppose the choice of anyone from outside the Department for the Tokyo post. At that time, Tokyo and Moscow were considered the two most attractive posts for career diplomats.

When the Harvard professor of Japanese studies, whose wife was Japanese, was first mentioned as a likely candidate for ambassador to Tokyo, the State Department rose in a body against his nomination. According to Arthur M. Schlesinger's *Thousand Days: John F. Kennedy in the White House*, the State Department tried to justify its opposition to Reischauer by quoting the Japanese Embassy as indicating disapproval of an American ambassador married to a Japanese. Perhaps this sort of opposition strengthened Kennedy's determination that Reischauer was the best man for the job.

Born and raised in Tokyo, fluent in speaking, reading, and writing the Japanese language, married to a Japanese, a distinguished scholar of Japanese history and literature, the new ambassador was affectionately dubbed *Edokko taishi* ("Tokyo-born ambassador"). What he said and did in making his rounds of all but seven of the forty-six Japanese prefectures, meeting more than fifty thousand Japanese of all walks of life during his more than five years in office, have already found a place in recent Japanese history. Here only a few examples must suffice:

—One of Reischauer's first statements, upon arriving in Tokyo in April, 1961, is that he feels as though he has come home.

—Shortly after taking up residence at the embassy, Reischauer quips to the Japan-America Society that his new home is in the same Tokyo ward where he was born.

—Reischauer displays his skill at bowling at the Tokyo International Trade Fair. American manufacturers of bowling equipment were struggling at the time to develop a Japanese market for the game, not yet so popular in Japan as it has since become.

—Reischauer expresses his admiration after riding on the still experimental "dream express," the bullet train of the Japan National Railways, which opened to public use in October, 1964. The fastest train in the world, the express travels the 320 miles between Tokyo and Osaka in three hours and ten minutes.

—Reischauer enjoys a meal of sukiyaki made with high-quality Matsuzaka beef in February, 1964. Shortly thereafter, the Japanese government lifts its ban on the export of Japanese beef to the United States.

—In March, 1964, Reischauer is stabbed by a deranged nineteen-year-old youth. The incident leads to the implementation of new measures to care for the mentally ill. Later, when the ambassador contracts hepatitis from a blood transfusion, a wave of investigations into the procedures for donating blood and processing it is set off. While recovering, Reischauer says from his hospital bed: "I have received so much Japanese blood through transfusions that I've now become truly part Japanese." Prime Minister Ikeda takes advantage of the first television transmission by satellite from Japan to the U. S. to apologize to the American people for the attack on Ambassador Reischauer.

Despite Reischauer's conviction that the basic Japanese and American aims and interests coincided, strains and tensions were developing between the two countries. In his view, the difficulties and misunderstandings were due as much to the "extremely unrealistic thinking of Japanese intellectuals" as to the fact that Americans limited their contacts largely to English-speaking businessmen and conservative politicians. He himself made a point of meeting and talking with Japanese intellectuals, opposition politicians, and common people. These efforts, sustained by the missionary zeal that was his birthright, won the epithet of the "Kennedy-Reischauer offensive." When told of the term, he claimed to be honored by it.

On a trip to Washington in July, 1963, Reischauer told Congress that the real enemy of the United States in Japan was classical Marxism, and that he would not miss the opportunity to attack it whenever he could. This prompted *Izvestia* to shoot back: "Once upon a time, Ambassador Reischauer's father founded a school for the deaf and dumb in Japan. What a pity he did not enroll his own son in it. Perhaps then the son was not quite so deaf to the feelings of the Japanese people as he now seems to be." It should be immediately clear who was on the defensive in this instance.

What finally stopped the "Kennedy-Reischauer offensive" was neither a Soviet counteroffensive nor an attack from the Japanese left, but, ironically, America's own foreign policy. The escalation of the

Vietnam war and particularly the start of the bombing of North Vietnam in February, 1965, touched off widespread skepticism in Japan of U. S. Asian policies and, indeed, of the moral integrity of the United States itself.

Ambassador Reischauer returned home to warn Washington of the effect the Vietnam war was having on Japanese-American relations. When he came back to Japan, however, he defended American policies in Southeast Asia and took the Japanese press to task for its partiality to North Vietnam. His "offensive" lacked conviction this time.

After J. Kenneth Galbraith, also a Harvard professor, resigned as U. S. ambassador to India in protest over the Vietnam policy, there were constant rumors that Reischauer was about to do likewise. But he stayed on at his post. He explained later that one reason for not resigning was his continuing love for Japan. Another was that his resignation, which would inevitably have been taken as a sign of his opposition to Vietnam policy, as Galbraith's had been, would have served only to disrupt further the troubled relations with Japan. Professor Masaru Ikei of Keio University believes the latter to be the chief reason that Reischauer refused to follow Galbraith's example. After Reischauer did finally resign in the fall of 1966, he began gradually to express criticism of Washington's Southeast Asian policies. Many Japanese today agree with Ikei that the ambassador long held such views, even while he remained in office.

The main reason that Washington could disregard Reischauer's warnings about the effect of Vietnam on relations with Japan was that the Japanese government continued to avow its support of U. S. policies. The ambassador's warnings were soon followed by a statement by Takezo Shimoda, Japanese ambassador to the United States, that "Japan was giving quiet support" to American policies. Which of these two ambassadors conveyed the real sentiment of the Japanese people? How, in the absence of a man like Reischauer, would Japanese public opinion have been reflected in American policies toward Japan? Kiichi Miyazawa, former minister of international trade and industry, praises Reischauer as the only foreign ambassador to be in communication with Japanese at all levels of society. The fact that he was able to keep up that sort of dialogue with the Japanese people raises the question of how future relations between Japan and America should be conducted, regardless of what the content of the future dialogue might be.

At sixty-one, Reischauer now lives in a suburb of Boston and holds the special academic rank of University Professor at Harvard. Disclaiming any intention of ever re-entering government service or of becoming an ambassador again, he continues to display all his former vigor in the private promotion of Japanese-American relations.

Straight Talk and Quiet Diplomacy

"RELATIONS between Japan and the United States cannot be considered apart from all of Asia. Henceforth, the two countries should cooperate in carrying out Asian policies." This was the theme of a speech by U. Alexis Johnson to the Japan-America Society in Washington shortly before he took up his new post as ambassador to Japan in the autumn of 1966. In plain words, he called upon Japan to awaken to the hard realities of the situation in Asia and to begin living up to her responsibilities as a member of the free world. This was a new voice in the dialogue between the United States and Japan. "My predecessor, Dr. Reischauer, and I are different men. Each of us has his own strengths and weaknesses. I intend to do things my own way. . . ."

Ambassador Johnson arrived in Japan amid a rising tide of public criticism of American intervention in Vietnam, especially the bombing of the north. At the same time, political slogans demanding the reversion of Okinawa had begun to be heard frequently. President Johnson had decided that the time had come for straight talking with Japan: Washington needed Tokyo's cooperation in pursuing its Vietnam policies and in defending the dollar. Ambassador Johnson had had firsthand experience in Vietnam, first as deputy ambassador to South Vietnam and later as assistant undersecretary of state. It seemed obvious that he had been appointed to toughen up the Japan-America dialogue.

The new ambassador was an unyielding hawk on Vietnam. This the Japanese foreign minister, Takeo Miki, found out during his first meeting with Johnson to discuss various issues. Only on the Vietnam issue were they unable to achieve any meeting of minds. At one point in their discussion Miki broached the idea of having both Hanoi and the United States brought to the negotiating table by a group of communist nations and a group of free-world nations, respectively. Ambassador Johnson, who had been wounded by an enemy bomb during his tenure in Saigon, dismissed the notion as "wishful thinking." According to Miki, Johnson told him that the war would never be ended by peace negotiations. The only course was to wait for the gunfire to cease spontaneously.

Early in 1968, the Japanese government announced, as a sort of trial balloon, that the prime minister would send a special envoy to Washington to discuss Vietnam. Ambassador Johnson's reaction was to go immediately to visit Prime Minister Sato at his Kamakura home to request that the plan be dropped. It was. This was how the United States did its "straight talking" with Japan. But Japan, for her part, did little or no "straight talking" to the United States—on either the Vietnam or the China issue. The "straight talk" strategy seemed very much like one-way traffic. It quickly became clear to most Japanese that the "honeymoon years" of the Kennedy era had ended. Ambassador Johnson's manner symbolized the new toughness of America.

"I believe in a quiet diplomacy," Johnson said at a news conference in November, 1966. "Any diplomatic moves that make a big splash in the newspapers will not be successful. Noisy publicity only hardens diplomacy and makes the solution more difficult." Seventeen months later he told foreign correspondents in Tokyo: "There is no room in diplomacy for sentiment or feeling." It was with this attitude that Johnson devoted himself to the business of his job.

In the autumn of 1967, Prime Minister Sato traveled to Washington to discuss the question of Okinawa's reversion to Japan. The Japanese side wanted a precise date for the reversion, to be announced in a joint communiqué that would be issued at the close of the talks. The American side had suggested the vaguer expression "at the earliest possible date" instead of a fixed date, but the Japanese again requested a more definite commitment. Flying with Sato's party across the country from the West Coast, Johnson gazed down at the Missouri River, as if to find the answer somewhere in its muddy waters, and expressed to the Japanese his doubts that President Johnson would go along with their wishes.

Miki recalls: "I knew that Mr. Johnson would join us in Seattle for the flight to Washington, but I didn't expect him to bring a radio-telegraph machine on board for communicating with Washington. Knowing that he was talking to Washington, we pressed for a definite Okinawa timetable during the in-flight conference. I'm glad we did." The key phrase that appeared in the joint communiqué that was finally issued was "within a few years." Sato took this to mean "within two or three years."

When the Nixon victory in 1968 brought a Republican administration into office, Ambassador Johnson did not disappear from the front

The Occupation and Its Aftermath

36. *September 27, 1945. Emperor Hirohito calls on General MacArthur. It was after this first meeting that the American supreme commander commented that the emperor seemed the foremost gentleman in Japan and decided to preserve his position as symbolic head of state.*

37–40. *Tokyo in ruins and reconstructed. The upper photograph on the facing page shows the extent of destruction caused by ten months of systematic fire bombing by American B-29s. Below is a view of one of Tokyo's newest skyscrapers rising above the city twenty-five years later. On this page are two views of the same spot in Shinjuku, one in 1945 and the other in 1971.*

41. March, 1946. The U.S. Eighth Army on parade at the Imperial Palace in Tokyo.

42. Joint administration in action. An American MP and a Japanese policeman join in directing traffic early in the Occupation.

43. The children of Japan were often the quickest to form international friendships. While their elders look on warily from a distance, these two do not hesitate to strike up an acquaintance with American GIs at Tokyo's Yasukuni Shrine.

44–46. *Feeding a starving nation. Food sent to Japan through such agencies as* GARIOA *and* LARA *was rationed throughout the country, but the supplies were never sufficient to feed all the hungry. Above, Texas rice and American canned foods being distributed during the summer of 1946. Below, children at Ueno Elementary School in Tokyo eating American rice for lunch.*

47–48. *Democratization in action. Two of SCAP's earliest directives, issued in December, 1945, required that Japanese women be granted suffrage and that farmlands be equitably redistributed. Above, women vote for the first time in Japanese history in the election of April 10, 1946; many went to the polls fearing that they would be scolded by MacArthur personally if they stayed away. Below (left), a Japanese farmer receives title to the land that his family has cultivated for generations as tenants. The land reform proved to be the most successful of the Occupation's many democratization programs.*

49. *"The flying fish of Japan." Hironoshin Furuhashi (right) and Shiro Hashizume congratulate each other after finishing first and second in the 1500-meter freestyle race August 17, 1949, at the AAU Swimming and Diving Championship Meet in Los Angeles.*

50. *Girls strolling in Tokyo in 1947, displaying the so-called "new look."*

51. *American movies reappeared in Japan in 1946, and long lines formed daily to see them. SCAP considered movies a useful medium for disseminating democratic principles. Japanese flocked to them as an escape from their wretched postwar life.*

52–53. *End of the Occupation. Above, Shigeru Yoshida and John Foster Dulles meet in 1951 in one of their many conferences to prepare for the Japanese Peace Treaty. Below, Yoshida signs the treaty in San Francisco on September 8, 1951, thus formally ending the war and beginning an era of confusion for Japan as she struggles to achieve genuine autonomy.*

54–55. Under the terms of the Security Treaty signed the same day as the Peace Treaty, the American military presence remained a continuing reality for newly independent Japan. Right, an Okinawan woman works her fields in the shadow of a huge U.S. transport plane. Below, a demonstration at Sunagawa, on the outskirts of Tokyo, where American attempts to extend the Tachikawa Air Base met with violent popular resistance that continued throughout the summer of 1955.

56–57. *The struggle over the Security Treaty renewal. On January 20, 1960, Prime Minister Kishi and President Eisenhower (above, flanked by Foreign Minister Fujiyama and Secretary of State Herter) signed an agreement to extend the Security Treaty for another ten-year period. The renewal and plans for an Eisenhower visit to Japan set off massive anti-war and anti-treaty demonstrations throughout Japan. Below, "demos" like this one occurred in front of the Diet Building almost daily during the summer of 1960, until Eisenhower's visit was cancelled and the Kishi cabinet fell.*

58–60. *When Presidential Press Secretary James Hagarty arrived in Tokyo on June 10 to prepare for the Eisenhower visit, his car was mobbed at Haneda Airport and he was forced to escape by helicopter. Opposition to the Security Treaty and to the presidential visit was not limited to leftists, but included all sectors of Japanese society that feared for the future of democracy in their country.*

61–62. *In February, 1962, Attorney General Robert Kennedy was sent to Japan by his brother President Kennedy to gather opinions of average Japanese people on problems of Japanese-American relations. At Waseda University he was engaged by students in an intense debate on the issue of U.S. bases on Okinawa.*

63. *President John F. Kennedy welcomes Prime Minister Hayato Ikeda to the White House at the beginning of their talks in June, 1961. Behind them are Secretary of State Dean Rusk and Foreign Minister Zentaro Kosaka.*

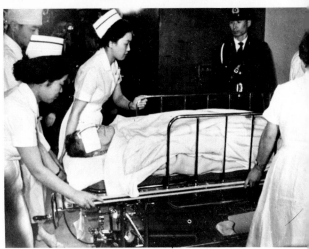

64–65. *Edwin O. Reischauer, the "scholar-ambassador, born in Tokyo," was perhaps the most popular American envoy ever sent to Japan. In the upper picture, he and his wife say good-bye to Japanese children after his resignation in 1966. Below, he is rushed into surgery at Toranomon Hospital following a stabbing attack on him at the American Embassy, March 24, 1964.*

66. *In November, 1967, Prime Minister Eisaku Sato traveled to Washington to ask for the return of Okinawa to Japan. Following talks at the White House with President Johnson, he returned to Japan with no more than an American promise that the Bonin Islands would revert to Japanese ownership within a year.*

67–68. *Two Nixon visits with the emperor. In November, 1953, Vice-President and Mrs. Nixon were welcomed to the Imperial Palace by Emperor Hirohito and Empress Nagako. On September 26, 1971, President and Mrs. Nixon returned the courtesy at Anchorage, Alaska, where the imperial couple stopped briefly on their way to Europe.*

69. *January 6, 1972. President Nixon welcomes Premier Sato to the western White House at San Clemente, California. The Sato visit was one of a series of summit meetings between Nixon and heads of state of the world's great powers, prior to the U.S. president's trip to the People's Republic of China.*

70. *American futurologist Herman Kahn is introduced to Prime Minister Sato in Tokyo in 1970. Sato had recently capitalized upon Kahn's optimistic predictions for Japan's future to win votes in a successful election campaign.*

71–73. *Japan in America. During the 1960s, Japanese products—material and spiritual—attracted increasing interest in the United States. Pictured on this page are the Sony show-room on New York's Fifth Avenue, a sampling of the American press coverage of novelist Yukio Mishima and his dramatic suicide of November 25, 1970, and young Americans meditating at the San Francisco Zen Center.*

ranks of American diplomacy. President Nixon, who admired his matter-of-fact manner of doing his work and appreciated his unyielding position on Vietnam, appointed him undersecretary of state for politcal affairs, a top position on the State Department's organizational pyramid. Just before leaving Japan, Johnson confided to a close friend: "Taking this new post is like going to the electric chair. I wish I could stay longer in Tokyo."

One day in the summer of 1970, the phone rang at the Japanese Embassy in Washington, and the caller was connected immediately with Foreign Minister Kiichi Aichi, who was then in Washington. "Hello, Kiichi. I want to talk to you about our real intentions. I'll be right over with Kissinger." Johnson's call came soon after the Japanese-American textile talks had broken down in disagreement. Never before had Henry Kissinger, President Nixon's special assistant, or Undersecretary Johnson visited a foreign embassy in Washington on business. But Johnson was determined to break the textile deadlock that was having such an ill effect on Japanese-American relations.

When Ambassador Reischauer left for home he had quipped: "From now on, I plan to act as unofficial Japanese ambassador to the United States." Washington gossip has it that Johnson, like Reischauer, cannot forget his Tokyo days.

Former ambassador Johnson began his foreign-service career as a language student in Japan in 1935. Today, he is considered the best-informed man on Japan in the State Department. "Having him in such an important post in the State Department is of great value to Japan," says Aichi. That is no doubt true, but official diplomacy is no longer the only effective channel of Japanese-American relations today. National assemblymen, businessmen, and public opinion have come to have more influence than ever before, as demonstrated in recent textile talks. Thus, "quiet diplomacy," emphasizing dialogue at the official level, is at a turning point. At this critical juncture, the man sent as ambassador to Japan, a nation of highly sophisticated public opinion, is Armin Meyer, a specialist in Middle Eastern affairs.

No More Special Considerations

"JUST TAKE a look at this chart. It should give you some idea of the problems America is up against," invited U. S. Ambassador

Armin H. Meyer, picking up a chart of Japanese-American trade. Its top right-hand corner was worn and covered with finger marks, evidently from frequent handling. The ambassador was using the chart to illustrate, in an interview with an *Asahi* reporter, the reversal in trade between the two countries since 1965 and the heavy adverse imbalance suffered by the United States.

The appointment of Meyer as America's sixth postwar ambassador came as a surprise to most diplomatic observers. This career diplomat, transferred from Iran, was coming to Japan with little knowledge of the Far Eastern situation. His harshest critics were quick to point out that he occasionally said "American relations with Iran" when he meant "with Japan." His immediate predecessors had each had some connection with Japan even before being appointed to the Tokyo post, and serving under them at the embassy were experts with close familiarity with the Japanese situation. The choice of Meyer to succeed Ambassador Johnson was unexpected, to say the least.

George Packard, a special assistant to Ambassador Reischauer, felt compelled to write in an influential Philadelphia daily that President Nixon was "slighting" Japan by his choice of ambassador. Packard went on to observe that voices in Tokyo had complained that Nixon was treating Japan like a horde of Arabs. Immediately after taking office, Meyer responded in print to Packard's article with the argument that at no time in the history of Japanese-American relations had both the Tokyo embassy and the State Department been staffed with so many experts on Japan.

It is rumored that during Meyer's first months in Tokyo some academics and diplomats would jokingly ask what the name of the present American ambassador was. If the ambassador knew about this, he did not seem bothered in the slightest.

Although Meyer will probably be remembered as one of the architects of the Okinawa reversion, he has devoted his greatest efforts to economic issues, and especially to explaining the American economic position to the Japanese. "Okinawa just happens to be important at the moment. In the long run, economic relations between the United States and Japan will prove more important," he comments. "Sometimes I wonder if the Japanese evaluate their economic power correctly. In 1970, for example, Japan produced four million cars for the domestic market. The United States produced eight million, but since the American population is about twice that of Japan, car production in proportion to population was about equal. The Japanese are also always complaining that their GNP may be high but their per capita income is really low; it seems to me, though, that income is steadily increasing and Japan is fast becoming a thoroughly affluent nation."

Every ambassador has a twofold mission. One of his tasks is to report accurately on local conditions. The other is to help explain his own country's attitudes and policies as fully as possible to his host country. This dual function remains the same no matter where a particular individual may be assigned as ambassador.

The Tokyo American embassy enjoys a high reputation for the accuracy of the intelligence it collects. It demonstrated its skill in reading the extent of the youthful dissident strength in the election of the Liberal-Democratic party's president in October, 1970. Takeo Miki was challenging Prime Minister Sato for the position and the embassy's political experts predicted that he would win more than one hundred votes. Although Miki lost the election, as predicted, he garnered 111 votes.

American policy toward Japan has always been based upon the intelligence provided by the staff of experts at the Tokyo embassy, and its fundamental objective has been to protect and strengthen Japan's pro-American conservative regime. On the Japanese side, naturally enough, there has been a tendency to depend on a certain "softness" or "special consideration" in the American attitude. This, in fact, has been a characteristic feature of Japanese-American relations since the war. But Ambassador Meyer, non-expert that he is, seems bent on shifting the emphasis of Japanese-American diplomacy. Rather than explaining Japan to Washington, he seems more determined to explain the United States to Tokyo. "Misunderstanding usually breeds trouble in international relations," he says. "I am trying to make the American point of view understood. Japan is an independent country, capable of making her own decisions; I am not trying to force an American line on Japan."

The forthright "Meyer offensive" may be viewed as a product of his personal nature and experience. A mathematics major as a student, Meyer tends to think of all power relations in terms of numbers. He also believes that the cool rationalism of the mathematician should prove of benefit to both nations in dealing with their mutual problems.

His presence in Tokyo may also be seen as reflecting the tide of the times. The American economy, being what it is at the moment, can hardly afford to allow Japan "special considerations" much longer. Japan, now a sharp competitor economically, is no longer the nation that she used to be either. Ambassador Johnson set the new tone of frank, straight talking with Japan, and Meyer is continuing in a similar vein.

The fact that the American ambassador is not a well-known figure need not be to his disadvantage. In fact, it would seem odd if the American ambassador, alone of all the foreign envoys in Tokyo, stood out with particular prominence. This is all the more true at a time when Japanese-American channels of contact have multiplied and the State Department is no longer the sole steward of relations between the two countries.

Dr. Reischauer's appointment as ambassador in 1961 was greeted with some trepidation in certain Japanese circles that feared he knew too much about Japan. It seems odd now that Meyer should be criticized for knowing too little. Some Japanese, however, welcome the new atmosphere that ambassadors like Johnson and Meyer seem to be creating in Japanese-American relations. "The United States is exhibiting the American habit of pressing its arguments without reserve until one side or the other wins out," comments Hideshi Maki, director of the South American Development Company and a friend of President Nixon's who has long hovered behind the scenes in dealings between the United States and Japan. "It's time that Japan abandoned her rather spoiled 'Oriental' insistence in seeking agreement in a spirit of mutual conciliation. It is important that each side try its utmost to achieve whatever it is after, and then, the argument over, be able to shake hands with the opponent and congratulate him on a good fight. Future Japanese-American relations would be much healthier if built on a foundation like that."

Ambassador Meyer's determination to drive home the American point of view should be taken by the Japanese as a challenge. Confronting so stubborn an opponent offers an opportunity to make clear to the United States precisely what Japan wishes to say, as well.

Military Diplomacy

DURING the late 1960s, the reversion of Okinawa to Japan developed quickly into the most important issue in Japanese-American relations. In January, 1969, a conference on Japanese and American policies for Okinawa and Asia was held in Kyoto with the purpose of aiding indirectly, through private discussion with influential Americans, government negotiations for the return of Okinawa. Two American military men were invited to attend: Gen. Maxwell D. Taylor, former chairman of the Joint Chiefs of Staff, and Adm. Arleigh A. Burke, former chief of U. S. Naval Operations. They had been selected first among possible participants by the conference's sponsors, who sought men with both some understanding of Japan and influence in the U. S. Defense Department. Both hawks, the two men expressed themselves strongly opposed to the return of Okinawa on a *hondo-nami* basis (that is, with a total absence of nuclear weapons and with American bases being subject to all provisions of the Security Treaty, as is true of the main Japanese islands). Doves at the conference, both Japanese and American, took great pains to alter the thinking of the pair on the issue. By the end of the conference, both of them seemed to be growing increasingly sympathetic to the dovish argument that whatever military losses the United States might suffer from a *hondo-nami* return of Okinawa would be more than offset by political gains. There is no way of knowing how the two acted after their return home, but many in the Japanese government credit them with a considerable role in the eventual reversion agreement.

Both the general and the admiral had long been familiar with Japan and Japanese affairs. Taylor had first come to Japan as a captain in 1935 to work as a language officer at the U. S. embassy. A very close associate of his at that time was Capt. Kazutsugu Sugita, a member of the American desk of the General Staff of the Japanese Imperial Army. Sugita, now an adviser to Mitsubishi Heavy Industries, recalls that Taylor spent a period of time with the Imperial Guard Artillery Regiment. "He was a very gifted linguist," says Sugita today.

During World War II, Taylor was in the European theater. In the last days of the Korean War, he commanded the Eighth Army. He was then promoted to commander in chief of U. S. Forces, Far East, and was stationed in Japan. As America's Far Eastern policies shifted during the fifties, Taylor devoted his energies to strengthening the Ground Self-Defense Force, which seemed to be replacing the American ground forces as they were gradually withdrawn.

Burke, as commander of a destroyer task force during the Pacific War, came into direct collision with the Japanese navy off the Solomon Islands. He earned the nickname "31-knot Burke" by his intrepid feat of making destroyers with a top speed of 30 knots run at 31. Soon after the war, he arrived in Japan as deputy chief of staff of the U. S. Navy, Far East.

One day former Vice Adm. Tadakazu Kusaka, who had commanded the Japanese Southeastern Fleet headquartered at Rabaul, received a visit from an American sailor. Announcing himself as a messenger from Admiral Burke, the sailor presented a basket of canned foods and a letter, and then left. The letter invited Kusaka to the Imperial Hotel. He went, fearing that he was to be questioned about war crimes. Instead, he was greeted by a beaming Burke. "I was so impressed with the Japanese navy in Rabaul," exclaimed the American naval officer. "I've been hoping to meet its commander ever since." Later, Burke visited Japan just to attend a meeting of the Navy Rabaul Society as the guest of former Japanese navy men who fought there; after the meeting, he joined his hosts in paying homage to the war dead at Yasukuni Shrine.

When the Korean War broke out, it was Burke's idea to obtain the services of the crack Japanese minesweeping unit for clearing mines from Korean waters immediately before the landings at Inchon and Wonsan. During the early Occupation, this unit had removed from Japanese waters thousands of mines dropped by B-29 bombers in the closing days of the Pacific War. Burke also enthusiastically encouraged the rebuilding of the Japanese navy under a plan that had been developed secretly by a group of former officers, including Kichisaburo Nomura and Zenshiro Hoshina. Perhaps he had forgotten the pacifist constitution promulgated after the war, or perhaps he was intentionally ignoring it in submitting to the American government the Japanese plan as one developed by the U. S. Navy, Far East.

Burke held the post of chief of U. S. Naval Operations from 1955 until 1961, and during that period he never wearied of repeating that to strengthen the Japanese Maritime Self-Defense Force was actually to strengthen the U. S. navy as well. Unstintingly generous with aid to the Maritime Self-Defense Force, he once even offered to donate an aircraft carrier to Japan. The offer was politely declined. "If I had to name one man as 'father' of the MSDF, it would be Admiral Burke without a doubt," says Rear Admiral Suteo Ishida, of the General Staff of the MSDF. He remained in close contact with Burke while stationed in Washington as a Japanese defense attaché.

Military men speak the same language, and can understand each other quickly, as politicians or businessmen cannot. This seems especially true of Japanese and American servicemen. The fact that they were former combatants seems to account for their closeness as much as postwar ties of friendship. Whatever the reason, there can be little question that Japanese and American men in uniform are better friends than Japanese and Americans in any other occupation.

Since American policy toward Japan is first of all military, the Defense Department plays an extremely important role in relations between the two countries. Likewise, personal contacts between Japanese and American military men continue to exert a formidable influence on Japanese-American relations. In September, 1966, while General Taylor was a special adviser to President Johnson after serving as ambassador to South Vietnam, he was visited by his old friend Sugita. The former officer of the Japanese army requested Taylor to use his good offices toward securing the return of the Bonin Islands to Japan. In May of the next year, former Vice Admiral Hoshina was asked by Prime Minister Sato to go to Burke with a similar request. "Since the Bonins were under naval jurisdiction, the prime minister believed that the U. S. navy would have the final word in the matter," says Hoshina. Such personal contacts between Japanese and American military men are referred to with appreciation by Hoshina as "shadow diplomacy" and by Sugita as "invisible diplomacy."

There are many Japanese who agree with former ambassador Koichi Asakai when he says that the presence of men like Taylor and Burke is beneficial to Japan because they know Japan so well. This may be true, but others are equally justified in wondering why Japanese-American relations must always revolve around military affairs, with military officers playing key roles. Seventy percent of the officers in the Self-Defense Forces have been trained in the United States. This fact may prove beneficial to future Japanese-American relations, but there is also the danger that "military diplomacy" will increase in importance as time goes on.

Toward Partnership

THE LATE conservative politician Ichiro Kono was as popular as he was tough. There was one American, however, whom even Kono held in awe. John Foster Dulles, architect of the San Francisco peace treaty and of the original Mutual Security Treaty and later President Eisenhower's secretary of state, was a tough customer for Kono as well as for every other Japanese official who had to deal with him. For the Japanese, Dulles symbolized America's position first as occupier and later, in the early years of independence, as protector of a small, feeble nation.

In 1954, a new cabinet led by Ichiro Hatoyama took over the Japanese government from the Yoshida regime, which had been dubbed a willing myrmidon of the United States. Hatoyama badly needed something in the nature of a diplomatic stunt to lend glamour to his new government. It was with that purpose in mind that three powerful cabinet members went to Washington to sound out Dulles's reaction to a revision of the security pact, an agreement that the

Japanese public was coming in increasing numbers to regard as an "unequal treaty." The three—Agriculture and Forestry Minister Kono, Foreign Minister Mamoru Shigemitsu, and Chief Cabinet Secretary Nobusuke Kishi—directed Dulles's attention to the rising influence of the Communists and other anti-American elements in Japan. "Without a revision of the security pact, it will be most difficult for the ruling party to score a decisive victory in the next general election," urged Shigemitsu.

Dulles listened with growing displeasure registering on his face. Then he warned the three cabinet men not to lose all sense of proportion. "It is premature to suggest revision of the security pact when your own constitution prohibits you from sending troops overseas," he counseled the visitors, and then he proceeded to lecture them for an hour before sending them home deeply disheartened. After that meeting, Kono's lasting impression of Dulles was of an austere and sharp-tongued old man.

Thus refused revision of the security pact, the Hatoyama cabinet's next move was to seek normalization of Japan's relations with the Soviet Union. The government appointed Hatoyama and Kono chief delegates to the Japanese-Soviet talks which were scheduled to be held in October, 1956. Before leaving for Moscow, however, Kono took the precaution of first visiting Washington to discuss with Dulles the resumption of normal diplomatic relations between Japan and the Soviet Union. After talking quietly in the modest study of his home, Dulles told Kono: "I think it will be all right. But be careful: the Russians are not above trying to sell you the same horse twice." Kono later said that it was with that warning constantly in mind that he exercised great caution in the subsequent negotiations with the Soviets. His trip to Washington is another illustration of America's continuing influence over Japan, in her relations not only with the United States, but with the rest of the world as well.

At about the same time, Yasuhiro Nakasone, later to become head of the Defense Agency, wished to visit the People's Republic of China. Told of an American law that denied entry to anyone who had been to China, he took the initial precaution of requesting from Ambassador John M. Allison an assurance that he would not later have difficulties visiting the United States. Allison communicated with Washington, and then told Nakasone that he had been granted permission, a special exception having been made in his case. Nakasone, wishing to be safe rather than sorry in the future, asked Allison to give him that assurance in writing, to which the ambassador obliged. Before leaving for China, Nakasone paid a farewell visit to

Foreign Minister Shigemitsu, who tried to dissuade him from making the trip. "You are embarking on a great misadventure," warned Shigemitsu. "This trip will impair your future relations with the United States and jeopardize your career. As a friend, I advise you not to go." Nakasone, of considerably more independence of spirit than the older diplomat, went to China anyway, feeling only pity for Shigemitsu's excessive concern for American sensitivities.

Aiichiro Fujiyama, who served as foreign minister under Prime Minister Kishi, experienced Dulles's intransigence in a number of head-on collisions. One unforgettable encounter, when the American secretary of state rendered argument all but impossible, occurred in New York where Fujiyama was attending a session of the United Nations. Late one night, Dulles came to his hotel to see him on important business: the United States wanted Japan to cosponsor a certain General Assembly resolution to which Japan was reluctant to add her support. After Fujiyama had declined the request several times, Dulles was unable to conceal his intense irritation any longer. Taking a pencil from his pocket, he tapped it loudly and impatiently on the table, as though somehow to lend greater strength to his arguments and thus force the Japanese foreign minister to do his bidding.

"By the time the first Ikeda cabinet took office in July, 1960, an atmosphere of greater equality had developed between Japan and the United States," recalls Zentaro Kosaka, Ikeda's foreign minister. "Still, we couldn't help feeling conscious of our debts under the security pact."

Japanese officials may have felt a new confidence that they were free to say anything they wished in negotiating with the United States; nevertheless, it is known that Ambassador Reischauer was often irritated with the incorrigible habit Japanese officials had of requesting preliminary conferences with him before taking a step on any issue, major or minor. He registered his displeasure by refusing requests for such talks to sound out American feelings on a particular issue, and would curtly tell Japanese officials: "That's something you will have to decide on your own." It is hardly surprising, then, that Reischauer's enormous popularity with the Japanese public was not shared in by the Foreign Ministry.

Each post-Occupation Japanese government has been determined to appear able to negotiate with the United States on equal terms, and each has coined its own curious catch phrase to characterize itself. The Kishi government spoke of "a new era in Japanese-American relations," the Ikeda cabinet called Japan "an equal partner," and the Sato cabinet has used the phrase "responsible partner." Japan also calls herself "a great economic power," and when Prime Minister Sato traveled to Washington in October, 1970, to break the deadlock in the textile talks, he claimed to talk frankly with the Americans, as though "frankness" itself carried a measure of prestige for Japan. Frankness in international negotiation might well be taken for granted, but in emphasizing the word, Sato clearly revealed his sensitivity to the criticisms that his government was still subservient to the United States.

The principle aim of U. S. policy toward Japan since the Occupation has been the perpetuation of a stable, pro-American regime. Taking this into consideration, Washington has often been willing to stretch a point and grant certain favors to Japan. The United States now feels that it has given enough, but it seems unlikely that its basic policy will change. The greatest concern of the American embassy in Tokyo at the moment is who will succeed Sato as prime minister.

Aware of the overriding American wish for stability in the Japanese government, Foreign Minister Shigemitsu had tried to bargain for a further revision of the security pact in return for a decisive victory of the ruling party in the next election. It was with the same awareness that the Kishi administration staked its survival on the abortive visit of President Eisenhower in 1960.

Clearly, the United States and Japan have both used each other out of self-interest. Such relations have created in Japan a situation where any objections to government policies are immediately interpreted as anti-American criticism. The ultimate question may well be asked: are such relations truly conducive to continued friendship between the two countries?

A Few Discordant Notes

"NEITHER paying lip service to my own government, nor concerning myself much with my personal popularity at home, I simply tried to do my best. That is the only way for a diplomat to gain the trust of the country to which he is assigned. I was sure I was right at the time, and I haven't changed my mind since." This is how Takezo Shimoda, former ambassador to the United States, evaluated his years in Washington in a recent interview with the *Asahi Shimbun*. He is now a justice on the Supreme Court. No postwar Japanese ambassador has provoked more controversy or angered his home government more by his independence at his post than Shimoda.

He first ran into trouble at home when he announced to Americans that the majority of the Japanese "quietly supported" U. S. policies in Vietnam. The Japanese government was disturbed again when Shimoda described its requests for the return of Okinawa on a *hondo-nami* basis as "wishful thinking" and "irresponsible diplomacy." Most recently, when the United States and Japan were deadlocked in the textile dispute, Shimoda stated publicly: "The United States has done so much for Japan on the Okinawa reversion issue. It is time now that Japan reciprocated by relaxing her inflexible position on textiles."

Utterances like these have provoked prominent politicians such as Chobyo Yara, chairman of the Ryukyu government, to snap: "What country does Shimoda think he's representing?" Another unidentified member of the present Sato cabinet has commented: "Shimoda's posture is in utter disregard of domestic public opinion and has proved a negative factor in relations with the United States." Koichiro Asakai, an earlier ambassador to the U. S., has commented more sympathetically: "Mr. Shimoda is by nature even-tempered and rather taciturn. It could only have been his sense of duty that prompted such statements from him." Shimoda had, for a time, served as Asakai's minister at the Washington embassy. According to Asakai, Shimoda repeatedly demonstrated his prudence as a diplomat by modifying the ambassador's more strongly worded dispatches to Tokyo, saying that they would only cause trouble at home. But as the cautious Shimoda advanced in rank, first to deputy foreign minister and finally to ambassador, he grew increasingly outspoken. Doubtless, he considered it his duty to edify the Japanese public, which continued to misunderstand the actualities of Japanese-American relations.

But even Prime Minister Sato eventually came to disregard Shimoda's warnings. The return of Okinawa, finally negotiated on the desired *hondo-nami* terms, seemed to discredit Shimoda's reading of American public opinion as not totally accurate. Nor did the fact that he was better known in the United States than in Japan seem particularly desirable to the Japanese government.

Government policies shift subtly with the changing winds of public opinion, and the primary task of the Japanese ambassador in Washington is to gasp quickly and accurately the drift of American public opinion as it relates to Japan. He is also expected to influence that opinion in Japan's favor whenever possible. The job is not made easier by the undefinable barriers that still seem to separate American and Japanese diplomats despite years of intimate contact. Americans continue to exhibit an innate neighborliness toward ambassadors from European or Latin-American nations. Toward the Japanese ambassador, however, there is rarely the degree of "closeness" that he may tend to expect. When important news is to be distributed, foreign ambassadors are listed in categories according to the order in which they are to be informed. All too frequently, the name of the Japanese ambassador appears rather far down the list in a category entitled "other friendly countries," even when the news may involve U. S. Asian policy. During the first few years following the end of the Occupation, the Japanese ambassador invariably had to make a special effort to arrange an appointment with the secretary or undersecretary of state, to say nothing of the president.

It was only when Japanese-American tensions became more conspicuous, during Asakai's tenure as ambassador, that the prestige of the Japanese embassy began to rise. With Japan's star in the ascendancy and with his own excellent command of English, Asakai was able to expand the embassy's network of information sources in Washington. During his six years there, Asakai's face became an important and familiar one to the U. S. government.

In one respect, Asakai showed himself notably arrogant: anyone declining an invitation to one of his parties or receptions was not invited a second time. This may have been akin to a trait common among Japanese government officials. Generally, diplomats and bureaucrats are punctilious about performing the minimum social obligations of their offices but are reluctant to invest extra time or money in persons or groups on the off-chance that they may prove useful on some future occasion. In Washington, however, it is just that sort of social activity that frequently pays off in opportunities to detect budding diplomatic problems at an early stage and to head them off.

Ryuji Takeuchi, who succeeded Asakai as ambassador in 1963, devoted his energies wholeheartedly to selling Japan to the Americans. To that end, he cultivated the friendship of executives of the *Washington Post* and made frequent lecture tours around the country. The times were propitious, for since the beginning of the Kennedy years the American people, from the president down, had begun to show greater interest in Japan's amazing economic expansion, and were also in a mood to listen to what foreigners had to say about the United States. On many occasions Takeuchi criticized America in his lectures, but would amuse his audiences with the remark: "An orchestra with one or two discordant notes seems to produce a deeper, more resonant sound."

At that time Americans were still willing to listen, but by the time Shimoda arrived in Washington in 1967 the mood had changed. Vietnam and the race issue had cast the nation into total discord and Americans now showed an undisguised aversion to criticism from outside. The actualities of the situation in the United States, and what he considered the general Japanese misunderstanding of them, proved increasingly irritating and frustrating to Shimoda. No doubt it was those feelings that colored his statements which proved so controversial at home in Japan. While it is true that binational relations can never be absolutely free of discord, it was unclear where Shimoda's first responsibilities lay—with the Japanese or the Americans. The position that he took—pro-American through and through—might well be interpreted as a mere reflex of the Sato government's diplomatic posture.

Several foreign ministers, when asked what sort of person was best suited to the job of ambassador to the United States, gave differing answers. Zentaro Kosaka said: "Now that the State Department seems to have become a minority voice in forming American opinion and policy, the Japanese ambassador in Washington should be someone capable of finding and exploiting new sources of information." Kiichi Aiichi added: "Future ambassadors should keep in touch with the wide circle of policy-making organs and influential congressmen, keeping in mind the constant turnover of the latter." Takeo Miki stresses the importance of correlating domestic and foreign affairs. "If future ambassadors are to conduct a diplomacy that reflects Japanese public opinion and receives approval at home, they will have to be as well versed in domestic affairs as in international matters."

It is clear, then, that the Washington post can no longer be considered merely a decoration automatically conferred on men who have served well as deputy foreign ministers.

"Connections" in America

IT WAS not long ago that former foreign minister Takeo Miki received a letter announcing the establishment of a new foundation in memory of Woodrow Wilson and asking him to join its board of trustees. The letter was signed by former vice-president Hubert Humphrey, chairman of the board.

"Congratulations on your re-election," wrote Miki to Edmund Muskie when the Maine senator and leading candidate for the 1972 Democratic presidential nomination was returned to the Senate. Miki once studied in the United States and continues to keep himself well versed in American political affairs. As these letters indicate, he maintains a close association with leading figures on the American political scene, particularly with Humphrey, who has been a friend for more than ten years. Both Humphrey and Miki are party men through and through, and both consider themselves liberals. In the last few years, both have also been engaged in tough election campaigns—one for the American presidency and the other for the leadership of the Liberal-Democratic party. "If we both win," they had encouraged one another, "Japanese-American relations should go very well indeed." But their optimism proved unfounded, for both their campaigns ended unsuccessfully.

Recalling his days as foreign minister, Miki acknowledges his debt to Humphrey for "a lot of help" in the course of the negotiations for the return of the Bonin Islands to Japan. During the autumn of 1967, Miki had preceded Prime Minister Sato to Washington—at the prime minister's request—to open negotiations on the Bonins. The initial talks had not gone well, and Miki grew increasingly dejected and uncertain of how to continue. But timely advice was forthcoming from his old friend Humphrey: "Try making just one more push." When Miki did so, he obtained U. S. agreement to return the islands. Sato had himself planned to pull off the diplomatic coup of obtaining the return of the Bonins when he visited Washington later in the year, but Miki's early success robbed him of this prize. Not surprisingly, certain tensions developed between the two politicians. The estrangement between Sato and his foreign minister culminated eventually in the showdown election in 1970 for the presidency of the Liberal-Democratic party. Miki lost his bid, and Sato maintained his hold over the party.

After his defeats in the presidential election of 1960 and the California gubernatorial election two years later, Richard M. Nixon went into temporary political retirement. Between 1964 and 1967, he visited Japan annually (twice in 1964), partly on business as legal adviser to Pepsico and the Mitsui Bussan Company's American affiliate. On each visit he was royally entertained in Tokyo's Ginza and Akasaka districts by what might be called a "Nixon Welcoming Committee," led by Mitsui Bussan executives. Heading the committee was former prime minister Nobusuke Kishi, whom Nixon had known since the 1960 revision of the Security Treaty. Kishi is also the brother of Prime Minister Sato, and as such remains a powerful force in the Japanese government; he considers himself the Japanese politician closest to Nixon. When the final stage in the talks on the Okinawa reversion question was approaching in the autumn of 1969, Kishi flew to the United States and played an important role in preparing the ground for Nixon's talks with his brother, the prime minister.

Thomas E. Dewey, the late Republican politician of great influence within the party, lost the 1948 presidential election to Harry S. Truman in a surprising upset. On the rebound, he groomed General Eisenhower for his successful bid for the presidency in 1952, and bragged afterward that he had "invented statesman Ike." It was also Dewey who helped Nixon—a Californian with few connections in the eastern power elite—to open his law office in New York and establish an Eastern foothold in preparation for his political comeback. In a sense, he performed a similar service for Ichiro Kono, who was an important Japanese conservative politician but who lacked powerful friends in the United States. Their association followed a long and painful political struggle for Kono, and the story is revealing of important tendencies in Japanese politics.

Although a leading member of the Liberal-Democratic party, Kono had long stood in opposition to the "mainstream" of the party led by Prime Minister Yoshida, who had been forging strong connections with American politicians since Occupation days. Japanese big business remained markedly cool to Kono and the conservative faction he led. As a result of his rivalry with Yoshida and the "mainstream," Kono fostered the resumption of normal Japanese relations with the Soviet Union, a position that served only to alienate him further from Americans. Still, realizing that a conservative Japanese politician without American ties would be forced into helpless isolation, Kono sought such connections. He was helped by Masaichi Nagata, president of the Daiei Motion Picture Company, who introduced Kono to Dewey. The pair hit it off well, and Dewey went to work on Kono's behalf.

In 1959, the Japanese government seriously considered Kono's proposal that Dewey be engaged as American legal adviser to JETRO (Japan External Trade Organization). This was the first suggestion that JETRO retain an influential American lobbyist. The plan was dropped after a month of debate in which numerous objections were raised to the retainer that Dewey requested—¥100,000

($278) per day. The plan also called for Sukemasa Komamura, later JETRO's chairman, to serve as Dewey's assistant. Komamura was board chairman of the Gosho Company and was a relative of Kono's.

"Mr. Kono and Mr. Dewey 'clicked' so well because they were both tough, down-to-earth politicians," recalls Nagata. Through his introduction, Kono also met Eric Johnson, president of the Motion Picture Society of America and an influential American business figure. Through Johnson's good offices, Kono later realized a long-cherished dream to meet movie star Deborah Kerr.

The intelligence on the American situation that Kono managed to gather through his own sources often differed from that coming through formal government channels. Occasionally, it was reflected in the Kishi cabinet's negotiations of the security-pact revision in 1960 and also in the Ikeda's government's diplomatic maneuverings with the United States. U. S. Ambassador Douglas MacArthur II is reported to have been annoyed more than once in talking to Kono during the security-pact negotiations because Kono seemed uncannily able to read the cards that the U. S. was holding. During a 1962 tour of the Soviet Union and Europe as Japanese minister of agriculture, Kono voiced an enigmatic prediction to his aides that some grave event was about to occur in Southeast Asia. As soon as the party reached Washington, it learned of the dispatch of American troops to Laos.

These anecdotes should illustrate the importance for Japanese politicians of maintaining fairly close connections with important American politicians. Whenever they visit Washington, conservative members of the Diet seek opportunities to meet with well-known American politicians and invariably are photographed with them. Back home, they distribute prints to their constituencies. Japanese politicians who have already managed to forge such ties try constantly to cultivate new ones. There is nothing wrong with seeking mutual understanding through such associations, but that is a far different matter from the tendency of Japanese conservatives to consider friendship with American politicians as in itself a special qualification for prestige. Politicians, conservative and progressive alike, have but a single master to serve: the people. The rather frenzied cultivation of political acquaintances in the United States seems an odd way of providing that service.

Three Foreign Ministers

THREE successive Japanese foreign ministers during the late 1960s deserve credit for their efforts toward developing a truly independent Japanese diplomacy. They staged no stunts, scored no spectacular successes; nevertheless, in the course of dealing with many different problems they were untiring in their pursuit of that single general goal.

The first of them was Masayoshi Ohira, foreign minister in the Ikeda cabinet, who negotiated a reparations agreement with the Republic of Korea in 1962 that paved the way for the reopening of normal diplomatic relations between Japan and Korea. There had long been something known as the "Korea Lobby" within the Liberal-Democratic party, because the normalization of relations with Korea, along with Okinawa reversion, was one of the most critical issues of post-Occupation Japanese diplomacy. Groups of Diet members were frequently flying back and forth between Tokyo and Seoul, attempting to make progress on the difficult problem. The unacknowledged leader of the "Korea Lobby" was Bamboku Ono, a senior member of the party. At the end of 1962, he led a group of fifteen or sixteen members of the Diet to South Korea to promote friendly relations between the two countries. Korean officials and the Japanese legislators feted each other at a series of parties. At one of them, Ono and his group learned of the agreement that Ohira had struck a month earlier with Chong Pil Kim, director of the ROK Central Intelligence Department. They were stunned, for they had considered themselves the main "bridge" of Japan-ROK understanding. The contents of the Ohira-Kim parley, conducted in Tokyo at Kim's request on his way home from a trip to the United States, had been kept virtually secret even from the Asian Affairs Bureau of the Foreign Ministry.

At the time, Prime Minister Hayato Ikeda had been out of the country and the Japanese government had not been particularly eager to finalize talks on Korean reparations. But the United States had been: the smooth operation of American Asian policies required that Japan, "the most prosperous nation in Asia," and the Republic of Korea, "the staunchest anticommunist nation," bury their differences and become friends.

"U. S. Secretary of State Dean Rusk seemed eager for an early reopening of diplomatic relations between Japan and Korea," Ohira recalls. To the opposition, Rusk's eagerness was considered "U. S. pressure." But unlike the Okinawa reversion question, the Japan-

ROK relations problem was one in which the American government could only appeal to Japan. "At no time since the war has the United States been in so weak a position vis-à-vis Japan as now," some members of the State Department are said to have complained. It may have been with the Japan-ROK problem uppermost in its thinking that the American government sent a group of cabinet secretaries, led by Rusk himself, to Japan in 1961, a year before the Ohira-Kim accord. The presence of so many important government figures, ostensibly to attend the meetings of the Japanese-American Joint Committee on Trade and Economic Affairs in Hakone, was widely believed to be an attempt to flatter Japan into compliance on the Korea issue.

Meanwhile, Washington's attempts to persuade Korea to come to terms with Japan were impossible to disguise. When Chung Hee Park, then chairman of the Supreme Council on National Rehabilitation, visited Washington in 1961, President Kennedy conferred with him twice. They had been scheduled to meet only once, and the second meeting bespoke extraordinary hospitality shown to the representative of a mere military regime. According to informed sources, immediately before the Ohira-Kim agreement the State Department had instructed the American ambassador in Seoul, Samuel Berger, to inform the Korean government that should Japan and Korea be unable to agree on reparations, Washington was prepared to deal with the problem as best it could on its own responsibility. The concessions that Korea finally made in her claims on Japan were not, to all appearances, unrelated to U. S. intentions.

In reaching this agreement with Kim, Ohira was, for all practical purposes, cooperating with American policy. But it was the same foreign minister who stuck resolutely to his stand for increased trade with the People's Republic of China in the face of clearly demonstrated American displeasure. One day during the second conference of the Joint Committee on Trade and Economic Affairs, which sat in Washington in 1962, Secretary Rusk and Foreign Minister Ohira met the press together. Reporters asked Rusk whether he had advised Ohira to stop Japanese trade with China. After hesitating a moment, Rusk answered that he had not. At a party that evening, Rusk beckoned Ohira into a small room and whispered: "Tomorrow's papers will carry my answer to the reporters, and it will make me unpopular in America. But that answer was an expression of my personal friendship for you."

Etsusaburo Shiina, who succeeded Ohira as foreign minister, signed the treaty that finally re-established normal relations between Japan and the Republic of Korea. It was Shiina's slow, easygoing, rather ponderous manner—concealing a very agile mind—that helped him weasel himself out of a variety of predicaments while in office. In one session of the Lower House Foreign Affairs Committee, the opposition attacked his treaty with Korea as being hardly more than an anticommunist military alliance, and asked his estimation of America's role in the matter. Shiina answered, in all seriousness: "I have always considered the United States a respected watchdog for Japan. I still do. We cannot forget our indebtedness to that watchdog for our security. But I know of no house that allows its actions to be determined by its watchdog, and I have no intention of doing the watchdog's bidding. We must not forget that, by acting on our own initiative whenever possible, we shall benefit the United States in the long run."

At a conference of cabinet members of the ten anticommunist member nations of the Asian and Pacific Council (ASPAC) in Korea in June, 1966, Shiina objected to a motion to include in the conference communiqué a statement of preparedness by the participating nations for an anticommunist confrontation. He was immediately rebuked by the delegates of Korea, the Philippines, Thailand, and Taiwan, who had made the motion. "Isn't Japan anticommunist?" they demanded. "And isn't she willing to declare herself as such?"

In his slow way, Shiina parried the charges and eventually managed to tone down the communiqué, which had almost amounted to a pledge for unified anticommunist military action. Later he commented calmly: "It seems terribly difficult for ten men to carry a single palanquin, doesn't it?"

But the performance of the Japanese foreign minister at the following ASPAC Conference, held in Thailand the next year, was far more independent than even Shiina's. Takeo Miki declared in unmistakable terms: "Japan will adopt a policy of peaceful coexistence with China." The "mainstream" faction of the ruling Liberal-Democratic party, which strongly influences Prime Minister Sato's actions, immediately criticized Miki for going too far in giving the impression that Japan might be conducting "dual diplomacy."

Many critics point to the security arrangements with the United States and argue that whatever independence Japan might achieve would be at best a limited independence, confined within the larger framework of American Asian policy. Nevertheless, it is clear that the three Japanese foreign ministers Ohira, Shiina, and Miki strove— each in his own distinctive fashion—for the independence of Japan's diplomacy as she pursued her delicate relations with the United States and the rest of Asia through the 1960s. Can as much be said of the men carrying out Japan's foreign policy today?

Canned Speeches or Real Dialogue?

"I SHOULD very much like to hear your opinions on Asian affairs." With these words an influential official of the Kennedy administration requested an interview with the elderly Kenzo Matsumura some years ago. Matsumura, who died in the fall of 1971, was then a member of the Lower House and a senior statesman of the Liberal-Democratic party. At that time, the United States was still adhering strictly to its containment policy toward the People's Republic of China. The American official, on his way back to Washington from a visit to the Nationalist government in Taiwan, was doubtless interested in the views of Matsumura, who was maintaining a thin but firm communication pipeline with Peking.

Matsumura engaged the finest suite in the Imperial Hotel for the meeting, and, as a special courtesy to his guest, had a handsome gold screen set up in it. When his American visitor entered, his hand outstretched to shake Matsumura's, the venerable Japanese politician greeted him with a solemn, low bow.

"The Chiang Kai-shek regime is doing well," began the guest. "I see no cause for anxiety over its political future."

"It is good to hear that," replied Matsumura. "Years ago, when a farsighted Japanese statesmen named Shimpei Goto governed Taiwan, he worked hard to make Japan's colonialization of Taiwan much more successful than the imperialism of the European nations. His efforts are apparently bearing fruit in President Chiang's successful administration of the island. If that pleases you, I am glad that Japan, by this 'historical coincidence,' can be of help to your country."

"Wouldn't you like to visit the United States, sir?"

"No, thank you, I think not. However, I do have a message for President Kennedy which I should like you to carry to him. Please tell him that Asian problems are Asia's concern. He should dismiss all fears about Asia from his mind, and devote himself to domestic affairs. . . . Also, if there is ever anything troubling you, please be assured that the doors of the Matsumura home shall always be open to welcome you." Matsumura's language was formal and polite, but he made his point frankly, without offending his visitor. Although totally unfamiliar with American etiquette, he received his guest graciously; all who were present were full of admiration for his manners.

In recent years there have been numerous official meetings of Americans and Japanese of both the government and parliamentary levels, but rarely have Japanese delegates matched Matsumura's style. In May, 1971, the third Japan-America Parliamentary Exchange Conference brought more than a dozen American legislators to Japan to trade views with representatives of the Liberal-Democratic party, the Socialist party, the Democratic Socialist party, and the Clean Government party. The Japanese participants, for the most part, were awkward and unpersuasive speakers. Either by common consent or simply because they didn't know how else to begin, most opened their addresses by acknowledging Japan's indebtedness to the United States and thanking America for fostering her spectacular economic recovery since the war. But then, the standard preamble accomplished, each speaker would launch into an emotional plea for special consideration on such issues as textile exports and trade liberalization. Such wide-ranging requests, without any comment on their background, were hardly likely to be greeted sympathetically by listeners already deeply suspicious of the Japanese economic offensive.

The initial acknowledgments of indebtedness were intended merely as indications of modesty. The Japanese failed to realize that they also amounted to invitations to their American counterparts to make certain reciprocal demands. Not surprisingly, most of the discussions ended with parallel insistence on both sides and no meeting of minds.

As usual, the Japanese delegates to the conference had been selected with consideration paid to maintaining intra-party factional balances. This led to a bewildering array of factional differences being laid bare in the presence of the Americans. For example, when one Liberal-Democratic dove took the floor to say that the China question could not be solved without recognizing Peking's claims on Taiwan, an LDP hawk was instantly on his feet exclaiming: "My colleague represents the minority view of our party!" Moreover, many of the speeches of the Japanese politicians were intended less for their foreign visitors than for domestic consumption in their electorates. Similar considerations are probably responsible for crushing a proposal made several years ago by the Lower House Foreign Affairs Committee that candid discussion between government and opposition be held behind closed doors. "Obviously, no one saw any point in talking seriously if his remarks would never reach the ears of the voters," comments committee member Hyosuke Kujiraoka.

At conferences of the Japanese-American Joint Committee on Trade and Economic Affairs and other binational organs, the Japanese delegates almost invariably read mechanically from prepared speeches. American delegates deplore the fact that the Japanese seem not to have improved in speaking techniques despite frequent exposure to such meetings. "I wonder when the Japanese ministers will begin to notice the pained boredom on the faces of American delegates when they start reading papers prepared by their underlings," says a Japanese interpreter who has attended Japanese-American conferences for more than a dozen years.

One reason for the awkwardness of Japanese politicians at speaking in public is that they receive little or no debate training in their youth. Another is that party men, most of them ex-bureaucrats or former union leaders, generally stop thinking for themselves at some point in their careers and count on the party to do all their thinking for them.

Far superior to the general run of politician-speakers were the Japanese delegates to the private Japanese-American conference held at the Center for the Study of Democratic Institutions in Santa Barbara in January, 1968. Doves from the U. S. Congress and the Japanese Diet sat down together to thrash out long-range views on the China problem. This time the speeches of the Japanese delegates impressed their American listeners deeply. They had obviously studied the problem thoroughly, had thought out what they wanted to say with care, and presented their views with forthright persuasiveness.

Since Japanese-American relations are not limited to diplomacy and official discussions of mutual security but involve the daily lives of all the citizens of both countries, direct personal interchange by individuals on all social levels is important. The official contact of politicians is bound to increase, but experience has shown that frequency of communication does not of itself lead to improved mutual understanding. A more important task for the future is to expand the channels of dialogue through which the people of both nations can strike responsive chords in each other.

Some Private Diplomacy

L ATE IN January, 1969, Santa Barbara, California, was hit by the heaviest rains in more than fifty years. Road traffic was disrupted and the airport flooded. But as the torrential rains fell, a group of prominent Japanese and American doves met in a private conference to discuss the Asian policies of the United States. At the reception ending the two-day conference, Tokuma Utsunomiya, who was largely responsible for organizing the meetings, spoke on behalf of all the Japanese delegates: "I hear that local townspeople are blaming us Japanese for bringing the rains to Santa Barbara. That's probably just a rumor fabricated by some militant right-wing group. We have brought no dark clouds with us. In fact, we came to join with Americans of good will in an effort to drive the dark clouds from the skies of the world. . . . I believe we have reached some satisfactory conclusions."

Japanese participants in the conference included Aiichiro Fujiyama, Munenori Akagi, and Masumi Ezaki. American senators who attended were J. William Fulbright, John Cooper, Mark Hatfield, and Alan Cranston. The main conclusions that came out of the discussions were that the American approach toward Asia, largely military, was badly in need of alteration, and that the policy of shutting China out of the international community should also be replaced by a more positive attitude.

These conclusions ultimately attracted more attention in the United States than in Japan. Most of the Japanese participants would agree with Utsunomiya when he notes that American policy moves since Santa Barbara seem to indicate a strengthening of the doves' influence on American foreign policy. Akagi has announced: "Recent developments, notably the reaction of the United States to China's 'ping-pong diplomacy' and the visit of American journalists to China, make me hopeful that the goals we talked over at Santa Barbara may soon be realized."

The private Santa Barbara discussions were planned by Utsunomiya, a freewheeling member of the ruling Liberal-Democratic party, and grew out of his conviction that an improvement in Japanese relations with China would have to be preceded by some preliminary Japanese-American understanding. In 1968, he wrote to influential members of the American Congress, setting forth his view that the stability of the entire Pacific region depended upon good relations among Japan, China, and the United States. When he received a number of sympathetic responses, Utsunomiya went to Washington to arrange with Senator Mansfield and other congressional leaders for the meeting that eventually took place in Santa Barbara.

Utsunomiya himself hoped to act as a bridge of understanding between the United States and China. He also believed that the surest way to cause a relaxation of Japan's rigid China policies would be to first bring influential Americans around to his pro-Chinese position. The private diplomacy exhibited at Santa Barbara and in the preparations for those meetings might be considered an unspoken indictment of the Japanese Foreign Ministry. At any rate, its implied purpose was to step in and supplement the official channels by opening paths where formal diplomacy could not immediately tread.

Two conferences, held at Shimoda in 1967 and 1969, were similar attempts at private diplomacy. Both the Japanese and American delegations, remarkable for their nonpartisan character, consisted of representatives from various walks of life: government men, businessmen, professors, and journalists.

The host organization was the Japan Commission for International Friendship. Its chairman, Tokusaburo Kosaka, president of the Shin'etsu Chemical Company, had been nurturing the idea of the conferences and planning them for more than seven years.

In 1960, while the Japanese nation was up in arms over the revision of the security pact, Kosaka happened to be in the United States on business. In Chicago, he had been surprised to see headlines screaming: "Riots in Japan!" He had grown increasingly uncomfortable as he saw his American business associates try to avoid mentioning the controversial issue. This alarmed him, for he knew that such reluctance to discuss the serious matters that were straining Japanese-American relations could only lead to greater misunderstandings and difficulties. When he later had the opportunity to talk with young members of President Kennedy's braintrust, he found that they knew very little about Japan but that they were eager to listen and learn more. These experiences prompted Kosaka to take upon himself the task of sponsoring a form of private diplomacy between Japan and America. His first move in that direction was to organize the reception committee that greeted the late Robert Kennedy when he visited Japan in 1962.

The question of Okinawa's reversion to Japan was discussed at one session of the first Shimoda Conference. During the recess that followed, Eiichi Nagasue, a former Democratic Socialist member of the Lower House, showed a dime to Sen. Edmund Muskie and told him that it was Okinawan money. The Senator examined it with some puzzlement, apparently not realizing that U. S. currency was the legal tender of Okinawa, and said: "Why, it looks exactly like an American dime. Is it real?" This was only one incident at the conference that served to make Muskie realize how little he knew of Japanese affairs. But apparently it also fired his interest. "When I met him at the second Shimoda Conference two years later, I was surprised at how much he knew about Japan," recalls Nagasue. "He had also begun speaking out on the Okinawa issue at home." Mentioning the example of Senator Muskie, a leading contender for the Democratic presidential nomination in 1972, Shigeharu Matsumoto, director of Tokyo's International House, agrees that the Shimoda conferences played an extremely important role in making Japan understood to Americans who previously had little knowledge of Japanese affairs. According to Professor Fuji Kamiya of Keio University, the conferences also impressed both the Japanese and American governments with the importance of private diplomacy.

But there are limits to what private diplomacy can achieve, and expecting too much from it leads only to frustration. In the years before Pearl Harbor, a number of influential Japanese devoted themselves to developing private contacts and attempting to improve relations with the United States; their hopes were shattered when their private diplomacy led nowhere.

"Actually, 'private diplomacy' is much too grand a term for this sort of thing," warns Tadashi Yamamoto, who acted as secretary general of the Shimoda conferences. "Think of it only as channels of personal international contacts." Even Kosaka, who had been so successful in recruiting Japanese politicians to come to Shimoda without regard for party ties or politics, seems to have recognized the limitations of what private diplomacy can achieve. He later ran for a seat in the Lower House on a Liberal-Democratic ticket "because I cannot content myself with being merely an 'adviser.' "

Eiichi Shibusawa, the great industrialist of the Meiji era, is still remembered for his sponsorship of private Japanese-American conferences during the first decades of this century. He used to say of these activities: "What I and kindred spirits are doing is akin to performing gymnastic exercises as an indirect cure for indigestion rather than taking medicine for it." His great-grandson, Masahide Shibusawa, has carefully studied the grand old man's efforts in the cause of private diplomacy and echoes his feelings: "Private diplomacy cannot be aimed at immediate national gains. It should be

[249]

devoted to achieving a long view of a variety of international problems. If intended only to serve the purposes of governments, it is
doomed to failure."

Diplomats of Commerce

IMMEDIATELY after the war ended, the imposing main building
of the Dai Ichi Life Insurance Company, located in downtown
Tokyo right across the moat from the Imperial Palace, was requisi-
tioned for use as General Headquarters of the Supreme Commander
for the Allied Powers (GHQ-SCAP). Taizo Ishizaka, president of the
insurance firm, was ordered to greet General MacArthur at the front
entrance when he arrived to take occupancy of the building. Ishizaka
refused. "And never once, in the six years that he sat in my office on
the sixth floor, did I go to see MacArthur," he chuckles today.

Ishizaka has been one of the giants of postwar Japanese business
and a leading participant in what might be called business's private
diplomacy with the United States. As president of Tokyo Shibaura
Electric Company (Toshiba), he settled a crippling strike and later
re-established Toshiba's prewar technological affiliation with General
Electric. Having led the company back from devastation to prosperity,
Ishizaka has been hailed as the "father of Toshiba's reconstruction."
His experiences of bargaining with the labor unions and negotiating
with General Electric made him a firmly, antileftist liberal and convinced him that the only hope for the rehabilitation of the entire
Japanese economy lay in American aid. The man who had refused to
greet the American general who conquered Japan was soon trans-
formed into a standard-bearer for economic cooperation between
Japan and the United States.

While most Japanese industrialists gleefully welcomed American
procurement orders during the Korean War as an economic windfall,
Ishizaka held to a critical, longer view. He compared the profitable
orders to mere aspirin given to the critically ill, and declared that the
Japanese economy could be reinvigorated only by a thorough overhaul
and by adopting the latest American technology and systems of
industrial management.

Toward that end he helped establish the Japan Productivity Center,
and as its president in 1955, he led the largest postwar Japanese busi-
ness-survey mission to the United States. When the group returned

home, Ishizaka stated in a speech that American business principles stressed the priority of management's responsibility first to the consumer, next to the shareholder, and then to the employee. This gave rise, almost immediately, to the catch phrase "the consumer is king," although ultimately it was the producers who profited. The success of that first survey mission sent hordes of Japanese businessmen traveling to the United States to pay tribute to American industry and to learn its techniques.

The "Ishizaka era" really began in 1956, when he was elected president of the Federation of Economic Organizations (Keidanren). His predecessor, Ichiro Ishikawa, had been experiencing difficulties holding the federation together, but things picked up dramatically when Ishizaka took over. He brought certain distinct advantages to the post. Unlike Ishikawa, who had been president of the middle-level Nissan Chemical Industries Company, Ishizaka was president of one of Japan's largest corporations. In 1956, Japan was also an independent nation; Ishikawa had become director of the federation in 1946, the second year of the Occupation. As the *zaibatsu* were being dissolved and large businesses split into small ones by Occupation policy, Ishikawa—like the country itself—was reduced to playing a constantly passive role. He worked tirelessly to obtain American economic aid for Japanese industries, but was usually frustrated by the small amounts that trickled in. Until he retired in 1956, Ishikawa was frequently abused by business leaders as being a waverer, indecisive and weak-willed.

Ishizaka took over with confidence and vigor. According to Moriyasu Minato, director of the Nikko Research Center, Ishizaka's assuming the presidency of Keidanren "marked the passing of the era of rehabilitation based on U. S. aid. It was the beginning of the 'honeymoon years' during which Japan sought a higher growth rate with U. S. capital and technological cooperation."

Since the United States was both customer and benefactor, Japanese industrial circles were more timid and more careful than even the conservative government not to disrupt Japanese-American relations. For example, when Prime Minister Hatoyama created a political furor in 1956 with his impatience to re-establish normal relations with the Soviet Union, Ishizaka and other business leaders demanded, with a unanimous voice, his immediate resignation. Members of the cabinet were furious with Ishizaka's insubordination and insult to a prime minister democratically elected by the people. More recently, Ishizaka bluntly told Prime Minister Sato, who was negotiating the reversion of Okinawa: "The island serves us like a watchdog, but is

[251]

fed and taken care of by the U. S. Why risk bruising our partnership with America by demanding that she give us back the watchdog so quickly?"

After occupying the chair of "business premier of Japan" for six terms, totaling twelve years, Ishizaka finally passed it on to Kogoro Uemura, who had long been vice-president of Keidanren. Throughout his tenure, Ishizaka had steadfastly rejected any identification with politics. Uemura, however, was formerly a ranking bureaucrat and has maintained his political connections; he has also acted as a channel of donations to politicians from business. Politics has inevitably begun to invade the domain of Japanese-American economic relations, and Uemura is considered the best person for the job he holds. In that he still attaches first importance to maintaining close relations with the United States, however, he follows the "Ishizaka line."

Recently, other men have also involved themselves in what might be called the private diplomacy of economic relations with the United States. The greatest difficulty that they are encountering is an "information gap," characterized by distorted estimations of Japan's economic position. In a 1964 speech entitled "The Myth and the Reality," which he delivered in New York, Yoshizane Iwasa, chairman of the Fuji Bank, said: "Americans underrate the strength of Japan. They do not take her fully into their confidence on major economic issues or on political problems involving Asia." This speech had great repercussions in both Japan and the United States. And yet, only two years later Tokyo University professor Motoro Kaji, who had accompanied Iwasa, revisited the U. S. and reported that "Japan's real strength was vastly overrated."

To avoid such distortions and information gaps, Iwasa sees the need for constant efforts to promote mutual understanding between the United States and Japan. "Between America and the European countries it is easily achieved, but we must strive constantly to maintain mutual understanding by various means and through various channels." Iwasa has recently played a major role in organizing a group of influential businessmen into what is tentatively called the Advisory Committee on Japanese-American Economic Affairs.

The emergence of China and other multilateral international issues will significantly affect Japanese-American relations during the 1970s. The private diplomacy of Japanese business will have to be modified accordingly. The next few years will be a crucial period revealing how far beyond their abacuses and their immediate profits Japanese businessmen are able to see.

Two Japanese Tycoons

MANY OBSERVERS of the Japanese economy make quick and easy generalizations about the manners and techniques of Japanese businessmen. This is a risky practice, because there is a great range of diversity that may not be apparent from too hasty a glance at the Japanese business world. Two noted businessmen provide ample illustration of that diversity. Both are well known in America, where they do an enormous volume of business. In their business policies, as in their personalities, the two could not be more dissimilar.

"I don't think the friction in Japanese-American economic relations is as serious as it's usually made out to be. After all, American exports to Japan have trebled over the past decade and Japan continues to be a vital business partner," said Akio Morita, vice-president of the Sony Corporation, speaking in 1969 at a hearing of the Joint Congressional Foreign Economic Policy Committee, where American senators, congressmen, businessmen, and economists had gathered to try to establish foreign economic policies for the 1970s. Morita is usually singled out as the Japanese businessman most successful on an international level. "Few are as complex free in dealing with Americans as he is," says Sohei Mizuno, president of the Arabian Oil Company.

Exports to the United States account for roughly half of Sony's total exports and about thirty percent of its total sales. Morita is the man the company must thank for this success outside of Japan. In 1953, he first arrived in the United States to try to develop a market for transistor radios. He was then executive director of the Tokyo Communication Industry Company, the precursor of Sony. Within three years he had made Sony a regular exporter to the United States. In 1955, he had received an offer from an American appliance manufacturer to buy 100,000 transistor radios on condition that Sony mark them with the American manufacturer's brand name. This huge order equaled Sony's total production for eighteen months, and the Japan office leaped at the offer. Profitable though the contract would have been, however, Morita persuaded the company to decline it; he valued the workmanship and quality of Sony's product too highly to let it bear another label.

For eighteen months, beginning in 1963, Morita stationed himself in the United States and personally directed an energetic campaign to sell Sony radios. He was already a vice-president and member of the board, and for an executive of that rank to manage an overseas sales campaign was in itself unprecedented. His success may have been due

[253]

in part to the flair of his manner and his way of life. He lived in one of New York's finest apartment houses, shopped with credit cards at Tiffany's and other elegant stores. He and his family socialized easily with Americans. In his office, he displayed the Rising Sun flag. A friend of his, critic Chieko Akiyama, claims that he got along so well with Americans "because he had none of the obsequiousness that Japanese characteristically display when interacting with Americans or Europeans."

Morita was also "American" in the way he ran his office. While many Japanese executives in America are apt to apply Japanese paternalism to their American employees, only to be considered "easy marks," Morita gave and demanded full value. "To be a successful employer in the United States, you must be tough enough to fire incompetents without compunction," says Jiro Tokuyama, former manager of the New York branch of the Nomura General Research Institute. "Morita commanded the necessary authority to keep American employees in line. He succeeded by hammering it into the heads of his employees that he was not to be made a fool of."

Some observers credit Sony's success less to Morita's mastery of American business techniques than to its good fortune in entering the American market when it did. It introduced new types of machines, still unknown in America, and unhindered by competition, trade practices, and conventions, Sony had a clear run of the market. Still, Morita's skills in taking advantage of that market are undeniable. He was the only Japanese whom Morgan Guaranty Trust Company of New York asked to join its international committee, an organ formed to advise the bank on managing its international business. Says John F. Loughran, a Morgan vice-president and general manager of its Tokyo branch: "Morita is thoroughly adept at American marketing and financing methods. He is without a doubt the ablest Japanese executive doing business with the United States. The products he sells are not low-priced by any means, but they have certainly enhanced the image of Japanese products in the eyes of the American public."

Yoshihiro Inayama, president of the Japan Steel Corporation, is precisely Morita's opposite. While the Sony executive sells and sells and sells to the United States, Inayama exercises cautious self-restraint. "The Japanese steel industry would not be where it is today if it had not been for exports to the United States," he says by way of explanation. "That is why we feel we should do business with America in a spirit of conciliation. The U. S. could ban the import of Japanese steel at any moment, but it doesn't. We must reciprocate by limiting our exports voluntarily, whether we like it or not. I am sure that such voluntary controls will benefit the industry in the long run." Inayama, who is also president of the Japan Steel Federation and managing director of the Japan Steel Export Association, made his first visit to the United States in 1957, on a mission to obtain scrap iron. A worldwide shortage of scrap iron was beginning, and Clarence Adams, President Eisenhower's adviser on economic affairs, scoffed at the notion of a steel industry that was dependent on imports for scrap. He advised Inayama to get hold of more iron ore and to build more blast furnaces, promising American money, technology, and coal for the purpose. Inayama took this counsel to heart, and soon after his return to Japan the industry began modernizing and re-equipping itself.

Some critics condemn the steel industry's attitude as servile devotion to the United States. The textile industry is one which feels particularly hostile to steel manufacturers. It consists largely of medium- and small-sized mills that must fend for themselves as best they can, while the steel industry is made up of heavily capitalized companies that have been reared with the tender care of the government. "The steel industry sells at prices dictated by American buyers," textile men charge. "It claims to be earning dollars from exports, but look how much it pays for raw-material imports. Its international balance of payments is in the red."

"Both the Japanese and American steel industries have a stronger sense of public service than any other industry in either country," observes Akira Harada, director of the International Trade Bureau in the Ministry of International Trade and Industry. "They are convinced that steel builds a nation and that the peace of the world depends on their cooperation."

Scholarly Exchange

NOT MANY foreigners have been decorated by the Japanese government, and still fewer have been thus honored more than once. Professor Maurice H. Seavers of the University of Michigan has received two decorations for his contributions to pharmacology in Japan and for his efforts against drug addiction. He was granted the Third Order of Merit with the Cordon of the Rising Sun in 1963, and four years later he received the Second Order of Merit with the Sacred Treasure. The recommendation for the latter decoration was signed by the presidents of the Japan Medical Science Association, the Japan Medical Association, and the Japan Pharmacology Association, as well as by the chairman of the Committee on Measures Against Narcotic Drugs. It was accompanied by another testimonial signed by the presidents of important universities throughout Japan; never before had so many joined in recommending a medal for a foreigner. The prime mover in gathering support for Seavers's second medal was Tsusai Sugawara, president of the Society Against the Three Evils (drugs, prostitution, and VD). Sugawara recalls that the Decoration Division of the Prime Minister's Office first rejected Seavers's candidacy for the second medal, saying that only Nobel Prize scientists and scholars could be considered for the Second Order of Merit. "I went directly to the prime minister and asked which was more important, winning a Nobel Prize or a genuine effort toward stamping out drug addiction."

Professor Tsuneyoshi Tanabe of Hokkaido University credits Seavers with revolutionizing pharmacology in Japan, changing it from a German approach to an American one. An unending succession of Japanese pharmacology students worked under him at the University of Michigan, so many that their apartments and furniture and some of their equipment were regularly handed along from one to the next. Seavers's former students now teach at twenty-three Japanese universities.

It is not only pharmacology students who have chosen to pursue advanced studies in the United States. Japanese students in nearly all fields have gone there, often with American financial assistance. Japanese scientists have craved the environment, facilities, and liberal grants offered by American universities, and in these scientists the American institutions have found valuable skills and abilities. Many Japanese scholars have remained to make permanent careers in the United States. The Institute of International Education estimates the number of Japanese scholars who decide to stay in the U. S. at twelve hundred each year, the third largest national group after British and Indian. The number of Japanese students arriving to work at American universities is four thousand each year, the seventh largest group.

Japanese-American scientific relations reached their apex in 1961, with the creation of the Japanese-American Committee on Cooperation in Science as a product of the Washington talks between President Kennedy and Prime Minister Ikeda. At the first conference of this committee, in Tokyo, the United States was represented by Dr. Harry C. Kelly, then deputy director of the National Science

Foundation. The Japanese delegation was headed by Dr. Kankuro Kaneshige, professor emeritus of Tokyo University, and included Dr. Seiji Kaya, president of the same university, and Kiyo-o Wadachi, then president of the Science Council. The Japanese government had initially intended to sponsor the conference, but Kaya and the others insisted on doing it themselves.

Kelly and Kaneshige had been friends for more than fifteen years, since the early days of the Occupation. Immediately after the war, the cyclotron at the Physics and Chemistry Research Institute in Tokyo was destroyed by order of SCAP. This had alarmed American scientists so much that Kelly had been dispatched to Tokyo to investigate the matter. He remained in Japan four years. One winter he went to Hokkaido University to check some apparatus related to the cyclotron that had been moved to Hokkaido for safekeeping during the war. While there he was caught in a heavy snowstorm and rescued by local villagers. Their kindness made him a passionate friend of Japan, and it was through his intercession that the buildings of Hokkaido University were spared requisition by the Occupation for use as a military installation. Later, Kelly helped create the Japan Science Council, hoping that it would strengthen the position of Japanese scientists. Kaya met Kelly daily to prepare for the formation of the council. Today he credits Kelly with having saved Japanese science, except for its aeronautics and nuclear physics branches, from the Occupation.

In the past ten years, the Japanese-American Committee on Cooperation in Science has conducted 308 joint-research projects—in such areas as the geology of the Pacific region, cancer, and agricultural chemicals—and has sponsored 175 seminars. During this decade, each country has spent about 5.5 million dollars on the committee. More than fifteen hundred Japanese and American scientists have visited each other's country. But some groups within the Japan Science Council have been critical of the fact that the committee has limited cooperation in science exclusively to Japan and the United States, seeing this as an academic equivalent of the binational security arrangements. The areas that the committee has selected to spend its funds on have also been under some fire. "My greatest concern," recalls Kaya, who represented Japan on the committee for nine years, "was to see that Japanese members of the committee cooperated with no feelings of inferiority. I was determined to maintain relations of equality and reciprocity between American and Japanese scholars. I tried to distribute the financial burden equitably, and took pains to select for research those areas that were of mutual interest."

[257]

Recently, scholarly exchange programs have begun to change drastically. The Vietnam war and the need for economic retrenchment are forcing sizable cuts in American research grants and scholarship funds for foreign students. At the height of the Fulbright program, about three hundred Japanese students went to the United States annually; in 1970, there were only thirty-five. Many Americans are saying that Japan is now quite wealthy enough to finance foreign study programs of Japanese students, and American members of the Committee on Cooperation in Science hope that future seminars will be held in the United States to save them traveling expenses. Such sentiments do not come exclusively from the American side. Professor Emeritus Chuji Tsuboi of Tokyo University, a leading advocate of scholarly exchange, comments: "Japanese students who want to study in the United States have fallen into the bad habit of relying entirely on American grants. It's time they began to pay their own way."

PART FIVE

America Views
a New Japan

Open an issue of Life, *the* New Yorker, *or almost any other popular American magazine and one is bound to come upon advertisements for Japanese products—whiskies, cameras, electronic equipment, cars—or for Japanese airline services, tours in the Pacific area, and first-class Tokyo hotels. Some of the products are clearly identifiable as Japanese by their names or by the design motifs of the advertisements. Many are not.*

The confusion over whether or not to conceal the national identity of Japanese products in an industry, which by its very nature is especially sensitive to matters of image, raises a question far transcending advertising itself: is Japan's name in America good or bad these days? Certainly, it is far better than it once was. In the late 1950s and early 1960s, when Japanese manufacturers began exporting their goods to the United States in large quantities, they were faced with severe image problems. The horrors of World War II were still fresh and painful memories in the minds of Americans, and the Japanese were considered a devious, warlike, and barbaric people. Moreover, Japan was widely thought of as the source of cheap, shoddy goods. In recent years, however, these images have to a considerable extent been shed, replaced by descriptions that tend to include terms like "diligent and industrious," "high-quality merchandise," "craftsmen of superb technical skill," and the like. There is genuine admiration among many Americans for Japan's traditional culture as well as for the energy and high rate of economic growth that characterize her modern society. Nevertheless, there remains a lingering suspicion and distrust. At the first hint of crisis in present-day economic negotiations, some older Americans are quick to remember Pearl Harbor and the war. Younger people, lacking direct memories of the Pacific War, are often heard to complain of misunderstandings and problems of communication that seem almost certain to arise whenever they deal with Japanese.

The articles in this section attempt to describe the Japan that exists in the minds of Americans today. The material in them is based largely upon the results of a Harris poll conducted especially for the Asahi Shimbun *early in 1971, and amplified by numerous interviews with people of all walks of life throughout the United States. The images that one nation may have of another are always difficult to pin down in any precise way and they are inevitably riddled with mistaken stereotypes, myths, and distortions. Nonetheless, commonly held notions that one people have about another are often as revealing in their inaccuracies as in their truths.*

Such fallacies are particularly striking in the case of the opinions of Japan held by Americans. For a country that has been bound so intimately to Japan for more than a quarter of a century, one might expect America to be much more knowledgeable in things Japanese and wiser in its evaluations of the Japanese people. But, while Japan's new image is a definite improvement upon that of former times, it is yet to be supported by much real understanding. Although penetrating and intelligent opinions were offered by several of the persons interviewed in the United States, most of the comments gathered were marked either by blindness, puzzlement, or a shocking ignorance. The existence of what David Riesman calls an "ignorance curtain" is largely to blame, and it is this curtain that may prove in the future to be no less dangerous than the political and military divisions that go under such names as Iron Curtain and Bamboo Curtain. But even worse than this ignorance of Japan, and perhaps the chief cause of it, is a wall of disinterest that seals off the United States from its Pacific neighbor. Whereas ignorance can be attacked by factual data, disinterest forms an almost impenetrable barrier blocking fruitful give and take with the rest of the world.

If the United States, the most powerful nation in the world, retreats behind the darkened shutters of isolationism, the entire world will suffer. In the long run, however, America will be the greatest loser of all. This is particularly true in its relations with Japan, a nation which it considers an ideological ally and a trading partner of exceeding importance. At a time in history when technology has made communication between nations easier than ever before, ignorance, disinterest, and false myths must not be allowed to block the way to genuine understanding and good will.

The "Ignorance Curtain"

"DO THE Japanese wear Western-style clothing?" Was this question being asked by a young schoolchild? No; incredible though it may seem, it came from the mouth of an educated American adult. Akira Iriye, professor of diplomatic history at the University of Chicago, was amazed when a neighbor of his, a geographer at the university, came to him with this ingenuous query.

At the beginning of a new term at Columbia University, graduate students intending to specialize in Japanese politics were tested on their general knowledge of Japan. Barely half of them knew who was prime minister, and most could not identify a single Japanese political party by name.

Of the 1,613 people aged sixteen or older interviewed in the Harris poll conducted for the *Asahi Shimbun* early in 1971, twenty-nine percent said that they had read books on Japan. American intellectuals, told of the figure, were skeptical. Professor Morton Kaplan, who teaches international politics at the University of Chicago, doubts that it can be accepted at face value. Professor Hans Baerwald, an authority on Japanese politics at UCLA, thinks the figure might be accurate only if the books read include such things as James Michener's best seller *Sayonara*. Their doubts seem to indicate how little the American general public is interested in Japan.

Are the news media any more interested? The head office of *Newsweek* clips every article on Japan that appears in the *New York Times* and the *Washington Post* and sends them to its Tokyo correspondent. "We send him the clippings once a week," says a *Newsweek* staffer in New York, "but a week's accumulation of news on Japan is nowhere near as much as the news of America printed in Japanese papers in a single day."

As a result of such limited coverage, a single news item can drastically alter the American public's view of Japan. As if rushing in to fill the vacuum, American papers play up any abnormal incident occurring in Japan. Yukio Mishima's hara-kiri, the fierce farmer-student battles against the requisition of land for the new Tokyo international airport at Narita, and the violent antiwar struggle of radical student groups have all received sensational coverage recently, but there has been almost no in-depth reporting of their background or of other Japanese news. "It is exaggerating only slightly to say that such incidents as these shocked the American public as much as might the discovery of a man from Mars deep in the mountains," comments John Young, head of the Japanese language department at the University of Hawaii.

Twenty students of the same university, all studying Japanese literature, were asked recently what they thought of the Mishima suicide. Most shrugged and called it an act of savagery or another symptom of the revival of Japanese militarism. "It was as though all America had decided to brand it that by common consent," observes Hoover Tateishi, a faculty member of the university. "But these were people who supposedly understood Mishima's literature."

The Japanese are supplied daily with full coverage of American news, including almost everything from hot pants to the full texts of the president's speeches. The news that Americans get of Japan, however, is spotty and fragmentary. When some event does make news, Americans have no store of general information or background knowledge to help them make a balanced judgment of the incident. A case in point is the recent failure of a staff member of the Japan National Tourist Organization (JNTO) to convince two worried Chicago parents that Japan was anything but a barbaric, terror-ridden country. Their daughter had earlier come in tears to the Chicago office of JNTO, saying that she wanted to go to Japan to join her fiancé, a Marine stationed at Yokosuka, but her parents would not hear of it. Would someone from JNTO try to persuade them that it would be all right? When the JNTO man met the parents they reminded him of the recent TV coverage of riots at Narita and the militancy of antiwar students, and insisted that no power on earth could persuade them to let their daughter go off to so perilous a country.

"Ever since Pearl Harbor, the Japanese have had a reputation in the American mind for erratic, unpredictable behavior. Our distorted and fragmentary knowledge of Japan, gleaned from scanty and intermittent news, only serves to reinforce that negative image," says a reporter of the *Washington Evening Star* who came to Japan to gather material for a special story in the spring of 1971.

In the past few years, the Vietnam war, the decay of the cities, and economic problems have forced Americans to turn their gaze inward, and they are growing rapidly less interested in the rest of the world. A Gallup poll taken during the invasion of Laos revealed that one out of every three Americans was completely unaware of that military operation. When President Nixon devoted much of an exclusive ABC-TV interview in March, 1971, to the issue of troop withdrawal from Vietnam, only fourteen percent of the prime-time audience was watching.

Professor David Riesman of Harvard University is troubled by what he calls the American "ignorance curtain" shutting its eyes off from the rest of the world, but doubts it will be possible to tear open a hole in it. "Once," says Riesman, "the United States managed to isolated herself from Europe, but not from Asia and Latin America. What we seem to be entering now is an era of total isolationism. If Americans ever become really interested in Japan, it will probably be only when the Japanese prejudices against her minority groups or against Korean residents develop into violent racial conflict. Paradoxically, then, the low level of American interest may be lucky for Japan."

Service as a Commodity

WHEN Japan Air Lines inaugurated 747 jumbo-jet service on its transpacific route, many Americans expected a speedy decline in the airline's fabled service. The more passengers in a plane, they figured, the less efficient the service must inevitably become. They were wrong. When a stewardess went from seat to seat taking orders for cocktails, one passenger expected to get his only after she had finished taking everyone's order. But unlike on other airlines, his drink was in his hand within moments. Amazed, he could only speculate on what sort of magic might have been used to prepare his drink so fast. Later he asked Akio Sakamoto, manager of JAL's Washington office, how it was done. Sakamoto only laughed and gestured with his fingers the way a baseball catcher signals the pitcher. According to Shigeo Kameta, JAL's general manager for the Americas, the airline operates on the principle that service is itself a commodity to be bought and sold. So do all American passenger airlines, but all of them are in the red and JAL is making money.

The San Jose branch of the Bank of Tokyo has more money on deposit than any other California bank. Executives of American securities firms often come to ask its secret. "Our only secrets are the close, familylike personal relations between our management and staff and our service to clients," answers manager Kaoru Murakami.

[263]

These days it is the rare American who does not complain bitterly of poor consumer services and their high cost. "Marry a mechanic" is solid advice to the prospective bride, for labor is poorly distributed and good repairmen are hard to find. Repair services are as costly as they are unreliable: service charges have risen by as much as forty percent since 1965, and commodity prices by twenty percent.

Accustomed to terrible service, Americans are frequently amazed at the treatment they receive in most Japanese restaurants in the United States. The moment he is seated, the customer is handed a steaming *oshibori* (a small towel, neatly folded and served on an attractive tray). When he has finished wiping his hands and face with the soothing towel, a cup of tea is brought, unasked for. Along with their generally reasonable prices, it is their pleasant service that Americans point to in explaining the success of Japanese restaurants in the United States. There can be no doubt that thoughtful service has the appeal of novelty for Americans.

More and more Americans are beginning to wonder if obliging customer service is not an element central to the dynamics of Japanese business and to the thought patterns underlying Japanese business techniques. Professor Philip Kuhn of the University of Chicago, an authority on Chinese philosophy, suspects that Japan has a "business culture" all her own. The traits and conduct of businessmen of a country are based not merely on economic rules but also on broad cultural assumptions that, in turn, have developed out of the national cultural tradition. The pleasing customer service that Americans comment on so frequently, says Kuhn, is only the small visible part of a huge iceberg hidden underwater.

"American businessmen can only do well in Japan to the extent that they grasp this point. Since Japan will continue to develop as a market for American business, research on Japanese behavior is an urgent necessity," comments Raymond Vernon, professor of international business at Harvard University.

Peter Drucker, author of the best-selling book *The Age of Discontinuity*, says much the same thing in a recent article in the *Harvard Business Review*. He notes that while it would be both foolish and impossible for the West to try to imitate Japan, Westerners would do well to study minutely the Japanese rules of conduct. Drucker pays close attention to the fact that a policy decision in a Japanese business firm is based on intra-organization consensus reached only after long deliberation. He also notes that Japanese employees work until the day they retire as though they were still being trained. He believes that this attitude of discipline and endless training has developed out of the feudal ethic of the samurai who worked tirelessly to perfect his skills in both military and literary arts.

But Americans are not altogether unanimous in their admiration for Japanese business manners. Samuel Yorty, mayor of Los Angeles, says: "In Japan, a deal is made while one is innocently drinking tea." Tom McCall, governor of Oregon, sees the point of a dagger sticking out from the cloak of formal Japanese politeness. Many Americans, surprised by differences between their own conduct and that of Japanese they meet, urge that greater efforts toward mutual understanding be made. Albert Craig, professor of Japanese history at Harvard, observes that one cannot tell a Japanese person that he is mistaken about something, even when he is. Americans, however, feel no inhibition about saying bluntly to one another: "You are wrong."

At JAL's staff training center in New York, Japanese and American employees are all trained together. The American employees find most incomprehensible the totally unaffected way in which their Japanese colleagues can ask passengers: "Would you like a cup of tea?" or "Is there anything I can do for you?" Making such offers is second nature for Japanese, and JAL places special emphasis on such unsolicited offers of service. "Our American employees find it difficult to imitate such behavior without appearing officious," says Mitsuo Yoshida, head instructor at the center. "For someone to intuit another's unspoken feelings is considered a sign of good will in Japan, but not necessarily in America."

"I don't want to say that Japanese conduct is absolutely unique," says Paul W. McCracken, chairman of the President's Council of Economic Advisers, "but there is no denying that Japanese act differently from us. First of all, there is a distinct hierarchy of rank and seniority in Japanese firms. Secondly, Japanese employees have a strong sense of identity with their companies. Third, they are disciplined. Fourth, they are savings-minded. These and all their other qualities cannot be covered by any easy theory."

Despite the European origin of the great majority of American citizens, there are numerous institutes in the United States conducting research on how best to do business in Europe. Vernon points to centers researching Britain and West Germany as examples, and finds it curious that there has been so little organized research on Japan. He himself has begun this research for the benefit of American businessmen who want to enter the Japanese market. Considering the problems of business relations today, it seems only natural that the study of Japanese personality should be initiated by economists investigating the "business culture." Their researches may well lead to a serious study of Japanese psychology as a whole. Gone forever is the day when the Japanese way of thinking could be dismissed as "inscrutable" and Japanese behavior regarded as a contemptible breach of Western etiquette.

Remember Pearl Harbor

"IT'S PEARL HARBOR all over again! They've taken us by surprise!" shrieked the lady reporter at a White House news conference on March 9, 1971. Presidential press secretary Ronald Ziegler had just announced that the Japanese government was unilaterally suspending official talks on the textile issue, a thorny problem that had been troubling both governments for some time.

Several months earlier, a Japanese trade mission led by Masao Anzai, president of the Showa Denko Company, toured the United States. At a reception in New York, one American executive, exasperated by Japan's laggardly trade-liberalization policies, exclaimed: "I just want to make sure you know that there are plenty of Americans who haven't forgotten Pearl Harbor!"

Whenever the slightest tension occurs in relations between the United States and Japan, memories of Pearl Harbor inevitably come welling up in the minds of Americans old enough to have lived through the war. Professor Akira Iriye of the University of Chicago says that Americans began to take Japan seriously only when they were engaged in a war with her. If Pearl Harbor first opened American eyes to Japan, it also left with them the indelible image of Japan as a sly brat, not to be trusted for a moment. The intensity of American hatred for Japan whipped up after Pearl Harbor is clearly revealed by the fact that seventy-three percent of the opinion sample in a 1942 poll branded Japanese as "sneaky." *Asahi Shimbun* correspondent Takeshi Fujikawa, who worked on a Honolulu newspaper during the war, recalls: "Every time my copy referred to Pearl Harbor as a 'surprise attack,' the term was corrected to read 'treacherous attack.' "

An American mother will tell her boy to pick on somebody his own size if he wants to fight. No competition is considered fair unless both parties are on equal footing. At least, in American society, where the competitive spirit is fierce, both parties are supposed to start from positions of equal strength. Americans, therefore, view Pearl Harbor largely as a moral affront, in which Japan broke the rules of the game.

[266]

The American movie *Tora! Tora! Tora!* did not draw well at most theaters across the country. In Fresno, California, which has a large population of Japanese-Americans, it played to full houses. On one occasion, whites beat up Japanese-Americans in the audience, and Tetsuo Imagawa, director of the Japanese language section of the National Defense Language Institute, mentions having received phone calls warning him to watch out if he went to see the movie.

F. Robert, a graduate of New York University who is now driving a cab in Hawaii, sounds like one in a million Americans when he justifies Pearl Harbor. Believing that military engagements can be evaluated only according to their success or failure, he says: "Surprise attacks have been made in all wars. . . . After all, Pearl Harbor killed no civilians."

To most Americans, Pearl Harbor was an infraction of the rules of war but Hiroshima was not. This sentiment is behind the inscription below an aerial photograph of Hiroshima in ruins that hangs today in the Truman Museum in Independence, Missouri: "The bomb dropped on Hiroshima three hours ago . . . was the largest in history. Japan started the war at Pearl Harbor; she has been repaid many times over."

"Maybe Pearl Harbor resulted from our having forced Japan into a corner," says a member of the White House policy staff. "But I believe that the atomic bombings were a necessary evil to prevent further loss of life . . . . After all, we didn't start the war." Whereas Japanese think of the dropping of the atomic bombs as a moral problem, Americans regard these weapons as no more than large bombs. Thus, sixty-four percent of the opinion sampled on the 1971 Harris poll commissioned by the *Asahi* could maintain that the bombs were "necessary and proper." Americans react differently to nuclear weapons closer to home, however. Plans to install antiballistic-missile sites in Montana, the Dakotas, and Massachusetts provoked fierce opposition among local residents, and the town of Indian Point, New York, has been up in arms for ten years against a scheme to construct an atomic power station nearby.

Professor Philip Kuhn of the University of Chicago tries to explain the apparently contradictory attitudes of Americans toward nuclear arms. "Americans who were asked by the Harris polltakers: 'Were the atomic bombings necessary?' might be moved by rationalistic considerations to judge them 'a necessary evil.' But if asked the more general question of whether they support the use of nuclear arms, Americans—especially the younger generation—would oppose them."

The 1970 American national census put the average age at twenty-seven, one year younger than the previous census. A generation which knew neither Pearl Harbor nor Hiroshima is steadily increasing in numbers, and the older generation, with its strong memories of the Pacific War, is decreasing.

The U. S. S. *Arizona*, sunk at Pearl Harbor with 1,120 men on board, remains where it lay after the bombs of December 7, 1941. On its bridge, which protrudes above the water's surface, there has been constructed a memorial to that day. "Let me tell you about Pearl Harbor . . ." began the young military officer acting as guide for a large group of tourists, including an *Asahi* reporter. Not once in his narrative did he mention the word Japan. The tourists eagerly clicked their "Made in Japan" cameras as he spoke.

Disappearing Stereotypes

THE PICTURE in the *American Educator Encyclopedia* showed a family dressed in Chinese clothes, seated in a Chinese room, bowing and burning incense before a Buddhist image. But the caption identified the family as Japanese and went on to say that the Japanese had always believed a goddess dwelled in each rice plant. When this odd set of confusions came to the attention of the Japan International Education and Information Center, it informed the editors of the encyclopedia that Chinese had been mistaken for Japanese and that there was no belief in Japan linking a goddess with rice plants. Nevertheless, the 1969 edition of the encyclopedia was published without correction.

Such gross errors are growing increasingly rare, and are by no means restricted to the United States, but for many people in the West the word "Japan" still evokes hardly more than Mount Fuji, geisha, jinrikisha, and hara-kiri.

In the 1930s and 1940s a series of American movies was made featuring Mr. Moto, a fictitious Japanese private detective. He had been invented to compete with Charlie Chan, the enormously popular Chinese detective. The tiny actor Peter Lorre, made up with slanting eyes, played the part of Mr. Moto with short, nimble steps and quick, jerky gestures. In the Harris poll taken for the *Asahi Shimbun* in 1971, American respondents were asked what associations first occurred to them at the mention of the word "Japan." Sixteen percent indicated:

"a short Oriental person with slanting eyes." Some admitted that this might be a lingering image of Mr. Moto.

Once such ideas are established in the popular imagination, almost no amount of factual information can correct their errors or distortions. Westerners, convinced that the East is a mystical realm of the spirit, find it difficult to grasp the realities of modern, industrial Japan. It is not unnatural that the Japanese should often try to turn popular misconceptions about their country to their own advantage. When the Takashimaya Department Store opened its New York branch in 1958, it intended to cash in on the exoticism of the Japanese image. The store was abundantly stocked with quaint Japanese wares: folding screens, works of art, crafts, textiles, porcelains, and the like. Contrary to all expectations, the merchandise did not sell. Admission-free exhibitions of Japanese arts and crafts drew large crowds, but few people bought. Takashimaya then decided to forget about being "Japanese," and converted itself into a general-goods store. The switch paid off and in a few years Takashimaya's New York branch, which had been operating at a loss, was out of the red. Today, the store on Fifth Avenue no longer attempts a Japanese atmosphere, but its management is not sure that this is right either. "We are exploring ways of adding more of a Japanese touch to the store again, but at the same time remaining commercial," says manager Yoshimasa Takehara.

When the Library of Congress established its Far Eastern section in 1930, librarian Shio Sakanishi was charged with the task of building up the Japanese collection. She soon realized from reading the literature on Japan that was available in the West that the country had been treated primarily as a land of tourism and quaint exoticism, or less charitably, as an international curiosity. To a great extent, that image remains current. During her long years in the United States, Miss Sakanishi took pains to correct mistaken ideas that Americans had formed about Japan. When she tried to wipe away the myth that the Japanese were a people of particularly loose morals and great promiscuity, Americans well read in tales about the Yoshiwara, geisha, and mixed bathing looked annoyed, as if she were spoiling their fun. "I'd prefer to think of Japan as the land of Mount Fuji, geisha girls, and all that," a Madison Avenue advertising executive told an *Asahi* reporter in a *sushi* restaurant in New York. "Although I must confess that it's people like me who have been pushing things like Coke and Nescafé in Japan ever since the end of the war."

Throughout the 1960s, the Japan National Tourist Organization advertised Japan abroad as "an industrial country with snow." Their posters did not show a single geisha or rikisha. It also stopped representing Japan as a land of contradictions, with the old and the new existing in dramatic juxtaposition—no more posters of the new "bullet train" racing past the foot of Mount Fuji. The idea behind the new advertising tactics was to eliminate the image of Japan as a semitropical, and therefore backward, country. It is hoped that this new image will crystallize at the Sapporo Winter Olympics in February, 1972, and pay off in increased tourism.

Gerald Curtis, associate professor of Japanese political science at Columbia University, believes that the emerging new image of Japan as an affluent nation is beginning to stick in the United States. Important factors contributing to the new image are the 1964 Tokyo Olympics, EXPO '70, Herman Kahn foreseeing the twenty-first century as "the Japanese century," and the great numbers of Japanese tourists. The 210,000 who now travel to the United States annually have surpassed the volume of British tourists, and are second in number only to visitors from all other countries on the American continents.

Albert Craig, professor of Japanese history at Harvard, says that his strongest overall impression of Japan is that she has grown rich. "When I was studying at Kyoto University around 1951, even distinguished professors would spend only about thirty yen each day for a lunch of whale steak. Every time I've been back since then, Japan has gotten a little richer, and I notice changes in the faces of Japanese people."

Japan's affluent new image has inevitably set off demands for a greater contribution to international society and for Japan to carry a larger burden of responsibility. There is always the problem of slogans distorting the total image of a country, but that may be less a danger now than it used to be. More and more young Americans are coming to Japan alone, and after traveling about the country, taking back with them a great variety of experiences of Japanese life. "As more and more young Americans come to know Japan, the foolish old stereotypes should quickly disappear," says Shin'ya Takahashi, manager of JNTO's Chicago office.

Seven-day Work Week

A MERICAN government and business offices usually remain fully lit well into the night, long after the working day has ended. The idea is to discourage burglars. Around eight o'clock, the cleaning crews arrive and can be seen from outside as they do their sweeping and dusting. In some offices, men can be seen working at their desks as the cleaners sweep around them. They are invariably Japanese, employees of Japanese banks or trading companies. The manager of the Portland, Oregon, branch of the Bank of Tokyo was caught in his office late one night by an *Asahi* reporter. "We're working against time to finish up our annual balance sheets," he explained sheepishly. "We don't always work this late."

Japanese work hard. That is the general belief of Americans, who are no longer known for their diligence, but the impression is far from new. In a 1942 poll conducted by Princeton University's public opinion research institute, respondents were asked to choose the attributes that best applied to Japanese people. Thirty-nine percent picked "hard working." At a time when intense anti-Japanese feelings were being fanned by words like "treacherous," "sly," and "cruel," at least four out of ten Americans were willing to admit that the Japanese were also diligent. Behind this feeling must have been the experience of hard-working Japanese-Americans.

"The only way Americans of Japanese origin can make a place for themselves here is by hard work," says Norman Mineta, gesticulating firmly with his fist. On April 13, 1971, Mineta was elected mayor of San Jose, California, by a record-shattering sixty-two percent of the vote, making him the first Japanese-American mayor of a major American city. The town's population of 450,000 includes only 12,000 Japanese-Americans. "It was by hard work, and only hard work, that I won white votes too," says Mineta. He worked until after nine at night, seven evenings a week, when he was deputy mayor. "My wife never once complained," he says with a smile.

Because the American work week is only five days, working seven days a week, and not minding overtime, would be a sure-fire way to get ahead, one might think. "But Americans have a deep-rooted feeling that the diligence of the Japanese makes for unfair competition. It's akin to the fear of losing," comments Gerald Curtis of Columbia University.

Shin'ichi Uozumi, president of the Dentsu Corporation of America, also puts in a seven-day work week. He wakes up in his Manhattan apartment at five every morning and immediately begins playing records of Japanese music. Then he takes a shower, booming out popular songs in a voice that reverberates through the bathroom. He next performs a series of special exercises that he calls "octopus dancing." He spends the next two hours reading, mostly news magazines or trade periodicals, but occasionally a best-selling novel, taking notes on whatever it might be. He walks to his office, and when asked how long it takes, he says: "Exactly two thousand paces." A pace-counter that he wears on his hip registers how far Uozumi walks as he makes his way through the valleys of skyscrapers: at the end of a day it usually reads more than ten thousand.

During the day, Uozumi receives guests and visits business associates. This keeps him constantly walking and talking. He sends his American staff home at five every afternoon, and then sits down to his desk work. If he has a spare moment, or if he feels drowsy, he is likely to pick up and translate some material that might prove useful for later reference. Thus he keeps at hand a constantly growing file of data for speeches on almost any topic. "I can't take it easy even on weekends. I still have so much to learn."

One meets such hard-working Japanese all over America. On the West Coast there is a salesman who spends time every morning thumbing through the yellow pages of the telephone book, selecting potential customers. He then sets out with a suitcase full of the wigs he sells, traveling all over the city selling, selling, selling. "If I could get my hands on a large enough supply, I could sell a Japanese wig to every woman in America," he boasts. On an Alaskan island, a young Japanese man living with his pregnant wife turns out to be the entire work force for a lumber yard. In a certain city, a Japanese dishwasher works so hard that his white fellow workers in the restaurant joke that it hurts their hands just to watch him.

Paul W. McCracken, chairman of the President's Council of Economic Advisers, showers praise on the Japanese for their diligence. He recalls a West German businessman saying that his counˈrymen had once equaled the Japanese in their capacity for hard work, but over the past ten years have slipped far behind.

A community of interests has led to solid and fruitful cooperation between Japanese businessmen and American Jews. Importing, brokerage, wholesale selling, and other distribution and service businesses in the United States are held largely in the hands of Jews. New York advertising agents estimate that as much as ninety-nine percent of American imports from Japan that require brokerage service are handled by Jewish merchants. Seventy percent of American travel agents dealing in tours to Japan and other tourist services are Jewish. The Japanese-Jewish success is sometimes referred to as "the J-J era." Recently Jewish organizations in the United States have begun studying Japan with great enthusiasm. One sponsors a regular series of Japanese movies.

Japanese businessmen, although frequently noted for their inability to assimilate themselves to their foreign surroundings, are reaffirming for Americans the image of the hard-working Japanese. The general social situation in the United States today serves only to cast the diligent Japanese into bold relief. "A major obstacle to becoming a postindustrial society is the loss of a sense of value for hard work," says David Riesman, Harvard University's famed sociologist. "It is the most serious problem facing America today."

Buy Japanese

A GREAT stir was created recently when the *New York Times* devoted front-page space to the story of a woman living alone whose apartment had been burglarized so many times that she felt safe only after sealing her door with eight separate locks. Apparently crime had made the city unsafe to live in. But in Portland, Oregon, a city of 400,000, no one even bothers to lock his car. Flowers are plentiful, and Portland is sometimes called the "city of roses." She enjoys an affectionate sister-city relationship with Sapporo. A portrait of Crown Princess Michiko hangs on the wall in the office of Mayor Terry Schrunk, and a large Hakata doll occupies a place of honor. It is a conservative city, and its people are friendly toward Japan.

A community unusually tranquil for a port town, Portland seethed with excitement over a recent fight to lure Japanese shipping. In 1970, six Japanese shipping firms announced plans to build piers in Seattle and Vancouver to handle containerized transpacific transport of the lumber and wheat that Japan imports from the American west coast in enormous quantities. Portland launched a drive to lure Japanese containerized ships to its harbor too. Despite the "Buy American" campaign, the city fathers bought a crane from Hitachi, Ltd. They also sent a mission to Tokyo to make "sales" calls on the six shipping firms and plead Portland's case.

Portland suffers from a certain geographic disadvantage: it is a river port, well inland from the Pacific coast. For that reason, the

Japanese shippers had selected the coastal cities of Seattle and Vancouver. But Oregon, with little industry besides commerce, depends heavily on trade with Japan. In 1970, $290 million in exports and $150 million in imports passed through Portland, amounting to about forty percent of the Oregon economy. When the Japanese shippers decided against using Portland, the Portland Port Authority and the Oregon Transport Bureau appealed the decision to the Federal Maritime Commission, saying it was a life-and-death issue for the city. The commission ruled against Portland on the grounds that the shipping firms were free to choose their ports. In a free enterprise system, they need follow only the economic dictates of cost and profit.

Portland then took its case to the Federal Court of Appeals. There was no great hope of success, but as the newspaper the *Oregonian* stated eloquently: "Oregon has never gone down to defeat without first putting up a good fight." Unexpectedly, this round proved favorable, for the court ruled to temporarily ban containerized Japanese ships from calling at Seattle until a public hearing was held in Portland and the city's case investigated further. That intermediate ruling was in itself a heavy blow to the shippers, for it would cost each of them nearly $300 thousand a month to keep their vessels out of Seattle. They decided to reopen negotiations with the Portland Port Authority, and finally reached a mutually agreeable settlement: an average of three ships would call at Seattle and Vancouver every month and one and a half at Portland.

The *Golden Arrow*, the first Japanese ship to arrive, steamed up the Columbia River proudly flying the Rising Sun flag. As soon as she entered the harbor, one of her containers was landed and hauled to Fifth Avenue, Portland's main street. There, apples, strawberries, and other fruit packed in the container were extravagantly handed out to local Japanese residents and to any Japanese-Americans passing along the street. The *Golden Arrow*, well pleased by the success of her call at Portland, later sailed for home with a load of American onions to relieve the current Japanese vegetable shortage.

The so-called "container-ships affair" had political ramifications that extended beyond the economic benefits to the city of Portland. The shipping agreement was reached on November 3, 1970—two days before the gubernatorial primary. It had been the understanding that the announcement of the agreement would be held off until after the primary, but Gov. Tom McCall wanted the news to go out the day before the primary. He turned to Keisuke Ochi, the Japanese consul general in Portland, for help in getting the consent of the Japanese shippers. Ochi put through a midnight international telephone call to

Yoshiya Ariyoshi, president of Nippon Yusen Kaisha (N. Y. K. Line), the company that had been representing all six of the shipping firms. Ariyoshi gave the go-ahead on announcing the settlement, and McCall went on to win re-election.

Successful political lobbying in the United States follows a fixed sequence, and any departures from the pattern may set sparks flying. Lobbying should first be conducted on the local level (among both local politicians and leaders of the business community), next at the national Congress, and finally with the executive branch of the administration. In her negotiations on the textile issue—a matter that former undersecretary of state George Ball called a local issue affecting only the South—Japan attempted to reverse the established order by linking textiles to the question of Okinawan reversion. The textile negotiations consequently collapsed in failure. Portland's success in the "container-ships affair" may be attributed to diligent lobbying that followed the proper channels. She first enlisted the assistance of Sen. Mark Hatfield and Rep. Wendell Wyatt, both close friends of McCall's. Later, at the Federal Court of Appeals, the city received behind-the-scenes help from the American consul general in Seoul, another friend of McCall's, who had earlier worked in the New York law offices of Richard Nixon and John Mitchell.

According to one influential Oregon businessman, the state has only one percent of the American population, one percent of the country's resources, and receives only one percent of local grants given out by the federal government. He feels that Oregon should seek economic advancement through closer ties with Japan, which is not much farther from the state than Washington, D. C. Oregon's neighbors, Washington and California, share this attitude, especially since both were hard hit by the curtailment of the federally funded program to develop the supersonic transport.

Unlike the overall U. S. trade with Japan, that of the Western states is marked by an excess of exports to Japan. Japan is a top-value customer becasue she can pay cash. "We welcome Japanese capital in Oregon," says McCall. "We don't mind if our Japanese imports increase. We know that we'll be left way behind if we stick too closely to the slogan 'Keep Oregon Green.'" The governor is now seeking to persuade Japan Air Lines to divert one of its three weekly flights to Chicago to Portland. "I don't want Japan to forget," he adds, "that we have as much self-respect as she."

Before the "container-ships affair," there had never been any real trouble between Japan and Oregon. "That incident showed us how serious the consequences for Oregon might be if Japan were suddenly

[275]

to desert us," comments the head of the Portland Port Authority. It is clear that if Japanese businessmen will respect local interests and sentiment and promote their affairs with care and consideration, the stage is well set in Oregon for further inroads of goods "Made in Japan."

Japanese Pianos
from Alaskan Woods

"USED to be just a fishing village. There was only one road, a thousand yards long or so, running right through the middle of town. What you see here now is all thanks to the Japanese company." This is how Mayor Shepherd of Sitka on Baranof Island in southeastern Alaska describes the town's spectacular recent development. Sitka is an old town, dating back to the days of Russian rule. Today, it is perhaps the only American town that depends exclusively on Japanese industry for its economic existence. Since the Alaska Pulp Company first began operations there in 1959, the population of Baranof Island has doubled to six thousand, and nearly half the people are on the payroll of the Japanese company.

The Alaska Pulp Company is a Japanese firm, but its local branch has been incorporated under American law. Cutting wood from the federally owned Tongass Forest nearby, it is a major supplier of Japan's synthetic fiber, paper, and lumber industries. In the late 1950s, when plans for the company's advance into Alaska were first announced, American paper industries opposed them strenuously. They were overwhelmed, however, by the local Alaskan enthusiasm for economic development.

"The piano sounding boards stamped 'Made in Japan' that are so well received at home and abroad are all made of Sitka spruce," says Kazuyoshi Hayashi, local manager of the Alaska Pulp Company. "They tell me that no sounding boards produce such beautiful sounds as those made of wood from mountains exposed to glaciers," he adds, giving a poetic motivation to what is in fact a hard, rough industry.

Alaska Pulp's Sitka branch has only nine Japanese on its staff; all its other employees—450 men on the factory labor force and 500 lumberjacks—are American. "After a couple of early strikes for better pay and working conditions, we learned our lesson. Work

[276]

management is now left entirely in the hands of American personnel. The Japanese staff retains top authority, but actually we just watch what's going on from the windows of our offices," laughs Hayashi in explanation of the company's system of indirect administration.

Whenever there is a fire in Sitka, Alaska Pulp's engines are called out to help fight it. When tourist boats arrive from the lower states, the company offers them the use of its pier. When there is a power failure in town, Alaska Pulp shares its power supply; its power station can generate 25,000 kilowatts, the town's only 14,000. Every year the company pays more than eight million dollars in wages, a figure nearly ten times the size of the town's budget.

"There is no question that Alaska Pulp has benefited our town economically, but I would also like to stress the cultural benefits that have come out of the Japanese-American contact," says Sitka school superintendant Havvik. He is referring to more than just the flower-arranging and doll-making classes taught by the wives of the Japanese staff members. Mayor Shepherd adds that he wants to take advantage of Alaska's unique history and location in making the island a meeting place of Russian, Japanese, and native cultures. The Eskimos of Alaska, with their black eyes and glossy black hair, do not look very different from Japanese. Perhaps this is one reason why the entry of Asians into Alaskan industry has not seemed as conspicuous as elsewhere in the United States.

Sitka is the only community in all of America where the Japanese language is part of the regular curriculum in elementary school. "Five years ago, we polled Sitka parents about whether Japanese should be taught in the schools," recalls Havvik. "All but two agreed that it should. We had a good laugh when we found out that the only ones against it were Japanese parents." It is the company that ordered textbooks from Japan and that pays the salaries of the Japanese teachers. "In view of Alaska's geography, it seems only natural that Japanese should be taught here. But we have also received inquiries from schools in Connecticut and South Carolina asking how to go about setting up Japanese-language programs," says Havvik.

The Alaska Pulp Company is booming and the town of Sitka is thriving, but what about pollution? "Alaska becoming contaminated by the present level of industry is simply out of the question," says one businessman in Juneau, the state's capital. But the smog and waste material produced by Alaska Pulp's factories have recently been getting critical attention from local fishermen and conservationists. "With the nationwide drive in the United States for environmental protection, Alaska Pulp may well come under fire," says Thad Poul-

[277]

son, editor of the *Sitka Sentinel*, the town's only newspaper. "I doubt very much that they have done adequate research on waste-disposal systems. New, strict water-purity standards are about to be established, and I do know that Alaska Pulp has set pretty low standards for itself. I would advise the company to devote as much effort to public relations as it used to in its early years here, and to work at keeping good relations with the local community."

"Right now we have no intention of making any direct attack on Alaska Pulp," says one leader of the local conservation movement, which has been very critical recently of the indiscriminate lumbering policies of the United States Forestry Service. "We expect the company to make wise decisions on the problem of waste collection. We don't really think that they will just sit back and do nothing until we start making a fuss about it. But still, Sitka shouldn't take any steps that might force Alaska Pulp to close down altogether."

Currently, the Alaska Pulp Company is also embroiled in a dispute with tax authorities over a difference of more than five million dollars in the evaluation of the firm's fixed assets. Thus it seems that the company, after more than a decade in Alaska, is beginning to encounter difficulties over taxes, pollution, and other problems that plague native American firms. Some friction is natural and inevitable. But if good relations between the parties involved are to be maintained, Alaska Pulp may be heading for a period of trial before all its troubles are settled.

"Pure-gold Americans"

IS THE "Go For Broke" fighting spirit of the Nisei 442nd Infantry Combat Team returning to reap laurels on America's battlefields? On March 2, 1971, Specialist Fifth Class Dennis Fujii, twenty-two years old, stood on the steps of the Hawaii State Capitol to receive a special citation of gratitude from the legislature. During the abortive Laos invasion, the "Sansei boy-hero" had given his seat on a helicopter to a wounded South Vietnamese soldier and had remained behind for five days at a point ten kilometers inside Laos. For those five days, newspapers across the United States acclaimed his heroism and demanded his immediate rescue. After he was rescued, he returned to Honolulu for a hero's welcome, wearing a Silver Star. The Royal

Hawaiian Hotel gave him a luxurious suite for nothing for two weeks. On the morning after receiving the citation, he was awakened by Vice-President Spiro Agnew on the telephone, relaying the congratulations, thanks, and pride of President Nixon, who had been steadfastly maintaining that no American ground forces remained in Laos after the operation.

Dennis Fujii declined the offer of a New York ticker-tape parade, preferring to return to his parents' home on Kauai Island. There the local press and the Japanese-language radio station KOHO had been deluged with praise for the young soldier from the Issei residents of the island. These first-generation Japanese-Americans called him "a credit to the Japanese" and "living proof that *yamato damashii* (spirit of Japan) is not dead!" At Waimeia High School, Dennis's alma mater, students asked him whether he intended to ride helicopter rescue missions again. "No thanks, not for me," he answered quickly. "From now on I'll stick to repairing 'copters on the ground. Another six months and I'll be out of the army. I want to come back and get a job as a fireman here on Kauai."

Dennis, obviously, is different from the men of the 442nd Infantry Combat Team who fought so hard to prove their loyalty to America. Nor does he consider himself the "pride of Japan," as he is dubbed by Issei. Gen. Ben Sternberg, commander of U. S. forces in Hawaii, came much closer when he called Dennis a "pure-gold American."

Carl Taketora Hirano, like Dennis Fujii, was trained at Fort Ord, California. He is the eldest son of Takatora Hirano, a Nisei, who runs the Ginza Restaurant in San Jose. But unlike Dennis, and unlike his own parents, Carl is Japanese by nationality: he happened to be born in Kumamoto. Nevertheless, he fought with the U. S. army until he was wounded near Danang in Vietnam and honorably discharged in March, 1971, with two Bronze Stars and three Purple Hearts. "I never once thought of dying for the United States," says Carl. "But once I put on the uniform, I had to act like a soldier. At the risk of being discriminated against, I was really fighting for Japan, because I didn't want to bring shame on the name of Japan. Why did I put on that uniform in the first place? Well, my parents . . ." He chose to leave the thought unfinished. Perhaps he was implying that he joined the army only to get the American citizenship that his parents so badly wanted him to have.

Asked what he thought of the My Lai massacre, and the trials that followed, Carl Hirano said without hesitation: "Anybody who criticizes Calley is a 'stinky.' If I had been in his boots, I would have done the same thing." Carl is only one of many Japanese citizens on permanent-residence status who, for one reason or another, are fighting in the American army.

There are also Americans of Japanese origin who were in Japan during the war and who were attacked or injured by their own countrymen. One is Mrs. Kayoko Shikamata, a Nisei teacher in a Los Angeles high school. Excusing herself quietly, she rolls up the sleeve of her blouse to reveal an ugly keloid scar on her right upper arm. She had returned to Japan with her mother, Mrs. Fusae Morimoto, just before Pearl Harbor, and was living with her parents in Hiroshima when the atomic bomb was dropped. Her mother describes their life after the bomb, and recalls the regular trips to the doctor in Hiroshima. "He would yank her hair every time we went, and then say: 'She's all right, I guess. Her hair doesn't fall out even when I pull it hard.' "

Mrs. Shikamata's younger brother, Koji Morimoto, was a year old when the bomb was dropped on Hiroshima. Growing up, he was often sick with pneumonia or indigestion, but regained his health after the family returned to the United States. In 1971, to his amazement, he was drafted at the age of twenty-seven. A back injury, suffered while practicing judo in high school, disqualified him, but he says: "I was just lucky." His cousin, Masashi Nakashimo, had just been killed in Laos at the age of twenty-three. His parents were often asked by other Nisei why they had let their son go to Vietnam. They cannot answer, but an even harder question to answer is what might be the purpose of the war itself.

Mrs. Morimoto and her two children are only three of more than sixty American *hibakusha* (atom bomb survivors) living in and around Los Angeles. They live quietly, trying to hide from the rest of the world their unspeakable experience of the bombs in Hiroshima and Nagasaki.

Japanese-Americans are, in many cases, torn between two consciousnesses. They are Americans and they are Japanese, and rarely do their surroundings permit them an identity that is not ambiguous. Historically and environmentally, it is difficult for them to determine their real identities. Japanese-American boys, like Dennis Fujii and Carl Hirano and Masashi Nakashimo, fight in Vietnam in order to fulfill their obligations as Americans. But even about such "pure-gold Americans" there are sentiments like those expressed in a letter to a Honolulu newspaper saying: "We should use more Asiatics like Fujii for service in Vietnam." Obviously the writer, clearly a white American, thinks of Japanese-Americans purely as Asians.

From Hawaii alone, eight hundred Japanese-Americans have been killed fighting in American uniforms in World War II, three hundred in Korea, and two hundred thus far in Vietnam.

The Rising Sun on Fifth Avenue

ALMOST any American housewife who uses soy sauce knows the name Kikkoman. This popular Japanese brand can be found on supermarket shelves all over the country. Names like Kikkoman, Honda, and Nikon (usually mispronounced "nigh-kon") have become household words in America.

"Only seven years ago, we threw a sakè party when our sales hit fifty cars in a single month," recalls Fujio Matsukata, assistant manager of the New York branch of the Toyota Motor Company. "These days we sell 17,500 cars a month. Volkswagen dealers all over the country are switching over to Toyota." Datsuns, made by Toyota's major Japanese competitor, are in such demand in California that one has to pay a premium to get one. Most other cars have to be discounted to keep the stock moving.

It was not so long ago that American importers, with the assistance of customs inspectors, would strip Japanese goods of brand names and any other marks that might identify their country of origin. "That is definitely a thing of the past," comments the director of the Portland Port Authority in Oregon. "Technological improvements and tired feet have done the trick," says Shin'ichi Uozumi, president of the Dentsu Corporation of America, accounting for the steady advance of Japanese products in America and for the disappearance of the stigma that used to be attached to them.

During the early 1960s, sales representatives of Japanese firms toiled mightily, trudging day after day from one retailer to another, demonstrating samples and begging them to put the wares on display for a week or two or to take them on temporary trial. This legwork began to pay off in the latter half of the decade.

Japanese automobiles had luck on their side when they first began entering the highly competitive American market. The age of multi-car families had just dawned in the United States, and Japanese manufacturers rode its first wave. A business recession was also under way, and the public interest was shifting away from the large, impractical American cars to small, economical foreign models. "The real deter-

[281]

mining factor was our successful development of small, economical cars that could also provide the speed and maneuverability needed for driving on American highways," says Kiesuke Ono, Toyota's New York manager.

Toyota's advertising in the United States consistently stresses the company's determination to improve the quality of its product. But, like most other Japanese companies—which pay a total of 30 million dollars for advertising annually—Toyota makes little or no mention of the fact that its cars originate in Japan. Americans familiar with Japanese products comment that though commercials for them frequently appear on television, only Japan Air Lines' advertising capitalizes on the fact that it is a Japanese company.

The Japanese Rising Sun flag flies regularly at two spots on New York's Fifth Avenue: the JAL office and the Sony showroom. But there the similarity ends, for the atmosphere inside the two offices could not be more different. JAL underlines its Japanese identity: decorations and displays are carefully designed to impart an aesthetic, Japanese feeling. After an observer passes the Japanese flag to enter the Sony showroom, however, there is absolutely nothing suggestive of Japan. Only English is spoken and the décor is as "international" as in any other such showroom. Sony deliberately avoided exhibiting at an Asian trade fair, called "From the Far Eastern Seas," staged in Minneapolis in 1970. The Sony Corporation considers itself an international unit, and apparently feels that excessive identification of its products with Japan might harm rather than help its sales. But few Japanese industries are quite as confident as Sony, despite Uozumi's contention that the image of Japanese goods as cheap but shoddy has disappeared in America.

Even Uozumi admits that only Japanese cameras and electronic equipment have attained so elevated a reputation that their manufacturers can actually begin to boast of their country of origin as do producers of French wines and perfumes, Scotch whiskies, and Danish furniture. The Matsushita Electrical Industrial Company, makers of products bearing the "National" trademark, is believed to spend as much as seven million dollars a year for advertising in the United States. According to Seiichi Kawagoe, head of Matsushita's American organization, however, the brand name is advertised but not the nationality. "By publicizing the Japanese origin of our products, we might court charges of dumping. . . . We once staged a show of Matsushita products at Macy's and were dismayed to find that the store had decorated the entire exhibition area with hundreds of Japanese paper lanterns."

The nationality of a piece of merchandise should not matter to the consumer, and yet Japanese producers are definitely apprehensive of revealing the origin of their products. Major consideration is taken not to irritate American competitors or labor unions in conducting their advertising. An odd sidelight is the frequency with which Japanese terms or cultural elements have cropped up in advertising non-Japanese products. A popular American line of men's cosmetics is named "Karate," and the Japanese sport, clearly associated with masculinity and strength, is the theme of the campaign advertising it. Travel agents frequently use pictures of *ikebana* (flower arranging) or *cha-no-yu* (tea ceremony) in advertising tours to Japan. Perhaps the most curious occurrence of a Japanese word in American advertising is found in the Boston posters for horse races carrying the legend: "Anyone who doesn't show up at the races is *bakatare!*" Japanese residents of the American town with a long tradition of elegance and quiet gentility are amazed to see this vulgar, and unusual, Japanese word that might be translated as "dumb clod" or "stupid jerk."

As Japanese products flood American markets, more and more Americans are unaware that the things they are buying are Japanese. Few Americans know that "Panasonic" and even "Sony" are Japanese brand names. Japanese travelers to the United States immediately notice Japanese products everywhere, but most Americans are either unaware or unconcerned. On the whole, they seem to feel neither antagonism nor any particular friendship toward Japan simply because they are buying and using so many things "Made in Japan."

A Language Few Can Speak

DURING the war, a half-believed myth circulating among American soldiers was that a foolproof way to lure Japanese soldiers out of hiding was to shout two words: "Hirohito, *bakayaro!*" ("Hirohito, the damn fool!"). Japanese troops were supposed to grow so incensed by this insult to their ruler as to lose their better judgment and come dashing out much as a bull rushes toward the bullfighter's red cape. One day, as the story goes, a Japanese soldier, lured out by this ruse, was about to be shot by an American when he quickly shouted back: "Roosevelt, *bakayaro!*" The Republican GI was so pleased by this bit of invective hurled at the Democratic president that he didn't pull the trigger, but greeted the enemy soldier with back-slapping glee.

Before the war, the United States had shown little or no interest in learning the Japanese language or anything of the philosophies or thought patterns that lay behind it. The official, government effort at education in Japanese had extended no further than sending three or four military officers to Japan as language students each year since 1918. In 1941, with threats of war with Japan visible on every side, the American government suddenly recognized the need for an army of men who could use the Japanese language. Several thousand educated Nisei were interviewed for jobs as language teachers, and eight were finally selected to establish an intensive language program. Thirty-seven days before Pearl Harbor, the language school began operations, with eight instructors and sixty students. "Producing Japanese linguists on such short order was a terrific job," recalls Paul Tekawa, Far East Division director of the National Defense Language Institute that developed out of the wartime Japanese-language program.

At first the institute taught only Japanese. Later it added other languages to its curriculum and today remains the nerve center of language study largely directed toward intelligence work. The history of the expansion of the curriculum subtly reflects not only changes in the character of the institution itself but the changes occurring in America's foreign entanglements. The institute added Korean to its program in 1945, Russian in 1947, and Vietnamese in 1957.

Interest in the study of Japanese in the United States waned after reaching a peak in 1950. It revived somewhat in 1959 when a new education law provided excellent financial grants for the study of "strategic" languages. As interest in Chinese soars ever upward, Japanese is again on the downgrade. According to John Young, head of the Japanese language program at the University of Hawaii, there are only 5,500 students of Japanese in America today. Harvard University, while increasing grants to students of Chinese and Near and Middle Eastern Languages, is expected to slash scholarships for students of Japanese by fifty-five percent in 1972. Several high schools, including a well-known pioneer program in Evanston, Illinois, will soon discontinue their experimental courses in Japanese language. Most programs lack sufficient funds to continue.

Ironically, however, while interest in Japanese declines among white Americans at large, Japanese-American communities are studying Japanese with increasing fervor. Hawaii alone has eighty Japanese-language schools, with a total enrollment of more than ten thousand students. This rather new zeal for learning Japanese is the result of merging the aspirations of Issei with the tendency of Nisei and Sansei to return to the Japanese cultural heritage in search of their identity. Younger Japanese-Americans do not seem to mind the heavy demands on time and energy that studying Japanese requires of them: they eagerly pursue the language alongside their regular school work.

The scene at Palama Gakuen is typical of the Japanese-language schools that are flourishing all over Hawaii. Young Sansei students step forward, one after another, lamely reciting short talks that they have painstakingly memorized in Japanese on such topics as "My Family" or "The Animals of Hawaii." Their Issei grandparents listen with eyes narrowing in delight. "Hawaii's first Japanese-language school opened in 1896," says Takeshi Fujikawa, Honolulu correspondent of the *Asahi Shimbun*. "Later it was closed under the Foreign-Language School Control Act born of anti-Japanese prejudice." The Japanese-Americans sued the Hawaiian authorities for what they considered an abridgment of their constitutional rights. Although other foreign-language schools were permitted to remain open, the schools teaching Japanese could reopen only when the lawsuit was won after a ten-year legal battle.

Today, wherever there are sizable communities of Japanese-Americans, Japanese-language education is flourishing—certainly a far cry from the days when critics predicted that the Japanese-language press in America would never outlive the Issei residents.

Radio broadcasting in Japanese is also on the upswing; Hawaii now has five fully Japanese stations, the West Coast four. Stations in New York and elsewhere now devote part of the broadcast day to Japanese programs. "Since we buy forty percent of our programs directly from networks in Japan, our audiences manage to keep abreast of Japanese affairs," says Yasuhiko Kagami, assistant manager of station Homecast, which serves all of southern California. "We also campaign against any incidents of discrimination suffered by Japanese-Americans."

Three years ago, KIKU TV station, the first Japanese television transmission facility in the United States, was inaugurated in Hawaii. It was rumored that the U. S. government was very reluctant to license so powerful a communications medium intended for the exclusive use of the Japanese-speaking community.

For Americans not raised in a Japanese-speaking community, the language remains extremely difficult to learn. "It is really hard for Americans to understand Japanese perfectly," sighs Tetsuo Imagawa, who has taught at the National Defense Language Institute ever since it opened. He might well have added that the mind of the language is as difficult to comprehend as the words. Only the very rare advanced student, he observes, can distinguish the difference of nuance in the two sentences, "Tori wa tobu" ("A bird is a flying creature") and "Tori ga tobu" ("Look, a bird flies"). Susumu Kuno, professor of Japanese linguistics at Harvard University, agrees that the *wa-ga* distinction is the despair of most American students. Other particularly difficult obstacles to fluent use of the language are the levels of politeness that are built into it, and the way Japanese people use "yes" and "no" differently from Westerners.

Even a fair command of the language does not necessarily enable a Westerner to comprehend the way Japanese people think. One White House staff member, supposedly well informed on Japan, observes: "We know, at least, that the Japanese sentence 'I will do my best' does not necessarily carry the firm commitment that the same phrase in English does."

An *Asahi* correspondent, sitting in on Vietnamese classes at the National Defense Language Institute recently, came away thinking: "Knowing an enemy's language may enable one to intercept his messages and understand his operational orders, but not necessarily read his mind. Understanding a language is one thing, but comprehending the heart of its speakers is a very different matter."

Japan Town

"IT'S THE same work that white folk do. But Japanese and native people get lower salaries for it. There's a double standard, and that's what I want to get rid of." George Ariyoshi explained, in faltering Japanese, his reasons for entering politics. In December, 1970, he was elected vice-governor of Hawaii. His platform had been one of honest action, and two of his campaign slogans were "No *uso*" ("No lies") and "No *shibai*" ("No phony theatricals").

When Norman Mineta ran successfully for mayor of San Jose in the spring of 1971, the opposition fanned resentment by asking repeatedly: "Why should our city be handed over to the Japanese?" Mineta had to fight hard to overcome the widespread racist feeling that it was foolish to elect a Nisei when white candidates were available.

Mineta and Ariyoshi are not the only Nisei who have risen to prominence in the United States. Sen. Daniel K. Inouye is probably the best known Japanese-American in the United States; he is joined in the House of Representatives by two other Nisei. Architect Minoru Yamasaki and S. I. Hayakawa, president of San Francisco State College, are two other distinguished Japanese-Americans. That these men all possess special talents is beyond question, but for many Japanese-Americans the driving force behind their success has been their resistance to racial prejudice. They have rarely made American whites the direct targets of this resistance, but instead have channeled the energy generated by antagonism into impressive diligence and a determination to be assimilated into American society.

The efforts of American Nisei are often blocked by formidable obstacles erected by the established society. Dr. Thomas Noguchi, who performed autopsies on the bodies of Marilyn Monroe and Robert Kennedy, was temporarily forced out of his $32,000-a-year job as coroner of Los Angeles County by jealous white doctors. It was only with the help of the Japanese-American community that he was later reinstated. James Yoshinaga, a city planner in Los Angeles, passed the necessary examinations for advancement three times, but he contends that his promotion was blocked by interference by his white colleagues. His case is now before the city council.

It is against the background of incidents like these that young Sansei are beginning to aspire to a new consciousness of their Japanese heritage. "I feel really relaxed coming here," says Mike Yanagita, a twenty-one-year-old Sansei who speaks only English, in the Japanese-American Community Service Center on the third floor of the Sun Building in Los Angeles's "Japan Town." His cheerful laugh does not conceal the deep feeling in his voice as he talks about his childhood. "My father always used to tell me to be a 'good American,' and whenever I played war games he told me I was fighting the Japs."

The Japanese-American Community Service Center was organized by a group of about fifty young people like Yanagita to help Japanese-Americans resist racial prejudice when they come up against it or to offer them material assistance if they need it. Moritsugu Nishida, the leader of the group, says: "Nothing is more desirable than a genuine fusion of Japanese and American cultures. But it is next to impossible for two cultures to coexist in a single person. We have to choose one way or the other." It does not necessarily follow that the JACS workers are attempting to isolate the young generation from the surrounding American community. Far from it. Their main work involves job placement, helping Issei, and counseling young people on drugs and draft resistance. They wear long hair, jeans, and rubber *zori*, and the walls of their offices are hung with posters of Che Guevara and the

AMERICA VIEWS A NEW JAPAN

Black Panthers. But in going about their work they are surprisingly unflamboyant and unradical. There is no suggestion of "Yellow Power," and the group maintains close contact with city authorities.

An interesting characteristic of young Sansei is their deep desire for solidarity with older Issei. In San Jose, a group of Sansei spends nearly every Sunday taking elderly first-generation Japanese-Americans on fishing trips or picnics. Once the group gave a birthday present of a washing machine to an old couple and received this good-natured thanks: "It's too fancy and expensive for us! We have a washboard at home and that's good enough."

Since Issei are often reluctant to talk about their painful past, Sansei groups have launched what might be called "Let Us Hear" campaigns. They are eager to learn the real facts of the struggle of early Japanese immigrants in the United States instead of simply the stereotyped success stories that are usually published. "We need the true story of the Issei community as a sort of springboard to discovering who we are," says Nishida.

Sansei are generally critical of their more conservative Nisei parents, calling them "120 percent American." Professor Hayakawa of San Francisco State they call a fascist. "They don't know what we went through during the war," remarks Sho Onodera, a New York Nisei who spent the war years in a relocation camp. Still, many influential Nisei lend their support to the urban redevelopment programs that are transforming the Japanese districts in a number of American cities. "Japan Town" in Los Angeles is undergoing massive changes, and a new area called "Sakura Town" is now being built in Denver, Colorado. Authorities of both cities give positive moral and financial assistance to such projects. George Umezawa, who works for the Community Redevelopment Agency in Los Angeles, says that the new "Japan Town" will become a life base for the local Japanese-American community. Alongside the soul-searching that young Sansei are undergoing, such projects might be considered community-wide attempts to forge a Japanese-American identity, forcing the community to re-examine its relations with American society.

The names the inhabitants use for the Japanese settlements shed some light on their view of themselves and their community. Issei traditionally call the Japanese area of downtown Los Angeles "Little Tokyo" or "Japan Town" out of nostalgia for their former home. Nisei tend to call it "First Street" without any particular national identification. Sansei and Yonsei (fourth-generation Japanese-Americans) have a much shorter name for it: "J Town."

[288]

Seeking the Serenity of the East

ONE DOES not have to go to a Japanese restaurant to find *teriyaki* in America these days. As a steak seasoned with soy sauce, it is turning up on menus in ordinary restaurants and diners all across the country. There is also fish *teriyaki*. From all indications, *teriyaki* is about to become a common English word.

Another Japanese word, probably even better known in America, is *hibachi*. It is included in both of America's two most recent dictionaries. But an American *hibachi* is nothing like the traditional Japanese brazier, used for warming hands but never for cooking. In America it has become a barbecue grill. "The Japanese call our sliced steak 'baabekew' and we cook our *teriyaki* on a *hibachi*," laughed UCLA professor Hans Baerwald as he offered an *Asahi* correspondent some "Made in U. S. A. *teriyaki*."

There is no necessity for using Japanese words for such things, but the tendency to do so may be a sign of the longing in many Americans, especially the young, for the mystery of the East. It is no secret that young Americans are intensely interested in all manner of the occult. "Psychedelic" shops or "head shops," crowded with young shoppers, are to be found all over the United States. Their atmosphere is always faintly Oriental or Orientalistic. Interspersed, with an incredible promiscuity, among posters, buttons inscribed with amusing or cultish slogans, strange articles of clothing, and sundries, are Japanese incense sticks, Thai incense pots, carved Indian stools, Chinese textiles, Japanese wind bells . . .

More and more Americans, apparently finding something lacking in their traditional European way of life and Christian morality, are turning toward the quietude of the Orient. Donald Scott, professor of the history of religions at the University of Chicago, says that no more than one student in four is seriously interested in Western European history. "Many start out by studying American history, but their interest soon shifts to the occult."

The single strongest cause of Americans turning inward and searching for spiritual harmony is probably the war in Vietnam. In the words of Elizabeth Gray Vining, the former tutor of the Japanese crown prince, the war is "the root of all evils." The sense of frustration that it has brought to the American people is growing so strong that it is forcing the government to plan for total withdrawal of American troops. It has also set off an economic depression, forcing major cuts in defense spending. These defense cuts, along with the satisfactory completion of a phase of the space-development program, considered the vanguard of American scientific research, have served to slow down or to halt altogether a number of research projects. As America seems to be entering a new era of introspection, Heisuke Hironaka, professor of mathematics at Harvard University, detects a clear shift in interest from natural sciences to the humanities.

A new enthusiasm for the irrational is a symptom of these tendencies. Many department stores display "adult pacifiers" next to their more conventional toys for children. Some harried businessmen buy so-called executive sandboxes and install them in their offices; to quiet their nerves they may take a few minutes away from their work to relax in these playpens. Many American housewives are enthusiastically signing up for yoga classes, as well as for judo or karate training. A unversity student at the Art Institute of Chicago, when asked why he was lying lazily next to a statue of a Buddha, replied: "I'm sharing the quiet with the Buddha."

It is hardly surprising that things Japanese—tangible manifestations of an Oriental approach to life—should appeal to Americans who are looking, even if only vaguely, for some mysterious essence that will bring them psychic stability. Americans looking at buildings designed by Japanese-American architects never fail to admire their "serene and simple lines" and gaze at them with a semireligious reverence.

But how deeply do Americans allow Japanese culture to take root in their minds? For one thing, they see little need to distinguish between what is Japanese and what is Chinese or Korean. For another, since the end of the war Japanese words have drifted in and out of fashion with considerable speed. Zen, *yugen*, and *shibui* were some of the earlier ones. "*Shibui* is no longer fashionable," says Baerwald. "The word was never really understood and it's now forgotten." Donald Shively, professor of Japanese history at Harvard University, adds: "In the days of Tenshin Okakura or Inazo Nitobe, the Japanese image could still be transmitted abroad in highly idealized form. Communication media are now far too sophisticated for that." Shively sees the current interest in the occult as inherently the same as the beatnik fad of recent decades.

Only time will tell whether the current fascination with things Japanese is no more than a fad in a regularly repeating cycle, a temporary panacea for psychic wounds, or a genuine and lasting interest that may eventually penetrate the American identity.

The Bus to Peking

A N OLD joke around Washington has the Japanese ambassador awaking one morning to find that the United States has overnight recognized the People's Republic of China. In a capital that has been humming with rumors ever since the first serves of the "ping-pong diplomacy" early in 1971, Ambassador Nobuhiko Ushiba might well be spending sleepless nights. But he laughs off the joke and says that America "has neither the power nor the inclination to recognize China right now."

When Chinese Premier Chou En-lai told the American table-tennis team that it had turned a new leaf in the history of Sino-American relations, Secretary of State Rogers immediately returned the serve by stating: "We are looking forward, rather, to a new chapter in the relations between the two countries." There can be no doubt, however, that both the people and the leaders of the United States welcome the change in the Chinese climate. President Nixon's recent statements to the effect that China must be brought into constructive relations with the rest of the world indicate as much. American historian and China specialist John K. Fairbank of Harvard University agrees that the relaxation of tensions between the United States and China is indispensable to keeping the rest of Asia friendly, and that an American withdrawal from Asia will be possible only if it can be assumed that Asia will not turn hostile.

According to the White House staff specializing in China policy, it is with these purposes in mind that the United States suspended its routine patrol of the Taiwan Strait two years ago and has since relaxed travel restrictions to China and the trade ban. The diplomatic break with the past represented by the Chinese invitation to the U. S. ping-pong team was the long-awaited first response to the American efforts. But Americans and others should not be overly optimistic about the improvement in the American-Chinese atmosphere. According to Undersecretary of State U. Alexis Johnson, it is no more than just that and does not necessarily indicate that Washington's recognition of Peking will be immediately forthcoming. The ultimate aim of American foreign policy is to keep Asia friendly, rather than to drag China into the power-politics game of the superpowers. Holding no trump card that will suddenly settle the Taiwan question, Washington can only maneuver within the overall framework of keeping up its good relations with its present Asian allies: Japan, Taiwan, and the Republic of Korea.

The American consulate in Hong Kong employs twenty-two Chinese-language experts to provide information about the mainland by translating newspaper and magazine articles, broadcasts, and even technical literature. Their translations are boiled down to thirty pages of abstracts that are delivered daily to the State Department. "Since China is still a closed society that does not give out information about itself, we must go to these lengths," says a State Department staff member. "But actually our major political interest is still in Japan."

Former ambassador Edwin O. Reischauer echoes this attitude when he says that for the United States "the China problem is really the Japan problem." But, due to a residue of memories of the fervent American missionary activity in China and the shock of the outbreak of the Korean War, popular and scholarly interest in China is probably about four times greater than that directed toward Japan. But the relative economic importance of Japan and China should be enough to reverse the ratio. According to Reischauer, the United States and Japan have far too much invested in one another for Washington to adjust its relations with China without any consideration for the position of Japan. Considering his close contact with the State Department, Reischauer's opinions may well be taken as official American views.

Immediately after the first word of China's invitation to the American ping-pong team flashed across the headlines of the world, both Pan American Airways and United Airlines petitioned for new air routes to Canton, Shanghai, and Peking. These applications by the two airlines are considered by the White House staff as no more than attempts to compete with Northwest Airlines's Taiwan route. Other American industries have shown surprisingly little interest in advancing into China. The major Asian market for American machinery, manufactured products, and resources is definitely Japan. "After all, what does China have to sell us?" asks one member of the White House staff.

Keisuke Ono, New York manager of the Toyota Motor Company, shares this view. "American automobile makers are not looking toward China as a new market," he says. "They are much more interested in the potential Southeast Asian market and in using Japan as a springboard to it." This casts a new light on the "free ride" interpretation of Japanese-American relations.

Ambassador Ushiba has worries other than waking one morning to American recognition of China. "Protected on one side by the American military umbrella, Japan is steadily increasing her trade with China. And on top of that, she is making the United States more and more impatient over her tardy capital liberalization schedule. A real resentment of American business interests toward Japan may well flare up when they wish to move into Southeast Asia in earnest," says Ushiba.

"Japan is far ahead of the United States in relations with China," observes one highly placed State Department official involved with Far Eastern affairs. "She is now doing a billion-dollar trade with China annually, isn't she? Our policy is to follow half a step behind the situation." Undersecretary of State Johnson explains the American position somewhat more clearly: "It's fine that Sino-Japanese relations are developing so well, and it may prove to the benefit of the United States in the long run. But we will never forsake Taiwan." By this he seems to be implying also that the admission of China to the United Nations could only be considered beneficial to the gradual easing of tensions with the United States.

Harking back to the Japanese ambassador's fictitious fears of being informed, after the fact, that the United States had suddenly recognized the People's Republic of China, a member of the White House China staff laughs: "You don't have to worry about missing the American bus. Even if you're waiting for it, it won't come by for a long time yet." This may be in jest, but could it be that the United States is actually standing at the bus stop waiting for a Japanese bus to take it to China?

(Editors' note: This article appeared in the Asahi Shimbun *on May 9, 1971. Just over two months later, President Nixon made his historic announcement that he would be the first American president to visit the People's Republic of China. On October 25 of the same year, China was admitted to the United Nations by vote of the General Assembly, dramatically altering the complexion of Chinese-Japanese-American relations since the original publication of this article.)*

The "Local Performance" Circuit

"MR. AMBASSADOR, we hear it's easy to get an abortion in Japan. What can you tell us about that?" Ambassador Ushiba was stumped when this question was thrown at him during a live televised interview in St. Louis in April, 1971. In Atlanta, a week earlier, he had been asked a similarly unexpected question on television:

"What do you think of the Lt. Calley court-martial? How would you compare it to the war-crimes trial of General Yamashita?" These are the kinds of questions that average Americans are asking about Japan. They demonstrate clearly how wrong is the notion that the only Japanese-American diplomatic problems are such issues as Okinawa and textile exports. They also show that the Japanese embassy in Washington cannot afford to communicate exclusively with the State Department.

"I believe in listening and talking to Americans at the grass-roots level, and I accept as many invitations for speaking engagements as I can," says Ushiba. He spends almost every weekend on the "local performance" circuit. During the first three months of 1971, he spoke at twenty-five different places: chambers of commerce, the U. S. Naval Academy, the Japan Society, local councils on international affairs, and the like. His staff is always hard-pressed, working against time preparing speeches for him. Everywhere he goes, television stations are waiting to interview him; they usually recruit professors and critics to hurl leading questions at him.

It was not so long ago, however, that Japanese diplomats in Washington considered their jobs well accomplished if all they ever did was press a large button labeled "The State Department." One even went so far as to say: "We are sent here as representatives of the Japanese government in order to keep in touch with the American administration. We do not want to offend the State Department by talking to the Congress." In contrast, the British and West German embassies had parliamentary attachés whose main function was to keep in contact with members of Congress and their staffs. No one, least of all the Department itself, commended the Japanese embassy for its unsolicited "loyalty" or "dutifulness" to the State Department. "Japanese diplomats just waste their time eating *soba* (buckwheat noodles) with pro-Japanese professors at social get-togethers, and neglect to maintain important contacts with Congress," says Hoover Tateishi, formerly on the staff of a congressman and now an instructor at the University of Hawaii.

But the Japanese embassy has turned over a new leaf. It has come to recognize the importance of private discussion with senators like Mansfield, Fulbright, Symington, Cooper, and Hatfield, who wield strong influence on American foreign policy. The embassy has also made efforts to develop contacts with leading members of the House of Representatives and with well-known journalists. What is the State Department's reaction to the new independence of the Japanese embassy? "We don't feel slighted," says one official of the Department. "If anything, Japan has not been publicizing herself widely enough. Her new attempts to venture further afield in influencing American popular opinion will only make our work easier." What he is probably implying is that when the Okinawa reversion issue comes up for debate, the State Department will benefit as much as Japan from Congress's deeper understanding of the Japanese situation. To prove this, State Department men and other diplomatic sources in Washington point to the Korean example. The ROK embassy took advantage of the arrival of a distinguished Korean political leader to deepen its contacts with Congress, and soon afterward won the passage of a Korean military-aid bill with amazing speed. Still, the same diplomats hasten to add that contact with Congress is one thing and negotiation is someting else again. Official diplomatic negotiations, they insist, should be conducted exclusively through one channel, and that is the State Department.

There are legitimate reasons for a nation's embassy in Washington keeping in touch with a variety of groups. First of all, the division of power between executive, legislative, and judicial branches of the American goverment is clear-cut. The executive's foreign policy will collapse immediately if vetoed by the legislature. It is essential that foreign diplomats in Washington try to assess the thinking of Congress. And the fact that Congress is but the mirror of local politics makes it necessary to maintain direct ties with local government, as well. Toward that end, Ambassador Ushiba would like to increase the number of Japanese consulates in the United States. There are now ten, and Ushiba feels that there should be at least two more: one in Atlanta, the heart of the South, and another one in the Midwest. But perhaps, before new offices are opened, there should be some investigation into what the existing consulates have been doing and how successfully they have gotten through to Americans at the grass-roots.

Another important reason for experimenting with new points of contact is the relative decline in the State Department's influence over the decision-making process in foreign policy and its lessened self-confidence. Things today are very different from the time when a strong secretary of state like John Foster Dulles personally took the helm of American foreign policy. Recently, foreign-policy decision making rests virtually in the hands of the president and his White House advisers. Policies on Japan evolved by the State Department are first discussed by a committee consisting of the deputy under-secretaries of the departments concerned and chaired by Marshall Green, the assistant secretary of state for East Asian and Pacific affairs. The views of this committee are then referred to the National Security Council, made up of the president and key cabinet members, and it is there that the final policy is determined.

The above may be the official policy channel, but the actual initiative in foreign policy has clearly, during the successive administrations of Presidents Kennedy, Johnson, and Nixon, been transferred to the White House. "The original site of the State Department building was a foggy swamplike area," reveals one member of the Department's Japan desk. "The Department's nickname, 'Foggy Bottom,' might be compared to Kasumigaseki ['Misty Barrier,' the location in Tokyo of the Japanese Foreign Ministry]. But today everyone speaks of 'Foggy Bottom' in a derogatory sense, as though our thinking is foggy as well," he concludes with a self-pitying chuckle.

Considering all of this, it seems that the Japanese embassy's recent attempts to change its posture and multiply its contacts may have come a little too late.

The Japan Lobby

"I'M WAITING for the day to come when a powerful Japanese financier or business executive sets himself up in a palace near Miami and leads a life of luxury, throwing around lots of money and meeting all kinds of people," sighs Kazuo Nukazawa, the Washington representative of Japan's Federation of Economic Organizations (Keidanren). He is saying that, although no Japanese lobbyist has yet established himself with quite such style or extravagance, it is no longer unusual to see Japanese business lobbyists around Washington. Most countries maintain a lobby in the American capital to promote their interests, and now that Japan's economic relations with the United States have become so extensive, she is no exception.

It is common practice in American politics for members of Congress to be petitioned by lobbyists for the passage or rejection of bills affecting the groups that employ them. Central and South American nations conduct particularly strenuous lobbying; each of these nations usually has only a single major export commodity—coffee or oil or sugar—and the country's economic life or death often depends on the extent to which the U. S. legislature sanctions the import of that product.

Since foreigners suffer from a lobbying handicap because of language difficulties and their inescapable conspicuousness, they usually employ American lobbyists. A 1938 law permits this if the lobbyists are registered with the Justice Department. The Japanese embassy, the Japan-America Trade Council, the Japan Trade Center, the Japan Woolen and Hemp Textile Trade Association, and other Japanese interests all have American lawyers as their lobbyists. Some of the law firms retained by Japanese interests are Stitt, Hemmendinger, and Kennedy; Daniels and Freehan; and the law offices of William Tanaka and Mike Masaoka. It has been estimated that more than one million dollars a year is spent on lobbying by Japanese groups.

In 1970, as the joint government talks on the textile issue seemed to be heading into rough waters, lawyer Stitt contacted Senator Wilbur Mills, author of the 1970 trade bill and an influential figure in determining American trade policies. Stitt, lobbying for the Japanese embassy, learned just how far Congress was prepared to go in making concessions on Japanese textiles.

"There is less and less cloak-and-dagger activity involved in lobbying these days," says Nukazawa. The lobbyist's job, basically, is to discover information and exchange it with rival lobbyists for their mutual benefit. "A good lobbyist is inevitably a kind of double agent," comments Nobuhiko Ushiba, Japanese ambassador in Washington. "He gets ten items of information but gives only eight in return," adds Nukazawa.

It has been estimated that as many as ten lobbyists hover around each American legislator. Influential congressmen are surrounded by more. Nearly half of the bills that go through Congress are thought to be ghost-written by lobbyists. If they are not actually writing bills, they are trying incessantly to influence congressmen on how to vote on them. Their tools are letters to legislators, testimony in committees, articles in newspapers and magazines, and private conversations with powerful figures. Lobbyists for foreign interests usually get the best results by joining forces with certain American groups that may share the same goals. For example, with the present tendency toward import restrictions, lobbyists for Japan, which desires to continue exporting to the United States, would do well to join hands with those American groups that are eager to promote imports. Examples of such cooperation are the meetings between the Japan-America Trade Council and the Emergency Committee for American Trade (ECAT), between Volkswagen manufacturers and American automobile importers, or between European dairy representatives and American agricultural bodies that benefit from using foreign dairy products. Nicknamed "horse-trading sessions," such meetings are for the purpose of exchanging information between American and foreign free-trade advocates. They have necessarily increased as the trend toward protectionism gathers momentum in the United States. The draft of Senator Mondale's free-trade bill is said to have been written at such a "horse-trading session." Experience with such meetings prompted the Emergency Committee for American Trade to sponsor a full-page advertisement in the *Washington Post* in October, 1970, urging Congress not to declare a trade war.

According to the *Congressional Quarterly*, foreign lobbying in 1970 equaled domestic lobbying in scale, intensity, and manpower. The pressure of lobbyists for foreign interests was especially conspicuous during the debate over the Mills 1970 trade bill; Japanese interests contributed to that pressure in large measure. During the final stage of the textile negotiations, lawyer Daniels, a lobbyist for the Japanese embassy, scored a hit by contacting Senator Mills and persuading him to consider a compromise plan—the inclusion of an escape clause in his bill. This paved the way for the voluntary control of exports by the Japanese textile industry. Washington sources rumor that Mills and President Nixon later agreed on the compromise plan over breakfast one morning in early March, 1970.

"The textile negotiations with Japan taught us a lesson," said one White House official. "We quickly established the International Economic Policy Council, because it was obvious that we needed an early-warning system." The White House was not alone in that view. Gov. Tom McCall of Oregon and Hoover Tateishi, an instructor at the University of Hawaii who used to be part of the brain trust of a congressman, both say that contacts with Congress should be exploited before any issue reaches the explosion point. Their warnings point the way to increased lobbying activity in the future. Ambassador Ushiba also has called for more Japanese lobbyists in Washington. He has suggested recruiting diplomatic bigwigs, including former Foreign Ministry men, to act as casual lobbyists making use of the great number of contacts that they developed during their careers. Moreover, in Japan's diplomacy with so diverse a country as the United States, it is important that she make her views known constantly in all quarters in order to avoid misunderstandings and unnecessary tensions.

Generation Gap in Japan Studies

"YOU'D LIKE me to name the American scholars who really understand Japanese politics?" responded UCLA professor Hans Baerwald to a question in a recent interview with the *Asahi*. He began counting on his fingers. "Well, let me see . . . there's Reischauer and Henry Rosovsky at Harvard, John Hall at Yale, Herb Passin and James Morley at Columbia, Marius Jansen at Princeton, Robert Scalapino at Berkeley, Robert Ward at Michigan, and Donald Hellman at the University of Washington. That's about all . . . but let me throw in myself to round it off to ten. That's ten out of a population of two hundred million," he laughed. Although the professors are less than a drop in the bucket numerically, they do have a voice in the making of American policy toward Japan. The State Department keeps in constant touch with them. "We regularly solicit their opinions by telephone and through conferences and informal lectures," says one highly placed official of the Department. "And we pay for them, too. I can't mention them by name, of course, but we do consult them. We are also in touch with twenty-five China specialists." The Japanologists and Sinologists who act as advisers to the State Department have been dubbed by the news media the "secret council," and no doubt many of the men named by Baerwald sit on this council.

Younger professors also cooperate with the State Department in varying degrees, but they cannot match in influence the senior men on the "council" who have a direct line to higher officials on the deputy undersecretary level and to the White House policy staff. The younger men are used more for long-range analysis of intelligence. Japanologists, so few in number and difficult to replace, are generally nonpartisan in that their influence extends to both Republicans and Democrats, and they enjoy a long life span in their roles as advisers. Edwin Reischauer, former ambassador to Japan and a star in the Kennedy firmament, has been credited with formulating much of the so-called Nixon Doctrine. He himself declares that the recent White House warnings about the revival of militarism in Japan "echo my views exactly."

Gerald Curtis of Columbia University is a member of the younger generation of American Japanologists. In a Greenwich Village coffee shop, with hippie types milling about, he talked with an *Asahi* correspondent about the differences that he sees between himself and the older scholars. "They have the advantage of personal ties and fairly easy communication with Japanese politicians, businessmen, and professors. But they are bound by a strong sense of comradeship and refuse to accept views that are very different from their own. When considering policies toward Japan, they cannot pick from a wide variety of possibilities in order to make the best possible choice. Some older scholars have argued too strongly, I feel, for the need for Japan to consult with the United States on almost every issue. China is a case in point. Assuming that there exists an implicit trust of Japan and a community of interest between both nations, then even if Japan were to move on her own initiative toward better relations with China, the U. S. is sure to benefit in the long run. But the older scholars cannot liberate themselves from thinking of Japan as a small child that we have to look out for, and that is where they are old-fashioned."

Later, the same correspondent spoke with Reischauer at his villa-like home surrounded by trees in a prosperous suburb of Boston. The former ambassador was clad in an elegant tweed suit. "There are outstanding young Japan scholars in the United States, men like Peter Duus, who teaches at Claremont Men's College, and Tetsuo Najita of the University of Chicago," he admitted. "But, by and large, young people define their specific fields, whether it's Japanese history or something else, too narrowly. And all they know about Japanese politics is the socialist line of thought that comes from Japanese intellectuals. I have urged that we discuss the China question with Japan before we open direct negotiations with China because I consider Japan vastly important to the United States."

Three years ago there came into being the Committee of Concerned Asian Scholars (CCAS), comprised largely of young students and scholars of Asian affairs who protested the alleged close cooperation of the Association of Asian Studies in the Vietnam policy of the American government. The older AAS is made up of eminent scholars, but recently many of its members who are Japan specialists have also joined the CCAS. Reischauer dismisses the CCAS as "primarily a group of New Left China scholars. Few of them know anything about Japan."

At the end of March, 1971, the more than two thousand members of the AAS convened in Washington for the association's annual conference. The CCAS submitted two "radical" resolutions to the group; one of them demanded an end to the training of Vietnamese policemen at the Vietnam Research Center of the University of Southern Illinois under the sponsorship of the Agency for International Development (AID). But the conference rejected the CCAS resolutions by a loud voice vote. The CCAS did not protest further. Later, Ryo Shirai, a research scholar at the University of Maryland and a director of the conference, speculated that the CCAS lost its determination for a showdown because many AAS leaders, including Reischauer, had already expressed strong criticism of U. S. Vietnam policy.

There does seem to exist a generation gap in American scholarship on Asia. On the one hand, there are the members of the older generation who, while they may understand Japan better, adopt an overly paternal attitude toward her. On the other hand, the younger men are equipped with precise knowledge of their separate fields—politics, sociology, history—but have yet to attain a fully rounded understanding of Japan. Professor Akira Iriye of the University of Chicago suggests that the only way to bridge the generation gap is to begin "to tap the latent interest in Japan shared by both American intellectuals and the general population." That is a worthy task, but there are great obstacles. First is the rapidly increasing interest in China rather than in Japan. Second is the fact that financial support for Japanese studies by the government and private institutions is being radically curtailed. As this situation continues, the number of American Japanologists, now set at only five hundred by the American Social Science Research Council, is bound to decrease even further.

Pinch-hitters Abroad

TURNING to the blackboard, Mitsuo Yoshida, chief instructor at Japan Air Lines's training and education center in New York, writes in large bold letters N-I-H-O-N-K-O-K-U. "This," he tells his audience at the initial training seminar for new employees, "is pronounced 'Nihon Kohkoo.' That is 'Japan Air Lines' in Japanese. Make it your first name. This word, written differently in Japanese, can also be pronounced 'Nihon Koku.' That means 'the country of Japan.' Better make that your middle name."

The close identification of company with nationality, exemplified in Yoshida's clever play on words, is not limited to JAL. Japanese enterprises active abroad, and Japanese individuals too, all carry—consciously or unconsciously—a huge invisible burden labeled "Japan." There are numerous other examples.

Nearly once every month, a Japanese vessel is caught fishing illegally off the Alaska coast. Each time, the U. S. Coast Guard, after pulling the ship into port, calls upon the Japanese-owned Alaska Pulp

Company in Sitka for help because none of the fishermen on board understand English. As soon as Alaska Pulp's general manager Kazuyoshi Hayashi receives a call from the Coast Guard, he drops whatever work he's doing, no matter how urgent it might be, and goes right down to the harbor. There he often finds the Japanese crewmen angling unconcernedly off the side of their ship. "It's really too much!" Hayashi exclaims. "They don't even know what they were towed in for." He does the necessary interpreting, intercedes with the Coast Guard, and usually ends up getting his countrymen off with no more than a reprimand or warning. "I'm really the Japanese consul here— without title or pay," he chuckles.

In San Jose, California, Kaoru Murakami, branch manager of the Bank of Tokyo, finds himself in much the same position. The Japanese-American population of San Jose celebrates New Year's with sakè parties, dividing into separate groups according to the Japanese prefecture that their forebears emigrated from: there are forty-six prefectures. The presence of Murakami, the local manager of the Sumitomo Bank, and their families is required at each and every such party because they are the most distinguished native-born Japanese in town. "We make the complete round, and are ready to pass out at the last stop," says Murakami, "but we want to oblige the community. We like to think of ourselves as unofficial Japanese consuls."

With minor variations in detail, Japanese corporations and residents in the United States pinch-hit for official government bureaus whenever the occasion demands. They receive nothing in return, but perform the service for love of Japan and a generous willingness to help their countrymen.

It is less easy to understand why their services should be necessary in places where there is a Japanese embassy or consulate. But they are. Late one evening, a tired young Japanese couple with a small baby walked into the Washington office of Japan Air Lines. The husband, an exchange scholar, had been studying at a U. S. university. As his term of stay had ended, he and his family had been about to board a plane for home at Logan Airport in Boston the day before. But they had been stopped at the gate by FBI officers on the grounds that they still owed the U. S. Internal Revenue Service some tax money. The professor had protested that he had paid all taxes and, besides, had obtained the required exit permit. The FBI would not listen. So the couple then took a night train to Washington to request help from the Japanese embassy. They received no assistance there, and were coldly turned away with the remark: "If it's got anything to do with money, let JAL help you." JAL immediately contacted tax officials, who checked their records and found that a mistake had been made. The professor and his family were free to return to Japan. They left with happy tears and deep gratitude to the airline. Masayuki Kishimoto, of JAL's Washington office, says: "We're not just an airline. We do everything."

Each and every passport issued by the Japanese Foreign Ministry contains this sentence inside its front cover: "The Minister for Foreign Affairs of Japan requests all those whom it may concern to allow the bearer, a Japanese national, to pass freely and without hindrance and, in case of need, to afford him or her every possible aid and protection." But Japanese diplomatic offices ignore this and often evade requests to aid and protect Japanese travelers; they usually have plausible excuses ready: not their jurisdiction, lack of funds, too small a staff, and the like.

When the Association of Asian Studies held its annual conference in Washington in March, 1971, the embassies of all Asian nations, with the exception of strife-torn Pakistan and Japan, threw parties for any scholars interested in the respective countries. They had asked the directors of the conference what they thought of the idea of holding such parties and had been assured that they would serve a useful purpose. The Japanese embassy declined to hold a party, claiming to be too busy with the Sakura (Cherry Blossom) Festival. A private Japanese institution stepped in and substituted for the embassy.

Professor Albert Craig of Harvard University compares this willingness of private Japanese organizations to fill the gap created by official coldness or disinterest to the spirit of a well-coordinated volleyball team. Every player on a volleyball team is ready to take a ball coming his way, regardless of what his assigned position might be. "This is something that Americans find hard to do," continues Craig. "Perhaps because we are brought up in a tradition of individualism, we tend to make sharp distinctions limiting the extent of our personal responsibility or authority."

"If an American office worker unexpectedly takes a day off," says banker Murakami, "his colleagues won't touch the work on his desk, even if it needs to be done urgently. His superior will have to take care of it."

"An American electrician," observes Alaska Pulp's Hayashi, "installs or repairs electrical equipment and does nothing else. An American painter only paints, and usually won't lift a finger to help another worker on the same job. That's why we need twenty or thirty maintenance men here when only two or three would be enough at home in Japan."

To such Americans, it may seem odd to see Japanese pinch-hitting and cooperating—although not always without complaint—as though private individuals expected to be called upon for public service as much as any official. Some Americans find this praiseworthy and attribute it to the "excellent qualities of the Japanese as individuals." But Tetsuo Najita of the University of Chicago recalls hearing one American remark: "The Japanese all act as though they had just come out of a totalitarian state like Russia." Such impressions are derived from seeing Japanese society within the geographical confines of the United States, where there are many obliging pinch-hitters conscious of their responsibilities to their countrymen. At any rate, it may seem difficult for Americans, with their singularly heterogeneous background, to comprehend that a homogeneous society like Japan is equipped with a strong sense of solidarity, whether its people are always conscious of it or not. It must also be hard to appreciate fully that each individual's sense of obligation is received without resistance and handed down from generation to generation.

A Wolf in Sheep's Clothing

"THE WAR in Vietnam would have been over a long time ago if Japanese troops had joined us," says George C. Wallace, governor of Alabama and a candidate for the American presidency in 1968. "Japan will soon have to take responsibility for defense against communism," says Los Angeles mayor Samuel Yorty, adding: "It is too expensive for the United States to go on holding a nuclear umbrella over Japan." He is, in effect, urging that Japan arm herself with nuclear weapons. Both of these men are American local politicians, eyeing the 1972 presidential election. Both are noted hawks, and at the same time, both are very friendly to Japan.

It is interesting that so many American hawks should be so well disposed toward Japan these days. One basic reason is probably that the hawks, with their paternalistic, protector instincts, find an agreeable protégé in Japan, a nation recently devastated by war. Another is that the hawks, with their intense hatred of communism, can see in present-day Japan a potentially strong anticommunist force. The general public in America differs from the hawks, however, in distrusting the notion of a rearmed Japan.

In a Harris poll conducted early in 1971, seventy-two percent of the respondents said that Japan should not have nuclear weapons, while sixty-two percent believed that a certain number of American bases and forces should remain in Japan. Of the latter group, thirty percent believed that the United States should leave troops in Japan "for general American security," and twenty-five percent urged a continued presence of American troops "in order to supervise and observe Japanese activities and prevent her from becoming a military superpower that might turn against America." Whenever the question of Japanese militarism arises, the general response seems to be a nervous shudder and a vague "Well, it's always possible . . ."

1970 was the year, exactly a quarter-century since the defeat of Japan, that voices were first raised warning of the revival of Japanese militarism. In America, the voices were heard on the highest level. At a foreign policy briefing for newspaper and magazine editors, a White House official said that if Japan ever came to feel the American presence in Asia undependable she would follow one of two possible courses: to rearm quickly or to collaborate with communist nations. Since even the latter choice would postulate militarization against the United States, either option made the revival of Japanese militarism unavoidable. These might be considered theoretical possibilities, especially if the position of the United States in Asia were weakened considerably, but coming from so high a source it seems reasonable to interpret these warnings as an argument, carefully calculated to appeal to laymen, justifying the retention of American military strength. The White House officer reinforced his argument by recalling that Japan had made two abrupt reversals during the past century. First, when Perry opened the closed doors of the country, Japan quickly forsook feudalism for absolutism based on the emperor system. Then, defeated in World War II, the Japanese switched from the emperor system to democracy. It was difficult to believe, he concluded, that profound philosophical beliefs were behind either of these dramatic reversals, implying that the Japanese could easily make a similar about-face at any moment in the future. This sort of forecast would seem rather convincing to an American public that already considers the Japanese an inscrutable people and that has strong memories of Pearl Harbor; Japan's flourishing economic presence in the United States also lends credence to these arguments.

Conversely, the American State Department chooses to regard the notion of revived Japanese militarism as unthinkable, and dismisses the possibility with a decisive statement that it has considered the situation coolly and thoroughly. "Japan's leaders and sensible Japanese citizens recognize that she needs a certain amount of conventional armaments in order to defend the main islands and Okinawa," say State Department officials involved in Far Eastern affairs. "But they would not think of developing a nuclear potential. It would be extremely costly, and serve only to shock the People's Republic of China, the Soviet Union, and even Japan's friends, paving the way to her own isolation."

While visiting the United States in the autumn of 1970, Yasuhiro Nakasone, director of the Defense Agency at the time, addressed himself to the fears of Japanese militarism in a speech at the National Press Club. "Japan holds yen in her right hand and Zen in her left," said Nakasone intending to amuse his audience with this felicitous phrase. But no one even smiled, and Nakasone lacked the persuasive power to convince anyone that he was anything but a wolf in sheep's clothing.

"The Japanese are always mentioning Sweden or Switzerland, and say that they wish their country were like them," comments a member of the White House staff for Asian affairs. "But those European nations are minor entities in international politics. A nation like Japan, a middle-class nation with huge economic power, can only be viewed with expectations mixed with suspicion." If Japan is to avoid the world's expecting too much of her, as well as viewing her with great suspicion, it will be necessary for her to clarify her diplomacy and back it up with specific, concrete supporting evidence.

A Limited Affluence

ONE MORNING in February, 1971, James I. Armstrong, dean of Middlebury College, visited the New York branch office of the Japan External Trade Organization with an urgent request. Severe financial difficulties were threatening Middlebury's esteemed Japanese language program with extinction after only two years in operation. Were there any Japanese funds to support the program? JETRO men pondered the question and went over a list of possible government sources, but none seemed likely to help the college. They then asked the Japanese Chamber of Commerce in New York whether it could raise the necessary funds from its members. The reply was that the government should be approached before money was solicited from private groups. Armstrong eventually returned home empty-handed and discouraged.

[306]

"Japan is now rich and should spend more" is a statement heard frequently all over the United States these days, and there is plenty of highly visible evidence to support it. Japanese tourist publicity during the 1960s depicted Japan as a thriving industrial nation; and then, reinforcing their image of Japan, Americans witnessed the 1964 Olympics in Tokyo, EXPO '70, Japanese products flooding American markets, and a booming Japanese GNP. It is difficult to convince Americans that Japan is anything but one of the wealthiest nations in the world.

"Harvard has given seventy thousand dollars in research grants to Japan for fiscal 1971," says Glenn Baxter, a director of the Harvard-Yenching Institute. "I believe that this money has been distributed to International Christian University, Doshisha University, and other Japanese schools through the East Asia Research Council. Japan gets one-fifth of Harvard's foreign grants, but in the future that figure is not going to increase. People in academic circles all over the country now recognize that Japan is rich."

Heisuke Hironaka, mathematics professor at Harvard, recalls his acute embarrassment upon hearing American professors say to one another: "Let's stop inviting Japanese professors here. They never pay for anything out of their own pockets." Hironaka feels that it is high time the Japanese rid themselves of the pauper mentality that they have clung to ever since the Occupation.

It is not merely the image of Japan as an affluent nation that makes American professors complain that the Japanese are freeloading. They themselves are suffering heavy cuts in research funds and other academic grants becuase of the American recession. Ten years ago, the National Science Foundation liberally distributed research grants to famous universities, urging the grantees to spend it quickly because there was much more to be given away. In recent years it has cut its budget drastically. Research grants and fellowship funds are withering away. Furthermore, the job situation in America has grown so tight that some Harvard graduates are forced to work as manual laborers. Many university professors, especially those in East Asian study programs, frequently complain: "Why doesn't Japan spend more money for cultural activities?"

One editor of an influential American newspaper compares Japan's recent activities to a man jumping up and down shouting how rich he is in front of the tax man, and then wondering how to escape taxation. The levying of taxes on Japan takes the form of expectations of her spending more on foreign aid, demands for capital liberalization, and fears and suspicions about the revival of Japanese militarism.

[307]

Within Japan, however, her image as an affluent nation is far different from the reality. Told that Japanese people are not really as rich as they are made out to be, one Japanologist snapped: "Then she ought to conduct a very different sort of propaganda campaign to convince us otherwise." But Kazuo Nukazawa, Washington staff representative of the Japanese Federation of Economic Organizations, says: "Trying to convince Americans that the size of Japan's dollar reserve does not tell the whole story is exhausting work. I tell them that individual Japanese still lead a hard life. I tell them how few Japanese have baths in their homes or how few Japanese sewers have adequate drainage pipes. But they won't believe it."

Erich Segal, popular novelist and Yale classics professor, is voicing majority opinion when he says: "The most important thing in Japanese-American relations today is to increase cultural exchange. The more the better. It will lead to better human relations, which will prove the key to better international relations." An American drama professor echoes the thought in saying that the successful meeting of different philosophies and ways of thinking is possible only through extensive exchange of aritsts, students, and scholars.

A Japanese version of the Fulbright academic exchange program would be most appreciated by many people. "Every American would jump at the opportunity to go and study in Japan," says Edwin Reischauer. But wouldn't Japan be injuring the pride of Americans by footing the expense of their studies? "Never! Not a bit!" laughs the former American ambassador to Japan.

The 1970 budget for the cultural-exchange program of the Foreign Ministry Public Information Bureau was about twenty-five thousand dollars. With the price of transpacific round-trip plane tickets fixed at roughly one thousand dollars, that amount certainly does not go far toward bringing to Japan the opinion-leaders of the world as the Bureau envisions.

Japanese travel abroad in droves on foreign scholarships or foreign invitations with monetary stipends attached. Clearly there is justification for the complaints that Japan takes much but gives little in return. The unfortunate experience of the Middlebury dean is but one example revealing a serious defect in the Japanese official machinery for encouraging cultural exchange. So long as the defect is left unremedied, Japan can only blame herself for the complaints about her tightfistedness that are coming in from America and the rest of the world. Perhaps, much of the blame for the general ignorance of Japan is hers as well.

[308]

Japan in America

ALL ACROSS the overwhelmingly vast American continent, people weary of the Vietnam war are turning inward, isolating themselves from the rest of the world. One might think that finding traces of "Nippon" in America at a time like this might be as difficult as picking up iron filings on a sandy beach. And yet, as a Japanese travels about the United States, he constantly encounters tiny bits of interest in Japan or attempts at imitating things Japanese, indicating that the American exposure to Japan is not really so slight as he might have thought. Usually he will find elements of both friendliness and antagonism mingled in the interest in Japan. The few anecdotes offered here should illustrate the strange mixture.

"Dear Mr. Sato." That was the salutation on each of a bundle of letters received by the Japanese consulate in Seattle from elementary school students in the town of Maple Valley. All the letters carried pretty much the same message: "We like Japan a lot. But we like whales a lot, too. We have heard that the Japanese are killing many whales. Please tell them not to." Fearing that the youngsters might have the idea that the Japanese were a particularly savage people, Consul Shigemi Hayashida replied immediately: "The Japanese are not the only people who kill whales. There is an international treaty about catching and killing whales, and the Japanese are acting according to that treaty." He has yet to hear from the schoolchildren again.

Costa Verde. These two words, meaning "Green Coast" in Spanish, form the name of a luxurious golf course south of Los Angeles Airport. Japanese capital bought it recently for more than two million dollars. Local Japanese residents, who had played regularly on the course, were jubilant, exclaiming: "Now we can play as much as we want." But the three hundred American former members of the club were considerably less pleased. "The Japanese think they can do anything with money," some were heard to grumble. An influential Japanese politician who had acted as a go-between in the transaction joked: "Now we can have a real Japanese colony."

Unpleasant Prospects. As Japanese investments in Southeast Asia keep expanding unchecked, the time is rapidly approaching when Japan will have to develop a huge armed power to protect her investments. This is futurologist Herman Kahn's prophecy in his recent

[309]

book on Japan. At a seminar sponsored by the Japan Society of New York, one professor of political science responded to predictions like this by admitting that Japan's overtaking the United States is a matter of grave concern to Americans. Most find nothing more appalling than the prospect of being surpassed by Japan.

Repainted Wall. On the fifteenth floor of the Kashima Building, towering high above "Japan Town" in downtown Los Angeles, there was a tiny repainted patch of wall facing the elevators. The Japanese consulate general has its offices on that floor, and still visible beneath the repainting on the wall was the word "Jap" scrawled in large, rough letters. "We have no idea who did it or why," said a spokesman for the consulate. "This is the first time something like that has happened in years."

Roses for the Emperor. A Japanese-American gardener in Portland, Oregon—the city of roses—read in a San Francisco Japanese-language newspaper that the emperor and empress grew roses as a hobby. He then and there decided to send roses from his garden to the emperor for his seventieth birthday in April, 1971. When informed of the offer, the Imperial Household Agency quickly replied that it was its practice to decline any gifts from abroad to the imperial family, except those sent by other heads of state. The gardener's go-betweens then came up with the proposal that the flowers be sent through the American ambassador as a gift from President Nixon. Portland Mayor Terry Schrunk was called upon to broach the matter to the State Department. When he called Washington, a Department spokesman cautioned: "In view of the present delicate situation with Japan, the State Department would not want to go so far." That's where it ended. The generous gardener withdrew his offer, and the roses were never sent.

American Sushi. "I eat here for nothing, so I can sometimes save as much as four hundred dollars a month. When I go back to Japan, I want to open my own *sushi* shop." Ken'ichi Nakashima, known to guests as Ken-chan, is a young *sushi* maker at the Kamehachi restaurant in Chicago. He spoke with humor, all the while casting sidelong glances at the American customers eating *sushi* or *hiya-yakko* (an appetizer of chilled bean curd) and sipping sakè. "Tempura and *teriyaki* are in American dictionaries, you know, but not *sushi*. I think I'll stick around in the States until *sushi* gets into the dictionaries." Ken-chan may not have to wait much longer. Chicago alone has thirty

[310]

Japanese restaurants, and in some places they are springing up at the rate of one a month.

Tofu.   The Japanese like to eat *tofu*, bean curd made from crushed soybeans, and it is also highly nutritious. "If they like it so much, why don't the Japanese buy more soybeans from us, and help adjust their export excess at the same time?" asks a high official of the U. S. Department of Commerce. Apparently he was not aware of the fact that Japan is already the world's largest purchaser of American soybeans. She imports three million tons of beans a year, four hundred thousand of them from the United States. All the beans that she buys from America are used to make *tofu*, and account for seventy percent of the imported beans used in making *tofu*; the People's Republic of China supplies twenty percent. When a Chinese trade delegation to Japan recently asked the *tofu* industry to buy more Chinese beans, the president of the American Soybean Growers Association in Hudson, Iowa, immediately put pressure on Japan not to buy from China. It was as recently as the Occupation that Japanese *tofu* makers first used American soybeans; the shipments of soybeans under the GARIOA program were the beginning of the large soybean-import trade.

Burning Energy.   Governor Tom McCall of Oregon sums up his feeling about Japan by comparing it to something that sets off shivers and goose bumps when touched. He adds: "Japan burns with a fiery inner energy. The time is not far off when she, the United States, and the Soviet Union will rule the seas." A drugstore proprietor in Plymouth, Massachusetts, responds rather differently. "A friend of mine who just came back from a trip around the world says the Japanese are clean, kind people. He thinks that West Germany and Japan are about the only decent places left. Well, America is a pretty good place, too, but I'd like to visit Japan someday and see it for myself."

PART SIX

The New Rivalry

"The third coming of the Black Ships!" screamed the posters advertising a popular weekly magazine, and Tokyo residents were surprised to see President Nixon glowering at them, pointing a menacing finger directly between their eyes. To one side of his baleful gaze was a drawing of the black warships that Commodore Perry had sailed into Edo Bay in 1853. A crisis had swept Japan soon after their arrival and another had accompanied General MacArthur, who led to Japan the second, metaphorical, invasion of Black Ships. The image has entered modern Japanese folklore as an ominous precursor of trouble with America and today, as Japan and the United States hurtle toward a new crisis in their relations, the Black Ships seem to be approaching once again.

An alarmist can discover crisis wherever he looks, to be sure, but there is justification today for serious concern. In 1971, during the short span of a single year, the Japanese-American relationship was buffeted so severely that even the most complacent observers of international affairs were filled with anxiety. Much of the sense of impending crisis felt by Japanese is due to the outdated manner in which the American government persists in regarding them. In its public statements the United States pays lip service to the fact that Japan is now a major world power—a fact, pure and simple, and one that needs neither explanation nor qualification—but its actions contradict its words and frequently relegate Japan to the subordinate position of a lesser partner, always ready to do America's bidding upon command. That the United States can move toward realigning its relations with China without heeding the interests of Japan, the third nation in the critical Far Eastern triangle, is remarkably callous. That it can proceed to take decisive steps to protect its own currency, again with little apparent regard for the Japanese economy with which it is so closely intertwined, is still more appalling. That it cannot effectively deny the

[313]

persistent and widespread rumors that nuclear weapons and poison gas are stockpiled at American military bases in the Japanese islands, in contravention of all public agreements between the two countries, gives final support to charges that the United States continues to consider Japan a sort of inferior, poor relation.

The Japanese, with their sensitivity to fine hierarchical distinctions, have long resented their subservience to the United States. It is true that they have benefited from the close relationship, but they chafe at the irony that much of Japan's unparalleled economic achievement since the war may be attributed to the instigation and encouragement of the United States. They have turned their subordinate status into a prod, using it to goad themselves to devote their full energies to catching up with America. Viewed by some Japanese as an overpowering colossus, by others as a benevolent employer or patron, the United States has been the dominating presence against which Japan has measured and defined herself. While it has not been her purpose to topple the American giant, Japan has struggled to emerge from its shadow and to achieve an equal footing with it. Now that these goals have been attained, the Japanese are incensed to see their hard-won equality so consistently denied by American actions.

This, in short, is the crisis that marks the present turning point in Japanese-American relations. Not simply a diplomatic crisis, nor a purely economic or political or cultural one, it affects all aspects of the increasingly complicated relationship. At this critical juncture, it is time that the two countries rethink and redefine their connections. The manner in which they go about this will depend as much on domestic as on international issues, since many of America's current difficulties with Japan are by-products of the various political, economic, and social problems it is contending with at home. For Japan as well, the ability to deal flexibly and realistically with new problems will depend on the extent to which her politicians can free themselves from past policies and outdated attitudes.

The articles collected in this section reveal the diverse ways in which Japanese society is affected by its sense of crisis with the United States and by its search for solutions. No clear, well ordered picture emerges, and prophecies of the future course of the Japanese-American relationship can be only fragmentary and partially reliable at best. One prediction that seems indisputable, however, is that the forthcoming association of Japan and the United States will involve increasing rivalry and intensified competition. For the security of the world as a whole, it is essential that this rivalry achieve an equilibrium that allows each party of the relationship its proper autonomy and yet is meaningful, harmonious, and profitable to both.

The Japan Branch of
the State Department

O N THE eve of the final stage of the Okinawa reversion talks, the
staff of the Treaties Bureau of the Japanese Foreign Ministry
worked late night after night. But despite its untiring labors, the
Bureau found it almost impossible to squeeze out a special allowance
of only about forty dollars from the Ministry to pay for dinners. "The
stinginess of the Ministry and the difficulty of raising so small a sum
is sure to jeopardize the morale of my men," complained Katsuichi
Igawa, chief of the Bureau. An officer was appointed to run about
from one office to another "negotiating" for the dinner money.

Bunroku Yoshino, chief of the American Affairs Bureau, was a key
figure in the Okinawa talks. Although, like every other bureau chief,
he has an official chauffeured car at his disposal, he still commutes by
train to and from his home in Yokohama because he would have to
pay the expressway tolls out of his own pocket and train fare is
cheaper. One might expect that he would receive a few words of
regret, if not an extra allowance to cover the tolls, but not at the
Foreign Ministry. There is no sentiment, no sympathy.

The Ministry itself has never received much appreciation from the
Japanese people, even before the Pacific War. It has frequently been
condemned as "a bunch of yes-men to the Americans." In the years
immediately following the end of the Occupation, the Ministry was a
rather insignificant presence, its functions limited largely to straight-
ening up reparations problems and other matters left over from the
defeat. Japan was then still a feeble, if sovereign, nation with the
shadow of the American colossus constantly hanging over her. Caught
between the strong American presence and the new postwar Japanese
nationalism that was gathering force through the struggle against
American bases, the Ministry was hard pressed to develop a popular
foreign policy. But even today, with Japan universally recognized as
a major power and a leading protagonist in the Asian drama, its
prestige has hardly risen.

One cabinet member has dubbed the Ministry "the Asian branch of

[315]

the State Department," and this name is echoed by similarly contemptuous phrases such as "the State Department's annex at Kasumigaseki" and "Foggy Bottom's branch office." It would not be surprising for such names to issue from the mouths of the opposition, but it is remarkable how little praise there is for the Foreign Ministry even within the government and the ruling party.

Recently, a short article written by an ambassador was circulated in the Ministry. Its thesis was what Vice-Minister for Foreign Affairs Shinsaku Hogen calls "the consensus of professional Japanese diplomats," namely, that no good can come of a diplomacy that panders to domestic public opinion. The Ministry's favorite example to justify this view is the dissatisfaction of the Japanese people with the terms of the Portsmouth Treaty, which ended the Russo-Japanese War in 1905. The widespread feeling that Japan had not received her due portion of war spoils exploded into riots across the country and the burning of the Hibiya Public Hall in downtown Tokyo. But, according to the Foreign Ministry, the public was unaware that Japan had nearly exhausted her supplies of ammunition, money, and military manpower and needed peace even more than Russia did.

In the 1930s, the public outcry against the spineless diplomacy of the Foreign Ministry served to encourage the usurpation of power by the military, which eventually plunged the nation into a disastrous war. The Japanese public does not realize, diplomats are quick to point out, that diplomacy is the art of compromise. Successful diplomacy would be impossible if the Ministry had to defer to the inflexibility of the public.

Postwar diplomats feel that their tasks have been made more difficult by the democratic system of government, in which diplomacy is inevitably mingled with domestic affairs. There is an abyss separating this position from that of former foreign minister Takeo Miki and other noncareer diplomats. Miki has stated that there can be no real diplomacy detached from public opinion and domestic affairs. It is this very detachment that the career men at the Foreign Ministry are so proud of, calling it "glorious isolation."

This difference in diplomatic philosophy has resulted in the initiative being taken by politicians inexperienced in professional diplomacy. It is they who have managed the major postwar international issues: the revision of the Japan-America security pact, the resumption of official ties with the Soviet Union, and the reversion of Okinawa. On each of these occasions, the Foreign Ministry has had to take the thankless "villain's role" of advising against negotiations by warning from the outset that the desired objectives were impossible.

Thus, to observers it has seemed that the credit for independent diplomacy has always gone to the nondiplomat politicians. Actually, however, the politicians are generally far more cautious about injuring American feelings than even the professional diplomats.

Hogen asserts: "Our diplomacy is not subservient to the United States. We say whatever we want to say." But former foreign vice-minister Shun'ichi Matsumoto disagrees: "Before the Pacific War, the Foreign Ministry was composed of yes-men to the Japanese military. Since the war, it has been so to the American military." Aside from who is right, it is a fact that Japan's postwar foreign policy has revolved around Japanese-American relations. The Ministry attaches first importance to the United States. Before the war, however, it held to a "Europe first" attitude. It has been argued that it was the very scarcity of Japanese diplomats well versed in American affairs that was largely responsible for the failure of the diplomatic maneuvers immediately preceding Pearl Harbor.

Japan's defeat and the American Occupation altered the characteristics of the Foreign Ministry noticeably. Diplomats skilled in English suddenly found themselves in the spotlight, conducting liaison with the Occupation through the Central Liaison Office (CLO). Since the Foreign Ministry had been shorn of all real diplomatic functions, the prewar European-school diplomats, fluent in German or French, found themselves with virtually nothing to do except occasional research. Even after the Occupation, former CLO men got the glamour posts. The star positions today are still related to American affairs, and the Washington embassy is manned by the cream of Foreign Ministry men. The ambassadorship to the United States is near the top of the diplomatic hierarchy; three successive foreign vice-ministers have been rewarded with the post upon reaching the top of the bureaucratic ladder.

"Postwar Japan has had no diplomacy," says Masashi Ishibashi, secretary general of the Japan Socialist party. If diplomacy is defined as the coordination of multilateral international relations and interests, then he may be right. Since the war there has been only coordination of relations vis-à-vis the United States. Japan's government leaders have not been able to ignore their sense of indebtedness to the United States for their national security. That is why, during the Okinawa reversion talks, they tried to lessen Japan's indebtedness and thereby make a good impression on the United States. Steps toward that end were the increase in Ground Self-Defense Force personnel, a concession on the textile import issue, and an advancing of the timetable for the liberalization of American automobile imports.

In the last analysis, Japan's present relations with the United States suffer from a critical inconsistency. All the while that she is representing herself as a major power and whipping up nationalistic feelings in her people, she cannot rid herself of the consciousness of bearing a debt to the United States for military protection. So long as this inconsistency persists, public criticism of the weakness and dependence of the Foreign Ministry will never let up. The source of the indebtedness is the Security Treaty; it is impossible to evaluate Japan's diplomacy today without taking into consideration how it is circumscribed by the security pact with the United States.

"An Ambassador Hears Only Lies"

"JAPAN'S postwar period will not end until Okinawa is returned to us." This statement has grown familiar and dull with repetition, but the Foreign Ministry was astonished when Prime Minister Sato first uttered it. "Our first reaction was that the statement would just get us into trouble," recalls Takezo Shimoda, former ambassador to the United States and now a justice of the Supreme Court; at the time, he was foreign vice-minister. "Mr. Sato had all the bravado of an amateur. Professional diplomats don't go around talking like that. At least not until they are reasonably sure of the success of negotiations over an issue of such magnitude." Shimoda was speaking in his office in the red brick Supreme Court building; stretching out on a sofa, he grew more animated as he continued. "I immediately dispatched the chief of the American Affairs Bureau to Okinawa to take the local pulse. He reported that the Okinawan people yearned for the return of the island to Japan. But majority sentiment within the Foreign Ministry was that Japan should not ask for Okinawa back while the Vietnam war was still raging, because the island was an important American supply base."

But the Japanese people were eager for the return of the island. Even U. S. Ambassador Reischauer traveled repeatedly to Okinawa —before Sato set foot there—and prophesied that the Okinawa reversion question would become the toughest problem in Japanese-American diplomacy. With such mounting interest in the status of the island, why did Foreign Ministry professionals seem so insensitive to the matter? Was it because of a lingering Occupation mentality, and their eagerness to avoid any issue that might conceivably displease Washington? Or was it still another example of the Foreign Ministry's determination not to be influenced by "vulgar, nonprofessional public opinion," as the professional diplomats put it?

The Foreign Ministry seems to regard the ability to grasp the pulse of public sentiment as but a minor talent. It ignores, or pretends to ignore, what the nation at large is thinking. One Japanese ambassador to the United Nations was even known to proclaim proudly that he made it a rule never to read Japanese newspapers. More realistic politicians condemn such attitudes as old-fashioned or downright arrogant. Former foreign minister Masayoshi Ohira, a party politician but not a career diplomat, says that the professionals are behind the times. "They won't realize that domestic and foreign affairs are separated for adminisrative convenience only. The two are essentially inseparable. Besides, diplomacy between countries like Japan and the United States, both of them democracies that respect freedom of speech, simply will not work if it ignores domestic opinion." Professor Yasuo Ishimoto of Osaka Municipal University agrees for a somewhat different reason: "With saber-rattling diplomacy out of date, the support of correct public opinion can greatly influence and benefit diplomatic negotiations."

Both Tokyo and Washington make it their first order of business to keep their relations friendly. Such being the case, the united, popular will that Okinawa be returned peacefully is an important trump card for the Japanese government in its negotiations. Are the professional diplomats not interested in joining the otherwise unanimous Japanese front?

At the third meeting of the Japan-America Parliamentary Exchange Conference in Tokyo in 1971, Japanese delegates referred to a ban placed on the import of Japanese mandarin oranges by virtually every American state, and asked Sen. Vance Hartke of Indiana to direct his good offices toward the easing or removal of the ban. "I've never heard of the ban," the senator responded with surprise, "but I'll see what I can do." After the day's session, a Liberal-Democratic member of the Lower House, concerned with agricultural matters, registered his fury over the inaction of the Japanese embassy in Washington. "We have emphasized it time and time again, and the Foreign Ministry is well aware that Japan would be willing to liberalize imports of American grapefruit if the United States would lift the ban on mandarin oranges," he fumed. "But apparently our embassy has done nothing whatever to make Japan's stand known to the Congress."

The most important tasks of Japanese diplomats in the United States are to grasp the real nature of the American situation and report it at home, as well as to argue their country's policies persuasively. As earlier articles have already demonstrated, official Japanese-American relations are no longer limited to politics, but have expanded into the economic and cultural realms, as well. But, unfortunately, not a few of the Japanese diplomats who aspire to posts in the United States lack the versatility necessary to the variety of their tasks. "All professional Japanese diplomats know Senator Fulbright as a critic of American Vietnam policy and they know of former senator Morse as a China-watcher. But I wonder how many know— or would even be interested in knowing—that the same Fulbright has tried to impose higher tariffs on Japanese turkeys or that Morse wanted to limit lumber exports to Japan. Maybe the diplomats think they needn't dirty themselves by keeping informed on economic matters, but international political relations are as much influenced by economic interests as anything else," comments an official of the Agriculture and Forestry Ministry.

It is essential that Japan's career diplomats be shaken out of their narrow professionalism and considerably broaden their outlook. It might even be helpful to offer high embassy posts to private citizens without diplomatic experience—to professors, for instance. "For the ambassadorial post in a centralized bureaucratic state like the Soviet Union, a man like Akira Iwai [adviser to the General Council of Japanese Trade Unions] would fit the bill perfectly. He already knows many figures high in the Moscow hierarchy." This suggestion comes from Tokusaburo Kosaka, a businessman who was instrumental in arranging the private Shimoda conferences, and more recently a rising force in the Liberal-Democratic party.

But there are few private citizens who are better suited to ambassadorial positions than the professional career diplomats, and it is unlikely that those who are would leap at the offer. "There is a saying that an ambassador hears nothing but lies," says Tetsuro Furukaki, the former ambassador to France, who had no previous experience as a diplomat. "The point is that an ambassador lets himself hear only what pleases him by meeting people exclusively at parties and official functions." And he adds that when dealing with Americans, who traditionally prefer ordinary suits to frock coats, "it is important to forget fancy diplomatic titles and meet them on a man-to-man basis."

Masao Tsuda, who served as Japanese ambassador to Argentina with no previous experience as a diplomat, recalls that a new first secretary arrived at the embassy and as much as told him: "Mr. Ambassador, I leave Argentina to you." He then proceeded to spend most of his time with the American embassy people in Buenos Aires, counting the days until he would be transferred to Washington.

"It seems to me that young men just beginning diplomatic training are growing more and more interested in the rest of the world, not just in the United States," says Taisaku Kojima, director of the Foreign Service Training Institute. "An increasing number of my students are seeking Asian posts, saying that they want to be regarded as trustworthy diplomats. A lot of them are studying Chinese." Kojima's institute includes as part of its curriculum some education in Japanese culture and industry through visits to important factories and to noted historic sites. "I remember a young diplomat many years ago who, unaware that Japan had steel mills, was inordinately impressed with the mills he saw in the United States, and became a passionate admirer of America."

A Fetish for Secrecy

DAWN. November 22, 1969. All Okinawa was holding its breath, waiting nervously for news of the Sato-Nixon joint communiqué, on which hung the future of the island. A special telephone connection had been set up to link the Tokyo Foreign Ministry and the Okinawa office of the Japanese government so that the communiqué could be relayed immediately to Okinawa. But when the news came from Washington, the Foreign Ministry held it up in Tokyo. Okinawans finally learned the contents of the communiqué from wire services, radio, and television. When Chobyo Yara, chairman of the Ryukyu government, met the press in his office he expressed irritation both at the lateness of the news in reaching Okinawa and at the fact that the communiqué needed so much clarification. "I can only conclude that the Okinawa people will continue to be subjected to discrimination, which they are expected to accept with patient sacrifice and passive resignation," he stated with exasperation. "If the Foreign Ministry had relayed the communiqué to Mr. Yara's office and explained the position of the Japanese government to him before he learned of it on television, he certainly would have been less angry.

The failure to do so was the single most unfortunate incident during my stay in Okinawa," says Sakae Kishi, former head of the Japanese government's Okinawa office and now chief secretary of the Home Affairs Ministry.

This is but one instance of the Foreign Ministry's odd addiction to secrecy and of its general tardiness in disseminating important information to the public. Diplomacy has long been thought of as a secret business, but the Ministry only courts ridicule by stamping almost everything "Confidential." A brief biographical outline of a foreign dignitary about to arrive in Japan will be marked "Confidential" when the whole world has the information. Digests of *New York Times* articles prepared by the Japanese embassy get the same stamp when they arrive at Kasumigaseki from Washington. Cynics laughingly observe that classifying such material "Confidential" is a precaution against revealing to the outside world the embarrassing truth that embassies cannot collect intelligence without depending on newspaper stories. The wife of a former foreign minister, about to embark on a trip abroad with her husband, was amazed to find that even the lists of clothing and personal effects she would be taking were marked "Secret."

"Secrecy may often be necessary in conducting delicate diplomatic negotiations, but even so, foreign policy must always be made clear to the people," says Hyosuke Kujiraoka, a member of the Foreign Relations Committee in the Lower House. "The Foreign Ministry simply does not make that distinction."

"Diplomacy has, for the most part, been conducted at the prime minister's office and at the Ministry," complains Zentaro Kosaka, a noncareer diplomat who served as foreign minister and is now chairman of the Foreign Affairs Research Council of the Liberal-Democratic party. "The ruling party is asked for its approval of some decision only after it has been made." While holding itself aloof from the ruling party, the Foreign Ministry maintains exceptionally close contacts with the prime minister. Copies of cables and important documents reaching the Ministry are sent daily to the cabinet secretariat, and high-level bureaucrats from the Ministry regularly sit in conference with members of the secretariat. They are also ready to come to explain specific matters whenever necessary. Even so, the prime minister's top aides admit to a number of grievances regarding the Ministry's secrecy.

So many of the documents that these aides receive are stamped "Confidential"—often unnecessarily—that they have to waste time trying to sort out the genuinely confidential papers from all the rest.

Occasionally, material that has appeared in newspapers comes to them with the "Confidential" marking. It seems that the Foreign Ministry has lost all ability to discriminate between what should be kept secret and what need not be.

The secretariat also complains that whenever important international events occur, the press invariably turns first to the prime minister's staff for comment. They are often routed out of bed in the middle of the night. The press obviously knows that it will get no information at all from the Foreign Ministry, otherwise the logical place to go. As a result, the prime minister's staff, although lacking the expertise of the Foreign Ministry men, are pressed to make comments based on little more than snap judgments or personal opinion.

The cabinet secretariat is also besieged by foreign visitors who have been turned away by the Foreign Ministry. Apparently out of timidity, Foreign Ministry men refuse to meet foreigners who come to Japan except those who present themselves through official channels. Perhaps they are afraid that they might involuntarily leak some secrets, or perhaps they just find it unnecessary to meet such people. "By now their timidity is a deeply ingrained habit, developed over the years, but there is no reason that they cannot be more open and outgoing," sigh members of the secretariat.

Trying to explain the timidity of the Foreign Ministry, former foreign minister Takeo Miki says: "Too many postwar cabinets put first emphasis on home affairs. Their foreign policies were based on domestic issues. The result has been that the Foreign Ministry, inexperienced in home affairs, has been led around by the nose so long that it has ceased to see its role in proper perspective." Surprisingly, Miki, not a professional diplomat, advocates a unity of domestic and foreign policy. His explanation is not altogether accurate. Actually, the cabinets—doubtless guided by instincts of self-preservation—selected for negotiation just those diplomatic issues that suited them, and then were able to flaunt what looked like diplomatic gains for Japan.

For example, the cabinet has reaped laurels for the Okinawa reversion agreement, boastfully describing it as a diplomatic victory for Japan and categorically denying that Japan was expected to reciprocate by making concessions on the textile issue. The breakdown of the textile negotiations was also proudly advertised as the first time since the war that the Japanese government had dared say "no" to Washington. No wonder that the professional diplomats have all but lost sight of their proper function, which is to decide what foreign policy is best suited to Japan and most consistent with her position in the international community. Moreover, inexpert in domestic affairs as they are, they have been afraid to speak out against government policy for so long that they have eventually stopped thinking for themselves. In the final analysis, then, perhaps it is the cabinet itself that the cabinet secretariat should blame for its grievances against the Foreign Ministry.

Ultimately, it is the Japanese populace that suffers most for the impotence of the Foreign Ministry. The government never tells the people more than it wants them to know, stirring them up to intense nationalism one day and leaving them skeptical and bewildered the next. Worst of all, they are contemptuously regarded as ignorant by the very diplomats and Foreign Ministry bureaucrats who have rendered them so by neglecting or refusing to keep them adequately informed. It has been said that unresolved problems of Japanese-Japanese relations led to the tensions and difficulties in Japanese-American relations in the years preceding Pearl Harbor. Is history gradually beginning to repeat itself?

Inter-Ministry Rivalries

IN DECEMBER, 1970, just as the textile talks between the United States and Japan—suspended in June and reconvened early in November—were drawing to an end, a staff member in the Ministry of International Trade and Industry (MITI) was reviewing the records of the negotiations. He scratched his head in puzzlement. Something didn't fit; something seemed to be missing. Was there some additional development that MITI knew nothing about? When he checked through a MITI official in the Japanese embassy in Washington, what he learned was inconclusive but led him to believe that Japan must have offered a major concession on the advice of the Foreign Ministry without first consulting MITI. He still suspects that the concession was a tacit, informal agreement to conduct item-by-item regulation of Japanese textile exports. This was something that the United States had been insisting upon, but which MITI and the Japanese textile industry had firmly resisted.

MITI suspects that it was on the advice of the Foreign Ministry that Prime Minister Sato had promised to reopen the stalled textile negotiations when he met with President Nixon in October. Foreign

Ministry denials have only intensified MITI's suspicion and resentment. The abyss of ill-feeling that had previously existed between the two ministries was further widened. ＊

MITI's position on the textile issue has always been that basic Japanese national interests can be safeguarded only by adhering to principles of free trade. In plain terms, its unabashed nationalism might be summed up as: "Japan is now a major economic power and will no longer continue to be just a yes-man to the United States." Against this, the position of the Foreign Ministry is that the interests of a specific industry might have to be sacrificed somewhat for the benefit of the nation as a whole. The Foreign Ministry was sensitive to the criticism frequently directed at Japan by other nations that she is too inflexible in demanding that she get her way on every issue. Since more than half of Japan's export trade is with the United States and with other nations with strong American ties, it pays for her to acquiesce obligingly to the wishes of these favored customers. Individual businessmen are accustomed to making certain concessions in the interest of pleasing their customers. Former ambassador Takezo Shimoda had obviously been following the Foreign Ministry line in requesting concessions from the Japanese textile industry during the negotiations and in predicting that the American government would impose restrictive import bills if concessions were not made.

MITI is notorious in some foreign circles for its fierce determination to strengthen Japanese industries. But the ministry apparently does not care if it incurs such international displeasure in the course of advancing the interests of Japanese business. On the other hand, the Foreign Ministry, which places primary importance on not ruffling the feelings of the United States, does not seem to mind being condemned as "spineless."

On the evening of June 20, 1970, Foreign Minister Kiichi Aichi and International Trade and Industry Minister Kiichi Miyazawa, en route to Washington for another round of textile talks that was to end in deadlock, met the press at the Mark Hopkins Hotel in San Francisco. Aichi had just arrived from New Zealand, having rushed to the United States to participate in the textile negotiations. He emphasized in the course of the press conference that his ministry and Miyazawa's were unified and of one mind on the textile issue. But he lost his composure when a reporter asked: "Mr. Minister, you keep harping on this unity, but to us you seem directly at odds with each other. What is this 'one mind' you're talking about?" At that point, Aichi could not refrain from chiding the reporter for his impertinence. As soon as

[325]

he had gotten off his plane, Miyazawa had informed him of the new proposals of the Japanese government, dictated largely by MITI, and the foreign minister was thoroughly exasperated. Sitting beside him at the press conference, however, Miyazawa seemed serene and undisturbed. He had come to the United States fully prepared for a breakdown in the negotiations. Four days later, in Washington, the talks were called off.

The sharply contrasting demeanor of the two ministers at that press conference in San Francisco bespeaks the difference in the attitudes of the ministries they headed. The Foreign Ministry always seeks agreement, first and foremost, in all international negotiations. MITI, however, feels it can afford to be rigid in its international dealings and can tolerate censure for causing ruptures in negotiations.

To be sure, there is nothing unusual about separate departments of the government disagreeing on international issues. But they must not allow their rivalry for prestige and influence within the government to interfere with reaching solutions to the problems at hand.

It is the general feeling of other departments of the government that diplomacy left entirely to the Foreign Ministry rarely works well. The Finance Ministry shares some of MITI's irritation with the Foreign Ministry. Haruo Nakashima, a finance official who served as minister of the Washington embassy for more than three years, sums up the attitude by noting: "Common nationality is not enough to insure communication. Experts on specific problems, even if they are of different nationality, invariably understand each other better than an expert and a nonexpert of the same nationality." A colleague of his, also with long experience in Washington, agrees: "In negotiating economic matters, discussions between the Japanese Foreign Ministry and the State Department are likely to founder. Since the former is probably being pressured by MITI, anyway, and the latter by the Commerce Department, direct negotiations between MITI and Commerce generally prove far more effective than the roundabout route via the Foreign Ministry and the State Department."

Masayoshi Ohira, a politician with experience both as head of MITI and as foreign minister, has declared: "This is an era in which diplomacy should no longer be relegated exclusively to the Foreign Ministry." Economic analyst Mitsuharu Ito brands the Foreign Ministry "thoroughly inept at handling economic affairs." He also criticizes MITI for failing to realize, as experts on international economics must, that no single nation can continue enjoying export excess forever. To further communication and to bring a measure of

[326]

flexibility to Japan's official economic dealings abroad, Ito suggests a lively exchange of personnel between the Foreign Ministry and MITI as well as appointing MITI men to ambassadorial and ministerial posts.

But realigning bureaucratic machinery and redistributing authority among the ministries will not be enough to solve international economic problems. Such matters, especially the problems of promoting orderly trade between Japan and the United States, are important political issues which directly affect the industries of both countries and influence the sentiments of their people.

To allow crucial international issues to be sucked into inter-ministry rivalry is both an irresponsible and a risky policy. Strong political leadership is essential to grasp accurately what is genuinely in the national interest, without being influenced by the tensions or competition between various ministries within the government, and to coordinate in advance the interests involved. It is high time such leadership was forthcoming.

Dangerous Ambiguities

ATOP MOUNT MINEOKA, near the southern tip of the Boso Peninsula, sits the radar site of the 44th Early Warning Group of the Air Self-Defense Force. In the murkiness of a mountain cave, a needle glowing pale white rotates continually around the face of the radar screen. The positions of aircraft in flight are flashed on a huge board. If an unidentified plane should be picked up by the radar, a large computer immediately dictates the best way to intercept or attack it. Mineoka is one of the radar sites "willed" to the Air Self-Defense Force by the American Occupation. The radar sites were built in Japan in the early days of the Occupation, just as the cold war was beginning. Later, they were transferred, one after the other, to the Air Self-Defense Force without cost. But even after the transfer, American officers were left on the radar sites as advisers and instructors, under the terms of the Mutual Security Treaty. The American officers withheld some information from their Japanese colleagues, including the movements of American U-2 planes over and around Japan. When certain unidentified planes showed up on the radar board, ASDF men would look questioningly at the American officers, who

[327]

would answer casually: "It's all right. That's a friendly special." This was known to occur often on many sites. Since the withdrawal of the last five American officers in the fall of 1970, all twenty-four radar sites have been manned solely by ASDF men.

The history of the radar sites symbolizes the growth of the Self-Defense Forces. Born as one link in the Far Eastern strategy of the United States, they grew to replace the gradually withdrawing American forces. To the Self-Defense Forces, the United States has truly been a parent who gave birth and succor. To date, arms and equipment worth over one and a half billion dollars have been transferred to them at no direct cost to Japan, and in addition, several thousand Japanese officers have been trained in the United States.

But all the while that the United States has been liberal with gifts of ordnance and education, it has also directed strong pressure on Japan to increase her own defense budget. "Every time a defense budget was determined," recalls former foreign minister Masayoshi Ohira, "the United States invariably indicated its dissatisfaction and protested that its ratio to the total budget was too small."

Today, for several reasons, the "parent-child" relationship between the United States and the Japanese Self-Defense Forces is fast approaching a major turning point. First, along with Japan's increasing power there has developed among SDF personnel a mounting desire for independence from the United States. Second, the United States has begun withdrawing more of its troops from Japan in accordance with the so-called Nixon Doctrine. The combination of these two circumstances seems certain to wean the SDF from Mother America.

The Ground Self-Defense Force stations one-third of its troops in Hokkaido, Japan's northernmost island. When firepower and armaments are figured in, the force in Hokkaido amounts to nearly half the GSDF's total fighting strength. The reason for this heavy concentration of strength is clearly that Hokkaido directly faces a menace from the north. "We have no particular confidence in the notion of joint defense with the United States," says everyone in the northern forces, from its commander down through the rank and file. "We are more conscious of the menace of the Soviet Union than we are interested in the United States," says a sergeant of the Seventh Division at Chitose. And a young platoon leader echoes: "The Security Treaty is based on the assumption that the Americans are to come to our rescue while we try to hold out in an emergency. But we cannot—and do not—count on that any more than you can rely on your neighbor coming to put out a fire in your own house."

The naive nationalism that is growing in the Self-Defense Forces is naturally stronger in its younger men. When a group of students in the Officer Candidate Schools was touring the Pacific War History Museum on a U. S. base in Okinawa, they confessed to feeling "a surge of surprised rage" upon hearing Japan referred to as "the enemy" by their American guide.

The Fourth Defense Program, launched in October, 1970, and requiring an expenditure of more than fifteen billion dollars over a five-year period, reflects another step toward weaning Japan's defense from the United States. In explaining the background of the new plan, Defense Bureau director Takuya Kubo remarks: "Up to now, the United States has always supplied everything that we needed for our defense. Our dependence on her has been unlimited and undiscriminating. The new plan postulates self-reliance, with American help limited to the nuclear-deterrent and the strategic-attack capability of the Seventh Fleet and the Fifth Air Force. But we will do everything else ourselves."

However, despite all the optimistic talk of "weaning" and self-reliance, the crux of the issue remains shrouded in ambiguity. The defense of Japan will continue to be shared, but to just what extent is unclear. For example, the Air Defense Command headquarters, which controls the radar sites, is housed in the U. S. Fifth Air Force Headquarters at Fuchu, Tokyo. The Fifth Air Force's jurisdiction also extends beyond Japan to Korea and Okinawa. In an emergency, both Japanese and American generals are supposed to command the air defense jointly. Naval operations also are to be commanded jointly. Where is the real line of demarcation between Japanese and U. S. commands? What will be the Japanese share of defense, and what the American? On critical questions like these, there are no clear answers. Nor has it been made clear in all the years that the Mutual Security Treaty has been in operation which party—the United States or Japan—will decide what constitutes an emergency.

There have been repeated instances of bickering in the Diet over the "prior consultation" phrase in the treaty. Which situations require the "prior consultation" of Japan by the United States, and which do not? At another key point in the military cooperation between the two countries there is dangerous ambiguity.

The Japanese-American Consultative Committee on Security, which is supposed to direct the actual operations of the pact, has met only once or twice a year in the decade since it was created. Each meeting lasted a mere two or three hours, and only broad issues like "the present Asian situation" were discussed.

At the present moment, as fears of the revival of Japanese militarism are intensifying in the United States and elsewhere in the world, it is clear that Japan has reached the point where further increase of her military strength must not be permitted without full clarification of the very foundation upon which her military structure stands.

An International
Division of Labor

" "YOU ARE hereby designated the State of Minnesota's ambassador of friendship and good will in Japan." Thus read the official-looking document presented to a leading Japanese businessman by the director of Minnesota's agricultural bureau in April, 1971, while on a trip to Japan. A similar document was given to another Japanese businessman at about the same time by the director of Illinois's agricultural bureau. Both documents were tokens of the esteem in which the American states held the two business firms as customers. Along with the certificates, both Americans spoke of the continuing research for developing products suited to Japanese consumers and invited the Japanese firms to make whatever requests they felt necessary. Minnesota and Illinois, both in the U. S. grain belt, recognize Japan as their biggest overseas customer. Japan imports nearly all the cereals she needs for food and fodder—corn, soybeans, wheat—and buys most of them from the United States. Japanese livestock farmers joke that three of the four legs on each of their cows or hogs have been fed on American food.

The hugeness of the flow of Japanese manufactured items to the United States—textiles, steel, television sets, even clinical thermometers—has brought about a souring of economic relations between the two countries. In 1970 alone, Japan sold $5.9 billion worth of goods to American buyers. But what is sometimes forgotten is the fact that she bought $4.5 billion that same year, including more than a billion dollars' worth of agricultural produce. No other country in the world buys as much from American farms. In the angry arguments over Japan's massive sales in the United States, another fact that is also unfortunately overlooked is the general satisfaction of American users of Japanese products and their desire to buy more. Tatsuo Goto, an executive director of Mitsui and Company, Ltd., was recently invited to a conference of American industrialists held in a suburb of New

York. He felt acutely embarrassed when a vice-president of U. S. Steel rose to complain of the five million tons of Japanese steel that were still entering the United States despite Japan's claim that she was voluntarily limiting her exports. But during a coffee break later in the day, Goto received a pat on the back from the president of a certain American oil company who told him: "Don't worry. We use Japanese steel pipe to pump crude oil from Alaska. The Japanese pipes are inexpensive and the best."

Amid the general cry for restricting Japanese textile exports, there were some voices in the American textile industry opposed to such controls. The sixth largest American textile manufacturer, Indian Mills (recently renamed Spring Mills as the result of a merger), buys a special synthetic fiber from Japan's Toray Industries, Inc., which it resells under its own brand name. Spring Mills apparently finds it more profitable to sell the Japanese fiber than to develop a manufacturing process of its own. It opposed the restricting of Japanese textile exports because it needed this Japanese product.

And despite the loud charges of dumping leveled against Japanese manufacturers of television sets, a steady stream of American purchase inquiries for large quantities of television tubes has been coming to Japanese makers of low-voltage appliances. "American importers of Japanese goods need them to survive," comments Toshio Doko, president of Toshiba Electric Company. "This is the kind of international division of labor that should be promoted."

More and more Japanese businessmen feel that the only way to avert economic friction with America is through establishing a division of labor that is mutually complementary, with Japan buying the agricultural produce that she cannot grow at home and selling the manufactured goods and technology that Americans need. They also urge a propaganda campaign to inform those Americans who are apt to complain about the amount of Japanese goods entering the United States without being aware of the beneficial aspects of trade with Japan.

When Sen. Strom Thurmond, a champion of trade protectionism, was in Japan in September, 1970, Japanese textile manufacturers suggested to him that the textile issue would best be settled by direct discussion between the Japanese and American industries. Thurmond himself was receptive to the idea, but the American Textile Manufacturers Institute shied away. After the possibility of such discussions was dropped, Kagayaki Miyazaki, president of the Asahi Chemical Industry, learning a lesson from this experience, suggested that Japanese business establish its own permanent lobbying organ in Washington. This organ, as he envisions it, would be manned by resident representatives of Japanese business who would keep in communication with American business, and would establish Japanese-American parliamentary contacts. Miyazaki believes that Japanese business would be well advised to invest liberally in a private diplomatic effort of this sort. The official Japanese embassy is limited in what it can do, but a commercial embassy would be able to serve the specific needs of the business communities of both countries as they arise.

Called something like "private economic embassy," a body like this might also help unify the divergent strands of individual Japanese industries. It could then convey a unified position to America through sources which benefit from Japanese-American trade, such as American farmers and users of Japanese steel.

Although Ryuzo Seshima, executive director of C. Itoh and Company, a major Japanese trading firm, believes that Japanese-American economic friction is "still only local and emotional," there is no more crucial time than the present to insure that the existing gulf is not widened further. It is not too soon to promote an "international division of labor" and to develop new channels of contact with the United States, not only for the good of economic intercourse, but also for the benefit of Japanese-American relations as a whole.

Computer Rivalry

THE MINISTRY of International Trade and Industry (MITI), the agency standing guard over Japan's trade liberalization program, has been visited, in an unending stream, by foreign capitalists seeking to open business operations in Japan. Prominent among the foreign visitors recently have been representatives of the American computer industry. It is no secret that American manufacturers are eager to sell computers in Japan, but thus far protectionist policies have prevented large-scale expansion. Resentment against these policies was voiced indirectly by Stephen Keating, the president of Honeywell Inc. (which had absorbed the computer division of General Electric not long before), to Morihiko Hiramatsu, director of MITI's electronics policy section. "We are most impressed with the size of Japan's market for computers," said Keating. "And we are also impressed with MITI's leadership in raising the Japanese computer industry to its present stage of development." When Hiramatsu mentioned the overcrowding of the industry, Keating complained that the situation in the American computer industry was even worse and invited Hiramatsu to come and reorganize it. The MITI man was not deaf to his visitor's implied displeasure with the tight barrier constructed by the Japanese computer industry, with MITI's assistance, to block any incursions by the American industry.

The American government has been adding its efforts to those of private businessmen seeking to sell computers in Japan. During the autumn of 1970, the Commerce Department staged a computer show at the trade pavilion in Harumi, Tokyo. With a backhanded compliment to Japan's advances in the electronics field, U. S. Ambassador Armin Meyer said: "Computers are the only electronic equipment that America sells more of than she buys. For the sake of continued Japanese-American friendship, it is my hope that Japan will buy more 'Made in U. S. A.' computers."

American manufacturers, especially in the communications industry, are now viewing Japan as the world's largest potential market. However, they know from their experience with transistor radios and color-television sets that if they do not move rapidly, Japanese technology will improve and Japanese manufacturers will soon be deluging the American market.

Changes in the attitude of American industry toward Japan were well illustrated in the contract revision negotiations between IBM and Japanese manufacturers held during the spring of 1971. Ten years earlier, the Japanese government had authorized IBM-Japan to produce computers. In return, IBM, sole investor in its Japanese branch, licensed to Japan certain basic patents over which it held exclusive ownership. When the contracts came up for renewal in September, 1970, IBM insisted that Japan license the patents for technological advances developed jointly during the intervening decade by MITI's Industrial Science and Technology Agency, the Nippon Telegraph and Telephone Corporation, and the Japanese computer industry. After six months of wrangling, an agreement was reached in March, 1971, obligating Japan to license the patents, for a consideration, as and when required. IBM thus obtained access to nearly nine hundred Japanese patents. Although it has found none of them immediately useful, the episode seems to indicate that even IBM, a giant controlling nearly seventy percent of the world's market for computers, has begun to grow edgy about the rising technological level of the Japanese industry.

Such nervousness, combined with a slowdown in the domestic market, is making the American computer industry impatient to get into Japan before it is too late. The Japanese action is a mixture of uneasiness and self-confident pride. Japan protects her computer industry because computers form the backbone of a society that has become increasingly "information oriented." According to Toshio Doko, president of Toshiba, "Sole dependence on imports for computers would subject our information-oriented society to American control." Behind this statement can also be detected an expectation that computers will follow color-television sets, automobiles, steel, and ships as a major Japanese export item.

But those are not the only reasons. Transistor radios bearing the brand name "Somy" (note the letter m) have recently been appearing on the Hong Kong market. They can be had for as little as five dollars apiece, and they produce a fine sound. The transistors in them come from an American-owned factory in Korea. Obviously, times have changed and Japanese electronic appliances on the international market are beginning to be threatened by products coming from countries with low-cost labor. "We should give up certain of our industries to developing nations and concentrate on new products that require greater research and technological input," comments Koji Kobayashi, president of Nippon Electric Company, Ltd.

Japanese industry has modernized itself rapidly by buying and adapting American technology. Japan has paid the fees asked by the patent owners, and the results have justified the price. But now Japanese technicians and designers have become confident enough of their skills to boast: "Give us money and a market and we will equal the Americans in technology." It won't be quite that easy. IBM spends approximately $416 million annually for research and development, nearly six percent of its annual sales. By comparison, Nippon Electric, Japan's foremost computer manufacturer, spends only a little over $16 million a year on research. In the technology trade, 1969 statistics show an import excess for Japan of nearly ten times: more than $366 million paid in license royalties as against about $44 million in royalties received for Japanese patents. "Japan is still a third-rate power in technological development capability," says Yukimoto Iwata of the Economic Planning Agency. "Private technological research has preceded government efforts. It is time there were more joint government-private efforts as in America and Britain."

American technology is bound to become harder for Japan to obtain. The United States, reassessing Japan's technological advances and adaptability, now considers her a formidable competitor and will grow increasingly reluctant to pass on newly developed technology to her. With this limitation on imported technology, Japan will have to rely more and more on her own resources. The mood of both the government and private industry is shifting toward larger investments in research and development than have been necessary in the past. "But we must be careful not to subordinate research and development to the interests of a specific industry," warns science analyst Yoshiro Hoshino. "Remember how Japan's efforts in the area of ocean development were transformed, almost before anyone was even aware of it, into a quest for oil resources?"

The first task facing government and private industry is to establish what their priorities in technological research and development are to be. Keeping both the international and domestic situations in mind, they should set objectives, select items for research, and proceed according to plans designed clearly in advance. Only in that way will the desired goals he achieved most efficiently.

Japan's Military-Industrial Complex

THE ATMOSPHERE in the director's office was tense as the top brass of the Japanese Defense Agency deliberated a question that was to have far-reaching consequences. Facing them was the decision of whether to import an airborne early-warning system (AEW) or to develop one in Japan. Some suggested initially buying a system and developing one later; others insisted that if a Japanese system were to be developed at all, work on it should start immediately. The final decision, handed down by Director General Yasuhiro Nakasone on April 1, 1971, was to go ahead with a Japanese AEW.

A single AEW site costs anywhere from sixteen to twenty-two million dollars. The contracts for importing a foreign system would have carried large profits, and American AEW developers and the trading companies that acted as their agents in Japan had readied themselves for fierce competition for the Defense Agency orders. They were clearly disappointed when the decision not to buy from abroad was announced. "We were forced into a sort of *sonno-joi* position," says Koichi Masumoto, an adviser to one of the trading companies involved, referring to the "honor the emperor, expel the barbarians" slogan of Japanese patriots during the early Meiji era. His trading company, Nissho-Iwai, had only recently lost the contract for the sale of Grumman F-2 fighter planes. "But we could hardly dispute the Agency's decision without appearing unpatriotic."

The decision to launch a domestic development program for the AEW brought the Japanese arms industry to a major turning point. Shigeo Natsumura, a former official of the Defense Agency, says that it marks the shift from an era of arms production carried out under foreign license to one of totally domestic production. In their infancy, the Self-Defense Forces received all arms and equipment from the United States free of charge. Later, Japan began producing arms under license from American manufacturers, copying their more advanced technology. This symbiotic system of licensed arms production linked the American and Japanese arms industries closely. There was a community of interests from which both sides benefited: the Americans received payment and the Japanese obtained arms and technology.

During the era of licensed production, Japan proved a most tempting market for the American arms industry. In order to manufacture F104J fighter planes, for example, Mitsubishi Heavy Industries paid Lockheed Aircraft a down payment of 1.5 million dollars, plus an additional thirty to thirty-five thousand dollars per plane. Furthermore, Mitsubishi bought from Lockheed all parts which could not be manufactured in Japan. For the first two hundred such planes—"the hundred-billion-yen purchase," as it was called—only forty-three percent of the parts could be made in Japan; all remaining parts were bought from Lockheed. Lockheed and Grumman had vied fiercely for the contracts for these planes and the negotiations had involved both Japanese politicians and the trading companies that acted as agents for the airplane manufacturers.

When Japan announced its plans to use the base air-defense ground environment system (BADGE) three American-Japanese teams— Hughes and Nippon Electric, Litton Industries and Mitsubishi Electric, and General Electric and Toshiba Electric—competed neck-and-neck for the orders. Similarly, when the surface-to-air system (HAWK) was under negotiation, Mitsubishi and Toshiba fought for the license held in the United States by the Raytheon Company. Thus, in Japan's case the term "military-industrial complex" might well be expanded to "Japanese-American joint military-industrial complex."

Now the "American" is to be dropped, and Japan's military-industrial complex is about to go it on its own. The Defense Agency's Fourth Defense Plan, announced in October, 1970, includes more than four billion dollars for arms (three times the arms budget in the previous plan) and more than 470 million dollars for research and development (three and a half times the previous figure).

[336]

"Dependence on imported arms limits our political independence," says a director of the Defense Production Committee of the Federation of Economic Organizations. "Only by making our own arms can we be sure of getting the real thing." But there are real problems. First, Japan still lags considerably behind the United States in arms technology. Furthermore, America never divulges her latest research or most up-to-date technology. It is all Japan can do to try to catch up to the next-to-the-latest advances. When told of Japan's intention to develop her own AEW over a six-year period with an outlay of more than thirty million dollars for research and development, an American expert told an official of the Defense Agency that the project was absolutely impossible. Such discouragement may be taken as a challenge. "We know that developing an AEW is no simple matter," says Tomio Tanatsugu of Toshiba's electronics department. "It will require the concentrated total effort and cooperation of every Japanese maker."

Second, arms production without foreign technological assistance is extremely costly. The supersonic high-performance training plane XT2 now on the drawing boards will require a projected expenditure of sixteen million dollars for development; planning a new jet transport plane would cost about twenty million dollars and a new-model tank more than five million. Even in mass production they might cost as much as two or three times more than imported weapons of comparable performance level.

For a variety of domestic reasons, the American arms industry is running into trouble. The prospect of losing Japan as a major foreign market will be an additional blow. "We can sense how restive American arms manufacturers have become lately," says an executive of Nippon Electric. "For one thing, their licensing terms are getting steeper and steeper." Late in 1970, when a licensing agreement between Kawasaki Heavy Industries and a major American helicopter manufacturer came up for renewal, the American company held out for higher fees. Kawasaki obliged.

Apart from technological and financial problems, a far more serious matter is now facing Japanese arms manufacturers. Confident of the skill and workmanship acquired during the years of licensed production, they are now calling for an easing of the ban on the export of Japanese arms. The government, rigid in upholding the ban thus far, is beginning to waver. The pressure of research and development expenditures is likely to make arms producers renew their demands for an expansion of Japan's defense powers and of her foreign markets as well. It is in the very nature of a military-industrial complex to enlarge itself continually once it has been set into operation. Even while Prime Minister Sato continues to declare to the world that "Japan will become a great economic power but not a military one," arms production continues to expand. Japan's failure to explain with convincing arguments why she must produce arms with her own resources and why she must expand her defenses will only confirm the suspicions of the rest of the world that she is well along the road to a new career as a military superpower.

Canned Pollution

"**W**HY DON'T you test some of this? It's still fish, even if it does come in a can." The young American professor's wife half jokingly handed him a can of tuna fish. It had been packed in Japan and bore the "Samurai" label. Her husband had been analyzing fish caught around New York, checking their mercury content. Antipollution campaigns had yet to begin and there was no public interest in this sort of research at the time. His university had no funds to finance his work, and he had to be content carrying out his analyses alone, with simple equipment. To help him, his wife had been angling in the Hudson River for samples, but recently she had not been able to catch much. The scarcity of fish led her to suggest that he try analyzing a can of tuna. He did, and detected mercury in it. Mercury was found in every can of tuna they had in the house. They bought all the different brands of tuna available in their supermarket, and found mercury in all of them, as well.

The young professor's research touched off a national alarm. The government acted quickly by prohibiting all further import of Japanese tuna, sending a fact-finding team to Japan, and imposing guidelines on the mercury content of tuna. The Japanese reacted in protest to each of these measures. Tuna is a migratory fish, they claimed, and not all canned tuna bearing Japanese labels is made from fish caught in or near Japanese waters. Furthermore, the mercury content of Japanese canned tuna was far below the guideline limits set by the U. S. government. As fears spread to Europe, American authorities began to relax the controls that they had initially set up in alarm, and soon the hue and cry over tuna died down altogether. Kanji Endo, an adviser to the Pollution Countermeasures Bureau, compares the behavior of the American government to a man swinging his fist in an impulsive burst of anger, but then not knowing whether or not to follow through and actually hit his opponent.

The rising American movement to oppose the export dumping of Japanese products in the United States is quickly beginning to realize that the best way to check the Japanese economic menace is to criticize Japanese "pollution dumping" at home. The uproar over contaminated tuna may be just one example of this trend. The United States is now eagerly advocating international pollution controls, but it has met with rather cold indifference to the issue in most countries. European countries lack the wide American spaces over which to spread their crowded factories. If they were to try to apply the stiff pollution controls demanded by Americans, factories would be forced to cease operating almost immediately. In fact, there is a strong suspicion in Europe that Americans are actually trying to erect non-tariff trade barriers by forcing European manufacturers to load the cost of antipollution measures onto the price of their products.

Japan is America's only ally in her campaign for concerted international pollution controls. In September, 1970, Prime Minister Sato and President Nixon exchanged messages pledging Japanese-American cooperation in combating pollution. The following May, Sadanori Yamanaka, director general of the prime minister's office, represented Japan at a Japanese-American conference on pollution. But conditions in the two countries are so radically different that it is questionable whether genuine cooperation in pollution control is possible. Japan has achieved her "economic miracle" by operating factories packed into a tiny geographical area with a greater density even than in Europe. Despite often repeated pledges of Japanese-American cooperation in the fight against pollution, Japan's stand on this question is actually far closer to that of Europe. Thus cooperation on pollution—like vague postwar pledges of cooperation in many other fields—is largely nominal. As far as pollution is concerned, there are actually more areas of conflict than of common interest between the governments of the two countries as well as between their respective industrial establishments. Even Yamanaka, an earnest advocate of pollution controls, had to emphasize at the conference the differences between the Japanese and American situations. Professor Raymond Vernon of Harvard University recognizes the possibility that the cost of environmental-protection efforts may act as a brake on Japan's economic growth. To the Japanese government and the business world, this is not merely a "possibility" but a matter of grave concern.

Returning to the young New York professor who detected mercury in canned tuna, when he sought expert advice for continuing his research he found none in the United States. He then went to Rome, seeking such advice among the participants meeting in an international conference on ocean pollution. He found scholars well experienced in the problems of mercury-contaminated fish. They were Japanese. From them he received abundant data on Minamata disease, which had killed or disabled numerous Japanese who had eaten contaminated fish.

Japan is nowadays so widely considered a "pioneer" in the pollution field that Japanese words have become part of the international language of pollution research. Japanese articles on ecological matters are being sent abroad as soon as they are written, without even being translated. *Kogai* (literally "public harm") is now understood by scientists all over the world as a synonym for environmental pollution. Professor Shigeto Tsuru of Hitotsubashi University is now trying to standardize the various English translations of *kogai* to "environment destruction" or ED.

International antipollution efforts, especially in the case of Japan and the United States, seem to flow in two clearly separate streams—government campaigns and private efforts. Ralph Nader and the American antipollution movement have served as strong stimuli to the popular campaign of Japanese citizens. When Nader visited Japan, however, the government did not greet him as the important envoy that he really was, but totally ignored his presence. It is also curious that a man like James Roche, board chairman of General Motors, who must hate Nader for plaguing GM with his one-share-stockholder campaign, should use some of his arguments in charging Japanese industry with unfair competition because it was not controlling pollution adequately.

Japanese industry may consider the Japanese delegates to the Rome conference as somehow treasonous, acting against the nation's interests and benefiting Americans in giving data on the Minamata disease to the New York professor. It may think of domestic antipollution campaigns in much the same light. But its view of "national interest" surely must be very limited. "Arguments in defense of national interests have consistently worked against effective pollution control in Japan," observes Jun Ui, instructor at Tokyo University's School of Engineering. "No one has ever benefited from self-sacrificing devotion to what the government has decided is the 'national good.' We must fight against pollution to the bitter end, and if our struggle benefits the United States as well, so much the better."

Nationalistic considerations of one country's interests pitted against those of another serve no purpose whatever toward cleansing our lives of the pollution that now surrounds us.

The "Johnny Walker Faction"

"**H**ELLO." "Hi." "*Komban wa.*" Japanese and American guests were gathering one evening in April, 1971, at the American Cultural Center in Fukuoka, where they were greeted by Alan Carter, minister for public affairs of the American Embassy. The occasion was a preview of a touring exhibition of contemporary American prints. Conversation, in English and Japanese, grew more and more lively as guests arrived and began circulating. Among them, an *Asahi* reporter spotted Densuke Nakashima, secretary general of the Western Japan Private Railway Workers Union, affiliated with Sohyo. He had recently led a strike of private-railway workers. "I get invitations from time to time, so I thought I'd just put in an appearance," he mumbled lamely as if to apologize for his presence.

"Mr. Nakashima is one of the union men who have been to America and who have been sympathetic associates of ours since they returned," explained the director of the Fukuoka Cultural Center. "We send them invitation cards to functions like this, hoping that it will give them the opportunity for informal reunions." He then showed the reporter a "Japan-America Labor Exchange List," revealing that some 120 leading union organizers in the Kyushu area had been to the United States on all-expense-paid junkets.

In 1962, Robert Kennedy, then attorney general in his brother's administration, visited Japan to take a reading of Japanese attitudes toward America following the massive demonstrations against the security pact in the summer of 1960. An important item in the report that he filed upon returning home was that the American government should take deliberate steps to cultivate Sohyo leaders. The fact that these union men were reputedly anti-American should not be allowed to prevent their visiting the United States on official invitations. Previously, invitations had gone almost exclusively to pro-American conservative groups, but the U. S. government wasted little time in acting on Kennedy's suggestion and began making contacts with Japanese progressives. Since 1962, an estimated 1,200 Japanese labor

[341]

leaders, many of them members of Sohyo, have traveled to the United States. Upon returning to Japan, many have organized fellowship circles and discussion groups.

Sohyo makes it a rule not to accept invitations to American social functions, such as the Cultural Center reception, but this stricture has not filtered down to union members on the local level. "Admittedly, America's early overtures had a real appeal for us," comments former Sohyo chairman Kaoru Ota, "but after Bobby was shot and American labor began to swing to the right under George Meany's leadership, the real aim of those trips began to come clear to us. When members of the Toyo Koatsu Industries union were invited to America, it became apparent that the trips were being used as a device for prying union men away from Sohyo." Sen Nishiyama, an American embassy adviser on public relations and cultural affairs, disagrees. "The only aim of the trips was direct person-to-person exchange on the union level. But I suppose that those unionists imbued with ideas of class struggle must view them as an attempt to destroy Sohyo's unity and to foster the development of American union practices, where labor and management cooperate more." However, Sohyo points to the establishment of Zemminkyo (National Council of the Chairmen of Trade Unions in the Private Sector) in 1969 as an example of the divisive effect of the trips to the United States. Most of the leaders of the new organization, which comprises the labor unions of the Nippon Steel Corporation and the Matsushita Electric Industrial Company among others, had been invited to the United States. Other labor leaders condemn their elitism, calling them the "Johnny Walker Black Label faction." Sohyo claims that the unions now affiliated with Zemminkyo, though once militant, have changed tactics and have begun agreeing to the programs for rationalization and stepped-up production that management had wanted. It also warns the new labor conference to beware of the "white hand" of American pressure.

Are labor leaders really so strongly influenced by their trips to the United States? Many members of the exclusive "returnees club" do not hesitate to speak ill of what they saw there. They are quick to criticize "the perpetuation of racism against blacks in American unions" or "the patronizing attitude of American union men toward us." It may well be that, as unionists, they feel compelled not to appear well disposed toward the United States.

American cultural-exchange officials can hardly be accused of selecting only those likely to prove friendly for trips to the United States; in most cases the actual recruiting is left to the unions themselves. This usually results in recommendations going to union leaders whose terms in office are about to expire. The American officials complain: "Since they retire soon after returning from their tours, they certainly can't be of much help to us even if we were out to Americanize their unions. We are always being scolded by higher-ups for not foreseeing this situation."

The times are changing and attempts to "brainwash" Japanese union men by offering them all-expense-paid trips to America are becoming out of date. Since 1970, under an experimental arrangement with the Americans, the Japanese side has been paying half the bill for such tours to the U. S. "Moreover," comments the labor counselor of the American embassy, "since union men in both countries are growing increasingly concerned with pollution and environmental problems, Japanese-American exchange might better be used for discussion of vital common issues rather than as a forum for ideological debate."

Regardless of motivations, the American government has demonstrated its eagerness to make American policies understood by Japanese union leaders. Has the Japanese government, on the other hand, shown even a tenth of such interest in informing American labor of its policies? Today American businessmen and union leaders alike are charging Japan with a passion for exporting her products at the expense of substandard labor conditions at home. But, despite such accusations, the Japanese government seems uninterested in inviting American union representatives to come and see for themselves the actual situation of Japanese labor.

In addition to the exchange of persons, another important task of the American information services is the dispersal of information about the United States through printed materials and films. Since translations of American books turn up in Japanese bookstores soon after—if not before—their publication in the United States, the embassy information services are now placing special emphasis on speedy delivery, having materials sent to Japan by air instead of by sea as in the past.

American information activity in the recent past might be compared to a preacher expounding the "blessings of democracy" and the "horrors of communism." But this too is changing. In April, 1971, the *Nichibei Forum* (Japan-America Forum), a magazine of information on America, was discontinued after running for seventeen years. It will soon resume publication, in altered format, as a journal dealing with problems that are common to both Japan and the United States. Whether the issues to be dealt with are problems of pollution, China, or the joint development of Southeast Asia, Japan and the United

ЕЕЕНTHE

States, as partners, should offer their wisdom mutually. Neither should seek to hide its own defects, and both should work at solving common problems together. It is to be hoped that the official information services of the American embassy and the Japanese people in contact with them see the situation in this light, and that future cultural exchange between the two countries is pursued in such a spirit.

Commercial Marriage Brokers

"MR. MATSUDA, let me introduce you to some people at Ford." Kohei Matsuda, president of Toyo Kogyo Company, responded with alacrity to this offer of an American embassy official in 1968. At that time, the Japan Automobile Manufacturers Association was sharply divided over a plan by the Ministry of International Trade and Industry (MITI) to reorganize the Japanese automobile industry, making Toyota and Nissan its two main pillars. The embassy man's casual introduction led eventually to the birth of a Toyo Kogyo-Ford joint venture, later joined by Nissan, to manufacture automatic transmission units in Japan.

"I only introduce people," laughs the embassy official, reminded of this incident. "In a way, I'm sort of a marriage broker." Judging by all the American-Japanese industrial marriages taking place these days, he must be doing a brisk business.

Not far from the American Embassy in downtown Tokyo is the United States Trade Center. Although officially an organ of the Department of Commerce, it is headed by the embassy's commercial counselor, John F. Shaw. The primary function of the Trade Center is to assist American businesses determined to get a foot in the door of the rich Japanese establishment. Every year it stages about ten exhibitions under the auspices of the Commerce Department. Its shelves are stocked with abundant data on international business: lists of American sources from which Japanese companies might obtain loans, credit reports on various American firms, literature on American business-management methods, and lists of American firms that have requested affiliations with Japanese companies in specific fields. Whenever such a request comes from America, the Center tries to make contact with an appropriate Japanese company in order to assist as a go-between in the American industrial advance into Japan.

Medium- and small-size Japanese firms often avail themselves of the services of the Center. "Small companies like us struggle constantly to find import agents," says one electric-appliance maker. "We have managed to make several import contracts thanks to introductions provided by the Center. We value their assistance very highly."

On a wall in Shaw's office hangs a chart that graphically illustrates American trade deficits. "From now on, we are going to try to sell more American consumer goods and leisure-activity goods to Japan," says Shaw, sounding every bit like an aggressive salesman. He is not the first American government official to act as pathfinder for businessmen seeking trade with Japan. One former section chief in MITI during the Occupation still remembers his amazement when a top economic adviser of General MacArthur's condescended to conduct an American fountain-pen manufacturer to his office. How many Japanese businessmen could expect service like that from their diplomatic representatives in the United States?

The general decline of the American economy in the past several years, combined with the miraculous growth of the Japanese economy, has intensified the crisis consciousness of the American embassy's economic officials. They are now making an all-out drive not only to put across particular business deals, but to sell the American economy as a whole. Much of their pressure these days is being directed toward an early liberalization of the import of American computers to Japan. Advancing further than is their usual practice, they are also probing MITI's basic policies and the general attitude of MITI officials. Naohiro Amaya, a MITI section chief in charge of long-term planning, says that he frequently gets searching questions about MITI's future industrial policies from inquisitive embassy officials. Recently, twenty MITI men were invited to the home of a high embassy officer for an open discussion and a free exchange of views.

This drive is being carried on by an embassy team of about fifteen men, including economic experts from the Commerce and State departments. Sometimes they are joined in their efforts by representatives of the Agriculture and Treasury Departments. They set off north and south across Japan, covering the entire country in vigorous and positive public-relations campaigns. Similar efforts are being carried on by the American Chamber of Commerce in Tokyo, with the aid of the U. S. Information Service. Chamber members have begun venturing far afield, to Fukuoka, Nagasaki, Shizuoka, Niigata, Sendai, and other industrial centers, urging local manufacturers and businessmen to engage in wider trade with the United States. Their

[345]

line of argument has been: "Well, Japan is now fully mature. It's time her doors were thrown all the way open."

It was not so very long ago that a deficit-ridden Japan was begging the United States to be lenient in setting criteria for dumping of Japanese export items and to remove all trade barriers other than regular customs duties. At that time, Japanese supplicants were told that such trade balances could not be set by two nations in isolation but must be adjusted overall. Commercial relations have now reached the point where Japan can use the same arguments vis-à-vis the United States. This reversal of the economic balance of power between the two countries, combined with the partial survival of Japan's protectionist policies, is making the United States so impatient and irritated that rumors now predict imminent restrictive measures being applied to the import of Japanese cars. Embassy officials, pointing to the high Japanese tariff and excise tax on foreign-car imports, have begun warning that Japan would be well advised to terminate this particular form of discrimination before it explodes into a major issue.

At this point, the United States is very eager to establish a foothold in the Japanese market for its computer and supersonic aircraft industries before Japan brings her own industries to a comparably high stage of development. It is clear that the United States will grow increasingly impatient if Japan continues to drag her feet on import liberalization.

"It will hardly be possible to eliminate friction entirely from Japanese-American economic relations," admit embassy officials, fully aware that their jobs are bound to grow much more difficult before they grow easier. "Our task is simply to reduce frictions to a minimum."

Random Thoughts from the Embassy

TWO AMERICAN embassy men sat down recently in Tokyo with an *Asahi* reporter to set forth their views of contemporary Japan and her relations with the United States. Both men, who shall remain unidentified, are career diplomats employed by their government to serve as its eyes and ears in Japan, reporting news as it occurs, and also as mouthpieces through which the American government can speak to the Japanese people. Their views are not necessarily to be taken as reflecting official policy. They are merely personal opinions that came to mind in the course of casual conversation. But they should be heeded. These men are not inexperienced in their jobs —one has been in Japan for ten years; the other, nine—and their random comments (paraphrased below, rather than quoted directly) offer a clue to the thinking of Americans who have been in the forefront of Japanese-American relations.

Problems seem to have a way of erupting suddenly and with little advance warning. For example, there was no pollution problem in Japan until the newspapers suddenly raised a hue and cry. Of course, the pollution itself had existed long before, but it was ignored. Now, historians can almost date the beginning of pollution to the month or even the day. The same is true of economic problems. In June, 1970, the textile issue got front-page coverage in the *Asahi* twenty-six times but only once in the *New York Times*. The textile trouble was the culmination of a series of economic problems between the United States and Japan going back over ten years, but no one paid much attention to them until the Okinawa reversion issue, an essentially political problem, came to a head.

Everyone was very worried that the 1960 security pact crisis might happen all over again in 1970. But, to our enormous relief, history did not repeat itself for once. The trouble that we'd been expecting in 1970 blew over in 1969.

Until the 1960s, only experts could handle Japanese-American relations. Things began to broaden a bit around 1970. Until then, the Japanese would grumble that too few Americans knew Japan well enough. But now that more and more ordinary American people are interested in Japan, the Japanese seem to be worried about it. Why worry? Take it as a challenge.

We are clearly entering an era of challenge, but we don't worry too much about the future of Japanese-American relations. After all, neither people are fools. The only totally trouble-free spot is the grave. Only in the grave are there no problems, no challenges.

A *Time* cover story on Japan evoked the widespread angry reaction that it was "full of prejudice and misunderstanding." Rather than get so worked up, we wish the Japanese would calmly think about why *Time* should devote so much space to Japan. Usually she gets only

[347]

about one-tenth of the space that Egypt gets in American magazines. The *Time* story on Japan contained much less misinformation than a story on Egypt would.

Recently, when Congress was at the height of a particularly stormy session, more than a dozen congressmen came to Tokyo to attend the Japan-America Parliamentary Exchange Conference. That would have been unthinkable ten years ago. But now American voters are interested in Japan, and some American legislators feel their political careers in jeopardy if they know nothing about Japan. The *Time* article and the coming of so many congressmen indicate that Americans are now in the process of getting to know Japan, a process which will, however, naturally involve fumbles and inadvertant mistakes.

In the past twenty-five years, the Japanese seem to have fallen into the habit of overreacting to the slightest friction in Japanese-American relations. Problems are bound to arise between the two nations, but it is not likely that they will shake our relations to their foundations. Remember the "chicken war" between the United States and West Germany? Or our difficulties with de Gaulle? They certainly did not destroy Washington's relations with either of those countries. We won't really begin to worry about our relations with Japan until visa applications drop off drastically or until Japanese students stop pouring into American Cultural Centers requesting information about scholarships to study in American schools.

We have noticed how stiffly two Japanese men, meeting for the first time, will exchange *meishi* (name cards), almost before they say anything. They are really trying to find out each other's station in life. Sometimes it looks as though one is bowing to the other's card, or to the title printed on it and the rank or social position that it indicates. Japanese tend to think of international relations in much the same way. They are constantly interested in the international ranking of their country. How many Norwegians would know their country's GNP ranking, or even care? We realize that the hundred years since the beginning of the Meiji era have been a history of national determination to "Catch up! Catch up!" but still . . .

We get the impression that, in all these years since she set out to become a modern state in 1868, Japan has yet to learn how to associate with foreign countries. We were startled, for example, at the excessively angry reaction here to an item in a British tabloid about the alleged cruelty of the Japanese to dogs. Everyone asked angrily: "What are they talking about?" and one department store that was about to open an exhibition and sale of British imports supposedly telephoned the British embassy to say that it would be canceled if the matter was not clarified. The whole Tokyo foreign society was as worried as the British embassy.

History tells us that Japan in the eighth century was as enamored of China as she was hostile to her. Today it is the United States that represents the "outside world" in the Japanese mind. We are perhaps sixty percent optimistic about the future of American relations with Japan; what worries us is whether Japan will become more international or nationalistic and chauvinistic in her relations not only with America but also with the rest of the world. We are more concerned about that than whether Japan will turn to the right or the left.

One final word will sum up some of the changes we've detected in Japan over the past ten years. When we first went traveling out in the country, we often had trouble getting *ryokan* (inns) to take us. We would ask *ryokan* men at railway stations, in Japanese, whether any rooms were available. "Full up" they would answer immediately, even though they were standing there with their flags touting for customers. These days *ryokan* men, spotting us getting off a train, rush up to greet us and try to drag us off to their inns. Times have changed.

The Socialists: America's Future Friends?

IN RECENT years, no Japanese political party has been able to remain absolutely firm in its attitudes toward the United States. The ruling Liberal-Democratic party, the Socialist party, and the other opposition parties are all shifting their positions on policy vis-à-vis America.

Ever since the breakdown of the textile talks, a certain note of irritation has underlined the words of LDP men when they talk about relations with America. About eighty of them assembled late in May, 1971, to oppose the liberalization of American grapefruit imports, and took the opportunity to berate the government for attempting always to turn a smiling face toward the United States. They insisted that party men be allowed to accompany the bureaucrats going to America to discuss the grapefruit issue, as though to intimate that the official government representatives would not stand firmly enough to suit them.

It is true that the Liberal-Democratic party has maintained a traditional friendliness toward the United States, but it is quickly receding. These days it is no longer unusual for hostile opinions to be expressed even in the party's prominent organs like the Policy Affairs Research Council and the Foreign Affairs Research Council. To be sure, some anti-American utterances may be simply ax-grinding by party members laying plans for the post-Sato years, but the tendency seems to be running deeper than that. Recently, when the Foreign Affairs Research Council was recruiting members for its Committee on Chinese Affairs, nearly one hundred party members of both hawkish and dovish sentiments stepped forward. The membership of the committee suddenly grew to surpass that of the council of which it is actually a part. "China is replacing the United States in more ways than one," observes council chairman Zentaro Kosaka with a wan smile. "The times are indeed changing."

Although the Liberal-Democratic party has been emphasizing good will with the United States ever since the end of the war, America does not rank tops in popularity even with party members. To everyone's surprise, a recent *Asahi* poll of the sentiments of LDP men toward peoples of other nations revealed that Americans were third in popularity, behind West Germans and Chinese. This would seem to suggest that the current of anti-American feeling within the ruling party is running deeper than anyone might imagine.

"Japan's attachment to the United States has been like that of a faithful employee to a good boss. It's oversimplifying things to call this recent turning away from the U. S. an anti-American revolt," comments Professor Michio Royama of Sophia University. "The government and ruling party must recognize that they, more than any other Japanese group, are responsible for the current difficulties in Japanese-American relations."

"The Socialists have certainly changed," remarked an American congressman after attending the third Japan-America Parliamentary Exchange Conference held in Tokyo in May, 1971. "At the last meeting they did nothing but insist that the Security Treaty be scrapped. This time, they didn't even mention it, but talked about all sorts of other things." In 1968, the executive committee of the Japan Socialist party had decided to refrain from participating in the first parliamentary exchange conference. "Talking with American legislators," the party had contended, "is tantamount to involving ourselves in the American imperialism that we are determined to fight against." Eleven years earlier, in 1957, a delegation of Socialists led by the late Jotaro Kawakami had visited the United States seeking conferences with American political leaders. Secretary of State John Foster Dulles had curtly dismissed them with an invitation to return when their party had come to power. "Since then," comments Torao Takasawa, director of the party's General Affairs Bureau, "we have avoided all formal contact with the United States and have regarded her as a remote foreign nation."

Refusal to meet with American legislators in order to avoid "involvement in American imperialism" may be considered by some a doctrinaire adherence to principle and by others a mere lack of self-confidence. But that is beside the point. More important is the fact that, ever since the Kawakami mission's fruitless visit to the United States, the Socialist party has been maintaining a "seclusion policy" toward America. However, its position as Japan's foremost opposition party makes it imperative that it see and deal with the United States as well as with the world's socialist nations. Yet hardly any of the members of the party's current Executive Committee have visited the United States in an official capacity.

Since around 1969, however, subtle changes have been coming over the Socialist attitude toward the United States. "I regret having dismissed America with so sweeping an opinion," says Toshiaki Yokoyama, chairman of the party's Election Committee; in 1969, he participated in a mass rally in Los Angeles against the Vietnam war. "While standing in the midst of several hundred thousand people, I felt a wonderful sensation that I have never noticed at Japanese demonstrations against the government. We can no longer discuss America in purely ideological terms." Ichiro Moritaki, professor emeritus of Hiroshima University and a member of the Japan Council Against Atomic and Hydrogen Bombs, seems to agree. After addressing the antiwar march on Washington in April, 1970, he said: "A change is taking place in the United States and I think, although I am not a Socialist, that the Japanese progressives are finally beginning to take notice."

At a time when even the People's Republic of China, the country most sharply opposed to the foreign policy of the American government, desires greater contact with and knowledge of the United States, it is unlikely that the Socialists will lag far behind. "We may continue with our opposition to American policies, but that does not mean that we should not deepen our contacts with Americans as much as possible," says Kanji Kawasaki, director of the Socialist party's International Affairs Bureau. "Mounting fears in the world of a revival of Japanese militarism and possible future shifts in American foreign policy may eventually render Japan's pacifist forces sympathetic to the United States." Keigo Ouchi, director of the party's Education and Propaganda Bureau, is also looking toward the future. "Sometime during the late 1970s or 1980s the world will be compelled to alter its values in international relations. In the building of a new, post-Vietnam Asian order, there should be an important opportunity for cooperation between the Japanese opposition parties, on the one hand, and the United States, on the other; both sides should work for the independent coexistence of nations without regard to their particular political systems."

"We are considering dispatching a special mission to the United States sometime in the near future," reveals Akira Kuroyanagi, International Affairs Bureau director of the Komeito (Clean Government party), a newly powerful opposition party that derives support from members of the Soka Gakkai religion. Statements like this and those of other political leaders indicate that the opposition is seeking new angles from which to view the Japanese relationship with the United States. Still, the Okinawa issue and the question of when U. S. bases will be removed from Japanese territory prevent overt friendship with America. It is unlikely that American policy toward Japan, with the Security Treaty at its nucleus, will change radically in the foreseeable future, and the possibility of real friendship between the Japanese opposition and the United States remains hypothetical at best. Nevertheless, a cool and objective examination of the future possibilities of Japanese diplomacy vis-à-vis the United States would not be a futile pursuit at the present time.

The Collapse of
Transplanted Rationalism

THE NAME on the door to a small office on the fifth floor of a building that stands half-hidden behind a coffee shop near Iidabashi station in downtown Tokyo reads: Society for Research in the Science of Thought (Shiso no Kagaku Kenkyukai). The office is furnished with only one desk and one telephone, and it is manned by a single clerk working there two days a week. Registered as a corporation, the Society has 241 members, whose collective careers represent an index to the thinking about America by Japan's progressive intellectuals since the war. The Society was founded in 1946, with seven leading intellectuals as prime movers in organizing it: Shigeto Tsuru (economist), Shunsuke Tsurumi and Kazuko Tsurumi (philosophers and social scientists), Kiyoko Takeda (social scientist), Masao Maruyama (political scientist), Mitsuo Taketani and Satoshi Watanabe (physicists). From the outset, the Society was to be the standard-bearer for a new "popular pragmatic academism," struggling against the rigid framework of Marxism and the German idealism that dominated the academic world.

The new direction of the "science of thought" movement attracted liberal intellectuals from widely divergent fields. Among those drawn to the Society's pluralism and the flexibility of new thought growing out of intellectual conflict were sculptor Taro Okamoto, playwright Junji Kinoshita, legal scholar Takenobu Kawashima, sociologist Ikutaro Shimizu, horse-race analyst Shunsuke Akagi, historian and professor of French literature Takeo Kuwabara, art historian and professor of education Saburo Ienaga, film critic Tadao Sahara, sportswriter Aromu Mushiaki, and communications expert Hidetoshi Kato. Such pluralism was encouraged in the Society by Kazuko Tsurumi, who had witnessed the vitality and dynamism of intellectual ferment in the United States during the 1930s. That had been a free and liberal time in America, with bold thinking directed from all sides to combat the Depression.

Despite its early admiration of the American intellectual scene, the Society's estimation of the United States changed with the shift of a liberal America to paranoid anticommunism during the cold war and the fighting in Korea. Many of the Society's members joined pacifist groups, including the Conference on Peace Issues, and the new strategy of the group was to "use one side of America as a foothold for attacking the other side."

During the mass demonstrations in 1960 against the Mutual Security Treaty, members of the Society who had studied in America issued the following statement, obviously directed as much to the Kishi government as to the United States: "We have studied the traditions of the United States and have a profound affection for the country. It is that affection which prompts us now to urge the Kishi government to sever its opportunistic ties with the United States and to seek a way to forge ties of genuine Japanese-American friendship."

The eight years following the San Francisco peace treaty and Japan's regaining her independence were termed by the Society a "political season," a time when politics received first priority in Japanese-American relations. It was that season that sapped the energies of the Society and ended with the 1960 struggle against the

[353]

security pact. The ending of the "political season" brought the final frustration of the Society's original aims. "But also during those years," says Shunsuke Tsurumi, "American positivism emerged as the mainstream of the Japanese academic world."

As the Society's reasons for existence grew increasingly ambiguous, the Japan "Peace for Vietnam!" Committee (Beheiren) came into being. The stimulus behind its founding was opposition to the Vietnam war, and its nucleus was the Koe-naki Koe (Voiceless Voice), a pacifist citizens' group led by Michitoshi Takahata, former secretary general of the Society. According to Takahata: "We asked Makoto Oda, the popular novelist, to head Beheiren because he had done nothing in the 1960 struggle against the security pact."

As an offspring of the Society for Research in the Science of Thought, Beheiren claims to be "a structure without structure." According to Oda: "We will welcome anyone simply on the basis of his opposition to the war. We don't ask about party affiliation or ideology." Beheiren carries on an active program of nonviolent civil disobedience, modeled upon the peace movement in the United States. In its early days it attracted wide popular support. Antiwar demonstrations used to include young girls in bluejeans, holding hands with their long-haired boyfriends, and also proper housewives with small children in tow. But as the Vietnam war dragged on, Beheiren began to change. "Today, Beheiren has become a youth movement on a limited scale," observes Kenji Muro, a member who formerly belonged to the Society. "It is now a cell of radical students who don't know where to go now that the campus rebellions have died down, and other individuals opposed to the war who are seeking some ideology to hang onto." Members of the original Voiceless Voice group no longer join Beheiren demonstrations.

"The first aim of the Society for Research in the Science of Thought was to transplant an American-style *gori-shugi* [loosely translated as rationalism] to Japanese soil," says Takahata. "But no matter how deeply its members dug into Japanese society, they failed to come upon a stratum receptive to *gori-shugi*." Many of the original members of the Society have regrouped themselves into the Society of Symbols (Kigo no Kai) and concentrate on the study of the writings of native Japanese thinkers such as Kunio Yanagita, Nobuo Origuchi, and Moto-ori Norinaga. "Through the study of Japanese thought," says Shunsuke Tsurumi, "we hope to bring the science of thought a new lease on life."

American Studies in Japan

"THERE has been something wrong with America ever since World War II," says Yasaka Takagi quietly. Now in his eighties, Takagi is a highly respected political scientist. "I can't help fearing that the ideals that the country was founded upon are being overthrown entirely. This is not an easy time for America. But I don't think that she has yet lost the ability to criticize herself. Since the majority of American young people still seem to value the spirit of the Founding Fathers, I'm still optimistic that America may right herself again. . . ."

It might be said that American studies in Japan began with Takagi, and it is no exaggeration to say that all leading scholars in this field today are his disciples. In 1918, a special course on the constitution, history, and diplomacy of the United States was inaugurated at Tokyo University. It had financial backing from an American banker who hoped that it might serve to improve strained Japanese-American relations. Takagi, a young official of the Finance Ministry at the time, was selected as the first lecturer for the course. For more than half a century since then he has served as an important link in the relations of the two nations.

It was rumored around Tokyo University that Takagi delivered his lectures from the same notes for more than thirty years. A tale like that would be a terrible discredit to any other professor, but for Takagi it is testimony to his dedication to Japanese-American relations and to his constancy of purpose through the difficult prewar, wartime, and postwar eras. During the war, when university students were being called into battle and had little time for classes when they were about to be conscripted, he condensed his lecture notes and distributed them to students. After the war, these condensed notes were published as a book on American civilization.

"For me, the ten years leading to the war were far more difficult than the war years themselves," he says, recalling his private efforts as a member of the Institute of Pacific Relations to steer Japanese-American relations back to a safer course. He worked tirelessly behind the scenes to arrange a meeting between President Roosevelt and Prime Minister Konoe. He wrote letter after letter to Ambassador Grew urging "self-restraint" by the United States. Recalling his anguish at seeing each of his efforts in the years before Pearl Harbor miscarry, he compares America's Vietnam adventure to

Japan's undeclared war with China during the 1930's and wonders if America in recent years has not become "Japanized."

At the bottom of Takagi's feelings toward America have always been an unbounded love and respect for the democratic ideals for which the country fought in its early years. His criticisms of America are born of his vision of the perfection that he feels it is losing and must struggle to regain. This attitude is shared by his former assistants at Tokyo University, Shigeharu Matsumoto, now director of International House of Japan, and Ken'ichi Nakao, professor emeritus of the university. These three men, the first generation of Japanese Americanologists, are bound by their conviction that America is basically "a good country of good people."

After the forced hiatus in American studies during the Pacific War, interest burst forth with extraordinary intensity. In 1940, only six students were enrolled in Takagi's course at Tokyo University. In 1946, several hundred signed up for it, and the university was hard pressed to find a classroom large enough to contain them all. Rikkyo University reopened its American studies center, which had existed before the war, and similar centers were soon inaugurated at Tokyo, Kyoto, and Doshisha universities. Programs were also begun at International Christian University, Tsuda College, Japan Women's University, and Tokyo University of Foreign Studies, as well as at Seikei, Saitama, and Nanzan universities. Nonacademic study groups were also popular, and an American Studies Society was launched as a fund-raising organization. The passionate enthusiasm for American studies during the years following the war quickly eclipsed research in all other foreign countries or cultures.

The foremost men in American studies today, scholars who attained their academic positions since the war, may be called the "second generation" of Japanese Americanologists. If there is any single characteristic unifying them it is a tendency to strive for a certain distance between themselves and the United States and to view America objectively and dispassionately. Professor Makoto Saito, who replaced Takagi in his position at Tokyo University, puts it somewhat differently. "They are turning away from America," he says. "Having come through the Occupation, we must now struggle to free ourselves from the extremely close bonds that joined Japan and America during that period." The first generation is apt to idolize and glorify America, but the second must be more analytic and matter-of-fact. "The tradition of American studies in Japan," observes Professor Yoshimitsu Ide of Japan Women's University, "has been influenced, in large measure, by the attitudes and preconceptions of native

[356]

American Americanologists. We now must do our own thinking in this field, independent of them."

A new school of American studies, one critical of the United States, is gathering influence in Japan today. It contends that earlier American studies in Japan, following the example of American scholars themselves, has ignored the problems of America's minorities—the blacks, Indians, and immigrant groups—and is in need of fundamental reform. The traditionalists have made a habit of criticizing the realities of American life as deviating from the spirit of the Founding Fathers. The younger scholars, by contrast, suspect that those long-touted ideals of American democracy are fraudulent, and that, rather than a land of liberty and equality, America has always been a land of racial discrimination.

Much the same attitude has also rapidly gained currency in intellectual circles in the United States since the beginning of the war in Vietnam. Such a radical revision of its assumptions regarding American history and society may be considered characteristic of a third group of Japanese scholars of American studies. One member of this group is Tomohisa Shimizu, a professor at Japan Women's University, who has been traveling regularly to the U. S. military base at Asaka in Saitama Prefecture making antiwar speeches to wounded Vietnam veterans. "Why did America start the Vietnam war?" he asks. "And why has she carried it on so long? Japanese Americanologists have given us no answers to fundamental questions like these." Yoshiyuki Tsurumi, an official of International House of Japan, directs similarly sharp criticism at American studies in Japan. "It is no more than the American view of America, or the view held by white Americans in the East."

At no point in the short history of American studies in Japan has there been so direct a clash of beliefs. To the plea of "first generation" scholars that America return to the ideals on which she was founded, young men retort that America was sullied from the outset. "America as she is must be destroyed and a new country built on the ruins."

Fading Nuclear Allergy

WHEN FRANCE launched a series of nuclear tests in the South Pacific early in June, 1971, an *Asahi* reporter went to get the reactions of the fishermen of Yaizu, where the biggest tuna catches in the Far East are brought into port. "Who cares?" they shrugged. "Our fishing sites are in the Indian Ocean and way down off the Australian coast, nowhere near the test areas. . . . Bikini? That's ancient history." Their indifference to the tests seems particularly remarkable when one recalls that Yaizu was the home port of the *Lucky Dragon No. 5*, the small fishing boat that had been contaminated by the "ashes of death" during American H-bomb tests at Bikini in 1954. That incident had touched off a passionate nationwide campaign against nuclear armaments. But now, only seventeen years later, Japan seems to be fast outgrowing her "nuclear allergy."

The once furious and vociferous outcries against American nuclear submarines in cities like Sasebo and Yokosuka, where naval bases are located, have dwindled to occasional small demonstrations that arouse little interest. And in Hiroshima and Nagasaki, only a quarter-century after the atomic bombs were dropped, survivors of the blasts complain that the horrors of their experience are being forgotten. Hiroshi Morishita, a high school teacher near Hiroshima who since the war has devoted his energies to educating others to the terrors of nuclear war, sighs: "Man can forget anything. When I read my old diary and come across a phrase like 'The whole sandy beach was covered with dead bodies,' I can hardly believe that I actually wrote it."

Should Japan possess nuclear weapons? "She should, depending on the circumstances," answered eight percent of the respondents to a 1957 poll conducted by the Hiroshima branch of the Japan Council Against Atomic and Hydrogen Bombs. "She should," answered twenty-one percent of the respondents to an opinion survey conducted by the *Asahi Shimbun* in 1968. "She should, for the sake of peace and security," answered thirty-one percent of those polled by Hiroshima Girls' Academy in 1969; the poll had been conducted among those alumnae who had been attending the school when the A-bomb was dropped on August 6, 1945. These figures are eloquent testimony to the decline year by year in the abhorrence of nuclear weaponry that Japanese people used to feel.

At its height, the Japanese campaign against nuclear armaments derived its impetus from memories of Hiroshima and Nagasaki, from Japan's renunciation of war, and from the repeated nuclear testing by the United States and the Soviet Union during the cold war. But even then, there was almost no anti-American feeling behind the virulent "nuclear allergy" of the Japanese people. Masaharu Hatanaka, director of the Japan Council Against Atomic and Hydrogen Bombs, represented only a tiny minority when he tried to foment anti-American sentiment by urging that the erring nations be carefully identified. The great majority of Japanese lent their energy toward working for a universal renunciation of war instead of singling out belligerent nations. In fact, surveys taken by teachers' unions in Hiroshima and Nagasaki have revealed that ten to twenty percent of middle-school students in those two cities do not even know who dropped the atomic bombs.

Japan is the only country in the world that has directly experienced the horror of nuclear devastation. Each time, in the bombing of two of her cities and in the exposure of her fishermen to radioactive fall-out, she has suffered at the hands of the United States. And yet, to the puzzlement of Europeans, the level of anti-American sentiment has remained remarkably low. Günther Anders, the Austrian Jewish philosopher, visited the Hiroshima Peace Memorial Museum and later asked its curator how the Japanese felt toward the United States. When he was told, his face turned crimson with rage. "Why don't they hate America? Why haven't they demanded greater redress from her?" he asked furiously, bursting into a torrent of vituperation against the United States.

Ichiro Moritaki, professor emeritus of Hiroshima University and a committee members of the Council Against Atomic and Hydrogen Bombs, recalls meeting Bertrand Russell at his home in northern Wales in 1957. The British philosopher speculated that the Japanese must burn with hatred for the United States. Moritaki said that rather than hating America, the Japanese were more concerned that no nuclear holocaust be permitted to occur in the future. "Can the Japanese really be of so noble a spirit?" asked Russell incredulously. It was but a casual conversation, but it left the two old philosophers surprised at the difference between the Japanese and the Occidental ways of thinking.

Why are Japanese feelings toward the United States so unvengeful? Scholars and atom-bomb survivors offer any number of reasons. Right after the war the Japanese were too hungry to think of anything but where their next meal was coming from. The Occupation imposed a total news blackout, which kept the Japanese ignorant of much of the tragic stories of Hiroshima and Nagasaki. U. S. policy toward occupied Japan was, for the most part, gentle and benevolent, for which the Japanese were grateful. The Japanese government consistently depicted America favorably, hoping to make the people forget the tragedy of the bombings. Many Japanese felt that to voice anti-American sentiments would be to play into the hands of the Communists. The Japanese take things philosophically and are quick to

[359]

resign themselves to what they cannot control. The Japanese are naively forgiving. There are other reasons, as well. First, the Japanese people derive a sense of satisfaction from the fact that international politics "bans" the use of nuclear weapons. Second, they have been able to advance their economic interests without the support of military strength.

In seeking the causes of the decline in the once virulent "nuclear allergy" of the Japanese people, one must look to the United States and to the Japanese government, which is always fearful that strong Japanese opposition to nuclear weaponry might run counter to American military strategies. But would it, in fact, prove so damaging to the long-term interests of the United States? Conversely, might not the very opposite prove to be even more detrimental? Japan's reduced abhorrence of nuclear armaments, combined with her present economic power and technological capabilities, may well shake her resolve not to make, possess, or import nuclear arms. The collapse of that resolve would certainly, in the long run, prove menacing to the United States.

Japan's prayers for the abolition and extinction of nuclear armaments—prayers symbolized by the thousands of folded-paper cranes made by children all over the country and sent to Hiroshima to decorate the bomb-memorial site—have tragically gone unanswered. Rather than disappear, nuclear weapons have continued their malignant spread. And yet, despite that spread, Japan's experience and Japan's prayers may have served as a remote deterrent to the use of nuclear bombs by the United States in Korea and Vietnam. If so, the terrible experience will not have been totally in vain.

Is it inevitable that Japan's nuclear allergy must diminish and eventually disappear? Can it yet be cherished and preserved? These are vitally important questions that the people of Japan must never stop asking themselves.

Thorns in Japanese Fingers

FOUR fire-breathing monsters attacked the foothills of sacred Mount Fuji one fine day in May, laying waste hundreds of acres of grassland in a few moments. This was no storybook incident, but the carefully staged grass-burning operation of four American tanks with flame-throwers mounted on them. The purpose of the operation that took place at the Kitafuji firing range in Yamanashi Prefecture was to facilitate the discovery of unexploded shells.

"How cruel!" wept groups of women as they watched larks fleeing in terror from their grassy nests, which were going up in flames. "Song My must have looked something like this!" The women, members of local associations of mothers and housewives, had gathered to protest the burning of the hillsides. For some of them, the burning of the grassland meant an economic loss, for they had gathered hay on those hills to feed their livestock. But, beyond considerations of economic loss, they were distressed at the destruction of their "spiritual home." Fuji is a sacred mountain, and its scenic surroundings are cherished by all Japanese. The assault on the mountain was painful even to the tiny spirits of schoolchildren of the nearby Ninno Elementary School, one of whom wrote the following verse:

> I never of looking on it, day in and day out,
> Mount Fuji, our most lovely mountain.
> Boom, boom, today again
> The firing of mighty cannons continues.
> If it is fired upon so much,
> I fear our poor mountain will be destroyed.

The Kitafuji firing range, more than sixteen thousand acres in area, lies surrounded by superb natural beauty between Lake Kawaguchi and Lake Yamanaka. It is fenced off with heavy barbed wire, and a sign in Japanese and English warns that trespassers will be prosecuted. Who would expect to come upon a firing range for heavy artillery in the midst of the scenic tranquillity of hills and lakes, pine forests and singing birds, at the foot of one of the world's most beautiful mountains? The stillness of the grove of massive, ancient cedars that surround the Asama Shrine, a sanctuary for climbers of the sacred mountain, is constantly shattered by the pounding of artillery.

Even local assemblymen affiliated with the ruling, pro-American Liberal-Democratic party have strongly advocated the removal of the range and the return of the area to Japanese hands. "Why carry on military activities in a place like this?" they ask. "Fuji does not take kindly to the Stars and Stripes firing upon it."

"It is the new nationalism, not leftist ideologies, that will decry the presence of American bases in Japan from now on," says Fuji Kamiya of Keio University. "Outcries against the Security Treaty have all but died down, but the longer U. S. forces remain in Japan the more discordant their presence will seem with their surroundings." In West

Germany, however, they are much better assimilated with the surroundings. American Undersecretary of State U. Alexis Johnson was asked at a hearing of the Senate Foreign Relations Committee in January, 1971, why U. S. bases in Japan were so unpopular while those in South Korea and West Germany were comparatively well regarded by local people. Johnson replied: "The Japanese do not feel the immediate menace and do not recognize the importance of the U. S. bases to the security of the entire Far East."

"The head-on clashes over the joint-security arrangements such as those that occurred at Uchinada and Sunagawa in the 1950s have disappeared," observe Shigemitsu Akanegakubo, former Socialist member of the Lower House and an opponent of U. S. bases in Japan. "Today's struggles are only to attack such base-connected nuisances as noise from jets." The subsiding of antibase tensions is due primarily to the reduction of the size of the American military forces stationed in Japan. The tensions have lessened, but they will not disappear as long as bases remain in Japan.

"The Americans live in paradise, while we're down here in hell," say some Yokohama residents, pointing up at a spacious U. S. military-housing area high on a hill overlooking the port. Within the fences surrounding the housing area there are green lawns and trees, but at the bottom of the hill people live in tiny wooden houses, crowded into narrow, dirty alleys. Yokohama's eighteen U. S. military installations occupy a total area of 1,580 acres.

"Of course, we have been pressing for the return of those tracts of property," says Ichio Asukata, mayor of Yokohama, "but we do not yell: 'Down with the Security Treaty!' That would not get us anywhere. The best way to achieve our goals is to explain the city's housing shortage and the resentment of citizens over suffering in the face of plenty; we also try to explain our plans for the use of the properties after they are returned to us." When he was a Socialist representative in the Lower House, Asukata was a dauntless opponent of the Security Treaty. Today he bases his actions more on the sentiment of the residents of his city than on abstract ideology.

Changes in the general level of the Japanese economy have had a decided effect on the attitudes of the people living around them toward the bases. The case of Sasebo Naval Base in Kyushu is a recent example. Late in December, 1970, a plan to transfer the U. S. Seventh Fleet from Yokosuka to Sasebo was abruptly dropped. Meanwhile, however, Sasebo shopkeepers had begun giving their stores a face-lifting in preparation for greeting the expected fleet personnel. When James Ashida, the American consul in nearby Fukuoka, visited

Sasebo to apologize for the sudden change in plans, he found Sasebo residents undisturbed and making long-range plans to rid themselves of dependence on the U. S. naval base.

The Girard case of only fourteen years earlier had brought a far less calm response from Japanese. Army Specialist Third Class William Girard had fatally shot a Japanese woman who was picking up used shells on the U. S. Army firing range at Soma in Gumma Prefecture. His trial in a Japanese court was attended by a nationwide furor, which did not abate when the American soldier was given only a three-year suspended prison term. Shukichi Sakai, the widower of Girard's victim, muses sadly: "In those days, everyone was so hard up that people had to risk their lives picking up old artillery shells to make a little money. Now, it's different. . . ."

Today, as the improved standard of living has begun to benefit people living on the periphery of American bases, they have come to resent the presence of the bases for reasons that are not simply economic. Many regard the continued existence of American bases on Japanese soil as a symptom of extraterritoriality. The Nixon Doctrine has brought about renewed cutbacks in the number of American forces in Japan, and there are predictions that Yokosuka and Sasebo will eventually be the only two American bases remaining. But even then, the presence of only two bases would probably continue to represent a danger signal in Japanese-American relations. "The retention of two naval ports by the United States would prick the pride of the Japanese like thorns sticking in their fingers," says critic Jun Eto. "They might conceivably trigger anti-American campaigns similar to those that have occurred in Hiroshima and Nagasaki."

If the United States intends to continue maintaining bases in Japan, it will have to devote greater efforts to winning the hearts of the people in the areas where the bases are located. Thus far, U. S. Far Eastern policy has placed primary emphasis on military affairs and neglected public relations. If this state of affairs continues, the bases may soon become something considerably more serious than thorns sticking in Japanese fingers.

Textbook America

"**B**OYS, be ambitious!" Leaving these words ringing in the ears of his students at the Sapporo School of Agriculture, Dr. William Smith Clark returned home to the United States in 1876. He had taught in Sapporo for only eight months, but his farewell exhortation to the young students of Meiji Japan won him lasting glory in the annals of Japanese education, at least until recently. In the years immediately following World War II, as many as fifteen grammar-school textbooks carried stories about Clark. But in 1970, his name appeared in only two sixth-grade textbooks, and the following year it disappeared from textbooks altogether.

During the early postwar years, textbooks were full of America. There were stories about traveling around the United States, descriptions of the TVA, episodes from American history, stories about small-town America, and biographies of famous Americans. According to Toyotaro Karasawa of the Tokyo University of Education, textbook space was allotted to forty-one famous Americans in 1956. Among the most popular were Benjamin Franklin, Abraham Lincoln, George Washington, Franklin Roosevelt, Thomas Edison, and Babe Ruth.

Since the late 1950s, however, references to America and Americans have been fast disappearing from the textbooks. The American influence, material and spiritual, that blanketed Japan during the Occupation years and the early fifties has faded noticeably. "It was inevitable," explains Kikuji Nakamura, a member of the National Institute for Educational Research, "that there be a reaction to the earlier adulation for everything American. But the sharp differences of opinion and conflicting attitudes toward America among Japanese adults have also thrown textbook writers and editors into confusion."

Despite the disappearance of America from their textbooks, however, Japanese schoolchildren seem to know more than ever about the country, and their interest in it has not waned in the least. America almost invariably ranks second—after Switzerland—on the lists of countries that pupils in elementary schools say they want most to visit. This was so in the years immediately following the war, and the United States has consistently maintained this position ever since. The three things about America that most interest Japanese schoolchildren seem to be the American form of freedom that produced Abraham Lincoln, the technological advances so dramatically displayed in the American space program, and the reasons that the country should be fighting in Vietnam.

In 1970, an opinion survey was taken of ninth-grade students of the Ichijo Junior High School in Utsunomiya. Given a list of positive and negative images to vote on, their attitudes were almost equally divided. Positive images included America's assistance in Japan's postwar rehabilitation, the frontier spirit and freedom of faith, highly developed science, and economic power. Negative images included inhumane acts in Vietnam, racism, the violence of American troops in Okinawa, and unilateral restrictions on textile imports from Japan. Only six years earlier, 250 students in the seventh, eighth, and ninth grades of the same school, asked to rate the merits and demerits of six foreign countries on a variety of issues, gave 245 votes favoring the United States and only 9 against it. Senji Suzuki, a teacher at the school, believes that the dramatic difference in the two polls shows the increased sensitivity of young Japanese students to news reports, especially news of the United States.

Folk singing is enjoying tremendous popularity among young people in Japan today, and the songs they most like to sing are the same antiwar songs that are heard at peace rallies all over the world. Many Japanese youths want to go to America to take part in peace rallies and sing folk songs there. "It doesn't necessarily mean that they know very much about the American peace movements or support them," comment some teachers. "They just say that it would be 'cool' to go to sing at rallies in the United States."

Most children in elementary and junior high schools are not very well informed about what is going on in the world. Their reactions to news are influenced largely by their home and school environments. But by the time they reach high school, students begin to show increasingly sensitive and independent reactions to the news they read and hear. "Japanese high school students," says Saburo Tashiro, a teacher at Toyama High School in Tokyo, "are definitely critical of the United States on four main issues: Vietnam, Okinawa, racial discrimination, and the atomic bomb. But they still praise the traditional optimism and cheerfulness of Americans and they respect the high level of American science. This has not changed. Most high school students are well disposed toward the United States. They have yet to develop any fixed ideology and they do not let their negative reactions to specific issues blacken their opinion of the entire society." Educators and psychologists who have studied the process by which political consciousness develops agree that young Japanese students seek a balanced view of the United States. Avoiding either outright rejection or passionate adulation, they try to see both the good and the bad in America.

It has been through the textbooks that they learned, in orthodox fashion, about the good side of America. The bad has come to them in fragments, from newspapers, magazines, movies, television, and hearsay. Their negative attitudes have not developed systematically through textbooks, but have been formed independently. Educators recognize that expunging all the glorifications of America from the textbooks will not encourage a balanced view, and feel that renewed efforts should be made to present an objective picture of the United States in books for young students.

Year after year, at least forty percent (the largest single segment) of the respondents in *Asahi* polls have indicated that the United States is the country whose friendship Japan most needs. China is usually given second ranking with around twenty percent. The ratio is nearly the same for all ages, whether the pollees are adults or young students. Such widespread feelings among the Japanese public that friendly relations with the United States are critical only increases the need for well-organized, systematic education through which the next generation can learn to view America objectively.

Youth International

"**N**O SOONER were they through customs in San Francisco than they dashed off to pay phones and started calling their friends. I was amazed. They felt no hesitation whatever about using pay phones for the first time in a strange land. I myself have been abroad any number of times, but every time I get more white hairs." Professor Michio Royama of Sophia University was telling of his experience leading a group of students on their first trip to the United States. After finishing their telephoning, some members of the group had apparently wasted no time in taking off for Las Vegas in rented cars.

A dozen years ago, Japanese students leaving for America on Fulbright scholarships were so nervous about leaving the familiar manners of home that they had to be coached in every detail of American customs and behavior, even to the point of being instructed in how to sit on a Western toilet. Most of them usually remained nervous until well after they had settled into their new American environment.

Times have changed, and today Japanese youths mingle with Americans almost as freely as if they were fellow countrymen. America feels closer to them than some parts of Japan, and when they travel off to the United States they feel none of their elders' nervousness about setting foot in a foreign land. Every spring, with the approach of summer vacation, bulletin boards at university campuses are covered with signs recruiting members for overseas-travel groups. Keio University alone has more than ten organizations that work overtime getting together summer trips abroad for students.

When the Japanese youths arrive in America, the sights greeting them are hardly different from those at home—highways and traffic jams, crowded cities and supermarkets. One young member of the Asahi Floating University's voyage to the United States in 1969 seemed to sum up the impressions of his fellow students when he exclaimed: "America is really to be pitied! She has nothing much of interest to show." Shin'ichiro Watanabe, a lecturer for the shipboard seminar, was compelled to snap back in annoyance: "Don't pretend to know so much. Remember, you've only seen a little of America."

"I've always felt America close to me," says long-haired folk singer Tomoya Takaishi. "That's why I went straight there when I sneaked out of Japan to see the rest of the world." All his money was stolen in Salt Lake City, and not knowing what else to do, he simply sat down by the side of a road. "I don't know what would have happened if this hippie hadn't come along and picked me up," he recalls, laughing.

Rock music, bluejeans, long hair bound with a rubber band—whatever it is that American culture means to Japanese youth, they take to it as naturally as breathing. Sportswriter Yukio Akatsuka points to American or Japanese words that have found their way into the speech of young people of both countries. "A lot of American girls used to call some boys that took them out 'NATO.' It stood for 'No Action, Talk Only.' It wasn't long before Japanese girls had picked up this bit of slang. Also, if you compare Japanese and American leaders of student movements, you'll see them using the same gestures and the same delivery when they give speeches. Neither Japanese nor Americans are imitating each other. The simple fact is that both think pretty much the same."

Whether out of sympathy or hostility for the United States, Japanese students these days seem most interested in the problems and current dilemmas of American society. Majors in American government at a Tokyo university were asked recently what interested them most about the United States. Most of them immediately mentioned the Vietnam war, the political and economic effects stemming from it, the antiwar movement, and the Black Power movement. "My students always want to do papers on America's race problems," says Professor Noboru Ito of Tsuda College. "I tell them that race isn't America's only problem."

An *Asahi* reporter, sitting in on classes at Tokyo University's

General Education Division, jotted down some things he heard students saying:

"American values are now in a state of conflict and disorder. New things are cropping up that we have trouble understanding."

"Hippies on the one hand, and 'middle America' supporting Nixon on the other—American society is much more complicated than it seems on the surface."

"American society seems to be confused, as though it were being tossed about helplessly in a whirlpool."

"I am most interested in the hippie values. And I think that Japan, of all other countries, is closest to the main currents of American civilization. Japan is now grappling with all the same problems of a modern, advanced civilization."

"I wonder whether America shouldn't thank her exploitation of blacks and underdeveloped countries for her wealth."

Masao Suzuki, twenty-two years old, is a senior at Doshisha University in Kyoto and a student leader of Beheiren (the Japan "Peace for Vietnam!" Committee). He once harbored an American army deserter from Vietnam. In 1970, he went to Cuba to work on the sugar harvest. In April of that same year he and others in the peace movement—including American students and teachers—staged an antiwar demonstration outside the U. S. marine air station at Iwakuni. Their rallying cry was not "Yankees Go Home!" but "GIs Join Us!" A year later, Suzuki and the antiwar groups returned to Iwakuni for a kite-flying festival followed by a rock-music concert. Antiwar GIs in civilian clothes joined the Japanese kids in the singing and dancing. "We feel no particular complex toward Americans," says Suzuki. "We have no illusions about them either. They are people like everyone else, and we can understand each other as human beings. I'm convinced of that."

Hideshi Kobayashi, Hiroshi Fujiwara, and Kiyoshi Fukuhara are recent graduates of the officer candidate school of the Maritime Self-Defense Force. During the summer of 1970—their last summer vacation as students—the three of them toured the United States at their own expense. They were hospitably received by students at American military academies. "We got along well with them because we were all soldiers or soldiers-to-be," agree the three men. "We believe that we should be able to get along equally well in the future too. It is between groups that there is the risk of misunderstandings arising. There should be opportunities for individual activities to influence diplomatic decisions and even military ones. We should also try to make positive personal contacts not only with Americans, but with Russians, and Englishmen, and everyone else."

Japanese young people today have few or no memories of their country's defeat in war. Lacking their parents' complexes, developed because of Japan's former backwardness among the civilized nations of the world, they feel no hesitation about mingling with American youths, just as though they were their own countrymen. The influence of American popular culture on the life of Japanese youth has been great, but they do not feel restricted by it in any way. The young Americans they meet are not so much foreigners as fellow human beings, seeking common goals. It is in their positive attitudes toward crossing foreign boundaries and deepening contacts with other people that the hope of the future lies.

PART SEVEN

Toward the Future

Premier Sato has stated on many occasions that Japan's postwar period will end only with the reversion of Okinawa. Whether or not his periodization is correct, it is noteworthy that it has taken over a quarter of a century for a Japanese leader to observe publicly that the aftermath of the Pacific War may finally cease to dominate Japan's view of herself and of her place in the world. The Okinawa milestone passed, Japan is now free to pursue a thoroughly new course, and the next quarter-century will doubtless witness a very different sort of intercourse between the two Pacific powers.

What will be the future of the Japanese-American relationship? Despite the current vogue for futurology and the plethora of statistics projected far into the future, no one can really predict what the quality of the future will be. Perhaps all that can be said with any certainty is that the critical importance of the relationship, both for Japan and for the United States, as well as for the rest of the world, will intensify as the two countries seek to adjust themselves to a new era of equality—and rivalry.

The articles in this final section attempt, at a time when both Japan and America are carefully reconsidering their priorities, policies, and goals, to look beyond to the problems that may confront them and the possibilities that may be available to them. Ironically, just as Japan is regaining national confidence and beginning to assume an international role commensurate with her wealth and dynamism, the United States, racked by internal dissensions that the bitter Vietnam experience has brought to a head, is turning inward, increasingly disillusioned with the global role she undertook so enthusiastically in the 1950s and 1960s.

What might be labeled the new Japanese assertiveness has thus far found expression chiefly in the economic realm, with businessmen carving out extensive markets for their goods all over the world. But the debates now going on within the Japanese government and the questions being asked by *the people indicate clearly that Japan will not remain reticent in other fields much longer. Should Japan press harder for a permanent seat on the U. N. Security Council? Should the "peace consitution" be revised? Should she scrap the Security Treaty with the United States and assume full responsibility for her own defense? Should Japan rearm fully, even to the point of producing nuclear hardware? What, ultimately, should be the political and military role of a nation that is already an economic superpower?*

Japan's answers to these questions will, of course, be greatly affected by the future course of American policies. In some ways, a United States weary and angry over the expense and frustrations of global leadership may be anxious to have Japan assume a share of the political and military burden, at least in Asia. At the same time, just as Japanese economic inroads have inspired concern in some parts of America, there are increasing fears of a resurgent Japanese military. The fears are shared elsewhere in the world, even in such staunchly anticommunist bastions as the Republic of Korea. In trying to allay such fears, Japan should keep before herself the example of the mistakes America has made as a superpower.

The basic problem of the future will be whether the United States and Japan can transcend such narrow-minded, nationalistic disputes as the thorny, but ultimately petty, squabble over textiles, and advance into a relationship of friendly competition and international cooperation. Japan's contacts with powerful neighbors like China and Russia, and with important trading partners such as the Common Market and the countries of Southeast Asia, will inevitably increase in importance. Many specialists in international affairs see this as a healthy development, arguing that Japan should be discouraged from giving disproportionate weight to her relations with America. In a widened, global context, Japan and the United States have much to offer both to each other and to the world. In the economic field, the two industrial giants have a unique opportunity to demonstrate to the world that a mutually profitable "international division of labor" is a viable alternative to the ugly trade wars that grow out of the insular protection of moribund industries. In the political arena, nonmilitary Japanese-American cooperation could be a vital factor in achieving stability and peace in Asia and throughout the world. The threats to harmony between Japan and America are greater than they have ever been before. But greater, too, will be the benefits to the international order of an effective resolution of their difficulties.

A Simulated Future

A GROUP of Japanese scholars and students gathered in Tokyo in June, 1969, to peer into the future. With the aid of a computer, and an expenditure of nearly three thousand dollars, they staged a two-day simulation dealing with Asia in the 1980s. Participating in the simulation were professors Kinhide Mushakoji of Sophia University and Kanji Seki of Tokyo University, other teachers, and nearly one hundred students specializing in international affairs.

Twelve nations were selected as models for the simulation: Japan, the United States, the Soviet Union, the People's Republic of China, Great Britain, France, India, North and South Korea, North and South Vietnam, and Taiwan. Each nation was given a code name (Japan was referred to as "Rio," for example, and the United States as "Jupiter"), and the students were distributed to the various countries with such assignments as prime ministers and ministers of foreign affairs, defense, trade, and the like. A secretary general of the United Nations was selected, as well as opposition leaders and newspapermen for each country. A classroom near the Tokyo University Computer Center was partitioned into separate booths for each nation, an international conference hall, a press room, and a control center.

The simulation was carried on for two days, each day divided into seven ninety-minute periods. It began with the ministers of each nation meeting in a simulated cabinet session to make policy decisions in accord with the current international situation as described in a scenario. The policy decisions—involving such matters as budget allocations, ratios of allocations to military purposes and domestic production, economic aid to foreign countries, trade volume, political relations with countries linked by alliances, and so forth—were then fed into the computer. The computer, which had been previously programmed and fed fifty other factors—the GNP of each nation, her total budget, her public-opinion trends, and the like—gave reactions to the policy decisions that had come out of the initial cabinet meetings. The reactions served as the initial conditions for the next simulation period.

In one example of the responses from the computer, a policy deci-

[373]

sion allocating too much of the national budget for military purposes and too little for domestic consumption caused a severe decline in popular support for the government; when the government support reached a certain low point, the computer estimated probabilities and flashed the signal: "Revolution!"

While the cabinet meetings were in session, an eight-nation disarmament conference was also in progress. When the conference received the emergency news that China had succeeded in developing an ICBM, it immediately responded by adopting a resolution to invite China to join the conference. Adding China to the international conference altered the preconditions of the international situation and consequently induced different responses from the computer to the policy decisions that were regularly fed into it.

The simulation, projected as far as the 1980s, showed one possible situation of the world fifteen years hence. Various other situations might also have developed, but it is interesting to examine some of the major revelations of this simulation. The developments of the 1970s and 1980s were described as follows:

—The United States became increasingly isolationist, and its relative position in international politics declined. The economy of the United States moved deeper and deeper into depression until the country was finally forced to turn to Japan for loans.

—Okinawa was received back as part of Japan, but the Security Treaty between Japan and the United States continued in effect. Japan continued to support the United States on the question of admitting China to the United Nations, but she declined American requests for loans.

—New regimes emerged in both North and South Korea. The two Koreas, rejecting intervention by the major powers, finally effected a reunification through the good offices of India.

—A coup d'état established a new regime in Taiwan. The new government then proceeded to initiate contacts with the People's Republic of China and unilaterally abrogated Taiwan's military alliance with the United States.

—The Paris peace talks broke down in failure, and at the end of the simulation, the war in Vietnam was still going on.

International-politics simulations, which Seki calls "a kind of toy," flourished briefly in the United States during the 1960s. But, discredited by the failure of the McNamara defense strategy in Vietnam and subjected to a rising tide of criticism that human beings cannot be measured and computerized, simulations fell out of fashion. Seki still maintains: "They are no more than toys, but they have their usefulness."

During the summer of 1970, one hundred young diplomats and scholars from fifty nations assembled in Vienna for a "United Nations university" to thrash out the Cyprus problem, using simulation techniques. They found them effective in discovering possible means of settling international conflicts. Simulations need not be limited to education and research, for the lessons derived from them may sometimes be useful in making actual policy decisions. After participating in a large-scale simulation at the Defense Industrial College in Washington in 1969, Hisao Iwashima, of the Japanese National Defense College, commented: "The simulation clearly revealed that an organization like the United Nations, though almost powerless, could still be effective in solving international issues. It showed also that nuclear bluffing did not always influence diplomatic negotiations in favor of the bluffer. This fact alone may lessen the feelings in some countries that nuclear power is a necessity. The development of a nuclear capability has the tendency of dragging a country to the brink of economic ruin. That impressed me very deeply."

"One of the first things revealed by simulations," says Sakio Takayanagi, an instructor at Chuo University, "is the thickly intertwined complexity of international relations. They also demonstrate how little any single nation stands to gain simply by pursuing its own interests. In that respect, simulations can prove highly enlightening for a country like Japan, which must rid herself of her self-centered view of international relations and take on a broader, more international vision."

For more than a quarter-century since the end of World War II, Japan's relations with the United States have been so close as to overshadow her contacts with all other nations. All major diplomatic issues—the Security Treaty, Okinawa, textile exports—have been of a binational nature, but now the time has come for Japan to break out of this limiting framework and to begin to function in larger, international circumstances. Perhaps simulations, requiring as they do a broad range of vision, may help Japan develop the multilateral formulae that will be necessary if she is to live up to her role as an important element of the world as a whole.

Outside Comments
on Japan's Future

"**WHAT** should be Japan's future role in the world?" The *Asahi Shimbun* recently questioned two distinguished American intellectuals on a number of matters related to this crucial issue. The two were Hans Morgenthau, professor of political science at the University of Chicago, and David Riesman, professor of sociology at Harvard University. Both of them have traveled widely and possess a vision that is broad and international in scope. Both have visited Japan. The present article is comprised of the questions they were asked and excerpts from their replies.

Question: Do you share the alarm, now growing more and more intense among critics of Japan, over a resurgence of Japanese militarism?

Morgenthau: I do not. Nobody knows what the future will bring, but at present I see no signs of a revival of militarism.

Riesman: I do not. I think there is a revival of Japanese nationalism and self-confidence which has healthy aspects; and, of course, there are some new strategic "realists" who would like to see Japan follow the lead of the militaristic powers, such as the United States and the Soviet Union. But, in spite of the flamboyant self-destruction of Yukio Mishima, I am not presently anxious about the revival of militarism.

Question: At present, Japan has no nuclear weapons. Do you think Japan should acquire nuclear weapons?

Morgenthau: Nuclear weapons for a nation such as Japan are not an asset but a liability. In view of her concentration of population and industrial centers in a small geographic space, Japan, by making use of nuclear weapons, would only provoke her own destruction. For this reason a Japanese threat to use nuclear weapons under certain circumstances would be ineffective. In this respect, Japan would be in the same position in which Great Britain, France, and China find themselves already. They divert large amounts of scarce resources for the development of nuclear weapons, and there is nothing they have done in foreign policy that they could not have done without nuclear weapons.

Riesman: I have argued since Hiroshima that nuclear weapons are self-destructive to the nation that possesses them. We Americans are less rather than more secure because of our possession of such weapons. Setting the example that they have, in the past, of disarmament, at least relatively, the Japanese in my opinion should continue their opposition to nuclear weapons rather than joining the so-called club, which is fundamentally self-destructive.

Question: As you know, the postwar Japanese constitution renounces war. At present, Japan has only self-defense forces that are limited to defense purposes alone. Do you feel the Japanese should continue this policy or not?

Morgenthau: Japan should indeed continue this policy because it best serves her national interest.

Riesman: As suggested in my answer to the previous question, I think that it would be unwise for the Japanese to go beyond the present so-called self-defense forces. I realize that we do not live in a world of order and security, but in one more closely delineated by Thomas Hobbes. Nevertheless, my experience of history and of life has convinced me that the military are in alliance with each other across national boundaries against their own people, not necessarily to engage in war but to enhance their status and gadgetry. At best this is an expensive luxury which is harmful to Japanese and world society; at worst, it is the beginning of the creation of a militaristic force in Japan of which there has already been sufficient experience.

Question: Do you believe that the United States should intervene to help Japan in the event of an outside attack upon her?

Morgenthau: The United States should indeed intervene in such a situation because it has a vital interest in the existence of a strong and independent Japan.

Riesman: The premises of the question are a world of disorder and great power anarchy. I do not believe that Japan must develop her diplomacy and strengthen her relations with all countries in the world, whatever their ideological posture. There is no road to safety. I could imagine a situation in which an attack on Japan should be resisted by the United States, but my impression of Southeast Asia is that American intervention has been more damaging than it could conceivably ever have been helpful. The Japanese should be glad to be spared from such a liberation! But American support for Japanese interests against invasion would seem desirable to me even though I am something of a pacifist and would prefer to see the Japanese concentrate on nonviolent defense of the Japanese home islands as a strategy that has never been fully tested in the world but tentatively adumbrated by what was done in Denmark under the Nazis and by Gandhi and his leadership in India.

Questioned further on the future of Asia and the Pacific region, Morgenthau indicated that he expected the United States to coexist with the People's Republic of China much as it does with the Soviet Union today. "Such a situation is likely to emerge," he added, "because it is a rational necessity from the point of view of American interests." Both he and Riesman favored improved Japanese relations with continental China leading to the restoration of diplomatic relations. Both of them also agreed that the United States should concentrate on helping Japan expand her economic activities rather than her military power, in such a way as to benefit the trade and development of Asia as a whole.

Asked for comments on the future of Japanese-American relations, Morgenthau replied: "The United States ought to continue the process of normalization of which the agreement on Okinawa is thus far the outstanding example. Normalization means the reduction of the American military presence to a minimum and the coordination of policies serving identical or parallel interests." To further understanding of Japan in the United States, Riesman encouraged the creation of more centers of scholarship dealing with Japan studies and an increase in the number of American newsmen able to speak Japanese and report intelligently on the complexities and intricacies of Japan.

Utopias Lost

PROFESSOR Yoshikazu Sakamoto was asked to comment upon the views on Japanese-American relations voiced by professors Hans Morgenthau and David Riesman in the preceding article. Now teaching international politics at Tokyo University, Sakamoto studied under Morgenthau at the University of Chicago in the mid-1950s, and they have been close friends since then. He first met Riesman at the first Dartmouth Conference on Japanese-American relations, held in New Hampshire in 1962. Both have been active in campaigns against nuclear armaments. The following is Sakamoto's response to the comments of the two American professors:

Over the years since the end of World War II, the United States has grown accustomed to its role as Japan's guardian. Now its relations with Japan, and with much of the rest of the world as well, are shifting from protection toward competition. Competition being the keystone of American society, Japan can expect Americans to view her with increasing severity as she reveals herself a formidable competitor. The United States also competes with the nations of Europe, but the similarity of their cultures tends to reduce feelings of rivalry between them. But Japan is the first non-European—or, in American parlance, Oriental—nation to attain a position of equality and significant competition with the United States. If it were military competition, Japanese power and ability would be denounced as "barbarism" in America. But what Americans are concerned about is not Japan's warring abilities but her business prowess, which has been tested by the standards of American commerce. They are growing nervous and bitter about it, and Japan must be prepared for the discord that is bound to result.

Professor Morgenthau and Professor Riesman both advise against Japan's arming herself with nuclear weaponry. But there are some officials in the Japanese government who insist that Japan exhibit, as a diplomatic expedient, her ability to develop a nuclear capability. That seems unreasonable to me. Recognizing the hardening American attitude that nuclear arms would prove of no value to Japan, I strongly advise these Japanese officials to reconsider carefully whether nuclear arms would serve any useful purpose at all, even as a diplomatic expedient.

Professor Riesman has raised the point that "the military are in alliance with each other across national boundaries against their own people, not necessarily to engage in war but to enhance their status and gadgetry." A major domestic problem now facing the United States—one raised by the Vietnam war, relations with the Soviet Union, and the projected American-Soviet disarmament—is how the American military machine is to be altered. Riesman's view, if expanded, is that an American pullout from Asia and a consequent expansion of Japanese military strength would not necessarily reduce the importance at home of the U. S. Army but would increase the possibilities of interdependence of the allied Japanese and American military machines. Thus, an expansion of Japanese arms would be neither helpful to military reforms in the United States nor good for future Japanese-American relations.

Both professors speak with reserve, no doubt out of a sense of international courtesy. They abstain from referring to the common charge leveled against Japan that she is getting a "free ride." But Japan cannot ignore the charge; it will prove harmful to the long-term expansion of the Japanese economy if Japan does ignore the criticism that she is taking "a free ride on the American defense bus."

[379]

Two very different routes to future amicable relations between Japan and America come to mind. One is to reduce frictions to a minimum without altering, in any basic fashion, the political and social systems of either nation. The other is to construct new, friendly relations while each nation is in the process of reforming itself. If Japan criticizes the United States, especially its relations with Asia, Japan will be compelled to reform herself, as well. Both countries would do well to reconsider what it means to be a major power in the world today. They should confront honestly the mistakes that America has made since the war, and rethink the responsibilities of a major power and the way such a power should behave.

In much the same way that America has viewed "Orientals," Japan's relations with Southeast Asia, at least in modern times, have hardly been conducted on the basis of mutual equality. The view of Japan held by a declining America should be taken as a warning to us. As China grows more powerful, similar relations will no doubt prevail between her and Japan. Thus China, in Japanese eyes, will seem much the same as we now appear to the United States. New Japanese-American relations demand that Japan consider the mistakes that America has made as a great power as though Japan herself might be making them.

The other course that Japanese-American relations may take depends upon increased person-to-person contacts between individuals of both nations. The importance of government-to-government contacts in international relations has decreased, and in no case is this more striking than in Japanese-American relations. The expansion of international relations on a nongovernmental level offers a clear indication of what the future will require. Both Riesman and Morgenthau say that they depend on newspapers, magazines, and friends for information about Japan. This sort of people-to-people exchange of information is meaningful and important. I believe that the world is in the process of forming interpeople, as distinct from international, relations. Such interpeople relations between the United States and Japan should be multiplied and expanded.

Interpeople relations will quickly reveal that the two countries share many of the same problems and that the irritation and frustration caused by these problems is also common to both. They will show also that the social mechanisms of both nations are designed to reveal their social ills speedily and unhesitatingly.

The anguish and frustrations suffered by both Japan and the United States stem from utopias lost. America's utopia is the spirit of its Founding Fathers, Japan's is her postwar peace constitution. The harsh contrast between such utopias and present actualities inevitably produces a profound frustration over ideals failed or unfulfilled. The futures of the two countries, and their relations with one another, must include thoroughgoing social reforms and attempts to return to their separate utopias.

The Closing Umbrella

ONE FULL-SCALE war in Europe, one in Asia, and the outbreak of a local brush fire anywhere in the world—preparedness for these two and a half conflicts was the fundamental impulse motivating American world military strategy of the 1960s. The Pentagon's defense report for 1971, however, seems to indicate a shift to a one-and-a-half-conflict strategy. Where have the fears of war been reduced? Which conflict has been omitted from the count? Defense Secretary Melvin Laird will not say.

"The reduction must be in Asia," suggests military-affairs analyst Hideo Sekino. "President Nixon has already made it clear that a pullout of American fighting power from Europe will not take place until the end of 1972, at the earliest." But neither is the United States contemplating a total pullout from Asia at the moment. "The United States certainly intends to secure its influence in Asia and to maintain to the end its own presence in an international political game that includes China," comments *Asahi* editorial writer Shizuo Maruyama. To support this view, he points to the fact that the Nixon Doctrine, announced in June, 1969, leaves room for "selective involvement" in future local conflicts that may break out in Asia.

Toward that purpose, the new American strategy for the Far East currently being mapped out may see the withdrawal of U. S. ground forces from the East-West contact points where flare-ups are most likely to occur, but the retention of the Seventh Fleet in Asian waters and the maintenance of an airborne striking capability on the chain of islands formed by the Philippines, Guam, and Okinawa. This strategy was demonstrated in part by a series of joint American-Korean air-transport maneuvers including Focus Retina (March, 1969) and Freedom Volt (March, 1971). But it remains doubtful whether the United States will be able to honor fully its commitments to its allies through a flexible and rather mild strategy of this sort. "In the last analysis," comments military analyst Makoto Momoi, "the

Nixon Doctrine amounts to a reservation that the United States will not automatically come to the aid of an ally involved in a local conflict, notwithstanding treaties it may have with that ally. We might better consider it a new American posture of 'selective noninvolvement.' "

Kiichi Saeki, director of the Nomura Research Institute, theorizes: "The United States will continue to hold itself responsible for the military settlement of the Vietnam war, but I believe that after fostering a situation in which the North will find it impossible to penetrate South Vietnam, it will leave the Saigon regime to determine for itself whether or not it can actually control the country. . . . The Nixon Doctrine is essentially an attempt to adjust America's national interests to its military capacities—that is to avoid getting involved in anything too difficult."

All these various analyses of the Nixon Doctrine would seem to indicate that guarantees of security by American military commitment are now in the process of being transformed into something far less substantial. "Behind this shift in strategy," comments Professor Donald Hellman of the University of Washington, "lies an assumption that China will be so busy with domestic problems for the time being that she will not develop a nuclear capability strong enough to menace her neighbors."

Whether or not Hellman is right in this view, the fact remains that the United States—while gradually closing the military umbrella it has held over its allies—expects a greater contribution from Japan toward the security of East Asia, especially the Korean peninsula. The statement in the joint communiqué signed by President Nixon and Prime Minister Sato in November, 1969, that the security of Korea was vital to Japan's own safety, seems to indicate the Japanese prime minister's acquiescence to American expectations of an increased Japanese role in Asia.

But from Korea, rather than a confident expectation of Japanese help should it be necessary, there comes distrust instead. Far from welcoming Japan's cooperation in the defense of Korea, Seoul newspapers have been deeply suspicious of any increases in Japanese military strength. Considering this Korean attitude, as well as the Japanese constitution and the pacifist sentiments of the Japanese people, Professor William Kintner, a specialist in foreign policy and military strategy at the University of Pennsylvania, is predicting the impossible when he visualizes Japan's assisting in the future defense of Korea.

"In the short run," predicts military analyst Hiroshi Osanai, "the

United States will count on Japan's building a great enough conventional fighting power for her to take over from America as a rear deterrent force in Southeast Asia. . . . In response to the expectations of the Nixon Doctrine, the fifteen-billion-dollar Fourth Defense Plan announced by the Japanese government in October, 1970, is but the first milestone on the road to Japanese arms expansion." The Defense Agency says in reply to that view: "The Fourth Defense Plan will provide only seventy to eighty percent of the self-defense strength needed to combat the anticipated threat of the 1980s. In the future, it will be necesary to secure a defense budget that amounts to at least one percent of the total GNP."

"It is easy to understand that the United States should be dissatisfied with Japan's remaining so lightly armed when she has grown so fat," comments Sadaichi Chikaraishi, professor of industrial management at Hosei University. "But if Japanese defense strength were allowed to expand in proportion to economic power, Japan would be forced to become by the 1980s a major military power, ranking behind only the United States and the Soviet Union. Such a situation would only intensify the suspicions of China and the nations of Southeast Asia. Since both hope and caution are mingled in American interests in Japan, our increased militarization would eventually widen the gap in Japanese-American relations as well. The heavily armed nations that are still bound by their 'cold-war mentality' are, without exception, facing monetary crises. Japan would be well advised to heed their example and limit the scale of her defense to that of the Third Defense Plan, which limits us to defending our territorial waters and no more."

In a symposium at the Tokyo American Cultural Center in June, 1971, Professor James Morley, director of the East Asian Institute at Columbia University, spoke of the need for a "double-pronged" Asian policy in the 1970s. A military equilibrium must be achieved, particularly with China, but at the same time, efforts should be made to lessen tensions among all Asian nations. But are both parts of such a policy really available to Japan at the present moment? So long as Japan's efforts to reach a military balance of power involve the negative factor of alarming her neighbors, Japan has no alternative to following only the latter course—that is, reducing Asian tensions through normalizing her relations with all nations.

Nonmilitary Cooperation

ON A RECENT visit to Japan, Professor Robert Osgood, director of the Foreign Policy Research Institute at Johns Hopkins University and a former member of the National Security Council, participated in a discussion on the roles of Japan and the United States in the future security of Asia with Junnosuke Kishida, editorial writer for the *Asahi Shimbun*. Hiroshi Shinohara, also of the *Asahi* editorial board and, like Kishida, a specialist in strategic affairs, served as moderator for the discussion and directed questions to both participants. A paraphrased transcript of the discussion follows.

Moderator: What is your forecast of the Far Eastern situation, as it involves Japan and the United States, during the 1970s?

Osgood: First of all, I do not expect any major military threat to arise in Japan, Korea, Taiwan, or their immediate vicinity. Since East Asia is still a volatile area, however, we cannot ignore the possibility of local clashes in Korea, for example, or of renewed Chinese hostility toward Japan. A weakening in confidence in the United States as a deterrent force in Asia, or a sudden American withdrawal from Asia, could bring a latent menace quickly to the surface.

Thus far, the United States has served as a stablizing factor in East Asia, but I expect that pressure will mount over the next ten years for a gradual reduction in the American military presence in this part of the world. The important question is how will both Japan and the United States cope with that contingency? Will they try to maintain American military strength against a possible attack on Korea or in order to insure the security of the Taiwan Strait? If so, how will Japan and the United States adjust the responsibility between themselves? Okinawa, as a base of American military strength, is for the defense not of Japan but of Korea. In case of an attack from the North, can the United States expect to use bases in Japan? Or would Japan prefer that the United States not be drawn into local conflicts like that?

Kishida: It will take a long, long time to do away with all unrest in Asia. Japanese cooperation toward that end is essential, but Japan's military role is very limited. The American military presence in Asia has proved to be a stabilizing factor in some respects, but it has also been a disturbing element. If an American withdrawal from Asia means only that the United States military presence will be replaced by Japanese military power, then the instability factor is sure to increase. Cooperation between Japan and the United States is unquestionably important, but if such cooperation emphasizes the military, then the cooperation itself becomes a disturbing factor.

Moderator: What changes do you expect in the military value of Okinawa after the island is returned to Japan?

Osgood: From the American point of view, Okinawa's primary military function is to allow the Seventh Fleet to operate effectively in Asian waters.

Kishida: I think that the military value will change. Once the island comes under Japanese sovereignty it will be impossible for American forces to count on unlimited use of its territory. I believe that this will compel the United States to pull back to the mid-Pacific and center its military deployment on Guam. Okinawa, in the overall strategy, will be reduced to a secondary position. At least, that is the most desirable way for Okinawan reversion to be accomplished. Since Okinawa is being returned for the betterment of future Japanese-American relations, in the long view the reversion should be accompanied by definite changes in the military role of the island.

Osgood: Regarding the use of the military bases on Okinawa, I think we ought to discuss constructive means of cooperation in the form of joint military action between the United States and Japan, based upon close and detailed consultation. Unless our two countries cooperate smoothly, neither the Seventh Fleet nor the American bases in Japan and Okinawa will be able to fulfill their functions of guaranteeing the security of Korea, Taiwan, and adjacent areas.

Moderator: How will a reduction of American forces, based on the Nixon Doctrine, affect Japan's role?

Osgood: Whether or not the Nixon Doctrine will prove to be of major significance to Japan will depend on three things. First, Japan's evaluation of the existence of a threat surrounding her. Second, whether Japan considers the reduction of American forces in Japan and Korea reasonable in light of her view of the possible threat. Third, whether or not Japan is prepared to take on a larger role in guaranteeing the security of the surrounding area.

Kishida: Without denying that force is necessary for maintaining security, it must be recognized that force does not consist exclusively of military might. Japan has grown increasingly aware of this fact. In addition to military power, the force needed to guarantee Asian security consists of economic strength, perceptive politics, education, and technological capabilities. Placing emphasis solely on military power will prove ineffective.

Osgood: Precisely. Future Japanese-American cooperation should emphasize nonmilitary aspects. It is in the nonmilitary realm that such cooperation is most vital to the stabilization of Asia. And, at the same time, if Japan is to enhance her position as an Asian power, a Pacific power, and a world power, she should avoid concentrating all her energies on relations with the United States and strengthen her ties with other nations, as well.

Moderator: How will the development of China's nuclear potential affect the general Asian situation?

Osgood: Asia will be affected more by the nature of China's foreign policy than by the scale or makeup of her nuclear weaponry. If China were to possess intercontinental ballistic missiles and intermediate range ballistic missiles by the late 1970s, anxiety would most certainly spread throughout Asia. However, China would probably be extremely careful in using her nuclear weapons as threats to back up policy bluffs. I expect that she will use her nuclear capacity with extreme caution, bearing fully in mind the four-sided political relations involving her with Japan, the United States, and the Soviet Union. Thus, I do not think that China's nuclear capacity will necessarily prove to be a disturbing factor in Asia.

Kishida: I agree. I think the limitations on what can be achieved by a nuclear capacity are becoming clearer and clearer. It has now become possible for non-nuclear powers to negotiate with nations, like China, that possess nuclear weapons. This makes it more important to understand the differences in the policies of each respective nation.

1985: A Trillion-dollar Economy

"THE REALITY was decaying, dingy cities where underfed people shuffled to and fro in leaky shoes, in patched-up, nineteenth-century houses that smelt always of cabbage and bad lavatories." Such was the bleak picture of the world of 1984 painted by George Orwell in his pessimistic novel. It is a far cry, indeed, from the optimistic prophecies of Japan in 1985 contained in a statistical forecast compiled by the Japan Economic Research Center early in 1971: "The gross national product per capita will exceed ten thousand dollars, the highest in the world. After taxes, the average white-collar worker will take home more than twenty thousand dollars. He will hold more than forty-five thousand dollars in deposits and other assets. More than thirty percent of his time will be spent on leisure activities, and only twenty-eight percent will be spent at work."

Which prophecy—Orwell's terrifying gloom or the cheerful comforts of the "trillion-dollar economy" projected by Japanese economists—will prove true for Japan over the next few decades? The great majority of Japanese economic experts and amateur futurologists are optimistic. Even Takeo Fukuda (former finance minister and at present foreign minister), who had long been sharply critical of Prime Minister Hayato Ikeda's rosy view of Japan's economic future, has come around: in 1969, in order to insure his political survival, Fukuda found it necessary to predict that Japan would attain the world's highest GNP by 1984 or thereabouts.

Japan's position as an economic superpower becomes even more striking when compared to the predictions made by the Economic Research Center of the GNPs that other countries in the world will attain by 1985:

	GNP (in $100 million)	GNP per capita
Japan	$16,502	$13,574
United States	27,757	10,750
Europe (total)	23,807	5,748
West Germany	4,744	7,677
France	4,929	8,733
England	2,466	4,165
Soviet Union	10,980	3,746
China	1,701	188
Southeast Asia	3,670	258

If statistics like these, as well as similar data compiled by the Economic Planning Agency and the Ministry of International Trade and Industry, prove accurate, what predictions can be made regarding Japan's relations with the rest of the international economic society? Her exports will total $150 billion in 1985, increased seven and a half times from 1970. There will be a slight decline in the proportion of exports to the United States and Southeast Asia and an increase in exports to other areas. There will be much-increased penetration of Japanese goods into the countries to which they are exported; by 1985, one out of every two manufactured objects a Southeast Asian uses will probably have come from Japan. The ratio of Japanese goods to the total imports of various parts of the world will rise. That ratio for the United States and China, now slightly over ten percent in each case, will rise to thirty and forty percent, respectively. In both Latin

[387]

America and Africa, where the ratio is now under ten percent, it will more than double.

Japan, for her part, will increase imports through trade liberalization and other means. It is estimated that as much as one-third of Southeast Asia's total exports will be to Japan. American exports to Japan should increase to fifteen percent. Japanese investments abroad, which now total more than two billion dollars, one-thirtieth of those of the United States, should increase tenfold, by conservative estimates, over the coming decade.

In such circumstances, the Japanese and American economies are expected to deepen their relations considerably. Japan will become a still larger market for American agricultural produce, large machinery such as huge passenger jets, and new technology. The export of Japanese machinery and manufactured goods will increase also, but it will continue to be products of smaller scale such as the radios and television sets that are already the pride of Japan. If both nations are content to refrain from involving themselves in unlimited sales competition and from imposing unreasonable import restrictions, striving instead to establish orderly and complementary trade relations on the principle of an "international division of labor," trade may contribute immeasurably to good relations between the two countries. Even cooperative Japanese-American economic efforts, such as the joint tapping of Southeast Asian raw-material resources should not be impossible.

To illustrate the new American confidence in Japanese goods, as well as the humor with which they are received, Toshio Shishido, director of the Nikko Research Center, points to a situation in a television comedy that he saw on a recent trip to America. Two clownish burglars were trying to jimmy the lock on a safe in a bank late at night. "Think you can bring it off?" one asked. "Sure," replied his sidekick, "this drill was made in Japan."

Although Japanese products have by now overcome much of their former stigma of cheap shoddiness, there may be other problems looming ahead, and Japanese should bear in mind that anti-Japanese tensions are likely to mount along with the expansion of the country's economic strength. "There is no industrial product that we have to buy from America because we can't make it here," says Ichiro Machida, director of the Mitsubishi Economic Research Institute. Many Japanese agree with him, and that fact alone signals the danger of future trade disputes. If Japan refuses to buy from the United States, and if her goods continue to permeate American markets at the present pace or at an increased rate, controversies like that of the still

[388]

unresolved textile issue are bound to occur with greater frequency. Moreover, such tensions may not be limited to Japan and the United States. In Southeast Asia, too, where Japan's presence is becoming more and more conspicuous, there is the constantly increasing danger of anti-Japanese sentiment flaring up with the fury contained in the invective "ugly Japanese." Still other, even more complicated conflicts of interest may well arise between Japan and the United States over the China market.

Since beginning her postwar recovery, Japan has rushed headlong along the path of economic self-development with little regard for "hazards" she may have been creating for other countries along the way. But now that her position as a major economic power is secure, Japan would do well to concentrate her efforts on acting with greater moderation and to behave as a responsible member of the international economic community, improving her relations with advanced nations and developing nations alike. Should she wander astray from her proper direction, obsessed with a compulsion to protect her domestic industries, she may experience—as has the United States—certain consequences that will not be of a purely economic nature. The challenge is new, but it is vital to Japan's survival and to the continued expansion of her economy. If she wishes to realize the trillion-dollar economy of the future, she must divest herself of her nearsighted, insular views of what is best for Japan alone, and contribute responsibly to the prosperity of the entire world.

The Gentleman from Japan

WHILE the textile issue continues to bedevil the troubled economic relations of Japan and the United States, the steel industry is usually pointed to as a model of good behavior. It has, so far, avoided direct conflict with American steel manufacturers, choosing instead to limit voluntarily its exports whenever any criticism was voiced against its export policies.

But, no matter how much the Japanese steel industry "protects" its American counterpart by keeping down its exports, is there any real chance that American steel manufacturers will become competitive enough to match Japan's low prices? The only conceivable way to make the American industry competitive is to put the Japanese on an equal level with them—that is, to raise Japanese prices despite their lower production costs. If Japan were to do that, would not some other country then rush in to undersell the United States? The only other steel manufacturers able to do this are those of the European Economic Community. With Britain in it, the EEC could become a formidable competitor for the United States. There is reason to believe—as the Ministry of International Trade and Industry does— that the United States may intend to make a common front with Japan against the EEC. That way, if the EEC were to try dumping European steel in the United States, America would have a partner in Japan, which could still undersell the EEC.

Given such speculation, it is not difficult to visualize also a scene of three gentlemen—Japan, the United States, and the EEC—shaking hands and establishing an international steel-price cartel. The image is borrowed from Professor Giichi Miyazaki, who has commented: "A long-range view of Japanese-American economic relations suggests that, if a conflict of basic interests were to arise, Japan is more likely to follow a conciliatory course than one that might lead to economic war. She has neither the intent nor the wherewithal to fight an economic war with the United States. Rather than fight, Japan will exercise such gentlemanly self-restraint as may involve her in an international cartel." Who would lose by forming so amicable a cartel? None of its members, and certainly not the gentleman from the Orient, who would be able to produce steel at the lowest cost.

The scene shifts abruptly to the comfortable home in Jakarta of an Indonesian economic official who spends all his time dealing with Japanese businessmen. The clock on the wall reads midnight as he arrives home from a long day's work. The official undresses for bed, swallows a few vitamin pills, sets his radio-alarm clock, and kisses his wife good night. It should be noted that his suit, shirt, necktie, and underwear were all made in Japan. He has ridden home in a Japanese car driven by a chauffeur wearing a Japanese wristwatch. His house is constructed of Japanese materials. The clock on the wall, the vitamin pills, the refrigerator from which he took a glass of cold water—they all were made in Japan. So was the radio-alarm clock next to his bed. The only Indonesian product in his home is his wife. This is the picture of the Japanese presence in Indonesia drawn by Jacob Utama, editor of the *Kompas*. He adds: "The term 'economic animal,' as applied to the Japanese, will soon find a permanent place in textbooks on international relations, alongside 'dollar imperialism' and 'Brezhnev Doctrine.' "

The Japanese presence has been commented upon by other Asian leaders with increasing frequency. "The problem for Asia in the 1970s will be not China, but Japanese economic power," said Indonesian Foreign Minister Adam Malik in November, 1969. "The drama of Southeast Asia is currently being rewritten to include ambitious new actors," noted Foreign Minister Sinnathamby Rajaratnam of Singapore in a 1971 New Year address, referring pointedly to Japan and the Soviet Union, as well as China and the United States.

"There are three factors behind the marked increase in Japan's economic activities in Southeast Asia," commented the *Hsing Chou Jih Pao*, a Chinese-language Singapore newspaper, in an editorial of February 9, 1971. "First, the international factors of the United States mired in the Vietnam war and the recession of British influence from Asia. Japan is being asked to take over from them. Second, the Japanese factor: Southeast Asia is becoming increasingly important to Japan as a source of raw materials for her industries, a market for her manufactured goods, and an object of Japanese capital investment. Third, the native factor of Southeast Asia's inescapable dependence on the advanced nations of the world."

If the volume of Japanese exports to Southeast Asia continues to increase at the present rate, Japanese goods may soon account for more than forty-five percent of the area's total imports. "When exports from one country to another exceed twenty percent of the importing country's total imports, it usually signals future friction between them," warns Professor Tadashi Kawada of Tokyo University.

"Nationalism tends to burn most strongly in countries with the greatest inferiority complex," says Professor Edwin Reischauer. "So long as Asia feels itself lagging behind the rest of the world, it will try to appease its sense of inadequacy with intense nationalism." If so, Japan, as the only advanced nation in Asia, can expect that nationalism to be directed against her. And, moreover, her chief rival for popularity in Southeast Asia will be China rather than the United States.

Commenting upon the Chinese economic competition that Japan is bound to encounter in Southeast Asia, Hiroshi Hashimoto, chief of the China Section in the Foreign Ministry, concludes: "In a popularity contest between China and Japan in Southeast Asia, China will represent herself as the people's candidate standing in opposition to rich, capitalist Japan." In a campaign of that nature, a high price tag on Japanese steel will give the opposition ammunition for its attacks on fat, capitalistic Japan. Thus, efforts to appear a well-behaved gentleman to the advanced nations will not necessarily result in making Japan's way easier in the rest of the world. This, perhaps, is the most critical dilemma of Japan's future.

[391]

The Chemistry of Superpower

SOME keen observers of the game of "diplomatic ping-pong" believe that America's quick return of Peking's opening serve represents an attempt to widen the Sino-Soviet split and thereby gain an advantage in the United States' own negotiations with the Soviet Union. The State Department is quick to scotch such rumors, however. "If such a side effect were to occur," says Assistant Secretary of State for Pacific and Far Eastern Affairs Marshall Green, "it would be just that: a side effect and not a motive. Our primary task is to maintain harmony with the Soviet Union."

American foreign policy has traditionally attached first importance to relations with the countries of Europe. "Even at its most isolationist, America never really took its eyes off Europe. An important element of that isolationism was the anxiety that Europe might grow strong enough to threaten the opening of the American frontier. But in American eyes," comments Makoto Saito, professor of American government at Tokyo University, "the affairs of Asia, even including the Pacific War, have always seemed somehow secondary."

After World War II, this geographical focus of American foreign policy shifted from Europe proper to the Soviet Union. The postwar world was quickly realigned into American and Soviet blocs, and the perpetuation of the line rigidly dividing them became a matter of overriding concern for both camps. "Between our country and the Soviet Union there is an implicit line demarcating separate spheres of influence," said Undersecretary of State U. Alexis Johnson at a Senate subcommittee hearing on Japan and Okinawa in January, 1970. "The basic premise of world peace is that neither nation overstep that line."

The central prop of this Pax Russo-Americana is a power equilibrium formed by the overwhelming nuclear supremacy of the two countries. Kiichi Saeki, director of the Nomura General Research Institute, elaborates: "The military bipolarity of the United States and the Soviet Union, based on their nuclear equilibrium, certainly has contributed to the construction and stabilization of the present framework of international politics. But we must not overlook the fact that the nuclear power balance is also based on the second-strike capability of the two great powers. Neither of them can unleash their nuclear might unless it is willing to be annihilated itself in a nuclear duel. In this respect, the Vietnam war has demonstrated the limitations of nuclear power."

Accordingly, the present American move toward curtailing military involvement in Asia is a recognition of this limitation on America's power. And yet, the United States is still committed to guaranteeing the security of the free nations of Asia. The White House staff for Asian affairs points to two conditions which must be met in order to plug up the gaps that would be created by an American withdrawal from Asia. The first is the rendering of American-Chinese relations nonhostile. The second is Japan's willingness to take on a degree of responsibility for Asian security that accords with her increasing economic power. As for the first condition, Kenjiro Miyaji, an *Asahi* editorial writer, thinks that "relations between China and the United States may progress at a faster rate than we expect. In the domino theory of the 1960s, China was viewed as the source of all threats. This fearful view was the psychological motivation for the American involvement in Vietnam. But the United States has also been long aware, I believe, of the axiom of international relations that, if a powerful nation exists, other powerful nations have to form diplomatic ties with it sooner or later."

The Pentagon papers, published amid great controversy in the *New York Times* and other American newspapers, lay bare certain facts which support Miyaji's views. For example, even while the United States was increasing bombing raids on North Vietnam, the United States delegate to the Chinese-American conference in Warsaw read a statement disclaiming any intention on the part of the United States to occupy the North and emphasizing that the sole purpose of the bombing was to prevent further infiltration of the South. Immediately afterward, a Canadian representative of the International Ceasefire Commission visited Hanoi to transmit this information. Premier Pham Van Dong declined to meet the Canadian envoy, however, saying that he had already been informed of the American position by the Chinese government—evidence, it would seem, that the Warsaw conference was functioning well as a diplomatic channel.

American policy toward the Far East has long revolved around China. During the war, the United States was defending "weak, helpless China" against "Japan, the strong aggressor." But with the Occupation and the removal of the fangs of Japanese militarism, the policy shifted. And after the Communists captured mainland China in 1949, the policy shifted even further, to the fortification of Japan.

What of the second condition of Asian security—increased Japanese responsibility—mentioned by the White House staff? "It is but an extension of the shift in American policy that began during the Occupation," comments Hajime Terasawa, professor of international relations at Tokyo University. Under those articles of the revised Secu-

[393]

rity Treaty dealing with the rest of the Far East, Japan is obligated to contribute to the security of the western Pacific. This obligation is justification for Japan's rearmament, with China viewed as the target. And the Nixon Doctrine's demands that Japan, as an affluent nation, begin to shoulder the burden clearly reveal that Americans still think of Japan as a military deterrent to be used against China.

If such is really the case, it points up the strong possibility that American Asian policy will continue to be inconsistent: China is still looked upon as a hostile nation, but friendly relations with her are being sought. "This inconsistency arises," according to Hans Baerwald, professor of Japanese politics at UCLA, "because the United States, while professing its recognition of the limits of power, still refuses to abandon its old power theories. The importance that the United States attaches to conciliation with the Soviet Union is an indication of the 'chemistry' of superpower. A superpower cannot extricate itself from the anomaly of keeping the peace by a reliance on military power."

"In the meantime, the nuclear era has undergone a fundamental change," comments Masataka Kosaka, professor of international relations at Kyoto University. "Military might has been replaced as the major motive force behind international relations, by something else." It should be clear that the proper course for Japan entails the rejection of military solutions to international disputes and the adherence to the spirit of the no-war clause of her constitution. By so doing she may yet challenge the perilous "chemistry of superpower."

The American Quest

A MERICAN society is currently undergoing changes so fundamental and so far-reaching that it is unlikely that the "power theories" of traditional American foreign policy will survive unshaken. Akira Iriye, a Japanese scholar who teaches American diplomatic history at the University of Chicago, has witnessed many of these changes firsthand. In the following article, written for the *Asahi Shimbun*, Iriye describes the changes in American society he has observed and comments on the direction that American foreign policy seems to be taking.

Japanese visitors to the United States these days are sure to note with surprise how greatly America has changed in only a few years. Such changes are certainly an essential element in any consideration of Japanese-American relations or the international relations of the United States in the 1970s. But just *how* has it changed? The answer to that question depends, of course, on the personal opinions and ideology of each observer, as well as on those particular aspects of America that he has happened to see.

When I look back over my eighteen years in the United States, I often wonder whether it is the country that has changed or myself. The America I encountered as a young foreign student and the country I see today as a professor are naturally not the same. In the course of studying and teaching American diplomatic history, I have tried to follow closely what Americans are thinking about the outside world, and have observed certain changes taking place in the country and in the attitudes of its people.

First of all, the position of the black man in American society has undergone a transformation that has had some effect on other countries' relations with the United States. Until only a few years ago, first-rate universities and famous prep schools were the exclusive preserve of the children of middle- or upper-class white families. Recently, however, it has become a widely held assumption that high schools and universities should admit black students in proportion to the percentage of blacks in the total population. More and more black students are also advancing into graduate schools and working for doctorates.

As the number of black students in universities increases and the educational level of American blacks rises, their presence has brought about fundamental changes in the traditional curriculum. Black studies or Afro-American studies are receiving increased attention and Occidental history and the classics—subjects which were firm pillars of the curriculum in the past—are suffering a marked decline in appeal. Almost every recent black applicant for admission to the History Department of the University of Chicago indicated that he wanted to major in American black history.

Thus, it is important for Japanese to bear in mind that, over the next several years, the educational level and political influence of American blacks will rise, but their primary interest will be in their own history and their own current affairs. They will be little interested in foreign relations in general, let alone Japanese studies or Japanese-American relations.

Most American students, black and white alike, are more interested than ever before in contemporary affairs and rather less in traditional history or classical studies. During the 1950s—when I first arrived in the United States—America was still suffering from the chaos of the postwar period, and Americans found some psychological solace in their spiritual ties with Europe. European history and classical literature were compulsory subjects for American students at that time. Likewise, American foreign policy, exemplified by the Truman Doctrine and the Marshall Plan, grew out of the historical and cultural connections with Europe. Americans felt a genuine obligation to contribute to the rehabilitation of Europe's war-shattered society and culture.

Now all this has changed. More students are interested in contemporary history than in premodern studies, in American society rather than in European civilization, and in social sciences rather than in humanities or the classics. It is difficult to make a sweeping analysis of how this change in intellectual preferences may influence American foreign relations. But one thing is certain: there is emerging a new generation, little interested in or influenced by the legacy of the past.

My third observation—related to the first two—has to do with changes in the American sense of responsibility or obligation to the outside world. A certain sense of mission has been characteristic of America's foreign relations. This sense of responsibility or obligation or mission has always been accompanied by an increase in military power. As Americans have been reminded time and again that their nation is a superpower, they have been exhorted to keep in mind both that power is accompanied by responsibilities and that the great American mission requires military might. This attitude has permeated every layer of American society.

The fine welcome once extended to foreign students was one expression of America's sense of responsibility for the well-being of the rest of the world. So were the strongly "realistic" theories of international relations propounded by American political scientists.

But that has changed, too, and the change reflects America's frustration over her foreign relations. The United States now receives foreign students less eagerly and less generously than in the past. Many Americans question whether their country has anything to teach the rest of the world. Even American specialists in international relations react critically these days to America-centered attitudes and to orthodox theories of power politics. They demonstrate instead a marked interest in studies that are sharply critical of American foreign policy of the past, and they are making efforts to establish a new brand of international relations, broadened to include economic and cultural matters as well as politics and theories of power.

It must be concluded that America, having been accepted—for better or for worse—as an unchangeable element in world politics over the past quarter-century, has come to an important turning point. Americans themselves will seek a new concept of foreign relations, free of past frameworks. The Japanese should not stand by as mere observers of this search. It is essential that Japan not shrink from extending full intellectual cooperation to Americans as they progress in their quest.

The Ghost of Dulles

"WE'RE STILL grappling with the ghost of Dulles," sighed an exasperated Japanese diplomat attending a joint Japanese-American conference that met at Lake Kawaguchi in the summer of 1971 to discuss the China question. American diplomats at the conference smiled their sympathetic agreement. More and more countries around the world were recognizing China every month, and the moment for the flag of the People's Republic of China to be hoisted at the United Nations loomed closer at hand. Still, the United States and Japan were bound by treaty commitments to stand by Taiwan against the Chinese mainland. It was easy for the diplomats who gathered at Lake Kawaguchi, both Japanese and American, to blame their predicament on Dulles, and to insist that the treaties which both countries had signed with the Taiwan regime of Chiang Kai-shek were born directly of Dulles's determination to contain the Communists. But is the former secretary of state entirely to blame?

Among the Japanese Foreign Ministry's top-secret documents, classified by the Ministry as "never for public view," are the minutes of a 1951 meeting between Dulles and Prime Minister Yoshida. It is common knowledge that Yoshida was forced by Dulles to choose a one-China stand for Japan in return for assurances that the San Francisco peace treaty would be ratified without any hitch by the American Senate. Yoshida had at first resisted, knowing full well that concluding a peace treaty with the Nationalist government of Taiwan was tantamount to recognizing that local regime as the legal government of all of China. But, according to reliable sources, Dulles persevered and at a secret meeting persuaded Yoshida to make a peace treaty with Taiwan that would recognize it as *a* government of China, not *the* government of China. The same sources quote Dulles as further assur-

[397]

ing the Japanese prime minister that he need expect "no serious objections" even from Britain, which had already recognized the Peking government.

Both Dulles, who was first and foremost a clever lawyer, and Yoshida, the canny diplomat, recognized the anomaly of the Japanese treaty with Taiwan. But successive, conservative Japanese governments have since transformed the initial ambiguity into something very explicit, deluding themselves into the fixed belief that the treaty amounted to Japan's recognition of Nationalist China as the sole legitimate goverment of all China.

Granted that at the height of the cold war Japan had little choice but to go along with the American containment policy by signing the peace treaty with Taiwan, it seems unreasonable to adhere rigidly to the anomaly when international tensions have eased. But there are reasons. First is the feeling of gratitude for Chiang's abstention from repaying Japanese violence with violence in kind when the Pacific War ended. Second is the lingering fear of the Chinese Communists, clearly a hangover from the cold war. A third reason is mercenary: some government leaders have "special interests" in Taiwan, and are able to peddle their influence in Taiwan to Japanese businessmen seeking concessions there; the Japanese concession to import Taiwanese bananas is but one example. In short, an anomaly developed by the cold war in the early 1950s is today propped up by sentiment and commercial interests. Dulles is certainly not to blame for this particular circumstance. No doubt it is this circumstance that makes the minutes of the Yoshida-Dulles meeting a "permanently secret" document.

Senator Fulbright and other prominent Congressional leaders have called for a thorough re-evaluation of the American Asian defense system, which was designed primarily for the containment of China. Professor Michio Royama of Sophia University agrees by saying: "Gone is the era of the cold-war diplomacy that forced rigid distinctions between friends and foes. We are now on the threshold of an age of 'mahjong diplomacy,' a diplomacy in which the separate Japanese-American, Chinese-American, and Japanese-Chinese teams will get along with one another, each winning points for itself." He is saying that the solution to the Taiwan problem will emerge only from a dynamic and flexible multilateral formula linking the United States, Japan, and China. However, it is impossible to predict the complicated formula with any precision, since the People's Republic of China, which has yet to make its debut on the international scene, is still a largely unknown quantity.

"So long as China refuses to abandon the idea of exporting revolution, Asian diplomacy will remain an insoluble equation from which only confusion will emerge," says Okinori Kaya of the Liberal-Democratic party. But in the light of Peking's "ping-pong diplomacy," the general view is that China's diplomatic policies toward Japan and the United States will probably be based upon the Five Basic Principles of Peace (including nonintervention in domestic affairs), which were enunciated in the 1950s.

"The anti-establishment diplomacy of the Cultural Revolution period, a diplomacy criticized by the entire world, does not reflect the true attitudes of China's present-day diplomacy," comments Mineo Nakashima, lecturer at Tokyo University of Foreign Studies.

While Wang Chiao-yun, deputy manager of the Chinese table-tennis team, was in Japan in April, 1971, Tokuma Utsunomiya, a Liberal-Democratic member of the Diet noted for his determined efforts at private diplomacy, requested that Wang use his good offices in persuading Peking to send a delegation to the meetings of the Japan-America Parliamentary Exchange Conference, scheduled to be held at Hakone in August, 1971. Ever since the private Santa Barbara Conference, which Utsunomiya arranged in January, 1969, it has been his chief purpose to bring the Chinese to a similar conference in Japan. He has not, as yet, received a reply from Peking to his invitation. This is but one example of the difficulties in actually carrying out peaceful coexistence with China at the moment.

"Live in Peking, and one cannot fail to be aware of the Japanese-American encirclement of China," says Kazuteru Saionji, a member of the *Asahi Shimbun* Research Council on China and Asia. So long as this sort of situation continues, it should prove impossible to induce Chinese to attend the sort of private conference that Utsunomiya has envisioned.

Diplomacy is inherently egotistical, and consistency demands that Japan concentrate, first of all, on improving her own relations with China instead of trying to act as a bridge between China and the United States. There are fears that normalized Sino-Japanese relations might jeopardize Japan's relations with the United States. But in the light of the apparent Sino-American rapprochement, it would seem far more sensible for Japan to take advantage of this opportunity to better her relations with the People's Republic of China.

In that case, what is to be done with the Security Treaty that binds Japan and the United States in a single military system designed to contain China? "Even the Anglo-Japanese Alliance, in effect from 1902 to 1922, served a military purpose only up to the Russo-Japanese War of 1904-5," comments Professor Hajime Terasawa of Tokyo

University. "Thereafter it remained as no more than a symbol of Anglo-Japanese friendship." Should it not be possible, then, to provide the security pact with a similarly symbolic identity and go on improving relations with China all the while?

The Future of the Yen

"WITH ALL these new books on revaluation of the yen coming out, I'll have so much reading to do that there won't be time for any vacation at all this summer," wailed a research staffer of a major Tokyo bank in midsummer, 1971. But the booksellers aren't complaining. "Fourteen different books on revaluation—ranging from theoretical economics to practical manuals on how to deal with the new yen when revaluation does take place—have come out in the past couple of weeks, and they are all selling like hot cakes," says the manager of one Ginza bookstore. Anyone who knows anything about money is in constant demand to explain how revaluation works and what it will mean. "I dictated a talk on revaluation and had the transcript distributed to all our branches," says Takashi Ihara, president of the Bank of Yokohama. "So many customers were coming in to ask tellers or bank officers how the revaluation would affect them." One economic analyst was even asked by an association of laundry-shop operators to give a talk on revaluation to its members.

As Japan's international balance of payments climbs higher and higher into the black, American pressures for revaluation of the yen mount in proportion to the red figures of its own international balance of payments. However, Japan's credits and foreign exchange reserves are now well above ten billion dollars, and to revalue the yen would cause such heavy losses to this reserve that the government can hardly revalue even if it wanted to. But the pressures are strong, and the crucial decision will come soon.

The yen is facing another challenge as well. The present international monetary system fixes the parity of non-American currencies with the dollar on the postulate that the United States will give, upon demand, an ounce of gold for thirty-five dollars. The trouble is that the governments and central banks of the nations of the world hold together more than twenty billion dollars in American money—twice the amount of gold held by the United States. This makes the dollar virtually inconvertible into gold, and consequently international con-

[400]

fidence in the dollar has fallen sharply. Only about six hundred million of Japan's ten-billion-dollar foreign reserve is in gold, the remainder being in American currency of lessened value.

The Japanese government is frequently advised in the Diet to sell some of its American money for gold or for a "stronger" currency like the West German mark. The government's stock reply: "It will be in the Japanese national interest to maintain and strengthen the present dollar-centered international monetary system. We will not ask to convert our dollar holdings into gold." Obviously, if every nation were suddenly to demand conversion of dollar reserves into gold, the result would be like a general run on a bank. The United States would throw up its hands in horror and the international monetary system would collapse overnight. But not every nation is as "nice" to the dollar as is Japan. The European Economic Community has begun moving toward establishing a standard international currency of its own. It will be at least ten years before this EEC currency completely replaces the mark, franc, and lira, but there is a strong possibility that when it does, it will become an international monetary standard every bit as stable as the dollar, if not more so.

If that happens, will Japan still be able to remain tied to the dollar simply because of the importance of her political and strategic relations with the United States? If she wishes to diversify her export outlets and sell more to Europe, she will be compelled to further her relations with the Common Market by divesting herself of dollar reserves and adding the new European currency to her reserves.

Moreover, if the current monetary chaos worsens and the dollar-gold convertibility is officially suspended, then the current parity of international currency will disappear. Each nation will then try to link its currency to the foreign currencies of its choice, eventually forming monetary or economic blocs. What course will the yen follow then?

Krokodil, the renowned Soviet satirical magazine, carried in a recent issue a cartoon showing a ship flying a flag marked $. It is flanked on one side by an EEC ship and on the other by a Japanese ship flying a ¥ flag. Japanese crewmen of the ¥ ship are struggling to transfer bolts of Japanese textiles to the $ ship but are being pushed back by the crew, who poke sticks and throw filthy water at them. But on the other side of the American ship, crewmen are busily loading goods marked "Made in U. S. A." onto the EEC vessel. American fuel overheats the boiler of the EEC ship and the heavy smoke from its funnel blasts the European crewmen overboard. The caption of the cartoon reads: "The Tranquil Sea of Capitalist Trade."

[401]

Japan is the nation that would suffer most from any severe disruption of economic exchange between herself, the United States, and the EEC. As a union of advanced nations, the EEC could manage with intra-EEC economic expansion alone. The United States depends only to a small degree on trade for its economic well-being. Japan, however, could not subsist without peaceful trade with the entire world.

A new prospect for the yen is its appearance in the international trade arena. Shackled by exchange control regulations, the yen has remained, and still remains, purely a domestic currency. But the possibility is now looming large that it may soon become an international currency. "Ideally, a nation's own currency should be used as her instrument of payment in external trade," says Shiro Inoue, director of the Bank of Japan. "The yen is becoming so strong that we should not be surprised if people abroad who have yen will want to use it," says Yusuke Kashiwagi, an adviser to the Finance Ministry. "And Japan will certainly welcome that," adding to speculation that the day is not far off when exchange control regulations will be relaxed. At that time, the yen may well become an international monetary standard like the dollar and the EEC currency now being developed.

Whatever the future of the yen, Japan would be ill-advised to form a yen economic bloc of an exclusive nature in Asia. That would only be courting bankruptcy, because of the inherent limits to expansion within a union of underdeveloped nations.

The only fully reliable statement that can be made about the present situation of the yen is that it is now facing trials that it has never experienced before. The problems are new, as new as the yen's powers and responsibilities in today's world. The course that the yen will follow into the future is still uncharted, but at no time has there been a greater need for clear economic vision based upon a sound judgment of the international situation and thoughtful consideration of national gain and loss.

(*Editors' note: This article appeared originally in the* Asahi Shimbun *on July 7, 1971. Slightly more than one month later, President Nixon dramatically announced a new policy for the dollar, setting in motion a series of international currency adjustments, including the revaluation of the yen.*)

"Post-America"

"**Y**OUR ISLAND used is to typhoons, and is hardly affected by downpours or heavy winds. But an enormous typhoon, the biggest since the war, is about to hit Okinawa. It started in Washington in 1969, gathered force as it crossed the Pacific, redoubled its velocity in economically powerful Japan, and is now about to descend on Okinawa with a fury that will tear asunder the beauty of your island and shatter the citadel of peace that you have erected here during the long years under foreign rule."

The prophet voicing this dramatic warning was Yasusaburo Hoshino, professor of constitutional law at Tokyo University of Arts and Sciences, while on a speaking tour of Okinawa during the summer of 1971 as a guest of the Ryukyu government. He found the response of his audiences all over the island encouraging. "We want to transform Okinawa from an outpost of war into a bastion of peace," was their common reaction. "We realize fully that, after the return to Japanese rule, our responsibilities as Japanese citizens living under the peace consitution of Japan will be heavy. But if the people of the main islands neglect or forget the terms of their own constitution . . ." Within that unfinished sentence are contained the Okinawan people's anxieties about the future and their feelings about the necessity of a thorough re-examination of Japan's present relations with the United States. They have waited patiently for the return to Japanese rule, but even more eagerly have they sought to cast off Okinawa's identity as a military stronghold. Still, despite their hopes to rejoin Japan as an island of peace, Okinawa will have American bases on it when the reversion is effected. As they become Japanese citizens once again, the people of Okinawa are asking that the Japanese government reread its own constitution and remind itself of the peace provisions it contains.

The people of Okinawa are not alone in their fears concerning the future military course of Japan. At the fourth Japan-Korea Ministerial Conference, held in July, 1970, Korean President Chung Hee Park told members of the Japanese cabinet: "If Japan is concerned about the defense of Korea, all we ask of you is economic cooperation. We seek no direct military assistance from Japan." Park was saying this at a time when it was clear that the United States would be cutting back on American military forces stationed in Korea. His point was underlined by an editorial entitled "Against the Veiled Expansion of Japanese Military Might" that appeared in a major Seoul daily in January,

1971: "The tragedy of a divided Korea—at which we cannot suppress our rage—stems, after all, from the militarist expansion of Japan. More than any other nation on earth, Korea is endangered by any increase in the military power of Japan." Five years earlier, at the first meeting of the Asian and Pacific Council (ASPAC) in Seoul, Japan was criticized for not fulfilling her obligations to the defense of Asia from communism and for concentrating instead on her own economic growth. Behind this sharp reversal lie the intensifying fears over the steady expansion of Japan's military establishment, an expansion clearly indicated by the announcement in October, 1970, of the Fourth Defense Program of more than fifteen billion dollars.

The Japanese-American joint communiqué signed in Washington in 1969 mentioned the conviction of the Japanese government that the security of Taiwan and Korea was as vital as Japan's own. Ironically, from Korea came the immediate response: "No thank you, we don't want the Japanese to take over our defense from the United States." The fears and criticism of Japanese militarism that are now being voiced so widely in Asian countries extend beyond the separate ideologies or political systems of those countries, and they are far more severe than most Japanese imagine.

Slogans that have gained popularity in Japan recently contain such phrases as "post-America" or "escape from the Security Treaty." Hajime Terasawa, professor of international politics at Tokyo University, comments: "I thoroughly abhor the attitudes behind such phrases. A phrase like 'post-Security Treaty' can be very dangerous." These phrases and slogans are backed by a kind of nationalism and pride in the new economic power of Japan. To the extent that they represent an emergence from a feeling of dependence upon the United States, such attitudes are shared by Japanese conservatives and progressives alike. But recently, there is a tendency to equate "post-Security Treaty" with "building military power through Japan's own resources," and it is this that men like Terasawa abhor. Others who oppose the security relationship with the United States hesitate to speak out against the Security Treaty for fear of being misinterpreted as advocating a strengthening of Japan's own military establishment.

This dilemma also affects American policies toward Japan. On the one hand, there is the insistence that Japan cooperate voluntarily in Asian defense and share the burden of insuring the area's security after the Vietnam war ends; on the other hand, the U. S. is reluctant to allow Japan to assume the burden too enthusiastically and develop a full-fledged military force. That would be tantamount to America's giving birth to an unwanted, devilish offspring in the western Pacific. In a sense, the United States and China have common fears regarding Japan: the United States fears that Japan may one day possess nuclear armaments and China worries about the general resurgence of militarism in Japan.

"It was the United States that gave Japan her pacifist constitution," says Makoto Saito, professor of American political and diplomatic history at Tokyo University. "Even though America herself has deviated repeatedly from its principles during the 1950s and 1960s, I wonder if she is not now anxious to have Japan return to the original purpose of the renunciation of arms in Article 9. Of course, it is difficult to say for sure, because America herself is in the midst of change." If that is true, the Security Treaty, which has been the cornerstone of the Japanese-American defense arrangement for the past twenty years, may become in the future a restraining force on the expansion of Japanese militarization.

Japan's actions and direction of the past decades have been determined almost exclusively by considerations of her own security and her economic interests. It is time that this changed and that Japan established a firm theoretical foundation for her diplomacy and her future role in the world. Her image as a nation dedicated to peace has been eroded by the winds of change. In order to rebuild that image she must concentrate the total economic power of her GNP, the third largest in the world, on a diplomacy of peace. An honest and far-reaching contribution to the peace and welfare of all human beings, unlimited by the framework of ideology—this ought to be the unshakable pillar of Japan's future foreign policy.

The Most Primitive Emotion

THE OLD stereotype of American blacks had them living in slums and dreaming of Cadillacs. Today, however, it is Japanese cars that catch their fancy. In fact, almost anything "Made in Japan" enjoys roaring sales among American blacks, and quality and price do not seem to be the only explanation for the phenomenon. More than one Japanese exporter has received letters from black leaders asking if there is not some way for them to import Japanese goods directly. "We hate to buy through white importers and let them make money out of us," is the sentiment common to most of the letters.

A Japanese student in West Germany was asked recently if he

thought Japan and China should forget past hostilities and become friends again. He replied, as every other Japanese intellectual would have, that they should, even if the two societies differed ideologically. "But that would make another alliance between yellow peoples!" exclaimed his German friend with asperity, much to the amazement of the Japanese student. Although the details vary widely, many Japanese have had similarly surprising experiences with European and American attitudes regarding race.

Racism, in international relations, usually runs deep below the surface like an underground river. But once it surfaces, its effects are rarely beneficial. Its appearance usually intensifies disputes between nations, and sometimes it triggers international crises. That racism casts a dark shadow over the tensions plaguing relations between China and the Soviet Union is by now common knowledge. At one point, it burst into the open only to exacerbate the Sino-Soviet quarrel. The insistent Chinese slogan "The east wind dominates the west wind" was attacked by *Pravda* as heralding the resurgence of the yellow peril. China immediately shot back that Soviet foreign policy had always been tinged with racial prejudices.

Following the Meiji Restoration of 1868, Japan struggled to overcome her backwardness as a "colored" Asian nation and to catch up with the advanced civilization of the "white" world. But her appearance in the exclusive club of advanced nations and her determined efforts to modernize herself were viewed by Western eyes as no more than cocky aping of Occidental manners and technology. Immediately, a barrier of racism was thrown up to keep Japan at a distance, and this in turn inspired passionate nationalism among the Japanese. Initially, Americans were comparatively well disposed toward Japan, but even they were to turn against Japan, shutting the Japanese out of their country with the Exclusion Act of 1924. This racist piece of legislation proved to be one of the underlying causes of the Pacific War. Indeed, the war itself might justifiably be described as a race war, for Japan's avowed aim was the liberation of greater East Asia from the yoke of white—particularly Anglo-Saxon—rule.

Can all this be dismissed as past history? Some American correspondents profess today to be surprised by the intensity of Japanese opposition to the war in Vietnam. "Why is the war so very unpopular in Japan?" they ask. "Why do even those Japanese who are ordinarily pro-American demonstrate against it time and time again? The war does not involve Japan directly. In fact, she is even making money from American procurement orders." The answer lies in racism. To the Japanese, the war in Vietnam presents the spectacle of strong whites bullying a weak yellow people. Learning of these Japanese sentiments must prove as surprising to the naive American correspondents as did the above-quoted German's response to the Japanese student.

The Pentagon papers published by the American press reveal that the matters of primary concern to the United States in its involvement in Vietnam are American prestige and American casualties. Scarcely any thought was given by the Pentagon to the destruction of life and property suffered by the yellow people of Vietnam. Futhermore, what is the world to think of the American system of justice, which sentences to death the crazed murderers of a white movie actress but shows wondrous leniency toward the officers and soldiers of the U. S. Army who slaughtered an entire village of Asians in Vietnam? On Okinawa, American military authorities loudly proclaim the harmlessness of American poison gas to the Okinawans in whose midst it is stored. Yet, at home in the United States, the same gas is considered too dangerous to be transported from one place to another.

No amount of discussion would suffice to determine whether or not racism is actually the force underlying all these cases. The roots of racism penetrate the human subconscious so deeply that some acts are liable to be considered racist even when there is no such intention.

It should also be remembered, particularly by Japanese, that racial issues are not limited to people of different race. Japan's victory over Russia in 1905 was the first case in history of a "colored" people overpowering a "white" nation, and a large and mighty one at that. If the rest of the world was surprised by Japan's victory, the nations of Asia and Africa were shocked. Later, during World War II, when Japan destroyed the British fleet in the Pacific, there was huge rejoicing in many parts of Asia to celebrate the collapse of British dominance in the Far East. But when the countries of Asia discover that the real purpose of Japan—the nation they look toward as the representative of their race—is to obtain for herself the status of "honorary white" (the classification actually accorded the Japanese in South Africa), enabling her to stand as a snobbish leader on the heads of her Asian colleagues, then their resentment and antagonism are likely to be hurled at Japan with an intensity far greater than any feelings they might direct toward people of a different race. The history of the Greater East Asian Co-Prosperity Sphere should prove amply the truth of this point.

Today, Japan is about to become a superpower, economically at least, on a par with the United States, the Soviet Union, and the Common Market. Will she be able to attain this elevated position without falling, at the same time, into the north-south syndrome by which the have nations of the northern hemisphere are separated by a wide abyss from the have-not nations in the south? Will she be able to escape the curses and reproaches of both the north and the south?

Many people hold that there is nothing to be gained by discussing the problems of racism. Racism is, to be sure, the most beastly and primitive of all human feelings, and the one least susceptible to reason. Yet it cannot be ignored. Elusive, volatile, and potentially terribly dangerous, racism must be prevented from exploding on the international scene. Japan must work with particular diligence to prevent such an explosion, for, should it ever occur, Japan is probably the country that would suffer most.

Chronology

1853   *July 8:* Commodore Perry arrives at Uraga with "Black Ships"

1854   *Mar. 31:* Perry concludes U.S.-Japan Treaty of Amity and Friendship (Kanagawa Treaty)

1856   *Aug.:* Townsend Harris arrives at Shimoda as first permanent representative of U. S. in Japan

1858   *July 29:* U.S.-Japan Treaty of Amity and Commerce (Harris Treaty)

1859   *June:* Ports of Kanagawa, Nagasaki, and Hakodate opened to international trade

1860   *Feb.:* First official Japanese mission sent by Tokugawa shogunate to Washington to exchange treaty ratifications; led by Niimi Masatoki, Lord of Buzen

1863   *June:* Shimonoseki Incident: Choshu forces bombard commercial French, Dutch, and American vessels anchored off Shimonoseki   *July:* American and French ships bombard Choshu in retaliation *Aug. 15:* British ships bombard Kagoshima

1864   *Sept. 5:* Allied fleet of American, British, French, and Dutch ships demolishes Choshu forts

1867   *Nov. 9:* Shogun Tokugawa Keiki announces an "imperial restoration"

1868   *Nov. 4:* Emperor Meiji departs from Kyoto to establish new court in Tokyo (the new name for Edo)

1871   *Nov. 20:* Iwakura Mission departs for U. S. and Europe with more than fifty Japanese students of Western institutions

1879   *July:* Former U. S. president Ulysses S. Grant visits Japan; meets with Emperor Meiji

1881   *Mar.:* King of Hawaii visits Japan seeking a member of the Japanese imperial family as consort for his daughter

1885   *Jan.:* First Japanese immigrants depart for Hawaii

1889   *Feb. 11:* Promulgation of Imperial Japanese Constitution   *Feb. 20:* Signing of U.S.-Japan Treaty of Commerce and Navigation

[409]

1890   *Nov. 29:* Convocation of the first Japanese Imperial Diet in Tokyo
1894   *July:* Outbreak of the Sino-Japanese War   *Nov. 22:* Revision of
U.S.-Japan Treaty of Commerce and Navigation
1897   *Jan.-June:* Dispute with U. S. over Japanese immigration to Hawaii
June: U. S. annexation of Hawaiian Islands
1899   *July:* Revised treaties of commerce and navigation with U. S., England, and France go into effect   *Sept.:* Open Door Policy announced
1904   *Feb. 10:* Japanese declaration of war on Russia
1905   *July:* Taft-Katsura Agreement recognizing Japan's interests in Korea   *Sept. 5:* Portsmouth Treaty ends Russo-Japanese War; demonstrations in Japan oppose the treaty as "humiliating to Japan"   *Sept.:* Edward H. Harriman visits Japan to establish a syndicate for joint Japanese-
American management of South Manchurian Railway
1906   *Apr.:* Japanese and Nisei children barred from San Francisco public
schools
1907   *Mar.:* Bill limiting Japanese immigration to U. S. passed in Congress
Oct.: Anti-Japanese demonstrations in San Francisco
1908   *Feb. 18:* Gentlemen's Agreement with U. S., whereby Japan agrees
to set quotas on Japanese immigration   *Nov. 30:* Root-Takahira Agreement on Japanese immigration
1909   *Feb. 3:* Land-tenure bill, directed primarily against Japanese immigrants, passed by California legislature
1910   *Aug. 22:* Japanese annexation of Korea
1911   *Feb. 22:* Second revision of U.S.-Japan Treaty of Trade and Navigation recognizes Japanese tariff autonomy   *Oct.:* Outbreak of anti-
Ch'ing revolution in China
1915   *Jan. 18:* Japan's Twenty-one Demands presented to China
1917   *Nov. 2:* Lansing-Ishii Agreement, recognizing Japan's special interests in China
1918   *Aug.:* Siberian Expedition   *Nov. 11:* End of World War I
1920   *Mar.:* Birth-control advocate Margaret Sanger visits Japan
1921   *Nov. 12:* Washington Conference opens (continues until Feb. 6,
1922)   *Dec.:* Four-Power Treaty signed in Washington by Japan, U. S.,
Britain, and France
1922   *Feb.:* Washington Conference treaties; Nine-Power Treaty
1923   *Apr. 14:* Abrogation of Lansing-Ishii Agreement   *Sept. 1:* Great
Kanto Earthquake
1924   *May 15:* Exclusion Act, largely anti-Japanese in intent, passed by
U. S. Congress
1925   *Oct.:* Locarno treaties
1930   *Jan. 11:* Removal of ban on export of gold from Japan   *Apr. 22:*
London Disarmament Treaty
1931   *Sept. 18:* Manchurian Incident
1932   *Feb.:* Lytton Commission visits Japan on way to Manchuria   *Mar.
1:* Establishment of state of Manchukuo; U. S. refuses to recognize its
legitimacy   *May 15:* May 15 Incident in Tokyo; assassination of Premier

Inukai   *Oct.:* Lytton Commission presents report to the League of Nations branding Japan aggressor in Manchuria

1933   *Feb.:* League of Nations accepts Lytton Commission report; Japanese delegation, led by Yosuke Matsuoka, walks out of League   *Mar. 27:* Japan's formal withdrawal from League of Nations

1934   *Dec.:* Abrogation of Washington Naval Treaty

1936   *Feb. 26:* February 26 Incident: attempted coup d'état in Tokyo by younger officers of Imperial Army

1937   *July 7:* Japanese and Chinese troops clash at the Marco Polo Bridge outside of Peking; beginning of war in China   *Nov.:* Japan signs mutual defense pact with Germany and Italy

1939   *May 12:* Nomonhan Incident: border clash with Soviet troops on boundary of Manchukuo and Outer Mongolia   *July 26:* Abrogation of U.S.-Japan commercial treaties   *Sept. 1:* German invasion of Poland; beginning of World War II in Europe

1940   *Sept. 22:* Japanese army advances into French Indochina   *Sept. 27:* Signing of Tripartite Axis Pact with Germany and Italy

1941   *Jan.:* Kichisaburo Nomura appointed ambassador to U. S.   *Feb.:* Foreign Minister Matsuoka makes plea for improved Japanese-American relations   *Mar.:* Matsuoka confers in Europe with Hitler, Stalin, and Mussolini   *Apr. 13:* Soviet-Japanese Neutrality Pact signed in Moscow   *Apr.:* Discussions in Washington between Secretary of State Hull and Ambassador Nomura regarding proposals for re-establishing friendly relations between Japan and U. S.; attempts to arrange a meeting between President Roosevelt and Prime Minister Konoe   *June 22:* Germany invades Russia   *July 2:* Imperial Conference adopts Outline of National Policies stating that "possibility of war with the U. S. and Great Britain is not to be ruled out"   *July 26:* Roosevelt freezes Japanese assets in U. S.   *Aug. 1:* U. S. announces oil embargo of Japan   *Aug. 18:* Meeting at sea of Roosevelt and Churchill; Atlantic Charter   *Aug. 28:* Ambassador Nomura delivers Konoe message to Roosevelt requesting meeting   *Oct. 16:* Resignation of the third Konoe cabinet   *Oct. 18:* General Hideki Tojo assumes premiership   *Nov.:* Saburo Kurusu sent as special envoy to Washington; meets with Roosevelt, Hull, and Nomura from Nov. 17 to Dec. 5. Hull notes delivered to Japanese government   *Dec. 1:* Imperial Conference makes decision for war with U. S.   *Dec. 7* (Dec. 8 in Japan): Air attack on Pearl Harbor; Japanese army moves into Malay Peninsula; Nomura and Kurusu meet Hull in Washington; Japan formally declares war on U. S. and Great Britain   *Dec. 8:* U. S. declares war on Japan   *Dec. 9:* U. S. declares war on Germany and Italy

1942   *Jan.:* Japanese army occupies Manila   *Feb.:* Japanese army occupies Singapore   *June:* Naval battle off Midway Island

1943   *Feb.:* Defeat of the German army at Stalingrad. Defeat of the Japanese army at Guadalcanal   *May:* Death of Admiral Isoroku Yamamoto in the Solomon Islands. Defeat of Japanese forces at Attu Island   *Nov.:* Cairo Conference, meeting of Roosevelt, Churchill, and Chiang

Kai-shek. Tehran Conference, meeting of Roosevelt, Churchill, and Stalin
1944   *June 6:* Allied landing at Normandy   *July 18:* Resignation of Tojo
cabinet   *July-Aug.:* Defeat of Japanese forces at Saipan, Guam, and
Tinian   *Oct.:* Naval battle at Leyte, Philippines   *Nov. 1:* Beginning of
air raids on Tokyo by U. S. B-29s based in Mariana Islands
1945   *Feb.:* Yalta Conference, meeting of Roosevelt, Churchill, and Stalin;
Soviet Union agrees to enter war against Japan   *Mar.:* Saturation air
raids on Tokyo   *Apr.:* U. S. invasion of Okinawa   *Apr. 12:* Death of
Roosevelt   *May 9:* Surrender of Germany; Japan declares determination
to continue war to finish   *May 11:* Japanese Supreme Conference for
Direction of War decides in secret session to request Soviet mediation in
ending Pacific War   *June 3:* Koki Hirota, former prime minister and
leader of Japanese peace faction, confers in Moscow with Soviet officials
June 21: Defeat of Japanese forces on Okinawa   *June 26:* United Nations
Charter signed at San Francisco   *July 13:* Prince Konoe offers to confer
with Stalin on terms for Japanese surrender   *July 26:* Potsdam Conference, meeting of Truman, Stalin, and Atlee; Potsdam Declaration lists
terms of unconditional surrender for Japan   *Aug. 6:* Atomic bomb dropped on Hiroshima   *Aug. 8:* Soviet Union declares war on Japan   *Aug.
9:* Atomic bomb dropped on Nagasaki; Soviet forces invade Manchuria
and Korea   *Aug. 10:* Japanese government accepts terms of Potsdam
Declaration   *Aug. 14:* Formal announcement of Japanese acceptance of
Potsdam Declaration at Imperial Conference; allied nations informed of
Japanese decision   *Aug. 15:* Emperor's broadcast to the Japanese nation,
announcing Japan's surrender   *Aug. 28:* First advance units of U. S.
Eleventh Airborne Division land at Atsugi airfield   *Aug. 30:* General
MacArthur arrives at Atsugi   *Sept. 2:* Surrender instrument signed
aboard U. S. S. *Missouri* in Tokyo Bay   *Sept. 9:* Announcement by Mac-
Arthur of basic Occupation policy for Japan   *Sept. 11:* SCAP directive
ordering the arrest of Japanese war criminals   *Oct. 4:* SCAP directive
removing restrictions on political, civil, and religious liberties   *Oct. 10:*
Release of political prisoners, including leading Japanese Communists
Oct. 11: SCAP directive ordering the revision of Japanese constitution and
encouragement of labor unionization   *Oct. 24:* Ratification of United Nations Charter   *Oct. 25:* SCAP directive prohibiting Japanese government
from engaging in diplomatic activities   *Nov. 6:* SCAP directive ordering
dissolution of *zaibatsu*   *Dec. 9:* SCAP directive ordering program of rural
land reform
1946   *Jan. 1:* Emperor's formal renunciation of divinity   *Jan. 4:* SCAP
directive ordering purge of all persons bearing responsibility for war
Feb.: Establishment of the Far Eastern Commission   *Apr. 10:* First Lower House election; women's suffrage in effect in Japan for first time   *Apr.
17:* Publication of draft of new Japanese constitution, including no-war
proposal in Article Nine   *May:* International Military Tribunal of the
Far East begins trials of Japanese Class-A war criminals in Tokyo   *June:*

Ambassador Edwin Pauley, special envoy of President Truman, announces reparations policy for Japan

1947 *Jan. 31:* MacArthur prohibits general strike scheduled for following day *Mar. 12:* Announcement of Truman Doctrine *May 3:* Promulgation of new Japanese constitution *June:* Announcement of Marshall Plan for European reconstruction

1948 *Apr.:* Russia begins blockade of Berlin. Economic and Industrial Advisory Mission visits Japan; announcement of four-year plan for Japanese economic rehabilitation *July:* SCAP directive deprives Japanese government employees of right to strike *Nov.:* Tokyo Military Tribunal announces verdicts on Japanese war criminals *Dec.:* Announcement of nine-point emergency program for economic stabilization

1949 *Apr.:* Formation of the North Atlantic Treaty Organization. Joseph Dodge, special economic adviser to SCAP, insists upon balanced budget for Japan. Currency conversion rate fixed at 360 yen per dollar *July-Aug.:* Shimoyama Incident, Mitaka Incident, Matsukawa Incident; facts of the three incidents, all involving sabotage of Japan National Railways, have yet to be explained; one view is that they were instigated by Japanese leftists, another that they were maneuvered by an American espionage unit to cast suspicion on Japanese leftists *Aug.:* Announcement of tax-revision program by SCAP *Oct.:* Establishment of Communist regime in China. Reopening of Japanese private trade

1950 *Jan.:* Omar Bradley, chairman of Joint Chiefs of Staff, visits Japan with other chiefs, and urges strengthening of U. S. military bases in Japan and Okinawa *June 6:* MacArthur orders purge of leadership of Japan Communist party *June 25:* Outbreak of war in Korea *June 26:* Further publication of *Akahata,* Japan Communist Party newspaper, prohibited *July:* SCAP directive creates Police Reserve Force. Formation of Sohyo (General Council of Japanese Trade Unions) *Oct.:* U. S. government announces seven basic principles for peace with Japan

1951 *Jan.:* MacArthur stresses necessity of Japan's rearming. Special Envoy Dulles visits Japan *Mar.:* First draft of peace treaty for Japan written *Apr.:* President Truman relieves MacArthur of duty as supreme commander for the Allied Powers *Sept. 8:* Signing of Peace Treaty in San Francisco; signing of Treaty of Mutual Cooperation and Security Between Japan and U. S.

1952 *Feb. 28:* Signing of Administrative Agreement between U. S. and Japan *Apr.:* Peace Treaty and Security Treaty go into effect; Japan signs separate peace treaty with Republic of China

1953 *Apr.:* Signing of Treaty of Friendship, Commerce, and Navigation between Japan and the U. S. *Nov.:* Vice-President Nixon visits Japan; first statements that the renunciation of war might be an error in the Japanese constitution

1954 *Mar. 1:* American H-bomb test at Bikini; Japanese fishing boat, *Lucky Dragon No. 5,* contaminated by radioactive fallout *Mar. 8:*

Signing of Mutual Defense Assistance Agreement between Japan and the U. S. *July 21:* Geneva Conference on Indochina ends

1955 *Aug.:* Foreign Minister Mamoru Shigemitsu visits Washington for talks with Secretary of State Dulles; communiqué on Japanese-American cooperation in the peace and security of the Far East *Nov.:* U.S.-Japanese treaty on cooperation in nuclear development

1956 *Oct.:* Prime Minister Hatoyama visits Moscow to sign joint Russo-Japanese communiqué as first step toward normalization of diplomatic relations *Dec.:* Japan admitted to United Nations by unanimous vote of General Assembly

1957 *Jan.:* Girard Incident: accidental shooting of an old Japanese woman collecting shells on a U. S. Army firing range; the incident and Girard's trial stir up widespread anti-American sentiment *June:* Prime Minister Kishi visits U. S. for talks with President Eisenhower *Oct. 4:* Launching of first Soviet satellite, *Sputnik* I

1958 *Sept.:* Discussions between Foreign Minister Fujiyama and Secretary of State Dulles concerning revision of Security Treaty

1959 *Mar.:* Inejiro Asanuma, special envoy of Japan Socialist party, visits Peking; delivers speech entitled "American Imperialism Is the Enemy of Both China and Japan." Tokyo District Court acquits defendants in Sunagawa Incident on the grounds that U. S. military bases in Japan are unconstitutional

1960 *Jan.:* Signing of New Security Treaty and related Japan-U. S. Administrative Agreement *May:* U-2 Incident; cancellation of scheduled U.S.-Soviet summit talks in Paris. Opposition parties reveal that U-2 spy planes are operating from U. S. bases in Japan *June 10:* Presidential Press Secretary James Hagarty arrives in Japan; mobbed at Tokyo International Airport by demonstrators opposed to Security Treaty; cancellation of Eisenhower's scheduled visit to Japan *June 15:* Massive demonstrations against Security Treaty and the manner in which Japanese government was forcing its ratification; 5,800,000 demonstrators protest throughout Japan

1961 *Apr. 19:* Failure of Bay of Pigs invasion in Cuba *Apr. 19:* Edwin O. Reischauer arrives as U. S. ambassador *May 16:* Coup d'état in Republic of Korea *June 3-4:* President Kennedy and Premier Khrushchev confer in Vienna *Nov.:* Joint Japan-U.S. Committee on Trade and Economic Affairs meets in Hakone for first time

1962 *Feb.:* Attorney General Robert Kennedy visits Japan *Sept.:* Secretary of State Dean Rusk and Foreign Minister Masayoshi Ohira confer on problems of Okinawa, Japan, and Korea *Dec.:* Second meeting of Joint Japan-U.S. Committee on Trade and Economic Affairs

1963 *Jan.:* U. S. nuclear submarines seek entry at Japanese ports; Japanese government allows entry despite vociferous public protest *Aug. 14:* Limited Nuclear Test Ban treaty signed by England, U. S., Soviet Union, and Japan *Nov. 23:* Television transmission via telecommunication satellite initiated between U. S. and Japan   *Dec. 31:* Announcement of joint agreement on reduction of U. S. forces in Japan

1964   *Mar. 24:* Stabbing attack on Ambassador Reischauer   *Apr.:* Japan joins Organization for Economic Cooperation and Development   *Aug.:* Gulf of Tonkin Incident; Congressional resolution authorizes "all necessary measures"   *Oct.:* Olympic Games in Tokyo   *Nov. 12:* U. S. nuclear submarine *Sea Dragon* enters Sasebo Naval Base

1965   *Jan.:* Premier Sato visits Washington for talks with President Johnson   *June 22:* Treaty signed between Japan and Republic of Korea   *Dec.:* Japan becomes a non-permanent member of the U. N. Security Council

1967   *Nov.:* Prime Minister Sato confers with President Johnson on the return of Bonin Islands to Japan

1968   *Jan.:* President Johnson emphasizes economic programs to protect the dollar in his State of the Union address. U. S. S. *Enterprise,* nuclear aircraft carrier, enters Sasebo Naval Base; widespread demonstrations in protest. Japanese-American conference in Honolulu to discuss measures to protect U. S. dollar   *May:* U. S. nuclear submarine *Swordfish* suspected of contaminating waters of Sasebo Bay by a radioactive leak   *June:* Formal return of Bonin Islands to Japan   *Nov.:* First election of government of Ryukyu Islands

1969   *Jan.:* First Japan-America Conference on Okinawa and Asia meets in Kyoto   *Apr.:* North Korea shoots down U. S. spy plane based in Japan   *July:* U. S. informs Japan of intention to remove poison gas from Okinawa. Premier Sato and Secretary of State Rogers meet to discuss Okinawa reversion issue   *Nov.:* Premier Sato meets President Nixon in Washington; joint communiqué announces reversion of Okinawa by 1972. North Korea, North Vietnam, and the People's Republic of China jointly denounce Nixon-Sato communiqué as an expression of militarism

1970   *Feb.:* Japan signs Nuclear Non-Proliferation Treaty   *Apr.:* Japan-China Memorandum Trade Liaison Council issues communiqué on commercial cooperation; China attacks revival of Japanese militarism   *June:* Minister of International Trade and Industry Kiichi Miyazawa meets with Secretary of Commerce Maurice Stans to discuss textile dispute; no settlement reached   *Oct.:* Meeting in Washington between Premier Sato and President Nixon   *Nov.:* Election of Okinawa representatives to national government. U. S. House of Representatives passes 1971 trade bill, including quotas on textile and shoe imports   *Dec.:* U. S. rejects final Japanese proposal on textile dispute. U. S. Treasury Department charges Japanese television-set manufacturers with dumping

1971   *Feb.:* Discussions in Peking between Japanese and Chinese government representatives Aiichiro Fujiyama and Wang Kuo-ch'üan   *Mar. 8:* Announcement of voluntary export restrictions by Japan Federation of Textile Manufacturers   *Mar. 11:* President Nixon rejects Japanese voluntary restrictions on textile exports to U. S.; presses for textile import quotas   *Mar. 12:* Japanese-U.S. govermental textile negotiations break down   *May:* Secretary of Commerce Stans denounces Japan's trade policies at open Senate hearing   *June:* Meetings in Washington between Japanese and American industrial leaders. Agreement for return of Okinawa signed simultaneously in Tokyo and Washington   *July:* Secretary of Defense Laird visits Japan, voices hopes for increased Japanese military capacity   *July 16:* Announcement of President Nixon's plans to visit China   *Aug. 15:* President Nixon temporarily suspends exchange of gold for dollars, imposes 10 percent surchange on imports and sets freeze on prices and wages   *Sept. 26:* Emperor and empress meet President Nixon briefly in Anchorage, Alaska, on first leg of their European trip   *Oct.:* People's Republic of China admitted to United Nations   *Dec. 20:* New currency exchange rates established by Group of Ten Conference of finance ministers; yen revalued from 360 to 308 per dollar

1972   *Jan. 6-7:* Prime Minister Sato confers with President Nixon at San Clemente, California; date of Okinawa reversion set at May 15, 1972; U. S. and Japan pledge cooperation in solution of China-recognition problem

Index

AAS, *see* Association of Asian Studies
Abe, Iso-o, 65
Abegglen, James, 5, 24
Adams, Clarence, 255
Advisory Committee on Japan-U.S. Economic Affairs, 252
Age of Discontinuity, 264
Agency for International Development (AID), 300
Agnew, Spiro, 279
Aiichi, Kiichi, 184, 225, 237, 325–26
Air Self-Defense Force (ASDF), 327–29; *See also* Self-Defense Forces
Aiura, Tadao, 99–100
Akagi, Munenori, 247
Akagi, Shunsuke, 353
Akanegakubo, Shigemitsu, 362
Akasaka Detached Palace, 53–54
Akatani, Genshichi, 139–40
Akatsuka, Yukio, 136, 367
Akiyama, Chieko, 254
Akiyama, Kunio, 105–106
Alaska Pulp Company, 276–78, 301–302
Allied Council for Japan, 119–22, 146
Allied Powers: in World War I, 87; in World War II, 111–13; on Allied Council, 120–22
Allison, John M., 214, 215, 232
Amano, Toshitake, 156
Amaya, Naohiro, 345
American Chamber of Commerce, 345
American Cultural Centers, 77, 341, 348, 383
American Educator Encyclopedia, 268
American Embassy, Tokyo, 103–104, 128, 214, 217, 220, 227, 343–44, 344–45, 346–49

American Social Science Research Council, 301
American Textile Manufacturers' Institute, 331
Ameya-yokocho black market, 124
Amis, Robert T., 175
Anami, Korechika, 116
Anders, Günther, 359
Anderson, Mori, and Rabinowitz, 33
Ando, Yoshio, 160, 195
Anglo-Japanese Alliance, 75, 399
Annie N. Brady Co., 55
Anzai, Masao, 266
Aoi Sammyaku, 135–36
Aoyama, Chise, 58
Aoyama Jogakuin, 58
Aoyama, Nao, 58
Apollo 11, 17
Arai, Ryuichi, 172
Ariga, Tadashi, 114
Arima, Yoriyoshi, 154
Arisawa, Hiromi, 195
Ariyoshi, George, 286
Ariyoshi, Yoshiya, 275
Arizona, 268
Armstrong, James I., 306
Article Nine (Japanese Constitution), 7, 131–33, 403, 405
Asahi Floating University, 367
Asahi Shimbun, 133, 143, 347, 358, 376
Asai, Kiyoshi, 183
Asama-maru, 103
Asakai, Koichiro, 121, 141, 158, 231, 235–36
Ashida, Hitoshi, 141, 189, 190–92
Asian and Pacific Council (ASPAC), 243, 404

The *"weathermark"* identifies this English-language edition as having been planned, designed, and produced at the Tokyo offices of John Weatherhill, Inc., in collaboration with the Asahi Shimbun-sha. Book design and typography by Meredith Weatherby. Text composed and printed by General Printing Company, Yokohama. Photographs engraved and printed in offset by Nissha Printing Company, Kyoto. Bound at the Makoto Binderies, Tokyo. The type of the main text is Monotype Bell 11/12; display type is Monotype Bell in various sizes.